TORIES AND DEMOCRATS

Tories and Democrats

BRITISH DIPLOMATS
IN PRE-JACKSONIAN AMERICA

By

William H. Masterson

Foreword by

Frank E. Vandiver

Texas A&M University Press
COLLEGE STATION

Copyright © 1985 by Orvetta W. Masterson
All rights reserved

Library of Congress Cataloging-in-Publication Data

Masterson, William H. (William Henry), 1914–1983.
   Tories and Democrats.

   Bibliography: p.
   Includes index.
    1. United States—Foreign relations—Great Britain.
2. Great Britain—Foreign relations—United States.
3. Diplomats—Great Britain—Biography. 4. Diplomats—
United States—History—18th century. 5. Diplomats—
United States—History—19th century. I. Title.
E183.8.G7M35   1985   327.41073   85-40046
ISBN 0-89096-224-3 (cloth). ISBN 1-58544-078-7 (pbk.)

Manufactured in the United States of America
First Paperback Edition

*To my daughters,
Amanda and Aileen*

Contents

List of Illustrations	ix
Foreword by Frank E. Vandiver	xi
Preface	xv
Acknowledgments	xvii
Prelude	3
George Hammond 1791–1795	8
Robert Liston 1796–1800	30
Edward Thornton 1800–1803	53
Anthony Merry 1803–1806	72
David Erskine 1806–1809	97
Francis Jackson 1809	121
Augustus Foster 1811–1812	144
Interlude 1812–1816	168
Charles Bagot 1816–1819	171
Stratford Canning 1820–1823	196
Postlude	223
Notes	225
Bibliography	259
Index	275

Illustrations

following page 78
George Hammond
Robert Liston
Henrietta Liston
Anthony Merry
Elizabeth Merry
David Erskine
Augustus Foster
Charles Bagot
Mary Bagot
Stratford Canning

Foreword

To those who knew Bill Masterson, this book will sound familiar—not in the sense of having heard it before, but in the sense of how Bill talked and of how his nimble mind worked. That was the first feeling I had upon reading *Tories and Democrats;* the next feeling was that happiness which comes with a sense of humor re-met.

Those feelings prompt me to write, not of the book—for Bill does that adroitly as he goes along—but of the author. I knew William H. Masterson for nearly thirty years; he was friend, companion, boss, ally, counselor, exhorter, comforter. Consider, then, that my recollections come from closeness and will reflect through that prism.

First, him: medium tall, not portly, energetic in step and gesture, Bill had sparkling, readable, kind eyes that accented a round face. He may have played poker—we never did—but if so, he would have been in trouble because he talked with his glance. He talked, too, with wit, hands, and body. A good storyteller in person or on paper, a lecturer supreme, Bill ranked among the two or three most popular teachers at Rice University.

A Houstonian, Bill went through local schools, graduated from Rice, and went on to history graduate school at the University of Pennsylvania. There he worked with Roy Nichols, whose witty world view fitted Bill's mind closely. Nichols, too, shared Bill's interest in early national history and let his Texas student study Tennessee in its forming years. A biography of William Blount emerged first as dissertation, then as acclaimed book in the Southern Biography Series, published by Louisiana State University Press. Writing deftly and with insight, Bill put Blount the man into his time and setting. That study reinforced a concern with the early national period and gave Bill a long research task which he pursued while filling various roles at Rice.

Rice in the 1950s and 1960s changed mightily, and largely because of Bill's vision and determination to enhance humanities in what was widely perceived to be a small technical institute. He had a large hand in luring me there in 1955, and he did it by reminiscing a little on the past, talking about present opportunities, and looking to a shining future. I believed him, that he would do the things he hoped, and thought the quest would be fun with him.

After returning from Pennsylvania to Rice's history department, Bill served a stint as assistant to President William V. Houston and that post gave an institutional view. Working full time back in the department gave Bill a chance to serve as motivator of humanities. Then came appointment as one of the first of a group of College Masters—his was Hanszen College—and almost constant involvement in student and administrative matters. That post also called on the considerable social abilities of Bill's gracious wife, and Vetta set a tone for college masters and their roles which carries to today.

Throughout these exciting assignments, Bill never lost interest in early American history. He and his family spent a year in England during the early 1960s; while there he did some of the research which makes this book so rich and informative. After that year "in the sources," a new Rice president asked Bill to become dean of humanities. The university had never had the humanities under separate administrative leadership, and the change suited Bill's temperament and conviction. Most of his colleagues nodded at his choice—he was logical, he had worked to bring the *Journal of Southern History* to Rice, had encouraged the selection of scholars in various humanistic disciplines, had, in effect, functioned as unofficial dean for some time. Under his benevolent hand, humanities and social sciences flourished. More than that, he helped shape a different view of Rice, one compatible with its name: The William Marsh Rice University for the Advancement of Letters, Science and Art.

Virtually at the pinnacle of his administration, Bill accepted a call to the presidency of the University of Chattanooga (later the chancellorship of the University of Tennessee at Chattanooga)—a halcyon day for him, a sad one for me. For a decade I heard often of his skilled handling of difficulties in Tennessee, and missed his humor every day. After superior service to Chattanooga, Bill retired in 1979, and moved to Austin, Texas, where he could use the University of Texas' library to continue his study for *Tories and Democrats*. Writing, beguiling as ever, did not prevent his becoming involved in teaching at St. Edward's University in Austin.

At last the book was finished. And almost coincidentally he was killed in a tragic accident. When I heard, I thought of a terrible void, felt quenched, bowed by the tumble of memories, lost without that wisdom and that wit.

When, a few weeks later, I read this book in manuscript, some of the hurt eased—his humor ran the pages, his shrewd ken of courage, heart, and motive, his belief in people and purpose and the general welfare. This book is not Bill, of course, but in it he gives his spirit, echoes his voice, and evokes the shade of a warm and gentle man.

Frank E. Vandiver

Preface

SINCE this book proposes to fulfill several varying purposes, some indication may be in order as to what these purposes are. Primarily this is an account of the lives—or mainly the American careers—of the first nine British envoys to the United States from 1791 to 1823. These men, eight ministers and an important chargé d'affaires, were not and were not intended to be portrayed as movers and shakers in diplomatic history. Policy was made and instructions were written in London, and the success of each envoy lay in the means and skills he used to carry out directions. His impact was not on events, but rather on the attitudes of men in both countries who shaped events. Though not primary figures, the ministers are mentioned in diplomatic histories and figure in monographs and, in two cases, in biographies. Their backgrounds and their consequent American performances have rarely been examined in much depth, and thus to present them in greater perspective is one objective of this work.

In addition, these men were professional reporters: both officially and privately they described the American people, their government, and their society. Visitors' and travelers' descriptions of pre-Jacksonian America are reasonably numerous, but these diplomats' perceptions are unique. Since almost all the envoys were the quintessence of British Toryism, disagreement with their hosts over social and political philosophies was inevitable. Tory Britain could cope with the storms of the French Revolution and Napoleon with some understanding, but the insistent nationalism of the militarily insignificant republic, like the pervasive Jeffersonianism of its society, constantly affronted the diplomats. They responded with warm and often perceptive comments on the young nation and its people.

Nowhere is the dramatic shift in Anglo-American relations after

1815 more striking than in Downing Street's choice of and instructions to the later ministers to America. No special relationship developed in these years, either nationally or personally, but the changes in British men and measures after Waterloo clearly reveal the new relations of His Majesty's governments both with Restoration Europe and with the Western Hemisphere.

Given the less than prominent public stature of all but one of these men, research on their lives has led me to great national repositories and libraries, small county and local archives, and private collections. The constant feature of these diverse experiences has been a warm interest and assistance that far transcended public service or private hospitality. The heartening assistance of so many people in two countries can be only imperfectly acknowledged here but imposes on me a commitment that may perhaps be met in some part by what follows.

—William H. Masterson

Acknowledgments

As is often the case with the research and writing of a book, the completion of this one involved many people. The staffs of the Library of Congress, the British Museum, and the London Public Record Office generously made books, documents, and manuscripts available to the author, as well as assistance in the gathering of material. Among the libraries consulted were those of the University of Tennessee at Knoxville, the University of Texas at Austin, and Oxford and Cambridge universities in England. A number of private individuals in England most graciously permitted the author to consult their heritage in documents and personal letters. The family of the author wish to express their deeply felt appreciation to all these and to the many colleagues, students, and friends who, by their interest and encouragement, assisted in the making of this book.

TORIES AND DEMOCRATS

Prelude

THE development of the Foreign Office that served the British Empire was highly ad hoc and evolutionary. Its pedigree was respectably ancient—the first mention of an official devoted to foreign affairs occurred in the thirteenth century. Three hundred years later, Britain's expanding relationships produced "northern" and "southern" departments, each directed by a principal secretary of the sovereign and concerned only with the nations in his geographical area. The British colonial acquisitions of the eighteenth century led to a brief experiment with a secretary of state for home affairs (Britain and Ireland) and a secretary for foreign affairs, the latter first filled by Charles James Fox.[1]

In 1784, the foreign secretary was served by a private secretary, two undersecretaries, and ten clerks. Under the pressures exerted by the French Revolutionary, Napoleonic, and Restoration eras, this small staff grew so that by 1832 it included twenty-three senior and junior clerks, librarians, précis writers, translators, and other various specialized employees, whose subsistence-level salaries were made endurable by an elaborate system of fees and perquisites.[2]

For more than twenty years the foreign secretaries and their growing clan had been migrating unpredictably between Cleveland Row, off St. James's Park, and the Cockpit at Whitehall. In December, 1793, they came to rest in a group of private houses in Downing Street, which the government first leased and then bought and threw together for offices. These old homes, the Foreign Office's official residence until 1861, were a peculiarly British combination of elegance and inconvenience. For decades the British Cabinet met here, and lesser offices were occasionally cleared to make space for elegant dinners. The secretary himself shared a private entrance with the undersecretaries and ambassadors and enjoyed a spacious second-story office with a commanding view of St. James's Park. His and other fine rooms were lined with handsome bookcases and graced by beautifully carved mantels and superb tapestries. In contrast, the clerks' offices were, in effect, hallways through which ministers passed. Books and papers were piled high on floors, and the unindexed and unregistered dispatches and other manuscripts were stacked in unlocked cupboards, later to be bound and sent to molder in damp basements. From the fourth-floor junior clerks' "nursery" to the cellars, privacy was a rarity. Doors were cut through walls and tapestries, and halls were partitioned with swinging doors. The whole clerical establishment consisted of dingy, shabby offices, uneven floors, corkscrew stairwells, and dark, labyrinthine passages, through which (the scene being British) pampered dogs wandered to perform tricks and seek biscuits.[3]

Since the Foreign Office, like the Diplomatic Service that carried out its policies, originated in the British sovereign's personal relationships with foreign royalty, it did not in the late eighteenth century regard itself as having much in common with other government departments beyond a somewhat reactionary philosophy. And it successfully resisted administrative innovations longer than any other area.[4] Hence, in an age of declining royal prerogative, the Foreign Office possessed the very mixed advantages of the closest relationship with the sovereign: both George III and George IV strongly influenced the appointments and decisions of foreign ministers.

The cabinet then met irregularly, and other ministers seldom read dispatches and other diplomatic papers. Thus, His Majesty's principal secretary of state for foreign affairs pursued his personalized and semiregal course primarily in relation to the prime minister and the king, with some attention to the War Office and the Admiralty. The foreign secretary sat in his office alone, summoning his undersecretaries by a bell. Castlereagh maintained this detached formality even with Undersecretaries Planta and Clanwilliam, who were personal friends of his; George Canning later relented to the point of summoning his aides by a messenger and allowing them to sit when there were no other ministers of state present.[5]

For decades nearly every foreign secretary was a peer or the son of a peer; there were no lawyers or professional diplomats. During the first forty years of Anglo-American diplomatic relations, the British foreign secretaries ranged in competence from the distinguished skill of Castlereagh and Canning through the dour proficiency of Gren-

Prelude 5

ville and Hawkesbury and the highly intermittent competency of Carmarthen and Wellesley to the flat inconsequence of Harrowby and Mulgrave. Though all except Fox were locked in the inexorable caste of social and political High Toryism, the best of the foreign secretaries stood far above the pious political amorality of a prime minister like Spencer Perceval. Even in crises of Anglo-American ill will, all of them rose above the opacity of the Tory backbencher ("the finest brute voices in Europe"), the venom of the *Quarterly Review*, or the coarseness of William Cobbett.[6]

By far the most powerful figures in the Foreign Office below (and sometimes even including) the secretary of state were the two undersecretaries, who under strong chiefs significantly affected the operations of the office and under less dominant leadership effected major policy decisions. Whereas the eighteen years between 1783 and 1801 produced only two foreign secretaries, the next nine years saw eight such ministers. This rapid turnover at the top naturally enhanced the authority of the relatively permanent undersecretaries, two of the strongest of whom, George Hammond and Joseph Planta, each held that office for more than ten years. Usually chosen from among the foreign secretary's personal or political friends and acquiring invaluable information from dispatches and personal mail, the undersecretaries in effect handled the daily operations of the office. They also maneuvered appointments and career opportunities for younger diplomats, especially those from abroad, from whom they received private letters seeking leaves of absence, changes of post, and financial assistance. They briefed diplomats departing for posts abroad and passed along to the secretary delicate suggestions from abroad concerning the handling of foreign diplomats. In sum, their personal influence was very considerable; hence, their individual and national prejudices had consequences as important as those of the secretaries themselves.[7]

The foreign secretary's instrument, the Diplomatic Service, was then regarded as technically separate from the Foreign Office, though personal interchange was frequent. In 1792 Britain had abroad three ambassadors, ten envoys extraordinary and plenipotentiary, and three ministers plenipotentiary. Most of the important missions—all of the ambassadorships and the most important ministerial assignments—were given for political or personal reasons to the relatives or protégés of the governing aristocracy. Decades later John Bright referred to the Diplomatic Service as "a gigantic system of out-of-door relief for the aristocracy of England." The monarch and his prime minister as well as party magnates were all involved in appointments, and the foreign secretary was lucky if he got a few appointments of his own to top posts. They were on the whole

> a hard-working and fairly intelligent set of men. Most of them were of true Tory stock and imbued with all its insular prejudices and pride. Their dispatches display a subconscious contempt for all that is not English. . . . They had no sympathy with the attempts of inexperienced men (notably Frenchmen and Americans) to work new institutions. The blessings of constitutional liberty they thought reserved for the aristocracy of Britain by the same divine wisdom which had given them their own jobs without the necessity of proving their capacity for them.[8]

Under the iron hand of Castlereagh and Canning, experienced diplomats such as Malmesbury, Keith, or Auckland might through ability or weakness or preoccupation create foreign policy; later an able ambassador like Strangford would be scourged for the attempt.[9]

Lesser appointees like the diplomats who were sent, usually unwillingly, to America before 1815 were much less competent and much more closely directed. Like his counterparts elsewhere, the minister to America regarded himself and was regarded in Britain as having three functions of descending importance. Primarily he was to induce the American administration to conform to British policy and interests, using means varying from diplomatic notes to bribery, threats, and even armed force, as directed by the foreign secretary in written instructions. Secondly, he was to cultivate those American political leaders best able to assist him in his primary objective. The ineptitude of the early ministers to America in this function led to serious consequences. In addition to these activities of persuasion and cultivation, a third task was to provide the Foreign Office with any information on or analyses of the American scene that might assist the foreign secretary to review and direct British policy toward America.

Unfortunately, most British ministers to America before 1812 chose to accomplish these aims through the "friends of Britain," that is, the Federalists. They never perceived or explained to their masters in London this steadily narrowing base from which they drew their information and conclusions. In addition, though the envoys kept closely in touch with American party politics as seen through Federalist eyes, before 1813 they never really understood American government, and especially the federal system. Americans themselves were then only slowly working out the implications of that system, and the Britons' perceptions of it were dulled by personal suffering.

John Quincy Adams doubted "whether any British minister who was ever here felt any wish to return after getting home[,] to come back *in the same capacity*. It is the real *purgatory*, and so is the condition of an American Minister to England."[10] The malaise of the British ministers in America did not arise from the same source as that which Henry Adams described for their counterparts in England: "feeling awkward in an English house from a certainty that they were not precisely wanted there, and a possibility that they might be told so."[11] Rather, the Britons' purgatory, like Dante's Hell, was composed of several layers—notably the American climate, the republic's social and political egalitarianism, its distance from England, and the absence of those niceties and assumed necessities of civilization that British diplomats customarily enjoyed in England or on the Continent. A further purgatorial level later evolved through the growing sense of a threatened rivalry with the young and bumptious nation.

In the first twenty-eight years of their formal peacetime diplomatic relations, Britain produced nine significant representatives (eight ministers and a chargé) in America. The length of their tours in America varied, but the average was three years. Of these nine men, seven of whom detested the United States, three were for most of their tenure regarded in America with a mixture of distrust, acceptance, and indifference; three (all prior to 1815) were cordially disliked; and three (two after 1815) were well liked. The chronology of their relative popularity indicates both a coming of age in American attitudes and a growing astuteness in the British Foreign Office. Overall assessment of the careers of the nine men reflects a reasonable achievement through more than thirty years of personalized diplomacy between two highly oppositional societies.

George Hammond

"In this wretched country whatever is done by government must . . . be materially regulated by the probable effect of the measures upon the minds of the people."
—Phineas Bond to George Hammond, 1794

IN early 1791, the nagging problem of accrediting a permanent minister to the United States of America was again troubling the government of George III. The prospect pleased neither William Pitt's cabinet nor the Foreign Office. Besides resentments lingering from successful rebellion, various rumors and facts about the former colonies were derogatory and depressing. America was five weeks away across a stormy ocean, its society was crude and sparse, and its few cities were said to compare unfavorably with many European villages. Its leaders had only two years previously launched a new federated government whose features were as inexplicable to many Britons as its success was problematical. Apparently at least half of the ascertainable American opinion had so opposed this government that the structure had been riddled with compromises, including a peripatetic capital to be located in several cities (one yet unborn) in the course of ten years.

Worst of all, since the Americans had included in their revolutionary manifesto a widely proclaimed defiance of the natural classes of human society, the new republic had become a haven for odious Irish immigrants. Such creatures as John Wilkes and Thomas Paine were regarded there with near veneration, and news of the political difficulties of the Republic's former royal ally, Louis XVI, had been greeted in some quarters with enthusiasm. There was, in fact, no assurance that an envoy from His Britannic Majesty would be properly received or his mission reciprocated.

On the other hand, British governments were accustomed to dealing with offensive peoples when the stakes were high enough, and in this case they undoubtedly were. Despite three carefully drawn stipulations in the Peace of Paris, the American states had not restored the confiscated property of British Loyalists, nor had any government in America compelled the repayment of pre-Revolutionary debts. Such delinquencies toward an unhappy band of British emigrés in Canada might be merely unfortunate, but when practiced against the great mercantile houses of London, Bristol, and Liverpool, the matter became critical.

Another financial pressure arose from rapid American expansion into the Mississippi Valley and resulting conflicts with American Indians. Simple justice as well as lucrative fur trade interests suggested that Britain's wartime allies should not be abandoned to American domination and exploitation. Powerful fur-trading enterprises centered on the still British-held military posts on the American side of the Great Lakes and in the dimly known world of forest and swamp in the south and southwest. In broader perspective, the whole American frontier from the Great Lakes to the Gulf of Mexico to Florida needed a closer surveillance than could be obtained from Canada.

Moreover, a Parliamentary committee on trade had recently recommended that Britain should regularize the lucrative Anglo-American commerce further but should on no account tolerate discriminatory American legislation. Reports were now reaching London, however, that an anti-British bloc in the American Congress, annoyed by Britain's refusal to open her West Indian colonies to American trade, evacuate the northwestern Great Lake posts, or send a diplomatic envoy to America, were planning to introduce the very inimical legislation that the committee had warned against.

From these various perspectives an American mission demanded attention from a British government under pressure to reduce internal taxes quickly. Hence, for the first time since John Adams had left London in 1788 after three years of furious frustration, Pitt's government in 1790 began a sustained consideration of the American mission.[1] The Nootka Sound controversy with Spain caused delays, but in 1791, the resignation of the pathologically dilatory Foreign Minister Francis Osborne enabled Pitt to place his own cousin, William Wyndham Grenville, now Lord Grenville, in the Foreign Office. Under that cold but able and ceaselessly active Tory, the search for a minister for America picked up momentum.

The new envoy was to be merely a minister plenipotentiary, a lowly rank in the second order of diplomacy, but there had never been a lack of candidates among lesser figures. Thomas Walpole, minister plenipotentiary to the Elector Palatine, was proposed, but declined. Thomas Douglas, fifth earl of Selkirk, a compulsive land speculator with large American interests, was a possibility, as was William Eliot, whose family could produce twenty Pittite votes in Parliament. Sir John Temple, the British consul general in America since 1785, would also serve, but dubious Revolutionary loyalties and suspected financial laxities made him unacceptable. Lord Dorchester, governor general of Canada, was considered, and George Beckwith, his go-between with Alexander Hamilton, had actively sought the position, as had Col. John Graves Simcoe, Dorchester's lieutenant governor for Upper Canada. Another hopeful contender was Phineas Bond, a former Loyalist who had achieved the consulship of the Middle Atlantic states and now urged both the necessity for a minister in America and his own capable availability. By October, 1791, however, it was known in America that the choice had fallen on a favorite protégé of Grenville's.[2]

The successful candidate owed his appointment to a temperament congenial to Grenville and to some accidental circumstances. Since matters connected with the treaty of 1783 were to be the principal agenda for the new minister, the powerful and intelligent Charles Jenkinson, president of the Board of Trade, counseled Pitt that someone connected with the formulation of that treaty would be most appropriate for the position. David Hartley, a British member of the 1783 commission, declined the new appointment but suggested his former secretary.

George Hammond, now twenty-eight years old, was the son of a respected senior merchant of Hull. After matriculating at Merton College, Oxford, young George had gone three years later with Hartley to Paris. During the negotiations he met both Franklin and Adams and attained the unusual skill of fluency in French. After the treaty meeting he returned to Merton for his B.A. and was elected a Fellow of the College in 1787. Seeking a diplomatic career and already marked as an Ultra-Tory, he was sent out by Foreign Secretary Osborne to be an attaché under Sir Robert Murray Keith, ambassador to the Court of Vienna. Keith, a kindly man, recognized in Hammond a well-connected protégé of the powerful and in less than a month wrote Carmarthen (secretary of state for foreign affairs) of his attaché's "modest, ingenious manners joined to an intelligent and well-cultivated understanding." Whether from the ingenious manners or from a shrewd desire to pass along a youth so dangerously well connected, Keith within another month was writing Carmarthen in support of Hammond's desire for "some solid establishment"—that is, a promotion—and within three months of his first appointment Hammond was promoted to secretary of legation at Copenhagen. The favor of both Carmarthen and Grenville continued to shine on the young Tory; in three more months he was secretary of the embassy at Madrid and within six months thereafter, in March, 1791, he received Grenville's official notification of his appointment to America along with a private letter urging an immediate return to England to prepare for the North Atlantic voyage before the winter storms made it dangerous.[3]

The choice of this spoiled, pompous, aggressive, and able young favorite was to produce long aftershocks. Picked for reasons to which his American tour was to prove largely unrelated, Hammond adversely affected Anglo-American relations long after he and the American tour were but mutually unpleasant memories.

In September, 1791, Hammond left Madrid for London to receive his credentials and briefing. He found Undersecretary Bland Burges dubious of the mission and keenly aware of "how very desirable it would be" that the Great Lake forts "should remain permanently in the possession of Great Britain," a view unpropitious for the settlement of a major American grievance. In deference to the undersecretary, Hammond took as his secretary of legation Edward Thornton, a twenty-four-year-old Cambridge graduate and tutor of Burges's eldest son, whose Ultra-Tory sentiments equaled the new minister's. After acquiring the servants, plate, and equipment provided by the appointment, Hammond joined Thornton en route to Falmouth, where they sailed on the mail packet in mid-September. A swift thirty-five-day voyage brought the men to Halifax. After recuperation they proceeded to New York and Philadelphia, arriving at the Quaker capital of the republic on October 21, 1791.[4]

The minister's arrival was viewed variously. Although Consul Phineas Bond had assured Grenville that advance news of the appointment had been received "very joyfully,"[5] the enthusiasm was noticeably restrained. President Washington was pleased but not overoptimistic, and a Quaker friend warned Vice-President Adams against the new arrival's designs. The French minister in Philadelphia, Jean de Ternant, understandably claimed marked indifference among the public.[6] Secretary of State Jefferson's friends were noncommittal, one of them merely commenting presciently of Hammond that "I hear he is a heavy man." Excited and nervous Tory hostesses of Philadelphia found the new minister to be a "tall, plump, rosy-faced young man; dressed with much elegance, and . . . at present more than a little cold and condescending in his manner." Hammond himself was pleased with his reception, writing Grenville that he had received "every mark of politeness and respect" from administration leaders.[7] To his mother he confessed that American society was surprisingly agreeable, that many of the leading families were wealthy, and since their members had often been educated or lived in England, "I have reason to think most of them are Tories at heart."[8]

But for Hammond the most congenial figure in Philadelphia was not an American Tory at heart but a most open and unmistakably English one. Consul Phineas Bond, the son of a wealthy Baltimore physician, had been educated in England for the law and then married and settled in Philadelphia, from which he had been driven for his British Loyalism during the Revolution. He had come back as consul in 1786 to negotiate for the payment of British debts. Family wealth, together with a lucrative law practice, had provided the consul with a well-staffed, elegant home complete with a fine library. He shared Carmarthen's and Hammond's tastes for art, theater, and High Toryism, and upon the minister's arrival he turned his home over to him as a temporary embassy, provided table delicacies, conducted spying operations, and dug out statistics for the minister's use. The consul's contempt for America was enormous, and he flaunted it on social occasions by parodies and sarcasms on American leaders so gross and virulent as to embarrass visiting Britons. Hammond was far too astute for this, but he secured promotion for the consul, obtained a leave of absence for him, and otherwise furthered his interests. Bond for his part visited Hammond's family while on leave and furthered the minister's standing at the Foreign Office. This close collaboration and its effects were noted by a French traveler, Moreau de St. Mery, who commented on Bond's hatred for his native country and that "his one noteworthy quality was his ability to influence Mr. Hammond. . . . The fact that he could be thus influenced says nothing for Mr. Hammond's ability."[9]

At any rate, the association with Bond coupled with his own close ties to Grenville completed for his lifetime Hammond's ideological structure. The three High Tories shared a vast capacity for work; all had able minds, fluent pens, and very little real humor. In particular,

Hammond derived little sense of proportion from a background of Tory Oxford followed by a gratifyingly swift series of promotions. Regarding any professional dissent as personal hostility, he was incapable of making tactical sacrifices for strategic gains; he devoted his professional career to the concept of the offensive defense.

His first moves in Philadelphia were intelligent. Although instructed by Grenville not to present his credentials until an American minister to Britain had been appointed, he realized that the American delay was not intentional. Accordingly, on November 11, 1791, he and Thornton were presented by Secretary of State Jefferson to President Washington. Hammond wore full court dress and Washington formal black velvet, but Jefferson, to the Briton's disgust, "was in plainest ordinary dress." The shorter, chubby Hammond described Washington as "very tall, florid, and somewhat angular in person, his voice high-pitched, but dignified and urbane in manner." The occasion went off well enough for the new minister to ask Grenville for a £200 increase in salary since he now expected his position to be "more stationary than I have hitherto been."[10]

Hammond's basic dilemma was not that his position was stationary but that it was equivocal. To Americans he was presumably a fully accredited minister sent to adjust boundary disputes and to bring about the British evacuation of American forts, to control Indian depredations in the west and southwest, and to make commercial arrangements to protect American ships from seizures, ideally even to secure their admission to British colonial ports. Actually he could do none of these. From Grenville, Hammond had a lawyer's brief to secure Loyalists' and creditors' claims and to do little else except prevent hostile Congressional discrimination against British ships and cautiously support Indian hopes for quasi-independence and a British protectorate. Firmly posited between these conflicting expectations, the minister was soon writing Undersecretary George Aust that "my situation here has been in many points of view critical and embarrassing."[11]

Normally a minister might mitigate such problems by a reasonably amiable professional relationship with the American secretary of state, but in Hammond's case this was quite impossible. Jefferson's admiration for the French republican experiment was as great as his indifference to Britain's most revered institutions. Also, the agrarian-democratic secretary of state indulged a penchant for philosophical comment that sometimes swept him to the point of sheer whimsy, though it also concealed a shrewd combative instinct. Nevertheless, Jefferson's patrician birth precluded his dismissal as mere rabble, to which British Tories like Hammond habitually consigned democrats. The secretary of state seemed designed by nature to infuriate George III's first envoy to America.

For almost eighteen months the two diplomats fenced over the real object of Hammond's mission. Jefferson soon suspected the close limits of the minister's authority, but pressed him for a commercial treaty and the evacuation of the posts. Hammond replied with charges of American treaty violations; thereupon, each fell to compiling examples of bad faith by his opponent's countrymen. Meanwhile Jefferson continued to urge on Hammond the American resentments at threatening Indian activity in Upper Canada, where Lieutenant Governor Simcoe was thought to be inciting the Indians to war, and in Florida, where William Augustus Bowles claimed British assistance in arms and money. As diplomatic civilities grew thinner, Hammond's hair-trigger combativeness became fully roused, and he began to give full credit to rumors of Jefferson's Anglophobia and bad faith. Fifty years later Hammond's secretary was to remember the bitterness of those clashes, recalling Jefferson's unorthodox publication of diplomatic notes and his "unfriendly temper and bitter zeal."[12]

It was not the cogency of his prolix notes that kept Hammond's mission useful to Britain but the unquenchable meddlesomeness of the American secretary of the treasury, whose Anglophilia and distrust of Jefferson made him the single most important circumstance in Hammond's American tour. The Briton was acute enough to perceive that Hamilton's invaluable help did not come merely from philosophical differences between cabinet members but also from the necessity of Anglo-American cooperation in commercial matters if the secretary's whole complex financial structures were to be successfully maintained. Already told in England of Hamilton's reliance on Britain, Hammond had the first of many long and confidential conversations with the secretary scarcely a month after his arrival. He reported himself delighted to find "my opinion of his just and liberal way of thinking fully confirmed."[13]

As the months passed, this way of thinking provided the minister with important information: that Hamilton supported British activity in American Indian affairs; that he felt the northern boundary problem easily solvable; that he would provide Hammond with data to combat

Jefferson's claims of British maritime depredations; that he accepted Britain's positions on Loyalists, creditors' claims, and navigation laws; that Jefferson's bias could not affect American foreign policy because it did not reflect the cabinet's views, and hence certain crucial diplomatic positions of Jefferson could be ignored in London; and that the two secretaries' positions were irreconcilable and Jefferson would soon resign. As these helpful conferences went on, Hammond's dispatches steadily laid the foundation of what were to become basic British axioms about Jefferson, that is, that he held a "rooted aversion to Great Britain" arising from personal debts in Britain and that he was unwavering as a tool of France and French interests.[14]

The Hamilton-Hammond entente was too obvious to be missed in Philadelphia. As early as March, 1792, Jefferson knew of Hamilton's betrayal of cabinet secrets to the minister. Ever since the Revolution, American officials had freely discussed secret policy with foreign envoys, but the 1790s saw some of the most savage political warfare in American history. While the success of the American experiment was still very much in doubt, the roles of administration and opposition were not well understood; political differences were universally ascribed to personal motives of ambition, envy, malice, sedition, atheism, and immorality. Newspapers routinely contained masterpieces of invective, and Federalists and Republicans alike were convinced that their opponents were the hirelings of France and Britain.

The Treasury Department was of course particularly suspect as a source of bribery; hence the well-known intimacy of Hamilton and Hammond seemed to confirm Republican fears. Several congressmen arranged a meeting with Hammond and charged him bluntly with partiality to Hamilton, whom they distrusted. The minister replied with equal directness that Hamilton was "more a man of the world than Jefferson" and "I like his manners better and can speak more freely with him. Jefferson is in the Virginia interest and that of France and it is his fault that we are at a distance." Grenville's protégé wrote to him plainly that except in cases of necessity he had little to do with the secretary of state, "as I cannot but consider him the devoted instrument of the French faction and . . . in two or three recent important cases acting officially in a manner diametrically opposed to the views of the President."[15] He did not add that this last "information" came from Hamilton. By 1793, when the gravest Anglo-American issues began to appear, Hammond had ceased to be the British minister to the United

States or to President Washington (of whom he did not always conceal a sharp dislike) and had instead become the British envoy to the Federalists and Secretary Hamilton.

This deflection of his mission in no way obscured the glitter of the minister's social progress in Philadelphia society. His presence at their parties provided tone if not warmth for Tory-minded hostesses, and official functions further crowded his calendar. Hammond joined various societies, attended sessions of Congress when his presence would not be misconstrued, and after Congress adjourned left the embassy in Thornton's care while he toured New York and New England. In October, 1792, he visited Mount Vernon. In Philadelphia, he and Thornton regularly dined with President and Mrs. Washington, the minister in resplendent court dress to "flatter" the president. Young Thornton found such occasions "of all others the most dull and unentertaining," since Washington's reserve chilled the party and produced "uncommonly phlegmatic and trivial" conversation until, in smaller after-supper parties, "the Secretary of State's strictures on monarchs began to throw a certain portion of animation into it."[16] On March 4, 1793, in the crowded little Senate chamber, Hammond and Thornton watched the president take his second official oath of office and make a short speech, an occasion in which the British flair for ceremony was noticeably absent.

Meanwhile, in a steady stream of dispatches to Grenville, Hammond was creating a twenty-year stereotype of America for the Foreign Office. The minister equated the Jeffersonian states' rights doctrine with French Revolutionary anarchy and American democratic rowdyism with the Parisian mobs. Success in their revolution, he wrote Grenville, had given the Americans "the dangerous notion of the equality of rights," and the southern states, "arrogant, luxurious, and incapable of energy," formed the base of Jefferson's party, which equated French with American success and through a "licentious" press attacked even the president. Personal and party combat would soon very likely lead to rebellion, which "the government has not the energy to repress."[17]

At the same time, Grenville from London was defining the issues for twenty years of Anglo-American controversy and conflict. In February, 1793, as Britain joined the European coalition against the French Republic, the serious questions were no longer the Loyalist debts and discriminatory duties that had brought Hammond to America, but the matter of the 1778 Franco-American alliance and the tortuous problems of American neutral rights in a world at war.

Because of delays in the mail to America, there was only vague information of the war as late as April, but Hamilton in his "candid conversations" had already assured Hammond of firm American neutrality. Meanwhile, although his attention was riveted on the European continent, the indefatigable Grenville sent Hammond instructions briskly disposing of American contentions on the nation's rights: free ships did *not* make free goods; foodstuffs of any national origin were liable to seizure; and Americans were advised to heed the proclamation of a blockade by which Britain would soon throttle the revolutionists. Details were spelled out by Orders in Council of June 8 and November 16, 1793, with later amendments. They provided for the seizure and sale to Britain of cargoes of corn, flour, or meal bound to France or her armies and for the confiscation of any ship with a cargo for the French colonies or for the use of these colonies. Hammond was directed to report on French ship movements and to press the administration to deny France the building, purchasing, manning, or equipping of privateers or warships and also to prohibit the sale of British ships captured by the French.

These and other orders slashing at America's lucrative West Indian trade and defining her neutrality in British terms were based by Grenville on his interpretation of Emmerich de Vattel and other international lawyers, whose diktat, like scriptural canons, could be variously interpreted. The British rendition, however, enjoyed the decisive assistance of the world's most powerful navy. The foreign secretary of course knew this, but he sincerely desired peace with America, and in none of his instructions did he achieve the later arrogance of the Marquis Wellesley or the self-conscious cleverness of George Canning. Unfortunately, his basic goodwill was dissipated in transition by his personal insensitivity and that peculiarly British air of long-suffering patience in dealing with the doggedly stupid, together with all those *formes d'hauteur* that Talleyrand noted as the trademark of Britain in dealing with Americans.[18]

Hammond seized upon the new course of action with all his native vehemence, and a torrent of his notes, memoranda, and protests poured upon the little State Department. Frenchmen and their ships became the common targets of the minister, Consul Bond, and the few British naval commanders yet in American waters. Hammond began to construct elaborate defenses for the infrequent but growing practice of British impressment of seamen claiming American citizenship, and he employed so many spies that Ternant complained, "The British minister has ten thousand eyes." London was appealed to for additional funds for espionage. When Jefferson reminded him that years had now gone by without British withdrawal from the northwestern posts, where Indian wars cost America "blood and treasure," Hammond caustically replied that His Majesty's ministers had more pressing matters to consider.[19]

In early 1793, before the diplomatic storm broke with full fury, Hammond achieved both professional and personal successes. The first concerned the long-awaited arrival of the French minister, Citizen Edmund Charles Edouard Genêt, as Ternant's replacement. Genêt's enthusiastic reception at Charleston and the ensuing anti-administration toasts and orations en route to Philadelphia eroded Genêt's fragile judgment. When faced with Washington's cool reception, Genêt plunged into wildly undiplomatic conduct and such flagrant assaults on American neutrality as to bring despair to France's American friends. Briefed confidentially on the administration's disgust, Hammond tracked the "violent Jacobin" with the passion of a wild game hunter, denouncing his "daring insults" to America, exposing his spies, and successfully instigating both a mutiny in a French squadron in the New York harbor and an assault on Genêt's house.[20]

Simultaneously, the British minister concluded a successful courtship. A year earlier a letter from Grenville to Hammond had introduced Andrew Allen, an American Loyalist returning on business, and thereafter Consul Bond had presented Allen's daughter Margaret, a renowned beauty, to Hammond. Margaret, who had been educated in England, became a favorite of Mrs. Washington's. But a junior diplomat's marriage, especially to an American, was a very delicate matter. Hammond wrote a letter to Grenville "soliciting your approbation" for "a matrimonial connection with a young lady at present in this country" and besought both the foreign secretary's approval and his sovereign's. Enclosed in his petition was a letter from Bond to William Hammond assuring the canny father that the marriage would be economical since Allen had a large estate and a bright future. The campaign culminated on May 20, 1793, when William White, Episcopal bishop of Pennsylvania, officiated at the couple's wedding in the season's premier social event. The brief honeymoon did not interrupt the minister's constant flow of complaints to Jefferson on subjects ranging from French privateers to Loyalist confiscations, but the couple did manage a quick trip to the site of the proposed new capital of Washington City, which impressed Hammond equally with its scenic beauty and its poor prospects.[21]

The marriage marked the last of the minister's personal happiness in America. In late summer Philadelphia was scourged by an outbreak of yellow fever, compelling Hammond's personal and official family to move to Lansdowne, Pennsylvania, for safety. Hammond described the outbreak with characteristic hyperbole as "the most malignant in its nature and the most extensive in its effect of any with which the human race has been afflicted in any country,"[22] as the fever cost the frightened household several severe bouts of illness and the lives of a steward and a maid. Soon thereafter reports arrived that a British-arranged truce in a Portuguese-Algerine war had opened the Strait of Gibraltar to Algerine pirates who seized American ships and carried seamen off to slavery.

Authorities as dissimilar as Consul David Humphreys at Gibraltar, Rufus King in New York, Christopher Gore in Boston, and Thomas Jefferson in Philadelphia agreed that Britain had arranged the peace merely to harass America's competitive commerce and that the Barbary cutthroats were "but the automatons of George the Third." In August and November, 1793, authenticated copies of Grenville's Orders in Council attacking Franco-American trade arrived in the American capital, and simultaneous reports told of British warships and privateers seizing American ships wholesale. Capricious condemnations of these vessels by West Indian prize courts were accompanied by American impressments into British warships. Even an American consul was seized and his papers confiscated.

As these tales reached the seaboard, infuriated mobs swarmed the streets of Baltimore, assaulted two British captains who had been French prisoners awaiting transport home, and stripped the ship intended for their return. A West Indian court's threat to Baltimore's war hero, Capt. Joshua Barney, brought such dire threats of retribution on Thornton, who had been sent to Baltimore as acting vice-consul, that Hammond ordered him back to Philadelphia, where even the minister and Consul Bond were receiving "very many indecent threats."[23]

Although personally courageous, Hammond drew from this excitement two conclusions, both wrong: first, that they represented the

American counterpart of the early French Reign of Terror, and second, that the administration did not share the indignation of the demonstrators. He was convinced by Hamilton that the cabinet desired a pro-British stance but that, as he wrote Grenville, "The domineering spirit of the agents of France," assisted by the anti-British southern states, defeated Washington's aims so that the administration, "instead of magnanimously avowing its inefficiency under the *present* constitution . . . to repress foreign insolence . . . endeavors to palliate its inability by half measures or to conceal its weaknesses. . . ." He therefore compiled a list of the states' pro-French violations of neutrality to "extort" from the administration "something like a confession of its own impotence."[24] George Hammond was neither incompetent nor stupid, but inexperience, nervous irritation, and arrogance prevented his recognition of an emerging national identity. Any minister of His Majesty who required of a government of the caliber of Washington's that it "magnanimously avow its inefficiency" and "confess its impotence" was dangerously out of touch with reality.

When Congress assembled on December 2, 1793, instead of confessing its impotence, the administration, through Secretary Jefferson, laid before the House a report on overseas commerce, stressing the restrictions with which it was burdened and suggesting countervailing duties against those nations refusing reciprocal reductions. A month later Madison followed with resolutions proposing the very discriminatory duties the threat of which had brought Hammond to America two years earlier. Worse followed. Jefferson had long outraged Hammond by publishing their diplomatic exchanges, and in the last days of his tenure in the State Department he laid before Congress printed copies of their entire correspondence on the northwest posts, showing that no progress had been made in that dangerous area. Hammond countered with an outraged note to newly appointed Secretary of State Edmund Randolph, who, he predicted to Grenville, would "improve upon the prevarication and subterfuge practiced by his predecessor."[25]

Unfortunately for Hammond, in Quebec, Lord Dorchester, governor general of Canada, had for some time felt that his thirty-year service in Canadian affairs conferred on him a power of divination wholly independent of the British cabinet's pacific Canadian policy. Hence in February, 1794, His Lordship, convinced of the inevitability of Anglo-American war, shared this insight with a considerable body of Indians and accompanied it with assurances that there was no Canadian-

American boundary at present but that one would be created after America lost the war. A week later Lord Dorchester ordered the bellicose Lieutenant Governor Simcoe to advance well into American territory and reestablish an abandoned fort at the Maumee Rapids, a particularly dangerous gambit since Anthony Wayne was moving from Cincinnati to establish American control over the northwestern Indians. Secretary Randolph therefore brushed aside Hammond's protests of Jefferson's publications and demanded an explanation of the warlike Canadian activities. An "acrimonious and intemperate man" in Hammond's view, the new secretary displayed a talent for acerbity equal to Hammond's own and a written style that probed the very limits of diplomatic allowances.[26]

So in 1794, an able if arrogant young Tory sent out three years earlier for different purposes found himself locked in a triangular dilemma between Anglo-French mercantile warfare, excitable Canadian officials, and an emerging American nationalism expressed in mobs, political societies, scurrilous newspapers, and congressional maneuvering. Helpless to change any of these, a more experienced diplomat would have sought if not to understand, then to conciliate; George Hammond could only attack.

To proposed Congressional duties Hammond was indifferent in public and threatening in private. To friendly Federalist Rufus King he admitted regret at Dorchester's bellicosity, but to Secretary Randolph he flatly refused to be questioned about it. He counterattacked on a broad front ranging from alleged American assistance to French privateers to Canadian incursions by Vermont citizens. Stung by Jeffersonian editors' descriptions of him as "an incendiary Jack-in-office" and "the British Solon whose function it is to lay down the law to subject peoples," Hammond demanded a federal libel suit against the editors as "indispensably necessary" to resist "the licentious torrent of abuse . . . from the public presses of this country."[27]

In diplomatic fencing, one wounds and is wounded, but Hammond's talent for personal offensiveness was striking, animated as it was by the flaming arch-Toryism of his close friend Bond. Mounting problems pointed up his personal deficiencies. "In addition to disliking Americans," a French visitor remarked, "his violent nature makes it impossible for him to hold his tongue, and frequently leads him to make mountains out of molehills." Tench Coxe wrote Jefferson that the minister's notes proved him "unfit for the management of affairs with this country." Randolph wrote Washington that "he seems to be exceedingly petulant; exposes many weak sides; does his cause an injury; thinks that it is something to say the last word however unimportant it may be. . . ." The president mildly agreed that "for reasons yet unknown," Hammond seemed to be "more captious than conciliatory." In private, Hammond's fury with the Americans dismayed even his devoted wife and Tory father-in-law.[28]

More remarkable tributes to the minister's unpopularity came from pro-British Federalists. Oliver Wolcott described him as "a weak, vain, and imprudent character, very much in the company and under the influence of sour and prejudiced tories who wish to see the country disgraced."[29] Fisher Ames believed that "he has sense and good principles, but he rails against the conduct of our government, not *oro rotundo* but with a gobble that his feelings render doubly unintelligible." Young Federalist John Quincy Adams unconsciously testified to Hammond's insensitivity in an account of a private dinner conversation. The Briton first attacked the mystic tie that binds all Adamses by inviting his Federalist host to disparage the Republican governor, Samuel Adams. Then, rebuffed in this, the minister remarked on how infinitely stronger the English government was than the American. According to Adams, he "wished well to our government and hoped it would continue. But he believed that two-thirds of the people were opposed to it whereas in Britain there was not more than a hundred hostile to their government."[30] It would have been difficult to invent a surer formula for antagonizing an outstanding young American nationalist like Adams.

The dangers inherent in having such a personally combative British envoy grew more apparent as Anglo-French mercantile warfare exacted its price in America. Both the English and the French capriciously seized American ships and cargoes for condemnation, but superior British seapower and a common language provided more opportunity for outrage. Arrogant British captains impressed seamen ashore, violated the neutrality of American ports and waters, threatened violence and blockade, and in general behaved as though dealing with the helpless natives of the African littoral. In response, furious citizens of New York, Baltimore, and Norfolk attacked landing parties, refused supplies, assisted desertion-minded British seamen, and tried to hale British officers before American courts. Democratic societies proliferated, and addresses poured into Congress demanding various retaliations. Amid speeches that Hammond called "disgraceful . . . to the lowest order of the community in any other country," the House considered bills for the sequestration of British property, commercial embargoes, and an army of fifteen thousand to fifty thousand men.

The angry Tory found himself both personally threatened and diplomatically besieged while, he wrote, "perpetually increasing . . . hostility to Great Britain pervades the whole of the continent." While legislators listened with approval to "insult and indecency," unchecked mobs threatened British ship captains, and the secretary of state answered his protests with "arrogance and menace" in "scurrilous and offensive language." Even Hamilton's Anglophilia occasionally cooled while the cabinet endlessly debated problems of captured vessels of both nations. In April, 1794, the minister somberly wrote about "the ferment in this country," that if it continued, he could not "be responsible for the preservation of the peace with Great Britain for any indefinite period."[31]

Fortunately for Anglo-American relations, that responsibility was not to be his. Federalist congressmen desperately sought to avoid open war, and in April the Senate confirmed Washington's nomination of John Jay as special envoy to England, seeking to achieve a treaty and to save the peace. Meanwhile, through the accidents of storms and mischance, none of Hammond's alarming dispatches written between February and May reached Grenville before June 10, 1794. Only then did Downing Street find that instead of the Anglo-American "harmony and understanding" that it professed to seek, there existed a fair possibility of American collaboration with revolutionary France.

To Grenville, therefore, the prospect of a treaty made in London between himself and the well-known friend of Britain, Jay, was attractive. Grenville perceived at once the necessity of calming matters by neutralizing Randolph and restraining Hammond. A stream of instructions therefore flowed from the Foreign Office. To curb Randolph's "spirit of hostility to Great Britain," Hammond was told to "converse confidentially" with Britain's friends in the administration so as to "either convince Mr. Randolph of the necessity of his adopting a different language and conduct" or else to destroy his influence. Dorchester and Simcoe were reined in. Hammond himself first received official approval for his conduct under trying circumstances "in which you have manifested great judgment and discretion while you maintained with a proper degree of spirit the rights of this country." He was then told to retreat on some minor points of neutrality, avoid correspondence with Randolph where possible, and refer differences to London to be settled by the treaty makers.[32]

The foreign minister's precautions were wise. The arrival of Rear Adm. George Murray with a squadron in American waters galvanized Hammond into hiring more propagandists, quarreling with Randolph over the sale of French prizes, and advancing new British legal claims. As he surveyed changes in diplomatic posts, he saw little good. In Paris, he told Grenville, America would soon be represented by James Monroe, "a man of moderate abilities and of embarrassed circumstances . . . long distinguished by his hostility to Great Britain." In Washington's cabinet Henry Knox would be followed in the War Department by Timothy Pickering, a man "possessing the most blind undistinguishing hatred of Great Britain," a misjudgment that ranks high among the most monumental made by British envoys.[33]

More serious was the impending departure of Hamilton, whose collaboration had so long helped the minister and who assured him that he would still remain helpful. Before Jay departed, Hamilton disclosed to Hammond that America would not insist on the free-ships–free-goods argument for which Jay was instructed to press and also that America would reject membership in a League of Neutrality, a sore subject with London.[34]

There the patrician and like-minded negotiators discovered by September, 1794, through sometimes tense but always polite sessions, that they could prevent the war that neither wanted. On November 19, they signed a treaty. Two days later a confidential note from Grenville suggested that the vitriolic diplomatic exchanges in Philadelphia arising from "personal animosities" should cease.[35] He assured them that the tone of Hammond's notes would be softened and asked at the same time for a similar reform in Randolph's. Next day Jay replied with similar hopes and added, "I have a good opinion of Mr. Hammond, more I really wish him well; the asperities, however, which have taken place lead me to apprehend that official darts have frequently pierced through the official characters and wounded the men." Hence he wished "Mr. Hammond had a better place, and that a person well adapted to the state of things [be] sent to succeed him." "Public and common good," he concluded, "is my object and motive." He also balanced a suggestion of more circumspection in the publication of diplomatic notes in

America with the further suggestion that the fiery James Hamilton, British consul at Norfolk, might also be replaced.[36]

Grenville took the suggestions in good spirits and on December 9, 1794, wrote a private letter to his protégé suggesting that since events in America had placed him "in a difficult and disagreeable situation . . . it will be by no means unpleasant to yourself to be relieved from it." Also, matters in America might best be served by "a person unmixed in the late discussions." He therefore sent Hammond a formal leave of absence and promised him another place in which his officially approved talent and zeal could be used. The formal leave, dated the next day, directed that before quitting America he present Bond as chargé d'affaires.[37]

A freakish fate ruled George Hammond's mission. The objects of his mission having been swept away within a year of his arrival, Hammond had spent three years in professional stalemate, personal dislike, and private fury. He was recalled to further the cause for which he had been sent. Nevertheless, in his last eight months in Philadelphia, Hammond attained professional and personal successes over his enemies and he returned home in triumph.

The turnabout came through routine wartime episodes: the captures of two ships at sea. In the first, His Majesty's ship *Tankersley*, bearing Jay's copy of his treaty and Hammond's recall, was taken by a French privateer. Hence the State Department was for four months ignorant of the treaty's contents, and Hammond did not learn of his recall until May, 1795. Meanwhile, the president and Secretary Randolph on March 7 received a copy of the deeply disappointing treaty. Submitted to the Senate for advice, the treaty was kept in debate in close secrecy until June 24, when it was ratified by the exact number of senatorial votes needed. A renewed effort at secrecy was defeated, and upon the publication of a précis the firestorm broke.

Future historians would debate the merits of the agreement, but to many contemporary Americans it represented American capitulations on neutral rights, Indian trade, boundaries, and the British Navigation System. Parades, editorials, demonstrations, and seething oratory swept along seaboard America, together with rumors of British bribery. Of course the slightest association with Albion's representative produced furious denunciations. At the same time, the arrival of a new Order in Council and the outrageous impressments, demands, threats, and attacks of British captain Rodham Home in Newport's harbor fed the flames. Amid this uproar, Randolph assured Hammond that the president would not sign the treaty without amendment of the Orders in Council and Article XII, limiting the West Indian trade. In July, Washington left the capital for Mount Vernon in considerable doubt as to the wisdom of the new agreement. In the same month public fury struck at Hammond and Bond. After a stormy meeting under Republican John Beckley, a crowd of three hundred or four hundred burned a copy of the treaty at Consul Bond's house, then streamed through the streets to Hammond's. There, while the minister and his frightened family watched from the windows, the crowd, according to Hammond's report, "arranged themselves in . . . the street . . . and after expressing their indignation by various noises" burned another copy.[38]

The minister's fury at the mob was mitigated by his recent acquisition of a devastating counterweapon. In a second sea encounter a British cruiser had taken the French packet *Jean Bart* and thereby placed in Grenville's hands the dispatches of Minister Fauchet to his government. In one of them the rambling rhetoric of the minister seemed to report a request by Secretary Randolph for a financial inducement to buy southern opposition to Britain. In May Grenville had sent Hammond a précis of the damning document and then a copy with directions to use them for the British interest.

On July 27, the minister reported the receipt of these instructions. He lost no time in inviting Secretary of the Treasury Wolcott to a small private dinner and in Thornton's company only, showed him the Fauchet dispatch. After further talk with the arch-Federalist secretary, Hammond gave him the original (in French) in return for an attested copy prepared by Thornton. Wolcott immediately convened the Francophobe Pickering and Attorney General Bradford, and after an amateur translation by Pickering they urgently summoned Washington from Mount Vernon and presented him with the dubious evidence and an accusation of Randolph as a traitor. The distraught president thereupon reversed himself and accepted the treaty, after which there was an emotional confrontation with Randolph, who, upon being accused of soliciting bribes, resigned in semiarticulate fury. On August 14, he informed Hammond that he had been overruled and that the treaty would be ratified.

Hammond's principal concern now was a quick departure with the ratified treaty before his part in the attack on Randolph became known.

Hence he immediately took his formal leave of Washington, presenting Bond as chargé. On the following day Hammond went to New York, hoping to confer there with Jay and Hamilton. On August 17, 1795, he sailed for Halifax on the frigate *Thistle*.[39]

As his ship left the harbor, Hammond could review his mission with satisfaction. Appointed, supported, guided, and protected from himself by Grenville, the minister had carried out the Pitt-Grenville policy of peace-with-rigor. He had attracted insult and hatred, but he had seen two American secretaries of state retire in bafflement. He had solved none of the problems of his original instructions, but they were deferred for arbitration by other diplomats. Meanwhile, American merchant ships faced the guns and boarding parties of the British fleet and the vagaries of British prize courts. In London a valiant but inexperienced American chargé, William A. Deas, faced Grenville's ponderous wrath almost wholly unsupported by an Anglophile Secretary of State Pickering. But in Philadelphia, Britain's chargé Bond could count on the sympathy of the most pro-British American cabinet yet created. So, as Hammond's ship approached the friendly shores of home, his peevish irritation faded, and a long-suffering wife wrote her father: "George has never been so attentive. . . . Ever since we left America he has been so changed. His cold, formal manner, *not only with strangers* has been thrown off and everybody observes how agreeable he is in company. . . . I don't think you ever saw him at his best in Philadelphia. I think we shall be very happy together."[39]

Grenville was quick with rewards. Even before Hammond's arrival in England, Bland Burges was bought out of the undersecretaryship of foreign affairs, which was awarded to the protégé in October, 1795, despite the only mild enthusiasm of his sovereign. There for eleven years Hammond profoundly affected Anglo-American relationships during three administrations by means of hard work, social acceptance, and unshakable prejudice. He bought a handsome house in Spring Gardens and entered into the high-spirited company of George Canning, Hookham Frere, George Ellis, and other rising Tories. He conferred officially with their powerful elders, Sir William Scott, Lord Hawkesbury, Henry Pelham, William Pitt, and others of the tight Tory coterie that governed Britain. As an expert on America he was consulted frequently, and he dispensed patronage and directed editors and journalists like William Cobbett. As his official stature increased, so did his girth, while his penmanship became so bad that George Canning pronounced it a form of cipher, and the younger diplomats secretly delighted in his unceasing pompousness. With Canning he was a moving spirit in founding the short-lived, vitriolic *Anti-Jacobin*, and he contributed to its pages such anti-Americanisms as to complicate the tenure of his successor in America. When the *Anti-Jacobin* foundered, the equally High Tory *Quarterly Review* was conceived at a dinner party in Hammond's home.

The former envoy never rid himself of three delusions about America: that inveterate American hostility to Britain arose from the self-interest of southern agrarian debtors and northern commercial rivals; that the American central government was too weak to control anarchic forces derived from France; and that American leaders were almost without exception hesitant like Washington, venal like Randolph, anarchic like Jefferson, or manipulative like Wolcott, and must therefore be controlled by threat or self-interest. Early in his undersecretaryship, Hammond clashed with John Quincy Adams in London. The Massachusetts man contemptuously delineated this "man of intrigue" and his "fawning malice." "I do see to the bottom of this Justice Shallow," he wrote in his diary, "but he knows not me." After further verbal combat, Adams noted that Hammond "came at last to a language not less intelligible, but rather more of unqualified acid."[40]

Hammond's long London service was interspersed with occasional brief Continental assignments. In 1806, when Foreign Secretary Fox hoped for an American rapprochement, he retired Hammond, who, however, came back as undersecretary under Canning's short administration from 1807 to 1809. Hammond later lived in high style in Paris for three years while serving on an Anglo-French war reparations commission. He retired in 1828 and watched his youngest son Edmund enter the diplomatic service and achieve a knighthood in a career that outshone his father's. In 1853, George Hammond died at the age of ninety.

Antagonism from Hammond's American mission never cooled. In 1814, at a watershed of Anglo-American relations, when Castlereagh offered him a position among the British negotiators at Ghent, Hammond had wisely replied that

my sentiments with regard to America are so well known both in that country and this and during my residence in the former I was necessarily so much engaged in hostile and irritating discussions . . . that if the . . . negotiations should fail I have little doubt that the failure would in a great measure be ascribed to me and the ministers . . . would in that case be exposed to censure for employing a person so obnoxious as I have been to the American government.[41]

This was the undersecretary who had briefed and prepared instructions for the four envoys who succeeded him in America. Of the four, two were, with himself, the most despised British ministers to America in half a century. A third largely ignored his instructions and admitted that he profited from Hammond's unpopularity. The fourth was recalled in disgrace for attempting to ameliorate the instructions made in part by George Hammond.

Robert Liston

"Much may be made of a Scotchman if he be caught young."
—Samuel Johnson

WHILE George Hammond sailed triumphantly homeward, Foreign Secretary William Grenville devoted such attention as he could divert from European warfare to maintaining the diplomatic headway achieved by Jay's Treaty. He chose age, temperament, experience, and Scottish scholarship.

Robert Liston, from an upper-middle-class West Lothian family, had been a first-rate scholar in languages, philosophy, and mathematics at the University of Edinburgh. There in 1772, a year before Hammond's birth, he was—by that combination of diligence and deferential good manners always impressive to academic faculties—chosen to be private tutor to the sons of Sir Gilbert Elliot, a friend of both the elder Pitt and the earl of Bute. Elliot's younger son, Hugh, on becoming minister to the Court of Bavaria, took tutor Liston there with him as secretary of legation and in the same capacity from 1772 to 1782 to the Court of Prussia.

In Berlin, Liston's debut with Americans was an unpropitious involvement in an attempt to burglarize the papers of traveling diplomat Arthur Lee. Nevertheless, the earl of Bute's son, John Stuart, took his fellow Scot with him to the Court of Madrid, and upon Stuart's return home in 1784, Scottish interests in Madrid secured for the former tutor the undemanding post of minister plenipotentiary there. Liston spent five uneventful years in Madrid. He relied on Consul General Anthony Merry at Málaga in commercial matters while he gave himself to music, reading, visiting, and the accommodation of important visitors.

From Madrid he was at age forty-six posted to Stockholm, where he built Listonhill, a comfortable private residence, and worked professionally with his benefactor, Hugh Elliot. The outbreak of Anglo-French warfare sent him in 1794 to Constantinople, presumably because of linguistic skill and savoir faire, but, though the salary was augmented by stipends from the Levant Company and the sultan, the cost of living there was one of the highest in the service. Liston, still unmarried at fifty, then lost his home by fire. A seasoned, urbane diplomat, he was available for further assignment before the close of a useful career.

In London, meanwhile, Jay was pressing Grenville to send to America a minister "possessed if possible of your prudence and self-command," and Gouverneur Morris also urged "a man of social temper."[1] An Anglo-Spanish war was an increasing possibility, and Spain was a neighbor of both Britain and the United States in North America. Grenville's remedy for dealing with diplomatic fallout from French Revolutionary explosions was an experienced envoy who would use personal influence among the American upper classes, utilizing treaties when they existed and the British navy when necessary. The pleasant, good-tempered, middle-aged Liston, who had been mentioned for America in 1783, seemed an excellent choice. Therefore, the foreign secretary raised the American post to envoy extraordinary and minister plenipotentiary (a slight elevation, but still a secondary rank); increased its stipend to £2,000 and contingencies; and called Liston from Constantinople in August, 1795, even before Hammond's return.

On February 22, 1796, during a brief visit to Glasgow between tours, Liston married Henrietta Marchant, daughter of Nathaniel Marchant, a physician living in Antigua. Henrietta, about forty, was a woman of minor financial means and major literary output in correspondence and diaries, who for some years had been devoted to the wandering and scarcely ardent diplomat. After the marriage, the legal arrangement, the collection of family books, pictures, and plate, the domestic staff and equipage, and interviews with Grenville and Hammond absorbed the few weeks until departure. The new appointee, at fifty-three, had little enthusiasm for the post and wrote a friend: "*Entre nous* I would much rather go anywhere else. A severe climate, hard work, and the being surrounded with ill disposed Yankee doctrinaires will at my time of life probably finish me off in a year or two. However Lord G very flatteringly says that I am the only man suitable; the French are making infinite trouble in that quarter and must be thwarted; so I suppose I must go."[2]

Liston chose Thornton, still vice-consul at Baltimore, as his secretary of legation. Undersecretary Hammond provided the fifty-gun frigate *Assistance*, and the official family—five servants including a maid, maître d'hôtel, and two footmen—embarked from Plymouth on March 18, 1796. The six-week voyage, which was stormy and complicated by an outbreak of smallpox and a scare from a French privateer, finally ended at New York on May 1. The taverns were full as citizens celebrated what Henrietta Liston called "the feast day of Saint Taminy . . . an American Indian chief of great renown and the titular saint of America." More important, their steward's reconnaissance discovered that news of a successful appropriations bill to carry out Jay's Treaty had made "the people's mind a little agitated"[3] and a mob was collecting, so the official party delayed disembarking and then went to the Belvedere Tavern, a mile from town.

Soon after the Listons' arrival, invitations arrived for social occasions whose splendor surprised them. An invitation from Consul General Sir John Temple produced a box at the New York theater, where Henrietta noted that "the usual offensive French music" was omitted in their honor. Henrietta recorded visits from Jay, "in dress and manner strikingly like a Quaker . . . his eye penetrating . . . his deportment grave," and from Hamilton, "lively and animated in conversation . . . gallant in his manners and sometimes brilliant in his sallies." She also found that her husband was well liked, "particularly as his predecessor Mr. Hammond was extremely unpopular, both here and at Philadelphia." At that capital the couple arrived on May 12, "well exercised" by wild American driving in a springless stage over roads that were "little if at all made and that little ill done."

The entourage was scattered over the capital until the departure of the Spanish minister provided a single dwelling, not very handsome but large enough for the household that continually grew. Almost immediately came Lord Henry Stuart, second son of Liston's patron, the earl of Bute. Lord Henry was a handsome nineteen-year-old without known vices or abilities, sent ostensibly to act as Liston's private secretary, but actually to be removed from London's temptations. Then, to save money, Secretary of Legation Thornton moved into the ministerial residence. A more rabid Tory than his chief, Thornton was personally attached to the family and, said Henrietta, "from having been long in this country" was "very useful to us."[4] Far less so was one Henry Brown, a ne'er-do-well friend of Henrietta's brother in Scotland, who made no contribution whatsoever.

On May 16, Secretary of State Pickering presented the new minister to President Washington, after which Thornton was presented and Mrs. Liston called on Mrs. Washington. Liston's popularity was immediate. Already advised by William Pinkney from London that the envoy was "a sensible well-informed man of pleasing manners and dispassionate temper whose . . . prejudices are in our favor,"[5] Federalists rejoiced in the amiable and relaxed sophistication and the gratifying style of living at the new embassy. Liston himself never felt Hammond's visceral aversion to all things not British and displayed tact and on occasion a mild sportiveness. He combined cultural interests—competence on the flute and an amazing number of foreign languages—with a healthy passion for good cheese and Highland "whysky." Henrietta was reserved but highly intelligent, possessing Scottish practicality, a genuine attachment to the natural beauties of the new nation, and a hopeful interest in its proximity to her relatives in the West Indies. A gracious hostess and a good diplomat herself, she praised when she could and reserved her more acid comments on the American scene for her Scottish correspondents.

Minister Liston wrote Undersecretary Hammond—much of whose advice he was wisely ignoring—that his own business would probably be confined to executing the Jay treaty and that "nothing is wanted . . . to keep this country on a footing of peace and good humour with Great Britain except a degree of civility and attention to justice on the part of our Sons of Neptune—but of these I have already had some reason to complain."[6] The Sons were, in fact, the principal threat to Liston's success. Already in July, 1795, Capt. Rodham Home, infuriated by British desertions, had imperiled ratification of the new treaty by threatening to bombard Newport, Rhode Island, by seizing and searching various American ships there and by otherwise violating American neutrality. In the same month, twenty American vessels in the West Indies had been stripped of their crews by another of Neptune's Sons. These and other reports filled the newspapers, as did Secretary Pickering's unavailing notes of protest.

Liston recognized the widespread American inducements to desertion, but he feared that callous British attacks by both warships and privateers would destroy chances for implementation of Jay's Treaty. Even Pickering, who surrendered on the rights of naturalized Americans, was infuriated by the mistreatment of American seamen, "the only subject," wrote Liston, "upon which I have never been able to bring him to speak with moderation." Noting that American fury was not confined to the "uninformed rabble of Philadelphia," the minister urged the Foreign Office to "remedy or at least mitigate this evil" and implored the Sons to use "forbearance and moderation."[7]

Neither appeal was successful. Captain Mowat, soon to replace a more temperate officer on the American Station, replied to Liston that "it is my duty to keep my ship manned, and I will do so whenever I find men that speak the same language with me, and not a small part of them British subjects."[8] Grenville, absorbed with the European conflict, brushed aside as notoriously fraudulent "certificates" of American nationality offered by Pickering and broke off discussions on the mutual restoration of deserters when the Americans linked the idea with efforts to curtail impressment. He also overruled Liston by refusing an American effort to place an agent in the West Indies as a resource for destitute or impressed Americans.

Aside from this naval stalemate, Liston fared well in his first year. Five British-occupied forts were handed over to American garrisons, and a beginning was made in the process of selecting arbiters under Jay's Treaty. Washington's Farewell Address strengthened the Federalists, and Liston skillfully handled the able if vain Rufus King both directly in America and via London.

The Listons and Washingtons maintained a mutual admiration unique among early diplomats and presidents. Nine years younger than Washington yet sharing with him much social and political philosophy, Liston was deeply impressed by both the president's dignity and his silence. He was, the minister told Benjamin Rush, "the only person he had ever known (and he had conversed with several crowned heads and many of the first nobility of Europe) who made *no* reply of any kind to a question that he did not choose to answer."[9] Henrietta spoke of "his face at the age of sixty-three rather pleasant, particularly when he smiled" and of "the dignity of air and manner" and "general coldness of his address." Mrs. Washington, though short and fat was "not without dignity, her face retaining the marks of delicate beauty and her voice . . . music itself."[10] At the Washingtons' invitation the Listons attended presidential dinners (Thursdays), levees (Tuesdays), and drawing rooms (Fridays). These last affairs were crushingly formal, each lady after a curtsy to Mrs. Washington being rather stranded in one location and able to speak only to her immediate neighbors. The president determinedly made the rounds with a word to each. After tea, coffee, cakes, and wine were served, the parties broke up in deference to the Quaker City's supposed disapproval of card games. The affairs, to young Thornton appallingly dull, were to Henrietta not "scenes of animation or hilarity" but were on the whole pleasant. At state dinners—gentlemen in full dress and clergy in canonicals—Henrietta, as the ranking diplomat's wife, invariably sat on the president's right, an omen for the future.

Still, Henrietta's modest social background made the demands of her new station depressing. For economy or other reasons she declined to give supper parties except when absolutely required, but instead held weekly drawing-room parties from seven until eleven, featuring tea, coffee, and the card tables denied Mrs. Washington by Quaker sensibilities. These affairs were widely attended, and Henrietta wrote with justice that her husband was "of no party" and "the greatest Democrates in town visit us, both English and American, not frogs." British radicals William and Joseph Priestley joined French royalist emigrés, Scottish travelers, congressmen, and cabinet members. The Portuguese minister's family were personal friends, and until Spain's alliance with France the lively, good-humored young Spanish minister Carlos Martinez d'Yrujo told his hostess he was determined not to quarrel with her "sooner than he was obliged." Liston in turn attended Priestley's lectures and was described by him as "a pleasing, liberal man" and a "gratifying change from . . . Mr. Hammond," who had subsidized Cobbett's attack on the philosopher. French minister Pierre Adet attributed his rival's popularity to other origins. Liston was, he wrote home, "an extremely dangerous man for this country" who knew American weaknesses. "I know twenty people who have brilliant equipages since they have been closely connected with Mr. Liston. Before his arrival they did not have the means to have a cabriolet."

If money was thus spent, Henrietta must have coveted it. Her Scottish soul was outraged by American prices and wages. The eleven American servants at the embassy, she wrote, would not "submit to anyone but myself," and she agreed with Priestley that "the servants alone are sufficient to render a native of Britain miserable in this country." She also found that foreign ministers were "esteemed lawful game here and there is less real principle . . . than I expected to find, particularly in the lower orders of the people," yet the door could be left unlocked all night, for "cheating not stealing seems to be the error in America." She confessed, too, that "American ladies dance better than any set of people I ever saw," the one advantage she saw of the French association. Her real passion was gardening, "one of the many things for which the people of this country have no taste yet," and she pined for "minced collops and Scotch hare soup . . . unknown in this country." Meanwhile, although Minister Liston's pay and accounts were far in arrears, he lavishly ordered silver services, coaches, furniture, and clothing.[11]

The summer provided a necessary break in official entertainment as officialdom fled the city's heat. The Listons took up residence in Germantown, but in August, with an entourage that included Lord Henry Stuart, Thornton, and a maid, they set forth on their first American tour. In hired carriages they battled execrable roads to Baltimore and Annapolis, through Alexandria and "a small town called George Town," to the site of the future national capital. Liston thought the site strongly resembled Constantinople, and Henrietta admitted it was "noble and beautiful" though in a six-mile circuit she saw only about one hundred houses and "cows feeding where streets ought to be."[12] After a three-day visit to Mount Vernon they returned to Germantown over roads that taxed the strength of four horses. By December they were reestablished in the capital.

Liston, meanwhile, observed the summer and fall elections with a philosophical detachment far removed from Hammond's frenetics. He reported "powerful instruments of defamation" used unfairly against both Adams (as a monarchist) and Jefferson (as an atheist). Witnessing the hired polemicists, bought votes, and intimidation of the nation's third presidential election, Liston commented wryly that "if the infant state of the society is taken into consideration, the advances . . . in the road toward corruption will be found to be as rapid as was to be expected."[13]

In fact, during the fall and winter of 1796–97, when Spain joined the French republicans and Bonaparte's Italian victories brought him to the world's attention, European events transformed Liston's mission as they had formerly recast Hammond's. The first British minister had come to clarify issues of the 1783 Peace of Paris but was locked in a siege of embattled arrogance over French revolutionary issues until rescued by Jay's Treaty. Liston was sent merely to implement that treaty, but the Directory's policies swept him to the very threshold of the triumph of Anglo-American military collaboration. The storms of Europe thus transformed the missions of the first two British ministers just as they were to defeat the efforts of the next four.

The first moves in the reorientation of Liston came from French resentment of Jay's Treaty and the actions of Pierre Adet, who in June, 1796, succeeded Joseph Fauchet. Adet immediately publicized the Directory's decision to treat American ships as that nation "allowed" Britain to treat them while authorizing French privateers to capture American shipping. He followed these with a well-publicized announcement of his impending return to France. Anti-French feeling rose accordingly. Adet then compounded his problems by engaging in an almost venomous published correspondence with Secretary of State Pickering, who, upon finding a correspondent as virulent as himself, cast aside impartiality for the rest of his life.[14] The correspondence with Adet, wrote Liston, "operated on Mr. Pickering a complete conversion, who is become one of the most virulent Anti-Gallicans I have ever met with." Washington, too, Henrietta reported, became "very much inraged" at the insults to himself and his people.[15] Liston's stock rose higher while attending social functions for the outgoing and incoming presidents. Meanwhile, the Directory ejected Minister Charles Cotesworth Pinckney from France and began a yet more anti-American policy of seizures and threats.

Then, just as his popularity soared, His Majesty's minister to America embarked upon a nearly ruinous enterprise. In November, 1796, there arrived in Philadelphia from Knoxville, Tennessee, one Capt. John Chisholm, a Scottish-born Indian trader, merchant, innkeeper, and handyman of Sen. William Blount of that state, formerly governor of the Southwest Territory. Chisholm accompanied some Creek Indians who sought the usual largesse from the national government, and for himself and his fellow former Loyalists Chisholm sought American citizenship. Both hopes were rudely treated by Secretary of War McHenry, and the innkeeper approached the minister with a proposal. He could, he said, enroll for His Majesty's service some one thousand former Tory land speculators and general adventurers in the southwest, together with some five thousand Indians already committed. Britain would "legalize" the expedition with temporary military commissions for the leaders, a cash advance, and powder, lead, blankets, and shirts for the Indians, together with some artillery and engineers and a frigate or two or three smaller vessels.

This force would attack Mobile, New Orleans, and Pensacola, seizing East and West Florida, while another group of Indians from the north under Joseph Brant would attack New Madrid on the Mississippi—in present-day Missouri—and then move on the Spanish silver mines of New Mexico and whatever else looked valuable. The Indians would be rewarded with movable loot and the renewal of British trading posts in the Floridas, while the gentlemen leaders would possess themselves of Spanish estates in Florida and Spanish silver. The Floridas and Louisiana would revert to British colony status, Chisholm would become Indian superintendent, common soldiers would receive land grants, Pensacola and New Orleans would be free ports, and the Mississippi River would be open to British and Spanish ships.

Nothing in the early history of the United States is more persistent than the myriad schemes by which small filibustering expeditions planned to seize imperial domains supported by large fleets conjured from vast distances. Eighteenth-century European wars had scattered throughout the American backwoods various aristocratic emigrés, alleged royalty, unemployed army officers, revolutionists, bankrupts, discarded heroes, and multinational outcasts. Elementary reason would show their logistics to be preposterous and their invariable dependence on Indian "allies" unrealistic, yet the exploits of Clive, Wolfe, and other heroes were fresh in men's minds. With such magnificent prizes as Louisiana and the Floridas in Spain's feeble grasp, frontier allegiances were precarious indeed. Governors, state legislators, congressmen, and even a vice-president staked their careers on schemes less realistic than Chisholm's. Moreover, Jay's Treaty and the election of Adams had convinced France's leadership that America was now irrevocably fixed in the British orbit. French policy therefore turned to the retrocession of Louisiana from Spain so as to threaten Canada and make France's West Indian island independent of the American trade. In Paris a succession of foreign ministers—Otto, Moustier, and Talleyrand—used various traveling agents, notably Victor Collot and Samuel Fulton, to make geographical, military, and political studies in Louisiana and the American southwest.

Thus, the sophisticated, experienced Liston was persuaded that an alcoholic, backwoods babbler whose sole qualifications for intrigue were boldness and imagination was "a man of good sense and judgment and of steady and determined character." The plan, the minister wrote Grenville, was of "easy execution" and "very inconsiderable" cost and would defeat French machinations "of serious not to say destructive consequences" to British prosperity.[16] In a series of meetings Chisholm glibly answered Liston's concerns about American neutrality and Indian atrocities. As the vision gained splendor (British ownership of the Spanish silver mines was now envisioned), Liston began writing Lieutenant Governor Prescott in Quebec about overland supply routes. On January 25, 1797, he reported the plan to Grenville in a cipher dispatch, followed by a slightly more cautious note on February 13. In March and April he wrote careful but favorable letters to Undersecretary Hammond. Meanwhile, Chisholm was giving new and disastrous dimensions to the plot. First he gossiped so freely that the plan reached Victor Collot and then Spanish minister Yrujo. Then the sometime innkeeper approached his patron, Senator Blount, who was now nearly bankrupt and deeply concerned lest his vast western land speculations totally collapse upon a French occupation of Louisiana. Blount immediately moved to take over the enterprise, and Chisholm, fearing this, told Liston that he was "irresistibly impelled" to go to London and present his case in person to the Foreign Office. Liston therefore advanced him passage money with a promise of more aid in London and provided introductions to Grenville, Hammond, and others, along with spurious mercantile letters to cover the intrigue. Chisholm left for London on March 20, 1797.

Within a month the minister's conspiratorial world collapsed. Almost before Chisholm left America, Grenville had read Liston's dispatches on the plan and summarily rejected the whole matter. The Foreign Office had no desire to jeopardize American collaboration against France by so unstable a scheme, and for a variety of reasons Liston was told to break off the matter with Chisholm. Unfortunately, Chisholm was now in London explaining his exotic plan to His Majesty's highly unenthusiastic secretary of state and spending Liston's money. Still worse, in the same disastrous month of April, Senator Blount wrote a letter to a Tennessee henchman and included the damaging statement that Blount would "probably be at the head of the business on the part of the British," and the letter fell into the hands of the Adams administration.[17] Liston had therefore given his approval to an intrigue now known to the administration and which was in effect if not in law a violation of American neutrality. Liston's reaction to this crisis was to urge Grenville to send Chisholm back "for the sake of appearances . . . and that he may have no . . . claims on me for considerable sums of money."[18] He then replied to a Pickering inquiry (compelled by Yrujo's suspicions) about British plans for an attack on Louisiana from Canada by a pious denial and sermon on the impropriety of violating neutral American territory.

The Foreign Office, however irritated, backed its minister, and when the American minister in London, Federalist Rufus King, mildly regretted that Liston had not informed the American government of "a scheme so mischievous and so hazardous to our peace," Grenville arrogantly replied that Liston had no right to do so since it "might have involved the proposers in much personal risk."[19] Grenville criticized Liston only for admitting the existence of the plot at all—an example of impolitic goodwill toward America that would not be repeated.

Fortunately for American self-respect, President Adams chose to lay Blount's intercepted letter before Congress, and the two houses began an investigation. Incriminating papers appeared: Blount's speculator-associate Dr. Nicholas Romayne, according to Liston "ended by revealing more than there appears to have been any necessity to do," copies of Liston's instructions to Chisholm were produced, and Chisholm's ship's owner revealed still more of Liston's part, leading to what the minister called an "exaggerated account" of his role.[20] While the House impeached Blount and the Senate sequestered his seat, Liston took his stand on Grenville's instructions, disapproving the proposal and his own contrived correspondence with Pickering over his part in the affair. To London he blamed the whole uproar on American pro-French and therefore pro-Spanish sentiment and urged that Chisholm, now fortunately in a Bow Street jail in London for debt, should be immediately returned to America. The secretary of state continued to support Liston's innocence, but the Spanish and French ministers excoriated both him and Liston. Republicans such as Jefferson, Madison, Monroe, Tazewell, and even Blount's brother Thomas were convinced of the British envoy's guilt. The party leadership demanded his recall. Henrietta blamed the whole uproar on French jealousy of her husband and the American "democrates" and admitted in letters home that "I cannot yet with perfect composure read personal abuse of my husband in Democratic news-papers."[21]

The worst feature of the whole affair for Liston was the loss of his earlier acceptance by men of both parties. Just a few months earlier Philadelphians had been infuriated by news that the French had ignominiously dismissed Charles Cotesworth Pinckney's mission seeking friendship, and as the number of American ships seized by the French rose sharply, Liston had written happily to Hammond that there would be no need for directions from home "if the French continue to do our business for us." "I am told," he continued playfully, "that Mrs. Liston makes converts of some by making their wives and daughters dance and play cards, and that others do the British minister the honour to think him a middling good sort of man."[22] Henrietta had then told her uncle that "the French have laboured for some time past to disgust and we to please; both seem to have succeeded beyond their contemplations."[23] Now, however, as Liston's defenses against the Chisholm revelations were widely unconvincing, the secretary of state, by upholding the minister's innocence, bound him to the Federalist cause as tightly as ever Hammond had been. A steady Republican press attack, wrote Liston, "asserted with equal insolence and perseverence [sic]" that "neither the secretary of state nor the president ever do anything without the previous opinion and advice of the British minister." More important, as more and more of his drawing-room guests were Federalists, the second British minister to America, like the first one, began to write dispatches from the Federalist viewpoint that were increasingly unrelated to the realities of American public opinion.

Personal troubles also irked the minister. By mid-1797, he had received no salary from either his Ottoman Empire or American missions. Only the patience of his London banker, loans from Bond, and a move to a smaller house in the suburbs kept the entourage in proper style. Henrietta's spendthrift brother and his wife descended on the Listons for a four-month visit. From home Liston heard of fleet mutinies, a falling stock market, specie failure, Wolfe Tone's Irish rebellion, and French army victories. In Philadelphia Liston's own efforts to resolve the impressment problem failed, and Congress not only embarrassed him with its investigations but also agreed with President Adams's proposal to send a conciliatory mission to France.

To escape these frustrations and to enjoy a diplomatic absence during the Blount investigations, on November 1, 1797, Liston left the embassy in Thornton's care and took his entourage on his second American tour. He and Henrietta spent five days with the former president at Mount Vernon. At Norfolk he put his family connections on a warship bound for Antigua. On a visit to the site of the new capital city Henrietta found "horses and cows feeding sumptuously in the principal streets."[24] The minister accepted the request of the embryonic city's proprietors to choose a site for a future British legation—a two-hundred-foot-square lot about halfway between the future presidential mansion and the capitol. These various matters attended to, Robert and Henrietta Liston plunged into an unprecedented thousand-mile journey to South Carolina.

It was a remarkable performance, faithfully recorded in Henrietta's diary. They slept in gracious mansions, rude cabins, and in open lofts near roaring fires to counteract icy blasts. Exotic foods intrigued them: canvasback ducks ("the best eating in the world"), wild turkey, and the ever-present pork ("delicious when roasted"), corn bread, and hoecake. They found that tea was seldom drunk outside the cities and that morning coffee was horrible everywhere, but apple and peach brandies were always available. In South Carolina rice and sausages replaced corn and hominy, and the travelers were deeply impressed with Charleston, "the only part of the United States where distinctions of rank are observed . . . and . . . [where] . . . a planter is a much superior being to a merchant." The "experience of always being received with cheerfulness and kindness" was a welcome change from Philadelphia, although one North Carolinian unaware of their identity commented to them on the "interference and influence of the British minister in Philadelphia." There they finally returned on February 11, 1798, and even the stout-hearted Henrietta admitted that she "prayed never again to travel in an American stage coach in winter." Though pleased to have made the odyssey, she vowed "few things could tempt me to repeat it."

Thornton had little to report after two and a half months except dreary complaints over prizes and false certificates and slow progress in the Jay arbitration committee. Yet within weeks British status changed with that bewildering speed that repeatedly confounded His Majesty's ministers in America. On April 3, the publication of diplomatic notes confirmed rumors that Adams's commissioners Marshall, Pinckney, and Gerry, after various indignities in Paris, had received French demands for indemnities and bribes. This, to a people who had suffered nearly $12 million in losses by assaults on shipping, in addition to national insults and the meddling of French envoys in America, produced the wild Francophobia of the famous XYZ affair.

"The dispatches from Europe," Henrietta wrote, "have acted like magic . . . every man speaking with a degree of violence at which I often stare with astonishment."[25] The commission in Paris was ordered home, a black cockade of national resistance appeared on hats, public addresses of support poured in on the surprised president, volunteer battalions marched, and Federalist gangs sought out and assaulted Republican editors and publicists. Frenchmen and other anti-Federalist foreigners prudently departed. Henrietta wrote that "almost Mr. Liston's whole time, as well as that of Lord Henry Stuart, is occupied in writing pass ports for those people who are now afraid to remain in the country, amongst . . . [them] the famous Volney." Congress, with a Republican minority reduced to delaying tactics, enlarged the army and navy, created a marine force, annulled the 1778 French treaty, armed merchant ships, prohibited trade with France and her colonies, and raised taxes for military purposes. It also altered naturalization laws and passed the notorious sedition legislation to eliminate dissent. Ultra-Federalists hoped for a declaration of war against the French republic but lacked votes for the ultimate breach.

In all this anti-Gallicism the Blount fiasco naturally faded and Liston's popularity rose with Britain's. The minister himself was convinced that arming American merchant ships would produce war, or at least an Anglo-American treaty, and, given wide latitude by Grenville to achieve these aims, Liston worked feverishly. He secured British convoys for American merchantmen bound for the Indies, arranged for recognition signals between British and American ships, and obtained naval guns, several thousand stands of small arms, and British working drawings for the American manufacture of cannon and shot. He even begged from home a limited supply of precious copper for sheathing American hulls and secured, in principle, a plan for British officers to serve for America on half pay. Like Hammond he purchased the pen of William Cobbett despite what he called Cobbett's style of "gross personal abuse." Unlike Hammond he enjoyed the closest collaboration with the American secretary of state, at whose request he refused safe conduct passes to foreigners marked for punishment or interrogation. Pickering's raging Francophobia was now so virulent that it even evoked some Federalist remonstrance, to which he replied that France, being an enemy of America, merited no diplomatic language. From France's ally Spain the secretary even managed to receive the surrender of disputed posts on the Mississippi "in a manner sufficiently ungracious," wrote Liston, "a task of no small difficulty." Meanwhile, he was gradually led to accept most British positions on maritime disputes, to depreciate the number of British-impressed American seamen, and to assist Liston in instituting a libel suit against Republican editor William Duane when that gadfly accused British officials of bribing Americans.[26]

Yet for all his tactical advances, Liston saw 1798 wear away in frustration. No Anglo-American alliance materialized, for reasons the experienced diplomat never understood. Others did. Louis-Guillaume Otto, the French diplomat who spent twelve years in America, in 1797 displayed to the Directory an insight granted to only one British minister to America before 1815 when he wrote: "Our agents wished to see only two parties in the United States, the French party and the English party; but there is a middle party, much larger, composed of the most estimable men of the two other parties. This party, whose existence we have not even suspected, is the American party . . . for whom preferences either for France or Britain are only accessory and often passing affections."[27] Liston, the one British minister to America to perceive this before 1815 (and the most officially condemned), was at this same time writing to his father to expect no Anglo-American alliance since "between one party hating us and the other being at bottom jealous of us, no great reliance ought to be placed upon their attachment." For America "an union with any particular nation will . . . lead her into schemes directly opposite to her interests."[28]

To the middle-aged and essentially eighteenth-century Liston, European diplomacy revealed that nationalism was a luxury reserved for powerful states, whereas weaker ones made alliances for survival. Liston therefore wrote in scorn and bewilderment to the like-minded Grenville of Americans' "overweening idea of American prowess and American talents" that led them to "the erroneous and impractical theory . . . that America . . . is independent of the rest of the world, and ought to reject foreign treaties." He was at a loss to explain to Grenville how a Federalist House Committee, by no means anti-British, wrote a report "disdaining a reliance on foreign protection, wanting no foreign guarantees of our liberties, &c."

Not comprehending dawning American nationalism, the minister was ill-prepared for the admittedly difficult task of assessing the nation's second president. To begin with, there was the contrast with the first president. Liston wrote of Washington's "natural dignity of person and manner" and Adams's "meanness in some things . . . awkwardness in everything and . . . neglect of the little proprieties of life" that produced "a degree of enmity hardly to be conceived."[29] When the president responded to the popular anti-Gallicism with a bellicose statement or two, Liston began to write home of Adams as "eminently calculated by his fortitude and genius to conduct . . . a necessary war."[30] This necessity was more apparent to the minister than to the president, however, and when Liston pressed him about an alliance he replied that the people were "deliberating upon that question" and he thought it unwise to "disturb their meditations."[31] Similar suggestions were turned aside, for Adams was in fact signaling a divergence of American and British positions and within a few weeks made his historic decision to send another envoy to Paris for a last try at peace.

As his hopes for a treaty faded, Liston failed to warn Grenville of the disappointment to come. Talleyrand's new amiability was dismissed as duplicity, as was George Logan's similar message since, wrote Liston, the Quaker came from a Philadelphia suburb "notorious for the prevalence of democratick and French principles in an indecent degree." Others who spoke or wrote of avoiding war were described to the Foreign Office as "the ignorant and the profligate" or those "who through timidity or indolence or avarice are anxious to avert . . . war."[32] When Adams sent William Vans Murray to Paris as peacemaker, Liston did not accept the Ultra-Federalist explanation of presidential senility, but rather saw timidity and failure to counsel with his devoted Abigail, who, in fact, thought more of Liston than her husband did.[33] A year later, in almost his last dispatch from America, the minister reported the preliminaries of the Convention of 1800 that de-escalated the war he had sought so actively to promote.

Unable to achieve his major goal of an Anglo-American treaty, Liston was nevertheless successful elsewhere. In Santo Domingo, then in full revolt against France and immensely valuable to both Britain and America for its sugar production, British and American policy differed. The revolutionary leader Pierre Dominique Toussaint L'Ouverture trusted American agent Edward Stevens while he was utterly dependent for supplies on the sufferance of the British fleet. Working between his bitterly anti-American compatriot, Gen. Thomas Maitland, the suspicious Toussaint L'Ouverture, and avaricious mercantile interests, Liston produced and implemented a delicate compromise that permitted supervised access to the island and minimized the spread of its slave revolt. He also allayed American suspicions aroused by the appearance of adventurer William Augustus Bowles, who claimed British support on the coast of Florida. In the complex Maine boundary dispute, a suggestion of Liston's broke an impasse, and the elusive St. Croix boundary was identified satisfactorily in 1798. However, the Loyalist debt commission from Jay's Treaty had no such success, and Liston, becoming embroiled and partisan, was sharply admonished by Grenville.

In the central issue of early Anglo-American diplomacy, Liston, though the most influential minister to America before 1815, was but another in a long line of failures. Publicly he steadfastly upheld his nation's position: that the number of bona fide Americans impressed on British ships was greatly exaggerated, that American courts unjustly condoned violence against Britons, and that American violation of Britain's justified Orders in Council naturally produced seizures and condemnations. Privately, however, the minister urged Grenville to force discretion on the Sons of Neptune because of the disastrous emotional and political effects of impressment and contested neutral rights. He also asked vainly for inquiries into the outrageously venal decisions by British vice-admiralty courts at Jamaica and Môle–St. Nicolas. Adm. Sir Hyde Parker, commanding the West Indian Station, tolerated every ship seizure and flagellation or worse for seamen. This brutal autocrat dismissed Liston's protests as irrelevant politics and threatened President Adams for ordering resistance. In turn, the minister wrote Grenville of the "moderation which I have in vain used my endeavors to obtain" and regarded such excesses as the most important element in the election of Jefferson in 1800.[34]

Ironically, the far more popular Liston did not close his years of American service in the triumphs enjoyed by Hammond but in personal and professional frustration. As Hammond had, the Listons fled from Philadelphia when, in 1798, the dreaded yellow fever broke out. When they returned from their sojourn in New Jersey, New York, and New England, the Listons found that "the air of Campagna in Rome has not been more fatal than that of Philadelphia or even New York has been." Disease had claimed the lives of both Republican editor Bache and his counterpart, Federalist Fenno, and had driven the Liston's closest friends, the Portuguese minister Freire and his family, from America.

Like Hammond, Liston looked upon the jungle politics and vitriolic press wars of the republic as "outrageous insolence," but since he was not a gut fighter like his predecessor, he was even less equipped to combat them. In September, 1798, William Duane succeeded Benjamin F. Bache as editor of the Republican *Aurora* and began a sustained attack on the minister as part of the fierce partisanship that made him the spokesman of the radical Republicans. His regular columns, "British Influence" and "More British Amity," rehearsed the real and imaginary British complicity in the Blount, Chisholm, and George Rogers Clarke intrigues in the west, detailed and enlarged upon maritime clashes, and provided constant "proof" of the minister's hand in everything from Algerine corsairs and the partisan performances of Pickering to wholesale corruption of Americans. This last was supposedly accomplished by a secret fund estimated from £150,000 upwards each year, and the editor tirelessly reminded his readers "how many snug things can be done in America for £228,000 sterling." When suggestions were solicited for titles to be purchased for the new congressional library, Duane suggested that in view of Federalist performance, Swift's *Art of Political Lying* and *Tale of a Tub* should be bought for Pickering and Machiavelli's *The Prince* for Secretary of War Dexter, "to be occasionally loaned to Mr. Liston."[35]

The minister contributed to the arsenals of his tormentors. In May, 1799, he entrusted his highly confidential letters to President Russell of Canada into the hands of an unlikely courier named Sweezy, notorious both as a former Loyalist and as a current horse thief. The "honest sheriff of Bucks county," as Duane called that Republican official, arrested Sweezy astride stolen property and opened the prisoner's luggage. Shortly thereafter Liston's letters appeared in the *Aurora*. Since they emphasized warm Anglo-Federalist cooperation and the likelihood of joint war against France, even Liston admitted that his letters injured him and advanced the Republican cause. Later the minister turned over to the British navy a captured British mutineer who claimed American citizenship; the navy promptly executed him, furnishing more grist for the *Aurora*.[36] At the same time another indiscreet Liston letter surfaced in London. In early 1798 he had written a Scottish friend, James Buchanan, parodying *Aurora* attacks by claiming to "lead Mr. Adams by the nose," hold conferences with his "bosom friend the Secretary of State," and "keep Oliver Wolcott McHenry right . . . but they are ready to go as far and as fast as I wish them to." Buchanan showed the letter in London, where it reached Minister Rufus King, whose furious letter to Pickering caused an agonized Federalist leadership caucus that ultimately excused the minister's heart at the expense of his head.

Colleagues in England also contributed to the minister's woes. Undersecretaries Hammond and Canning had led a group of schoolboyish wits in establishing the High Tory *Anti-Jacobin Review and Magazine*, the September, 1799, issue of which contained what Liston called "gross abuse of the character and political conduct" of President Adams and "a very harsh and exaggerated picture of the internal state of this country." Called to account by Adams, who had by request earlier assisted him in libel suits in Philadelphia, Liston explained British freedom of the press to the president but admitted to Grenville that he brought but little conviction.[37]

The Federalist leadership whom Liston and his friends were thus parodying, although it represented the principal hope for Anglo-American collaboration, was meanwhile publicly committing political suicide. The obstructionism of second-rate cabinet members Pickering, McHenry, and Wolcott finally drove the president to force McHenry's resignation and to dismiss Pickering, thereby destroying his own chances for reelection and Liston's for further progress in America. The president in fact declared war on his party's ultras by repeating charges that they were "a faction led by British influence and British intrigues." Even the new secretary of state, John Marshall, once stoutly anti-French, now took Liston to task about William Bowles and about naval matters in a way that indicated no great faith in British friendship.[38]

Although beset with problems, the Listons kept up their stylish program so gratifying to social Philadelphia. Dinners, balls, and at-homes followed one another hectically. Liston himself pursued interests in the American Philosophical Society. He and Henrietta entertained and sat for portraitist Gilbert Stuart and exchanged hospitality and presents with Benjamin Latrobe. They continued to enjoy Priestley and refereed the polemics between friends William Cobbett and Benjamin Rush on yellow fever remedies.

The real escape from troubles for both Listons was travel. In 1799 they undertook a formidable trek in the New York wilderness. The party included Secretary Thornton, Lord Henry Stuart, Henry Erskine (nephew of a Liston patron), and a New York merchant friend. Armed with passports from Governor Jay, they plunged into the New York wilderness, visiting Lake Champlain, Fort Ticonderoga, Lake George, and a Shaker community, and then set off for a month's travel to Niagara Falls. "There is perhaps no country where curiosity pays higher for its gratification than America," Henrietta wrote, and the party paid heavily.[39] After 200 miles along the Mohawk they struggled for days up creeks, rivers, and lakes to reach Lake Ontario. There, in "a little bateau rendered commodious by an awning," they sailed along the almost entirely uninhabited southern shore. They moved by sail or by rowing, and in the latter His Majesty's minister took his turn. At night under an oilcloth tent and by the light of a candle stuck in a bottle, the minister's lady prepared a supper of tea, salted meat, fish, and occasionally venison bought from passing Indians; then they retired to a mattress under an awning. After 170 miles they reached Niagara Falls where, Henrietta wrote "description fails . . . they must be one of the most beautiful and sublime objects of the kind in nature." The indomitable Scotswoman "did what few women attempt . . . to go down to the bottom . . . and I thought I never should have recovered the use of my legs." Three days later they went to Albany, and then to Trenton, New Jersey, for a last unavailing effort to help Ultra-Federalist leaders block the departure of Adams's new envoy to France.

Diplomatic routine was dull after the wilderness venture. Newspaper attacks had redoubled after the Sweezy affair, cries of "British influence" had defeated a strong Federalist candidate for governor of Pennsylvania, the Loyalist debt commission had broken up in failure, and tales circulated of maritime atrocities. In October, 1799, the Listons visited the Washingtons at Mount Vernon, noting that illness and "approaching deafness" depressed the president's spirits and that he was preparing the family burial vault.[40] Two months later they attended the funeral, and Liston wrote of the "irreparable loss" to the permanence of the Union. They later visited Mount Vernon again to call on the widow, who was "grieving incessantly" and "impatient for death."[41]

These defeats and losses depressed the minister physically and psychologically. Even before the northern trip he had asked Hammond privately to "prepare the way" for a leave of absence, and in October he made a formal request of Grenville. He cited "a disease of a paralytic nature" causing swelling and numbness in his legs and made worse by the "intemperance of the seasons in this country," so that English medical attention was necessary. He also argued that his "small property in Scotland" had suffered from his absence and that the cost of living in America had prevented his saving any money. He concluded with a request to be absent from the capital during the hot months and for a conditional leave to return to Britain in the winter of 1800.[42]

In fact, though he was suffering from some circulatory problems and from a very acute terror of yellow fever, Liston had another reason for terminating the American tour. Congress and the administration had now agreed on the move to the new and very raw federal city in June, 1800. Although Liston enjoyed travel in the wilderness, he had no intention of practicing his profession there. Also, the increasingly violent schism between Adams and the Ultra-Federalists portended either a Republicanized Adams or a Jefferson in the presidency after 1800, and between either of these and the Ultra-Tory British Foreign Office, a minister in America could expect little success.

Grenville, meanwhile, had been profoundly shaken by the democratic uproar in the young republic and the evident growth of Jefferson's Republicans. "The whole system of the American government," he wrote to his minister, "seems to me to be tottering to its foundations," and he doubted the government's ability either to carry out diplomatic commitments or to maintain order. He therefore felt "it may become necessary for us to reconsider our system . . . with respect to that country." He assumed that Liston would not wish to return to America, "nor is it desirable that you should," and while regretting the deterioration of relations, he concluded somewhat ominously that "where we cannot controul events we must . . . regulate our conduct according to them."[43]

Liston was pleased with his leave (the customary means of ending a mission) but disturbed by the foreign secretary's pessimism. He wrote in reply the most prescient dispatch from a minister in America for years to come. Urging a continuation of Grenville's policy of accommodation, he foresaw a North America "covered with friendly though not subject states, consuming our manufactures, speaking our language, proud of their parent state, attached to her prosperity." War, he wrote, would hurt Britain's navigation and cause "the propagation of prejudices which it may be impossible to eradicate." The American government "does not strike me (with the near view I have had of it) as being in so perilous a situation as is imagined in Europe." It would "get on well enough" if at peace and might be strengthened by war, and its "rulers are certainly in earnest in wishing to be well with us and it appears to me *possible* to arrange our difficulties."[44] Unfortunately, this prevision of the kindly minister was heresy to his successors and was shared by almost no British foreign secretary before 1815.

The envoy chose to delay his departure until fall, as he had permission to escape Philadelphia's heat. Liston awaited the outcome of the latest mission to France and congressional adjournment while dining with Federalists, crating pictures, and exchanging hospitalities. The president's lady sought to acquire his coachman, and his furniture sales were disappointing. He saw the government's plans to move to the new capital as contributing to the future stability of the Union, but he himself made only two brief visits there. He was Jefferson's guest at Monticello. After writing to Hammond that as "I cannot die in peace without seeing Canada," he determined to "run as far as Quebec and back again"; Liston in fact included Montreal in a swift "run" that ended at Tunnicliff's Hotel in the federal city. From there he reported the president "extremely well-lodged in about one-half of the Palace" hastily fitted up to receive him, and both houses of Congress "sufficiently well accommodated in one of the wings of the edifice . . . to be denominated the Capitol."[45]

In late November he took formal leave of the president and presented Thornton as the chargé. He also wrote former Secretary Pickering a warm letter explaining that he had not visited at his farm because he did not wish to arm "the abandoned editors of the Democratic prints," and he urged moderation on the splenetic Yankee while sending him prayers for his health and happiness.[46]

Rumors in Philadelphia said that Anthony Merry, Liston's former consular colleague in Spain, would succeed him in America, but the weary minister did not await Merry's arrival. The new admiral on the West Indian Station detailed the *Andromache* to bring the Listons to Antigua, and on December 2, 1800, they sailed from Philadelphia. Thereafter, Henrietta's severe illness detained them a week in Norfolk before a short voyage brought them to Kingston. In May, 1801, in much improved health they were back in England.

At home they settled at Millburn Tower, near Edinburgh, enjoying their gardening, books, and trips to the capital. In 1803 Liston resumed diplomatic duties by a tour at The Hague and after retirement was sent in 1812 on a diplomatic holding action to Constantinople after others had refused the post as unpromising and unrewarding. There, until Liston's recall in 1818 when he was seventy-six, the old couple kept an estate reminiscent of their early days. As in the latter days of his

American tour, his moderation was increasingly out of touch with the newer, more vigorous, and less conciliatory trends at the court and Foreign Office. Liston then spoke ten foreign languages, played the flute for relaxation, and in both the Ottoman Empire and Scotland kept up a correspondence with Americans. He was visited by Sir Walter Scott and a series of other Britons and Americans, all of whom Liston charmed by his courtesy and good humor. His later years brought recognition. He was a Privy Councillor in 1812 and was awarded the Grand Cross of the Bath in 1816. Robert Liston died at age ninety-four at Millburn Tower, six years after the indomitable Henrietta. Both Listons were the most perceptive, kindly, and humane of His Majesty's early representatives in America.[47]

Edward Thornton

> "What will be the language, or what the national character of a people composed of such heterogeneous particles, collected and huddled together from all parts of the world, it is impossible to say."
> —Edward Thornton to James Bland Burges

WHATEVER their trials, George Hammond and Robert Liston endured their American years with the physical advantages and social amenities of Philadelphia, until lately the second largest city in the British Empire. Moreover, both Hammond's fiery assaults and Liston's more diplomatic maneuvers were directed at governments with conservative Congressional majorities and somewhat sympathetic Federalist administrators. Then partly by chance and partly through Tory Britain's increasing aversion to a Jeffersonian administration, a lowly chargé d'affaires was for three years left to face social gaucheries and political animosities in the world's most primitive capital to which a British minister was accredited.

The quiet chargé into whose hands the happily departing Listons thrust the American mission was the son of William Thornton, a modest tradesman in Kingston-upon-Hull, Yorkshire. The elder Thornton had emigrated to London to become an innkeeper but died suddenly at thirty-one, leaving five motherless children to subsist on a meager estate. Medieval philanthropy customs rescued the family when their guardian placed Edward Thornton and an older brother in the Latin and Upper School divisions of Christ's Hospital, a London charity school. Under able tutors the boys excelled, and upon graduation Edward considered a career in the church, less from piety than from a desire to stay in school.

At nineteen and on the Hospital's charitable foundation, Thornton entered Pembroke College, Cambridge, where he won mathematics honors and a Latin prize and, for the only time, met his idol, William

Pitt. However, he failed to win a scholarship and so thankfully received appointment as personal tutor of the eldest son of James Bland Burges, member of Parliament from Cornwall. The shy, stammering young teacher became an intimate of the family, and when Burges became an undersecretary of state and acquired some patronage, he offered Thornton a secretaryship of legation, either with Francis James Jackson, returned from Berlin and intended for Warsaw, or with George Hammond, about to depart for America. The future was to prove both choices inauspicious, but since the Warsaw position did not materialize, Thornton went to America with Hammond, whose arrogance, though equaling Jackson's, was accompanied by a shrewder intellect. More important to Thornton at the time was that the American mission required no expensive court dress.

The young secretary's natural Tory cast of mind was firmly set by his years with Hammond. Personally and professionally Thornton shared his chief's profound disdain for the republic and its citizens, especially for the vocally democratic. He never forgot his formal presentation to President Washington by a secretary of state who not only "stood by in the plainest ordinary dress" but who "both then and afterwards appeared to make a republican virtue" of the contrast. In the Hammond-Jefferson diplomatic duels, Thornton spent hours copying his minister's litany of complaints, which, he wrote home privately, evoked "petulant" and "feverish" replies from Jefferson, showing a "bitterness of temper and . . . of feeling into which a public man at least ought never allow himself to be betrayed." By the outbreak of the Anglo-French war in 1793, Thornton was convinced that Americans applauded the excesses of the Reign of Terror. His humor was unequal to the sight of Americans self-consciously addressing one another as "citizen" or of a congressman who, he wrote, "in the very spirit of Cromwell" moved to melt down the House's mace as an aristocratic symbol. American conceit, he fumed, together with the fires of the French Terror had produced scenes "in which it was hardly possible for an Englishman to be present without feeling his blood boil" at the insults to Britain and "effusions of malicious hatred."[1]

Thornton's experiences in Baltimore as vice-consul were the result of a letter from Undersecretary Burges to Consul Bond introducing Burges's protégé as one "in whose welfare I greatly interest myself."[2] This hint was quite enough for Bond to appoint Thornton—with Hammond's consent—to the hotbed of violent republicanism in Baltimore, a city unrestrained by the presence of the central government and constantly agitated by waterfront incidents. When the new vice-consul responded with what Hammond called "a zeal and alacrity highly commendable," it was inevitable that he would be recalled to the safety of Philadelphia. In quieter days Thornton returned to Baltimore; even so, he wrote Burges that "solitude or insult is almost my only alternative."[3] His revenge came when he attended the dinner party at which Hammond showed Fauchet's dispatch to Wolcott and two days later when Thornton prepared certified copies of the dispatch that brought Randolph's ruin.

But in spite of his private resentments, Thornton was too lowly in rank, too politic, and too good-tempered to display them in public. His fellow countryman Thomas Twining, who visited Baltimore in 1796, contrasted Bond's sneering malice with the tact of the young vice-consul, with whom he spent one evening of "patriotic and temperate festivity" at St. George's Society and another reminiscing about Pembroke College. Thornton himself wrote Burges that while "I always argue, perhaps with improper warmth," yet "I keep good humor and express spleen frankly," and "so make friends." "I fear," he added playfully, "I am growing vain and insolent and wish to return to England to learn humility as young men do with their betters there."[4] Meanwhile, he visited the coffeehouses of Baltimore and Philadelphia, gathering and dispensing gossip. Thornton managed to retain the goodwill of such different friends as William Cobbett—for whom he later tried to obtain assistance and recognition in London—and Gilbert Stuart.

Although all his life he credited his training to Hammond, it was actually Liston who taught him most. The Scottish minister became fond of his young fellow scholar and recalled him from Baltimore to become both personal and embassy secretary and tutor to young Henry Stuart. Thornton traveled with the Listons to Mount Vernon, New York, and Canada and in 1797 took over the embassy while the Listons escaped the embarrassments of the Blount-Chisholm affair by their long southern tour. Upon their return, Thornton left America for his long-anticipated leave of absence. Henrietta Liston introduced Thornton to her uncle in Scotland as "sensible and intelligent as well as extremely worthy" and safe to introduce to society since "in politics he is clean and sound, and indeed Mr. Liston has been at some pains to check his warmth on that subject."[5] The secretary used the occasion to aid the Listons' campaign for their recall and perhaps also to placate a foreign secretary annoyed by the minister's indiscretions with Chisholm.

From April to late summer Thornton conferred at the Foreign Office, visited his and Liston's kinsmen, and received the coveted Fellowship of Pembroke. On his return to Philadelphia he was, despite his prejudices and junior status, the best-informed man in either country on the personalities and attitudes of the Anglo-American leadership. He shared with Liston the hopes and disappointments of the XYZ crisis, and when the "honest sheriff of Bucks county" seized the minister's ill-chosen emissary to Canada, Thornton carried a new diplomatic cipher to Quebec to preserve official security. In November, 1800, he joined the minister at Tunnicliff's Hotel in the wilderness capital to witness the opening of Congress's first session there. His chief then presented him to President Adams, after which the diplomats returned to Philadelphia, the senior to pack and the junior to wait hopefully for the early arrival of a new minister—a vigil that was to last three years.

It was well for the young Tory that he was spared the knowledge of this delay, since beneath amiable manners Thornton held a vast contempt for his hosts. To patron Burges he excoriated the Americans' "vanity as a nation" that "tinctures the whole of their character. Even in their sole national talent—mechanics—they [Jefferson and Rittenhouse in particular] borrow, or rather steal, the models of our machinery, add some small improvement, and call the whole their own invention." He found nothing in American politics or literature, and the emerging American language enraged the young academician. "They plead, I presume, revolution and the rights of man for these innovations . . . and the liberty of talking in bad English is I suppose considered as indefeasible as that of doing wrong when the people unite in such a resolution." Since Americans retained "all the local idioms and barbarisms" of the countries they came from, a "barbarous dialect becomes a national language and its corruption is perpetuated."[6]

This hapless people's leaders also roused his scorn. Washington was vain, cold, phlegmatic, indecisive, and overcautious. "He is a man of great but secret ambition," wrote the chargé, and "I have never heard of any truly noble, generous, or disinterested action of his." John Adams suffered still more; Thornton saw him as vain, literally uncouth, wavering in policy, influenced by his wife, and politically imbecilic. As for Jefferson, the arch-enemy of British Tories who became president on March 4, 1801, the first British representative to deal with him never perceived the contrast between Secretary of State Jefferson's approval of republican France in 1790 and President Jefferson's distrust of Napoleonic France in 1801. The Virginian's "bitterness and hatred of Britain" remained an unwavering constant in Thornton's assessment, explicable mainly by defaulted personal debts to British merchants. From Jefferson's informality in dress and manners to the busts of Franklin, John Paul Jones, and Lafayette in his home ("the first had talents without virtue, the second *deserved* hanging, and the third may yet meet with that fate"), nothing about Jefferson was acceptable to Thornton. Even the new president's language was "stilted and high-flown," and his public correspondence displayed a "want of prudence."[7]

The young chargé, so free with his strictures, was himself an odd mixture of prejudice and amiability, of carelessness and self-conscious scholasticism. His perceptive dispatches were set forth in a penmanship criticized at home as "slovenly," and he was once officially reprimanded for packing tea in his dispatch boxes, since one packet burst and "defiled an autograph letter from His Most Faithful Majesty of Portugal." Despite his humble origins Thornton was curiously independent, and in his later years he was to receive fierce official rebukes and once was recalled in disfavor. As chargé in America he was saved from the debacles of his successors by a higher intelligence and a lower rank, as well as by lessons in tact from the Listons.

More important, a temporary lull in the war and the presence in London of Federalist Rufus King as American minister meant that Thornton was given few significant duties to perform. Despite the almost simultaneous change of administrations in London and Washington, a period of calm descended, unknown in Hammond's stormy tenure and unusual in Liston's more placid one. Addington's feeble administration existed in 1801 and thereafter on the sufferance of Pitt; its foreign secretary was Robert Banks Jenkinson, currently Lord Hawkesbury. Jenkinson, although only thirty, had the procrastinating habits of a dotard, and his talents, other than those of placeholding and survival, were almost wholly devoted to combating the rising power of First Consul Bonaparte. He and the rest of the cabinet therefore let Anglo-American relations float quietly. Thornton received only three formal instructions from London in 1801, seven in 1802, and six in 1803.

Liston's hopes for a clash with France had died on September 30, 1800, when the quasi-war closed with the Treaty of Mortfontaine. Immediately thereafter, however, Bonaparte's Marshal Berthier at San Ildefonso obtained the retrocession of Louisiana from Spain, thereby reopening the prospects of Franco-American war. Thus, Napoleonic plans for North America, not the initiatives of British diplomacy, were to shape Thornton's three years as chargé in the republic. Nevertheless, these years were important to both nations for the formation of attitudes as the Jeffersonians assumed power. Whatever Thornton's significance was to be, it was an unhappy young diplomat who arrived on December 19, 1800, at the primitive new capital.

To Thornton, as to his successors, the federal city represented the culminating absurdity in a nation cursed by intolerable climate, social egalitarianism, and radical democracy. At its debut in 1800, Washington received unanimous derision as having "the name of a city but nothing else." "It is," Albert Gallatin wrote his wife, "hated by every member of Congress without exception of person or parties . . . around the Capitol are seven or eight boarding houses, one taylor, one shoemaker, one printer, a washing woman, a grocery shop, a pamphlets and stationery shop, a small dry goods shop, and an oyster house. This makes the whole of the city as connected with the Capitol."[8] Between this cluster and the president's house lay a swamp crossed by a causeway called Pennsylvania Avenue, but where not a single residence existed. There were, in fact, few houses anywhere, and as Oliver Wolcott wrote his wife "these small miserable huts . . . present an awful contrast to the public buildings." Over an area nearly the size of New York City, he continued, there was not "a fence or any other object except brick kilns and temporary huts for laborers."[9]

Not only the scarcity of houses but also the distances separating the few clusters aroused sarcasm. The mile and a half between the presidential "palace" and Georgetown contained public offices and a scattered fifty to a hundred houses. Georgetown was more than three miles from the Capitol, and the unimproved roads were as uncomfortable by day as they were dangerous by night. Six or seven fortunate congressmen lodged in Georgetown, three or four more near the presidential mansion, and all the rest were crowded "like scholars in a college or monks in a monastery"—ten to twenty in each house and two or more to a room—in the eight boardinghouses near the Capitol. Gouverneur Morris expressed his colleagues' disgust: "We need only houses, cellars, kitchens, scholarly men, amiable women and a few other trifles to possess a perfect city. . . . This is the best city in the world to live in—in the future."[10]

The economic visions of the first president for his namesake city were also shared by others. Wolcott reported that "the people are poor, and as far as I can judge, they live like fishes, by eating each other." Near the Eastern Branch of the Potomac stood "a very large but perfectly empty warehouse, and a wharf graced by not a single vessel." Greenleaf's Point, separated by a large swamp from the Capitol and its little village, presented, Wolcott wrote, "the appearance of a considerable town which has been destroyed by some unusual calamity. There are fifty or sixty spacious houses, five or six of which are inhabited by . . . vagrants . . . but there are no fences, gardens, nor the least appearance of business."

The raisons d'être of the new city were two unfinished white citadels rising from opposite shores of a swamp, contrasting sharply with the clusters of frame houses, stumps, woods, brush piles, swamps, and dusty rutted tracks called avenues. On the principal hill the high freestone Capitol represented the northern element of two proposed wings. Both legislative chambers were smaller and less convenient than their counterparts in Philadelphia had been, and the representatives' temporary quarters were considerably less elegant than the colonnaded arches and gallery of the Senate chamber.

A mile and a half away, the presidential mansion on its hill was already built and of ambitious size—"big enough," said Jefferson, "for two emperors, one pope, and the Grand Lama into the bargain." It towered above a welter of old brick kilns, workshops, rubbish, and pits of water at symmetrical but inconvenient distances from the humbler brick departmental offices. Inside the president's home, only six of the thirty rooms had been made somewhat habitable. Abigail Adams needed all the family fortitude to receive social and state visits when not one room was finished, the main stairs were not yet raised, the bell pulls were unhung, and the walls remained persistently damp from plastering. Sufficient candles, lamps, and the thirty servants required for the establishment were far beyond Adams's finances. The district's laborers had more bids than time, so that in the forested capital neither immigrants nor speculating citizens could be hired to cut or cart wood for the mansion's twelve fireplaces. "We have indeed," wrote the First Lady, "come into a *new country*." Sturdily she praised the natural beauties of the new capital and kept a brave face to the public while she received the news of the Republican victories in New York and South Carolina that would terminate her husband's public career. "If they will put me up some bells and let me have wood enough to keep fires, I design to be pleased," she wrote her children. "I could content myself almost anywhere three months."[11]

During these last months of the administration, Thornton chose not to join the eight hundred government employees and their families already resident in the federal district. Instead he kept the embassy in civilized Philadelphia, explaining to London the faster reception of news there and greater proximity to potential naval disturbances. The political arena, however, was now the wilderness "encampment," so during Congressional sessions he took rooms in Georgetown, the "court end" of the capital, which, though three miles distant from the center of action, was a compact settlement of some upper-class people. Settled in, Thornton paid his respects to the president and reconstituted cabinet and took up his daily rounds of duties.

Although Thornton was nominally responsible for the consular corps, such veteran consular officials as Thomas Barclay for the eastern states, Phineas Bond for the middle and southern, and Thomas MacDonald for New England, along with vice-consuls Gabriel Wood at Baltimore and Benjamin Moodie in the Carolinas, neither needed nor accepted his supervision. Thus, Thornton's primary function was to travel between the little groups of buildings gathering information. From this he directed to London a series of dispatches of remarkable insight and unusual literary ability that were worthy of more attention than either Hammond or Hawkesbury likely accorded them. His missives were marred only by that inveterate hostility to American democracy and its practitioners that was fully shared by his London masters.

From Philadelphia he had already warned London of a probable Republican victory in 1800. But in Washington he learned that the House Federalists might use the tied electoral count to defeat Jefferson if Burr would agree to "certain conditions." Ultra-Federalists painted the New York Republican to Thornton as "possessing talents at least equivalent to those of Mr. Jefferson with greater energy and consistency of character; and unbounded ambition, little scruples about obtaining his object and . . . (unlike Jefferson) actuated by no extravagant partiality for France and no inveterate hostility to Great Britain." Confined to days of ceaseless political agitation by lack of other diversions in their raw new capital, adherents of the angry Jefferson and the curiously enigmatic Burr trafficked in rumor and threat. Though Thornton was not as privy to High Federalist strategy as Liston had been, he nevertheless reported with remarkable accuracy. He never doubted that Burr seriously aimed to defeat Jefferson, and he attributed the former's strength to a "systematic and inflexible opposition to Virginia's political dominance."[12]

Several days after Jefferson's triumph on February 17, the chargé attributed the victory to Burr's tactical indecision and Federalist distrust of a man "at best but . . . the less of two evils."[13] By special vessel Thornton reported the election result to London where the news further depressed the money market. Meanwhile, he managed a final informal conversation with former President Adams, for whose political acumen he had only contempt and whose staunch commitment to American nationalism he understood as little as had Liston.

On March 4, 1801, the Tory chargé with his fellow diplomats witnessed Jefferson's simple inaugural—a trying experience. Nothing in that heyday of republican spirit was acceptable; the inaugural address was overcharged with conciliation and philanthropy yet contained bitterness, and the president's walk in ordinary dress from Conrad's boardinghouse to the Capitol accompanied only by a few associates was pure affectation. When both before and after the inaugural Jefferson in private talk with the chargé sought to dismiss his reported antipathy to Britain as "newspaper trash" and to assure the envoy that his personal admiration for the former Republic of France was now long dead, Thornton merely reported that the president had "taxed his imagination to supply the deficiency of his feelings."[14]

As a revolution in social usages began, Thornton was aware that they constituted deliberate presidential policy. However, instead of perceiving them as a popular response to American democratic sentiment, he accepted Federalist explanations of presidential malignity and frailties. Thornton explained the president's sending his message to Congress by messenger instead of delivering it in person as an act denigrating British and Federalist precedent that would fail "through the natural vanity of the Americans." Jefferson refused to designate regular levee days, receiving, said the disgusted chargé, "with the most perfect disregard for ceremony both in dress and manners all whom business or curiosity sent to the Palace." From a Virginia aristocrat who had been an envoy to Louis XVI's court and advisor to Washington on protocol, this could only be "affected humility," "pride," and a bid for popularity, particularly since the diplomat found Jefferson's household cost more than Washington's had and was "better arranged than Adams'."[15]

In political matters, too, the young diplomat clouded a naturally acute perception with malice and misjudgment. Noting Jefferson's real sensitivity to praise and criticism and his interest in science, Thornton concluded that the president's Anglophobia arose from French acceptance and British disregard of his scientific pursuits: thus, since "the dearest rewards of his scientific labours would be the panegyrics of . . . the people of England," Foreign Secretary Hawkesbury should plant such panegyrics in British journals. The young Pittite saw Madison and Gallatin as rivals in the new administration but felt Gallatin would win through his "superior art and above all . . . greater force and decision." The diplomat understood British political patronage, yet, sniffing Anglophobia in every breeze, he viewed Jefferson's rather mild displacement of Federalist officeholders as "extreme bitterness and the appeal to antient prejudices which . . . leave . . . little hopes . . . of anything like a generous settlement towards other nations."[16]

In the fall elections of 1801, Republican strength grew with Middle State victories; Thornton admitted that there were indications that even New England had not "entirely escaped the contagion of these principles." Republicans in fact captured both House and Senate, and Pitt's young follower in America expected a vast accession of authority to the central government. Instead, in the ensuing session he saw a states' rights Congress reduce the army, navy, and diplomatic corps; attack the mint; cut taxes; and reduce presidential patronage by repealing Adams's Judiciary Act. Since federalism's concept of balanced governments was incomprehensible to the young Tory, he could only explain this renunciation of power to London as either a sacrificial offering to Virginia, to which Jefferson "from timidity or easiness of disposition" was renouncing authority "in a way very little resembling the course of human actions," or as an example of the "vicious extreme to which the extravagant doctrine of modern republicanism may carry a people."

Disregarding Liston's visions of a stronger Union, Thornton returned to Hammond's disunion thesis: that the pro-British north, blocked by geography from western expansion, was nevertheless more powerful through its "natural love of order and enterprise" than a south of "corrupt and profligate manners." Hence, after the last southern Federalist had lost his seat in Congress, the states north of Delaware or the Hudson River might well "quit a Union that deprives them of their just ascendancy." Thus, informed mainly by a desperate Aaron Burr and a dwindling band of frantic Ultra-Federalists, the first British envoy to Republican America reported in the midst of the most popular of all early American administrations that it was losing public favor, that its laws were made coherent only by Federalist amendments, and that its actions were received "apathetically" by a nation quite possibly on the verge of dissolution.

Thornton's curious overview of the American republic, reinforced by Undersecretary Hammond in the Foreign Office, cast in granite several British delusions of ominous portent: of American weakness and the wavering characters of the third and fourth presidents, of the moral superiority of the north and the Anglophobia of Southern Republicanism, and of a probably fairly immediate disunion. Yet to do him justice, Thornton forecast a Republican ascendancy of at least ten years, a vast western growth, and an early march northward of states' rights doctrine. Further, despite his personal distaste for the philosopher-president, Thornton almost alone among early British representatives did not distort Jefferson through sheer ridicule.[17]

In part, Thornton's perception was the result of the shared interests of president, secretary of state, and chargé in scholarship and chess. Also, Jefferson and Madison were unfailingly amiable and accessible to the young envoy, perhaps feeling less need for caution with this junior diplomat and responding to Thornton's outward display of courtesy and deference.

More important, the force of mutual national interests drew the men inexorably together. American eyes were fixed on France in Santo Domingo and on Spain in Louisiana; in both places British policy paralleled American. In London the Foreign Office was absorbed with prospects of European peace, from the initial negotiations in the summer of 1801 to the final Peace of Amiens in March, 1802. In Washington the president had already rejected the proposal to join a north European league to enforce broader neutral rights, and like Adams before him, he sought to check attempts to stir up sedition on the Canadian border by Ira Allen, who, in Thornton's Gibbonesque prose, "would not scruple to set the whole country aflame for the sake of sharing in the plunder of a single village." Also, the State Department and the Foreign Office worked together to reduce discriminatory duties. When the Pasha of Tripoli declared war on the United States by cutting down the flagpole bearing the national emblem, Hawkesbury told Rufus King in London that British naval facilities would be made available to American warships and supplies would be furnished at cost. And on January 2, 1802, the foreign secretary sent Thornton a copy of his convention with King that settled the long-delayed Loyalist debt problem by an American lump payment of £600,000.

Even in the troubled areas of maritime rights and impressment, the mild skirmishes of Thornton and Madison, though they lacked the accommodation of Liston and Pickering, had none of the abuse of the Hammond-Randolph exchanges. While war lingered in Europe, profits dulled American anger, and the Peace of Amiens somewhat lessened Britain's maritime urgencies as to both manpower and ships. The London negotiators could make no progress in the impasse between Britain's pressure for mutual restitution of deserters and American demands for the abolition of impressment, but the pacific Addington administration discountenanced the most flagrant injustices of the West Indian prize courts, where most friction arose.[18] In such circumstances Thornton could maintain an agreeable display of good-natured cooperation when he visited the secretary of state, and the pleasantly reticent young chargé was welcome both in private homes and in the official if highly informal affairs at the "Palace." For most of his tour he was saved from the professional difficulties of his predecessors and the failures of his successors.

New twists of European politics in fact raised even happier possibilities to the chargé. American and British statesmen alike believed France's first step in repossessing New Orleans and its vast hinterland would be a reestablishment of French authority in rebellious Santo Domingo. American suspicions were confirmed when the preliminary peace in October, 1801, allowed Napoleon to dispatch his brother-in-law, Charles Leclerc, to that island, where he slaughtered the blacks and abused the Americans. In Washington, France's chargé, Louis André Pichon, asserted in vain that Louisiana had not been retroceded to France, and Thornton found himself in Liston's old role of administration favorite. By March, 1802, the president was warning Pichon of American anxiety and describing these warnings to the British chargé, who wrote Hawkesbury of "conversing freely" "on many occasions" with the president. Jefferson, reported Thornton, regarded retrocession as "a certain cause" of war and believed that if America alone could not expel France it "must have recourse to the assistance of other powers, meaning unquestionably Great Britain." Meanwhile, as the president got nowhere with his attempt to enlist Napoleon's aid in obtaining Spain's cession of the Floridas to the United States, attacks from the president echoed in the Republican press. Thornton wrote delightedly to Hawkesbury that "without pretending to say that this party is cured of its bitterness against Great Britain, I can safely venture to assure your Lordship that its predilection for France scarcely exists even in name."[19]

Presidential attention to the Briton became so marked as to bring envious remarks from former favorite Pichon, and though the young Tory remained skeptical of both the president and his politics, in September, 1802, he made the ritual visit to Monticello. There he spent three days, at times with other guests—Bishop Madison, the secretary of state, and federal city commissioner William Thornton—and there the president opened his library of books and maps to the Cambridge diplomat.

In the autumn of 1802, western pressures came to a head. In November Leclerc in Santo Domingo was fighting desperate blacks and yellow fever, and in Paris, Livingston was reporting no success in the Florida negotiations. Territorial governor William C. C. Claiborne wrote from Mississippi that Spanish Intendant Juan Morales at New Orleans had closed that port to all but Spanish vessels and had canceled the right of deposit (transshipment) essential to the western region's economy. This seizure of the western jugular with the possibility of immediate French reoccupation produced a national explosion, called by Consul Bond as great as any since the Revolution. To the president, of course, the threat was more than a Spanish one. Westerners talked of filibusters, and Federalists who sensed a popular issue offered resolutions for armaments and war and berated the administration for its inaction. To every politician in the wilderness capital, all this meant the serious probability of an Anglo-American alliance. Spain's minister, the Chevalier Carlos Martinez d'Yrujo, joined Pichon in assurances of the status quo, but the storm raged on.

Thornton himself hopefully chose to regard the closing of the port as officially inspired by Spain and as a prelude to war or the American seizure of New Orleans or both. Whereas the careful Madison always spoke guardedly, Jefferson speculated so frankly on a forcible seizure of

New Orleans that Thornton urged Hawkesbury that Britain should "have some share in the delivery of this Island of New Orleans to the United States" (America would take it anyway), so that "His Majesty's Government may hereafter attach still more this country to our interests . . . a very great change has gradually taken place in the opinions of all ranks in this government in favor of Great Britain."

The administration's nomination of Monroe to join Livingston in Paris in a last attempt to purchase New Orleans did not disturb the chargé's optimism. He offered Monroe the use of a ship, provided him with an introduction to Britain's Ambassador Whitworth in Paris, and suggested that Monroe proceed to London to discuss with the ministry the joint navigation of the Mississippi. He knew that if the French arrived in Louisiana, a seizure of New Orleans would be the most popular action that Jefferson, a president highly sensitive to popularity, could take. Therefore, the president's famous assurance that America would never give up the right of navigation and would in case of war "throw away the scabbard" meant Anglo-American collaboration to Thornton just as surely as the Congressional military measures of 1798 had meant war to Liston.[20]

Mingled with his continued criticism of Americans and their rulers, in Thornton's dispatches there appeared admissions that common language, habits, interests, and education were producing between Americans and Britons "a closer connection and friendship than either is aware of or is perhaps willing to allow." Western America's acceptance of Jefferson's negotiations over the Mississippi port instead of an insistence on a Federalist-inspired war was "the surest pledge of the continuance of his authority and the death blow of the Federal party."[21]

This new Anglo-American cordiality saved Thornton from his predecessor's temptations and his successor's blunders in western conspiracy. Ever since the 1800 election Aaron Burr had attracted Thornton's interest. Daring, devious, at odds with the Republican leadership, and clearly seeking "a more extensive field for his ambition," Burr represented a potential British ally—an able Federalist-oriented leader if the Union endured, or if it collapsed, a commander for the western segment. But by 1803, the Anglo-American entente was Thornton's first priority, and when Burr henchmen Jonathan Dayton and James Ross approached him about British interest in their western trip, Thornton declined to support a plan inimical to an administration moving toward a British alliance.

For the chargé personally, the prospect of this alliance offered an opportunity. By March, 1803, he had endured an eleven-year tour of duty among people he disliked in a republic he despised. Homesick and somewhat touchy over his personal financial status, he wrote London that the prospective alliance demanded "a more elevated character" to support the interests of Great Britain, "accompanied by all the outward circumstances or advantages which ought to distinguish the representative of His Majesty." Such a minister should command "opulence and even splendor," thus appealing to the "predominant features" of American character—"vanity and self-approbation."

Such wealth was especially necessary in Washington, where "almost every important person was a visitor" and influence required very extensive hospitality. The proud young chargé assured Hawkesbury that His Majesty's interests had not suffered since Liston's departure, but though the administration had shown him every attention, he was embarrassed in a land where "no ideas of respect or consideration for an office can atone for the want of wealth" and where even with what would have been a "decent income" elsewhere he had not been able "to show the slightest hospitality to a passing Englishman." He admitted the difficulty of finding a wealthy diplomat to go to a country where he would find "few men of education with whom to associate and still fewer (if I must speak freely) with the sentiments of gentlemen." The new, wealthy minister must, he concluded, be of such rank as not to be "afraid of debasing himself by a great degree of condescension."[22]

The British ministry that received these revealing admonitions had no intention of heeding them. For six months it had moved more slowly toward Anglo-American entente than had Thornton's imagination. The Addington ministry, if it meant anything, meant peace with France, on whom or on whose ally several Americans were (by Thornton's account) contemplating an attack. Still, when Thornton was writing his advice on a wealthy successor, Livingston was approaching Lord Whitworth in Paris, and from Madrid Minister Hookham Frere was reporting hints from Minister Charles Pinckney on joint action against Napoleon. More important, the fragile Peace of Amiens was fast dissolving in mutual distrust and treaty violations. So despite the distrust of such Ultra-Tories as James Harris, earl of Malmesbury, to whom Americans never ceased to be a "mean, illiberal, shabby people," their minister Rufus King was approached by Hawkesbury on a proposal that Britain seize and hold New Orleans in trust for the Americans, which was essentially Thornton's proposal of three months before.[23]

But the junior British diplomat in Washington was to see his hopes dashed as Liston had in 1798. While King and Hawkesbury talked collaboration, Thornton in March, 1803, saw and mailed to England a notice that Intendant Juan Morales's closure of New Orleans was unauthorized. In the next two months it became clear that a frontiersman attack on New Orleans had been effectively forestalled just as Burr's agent Dayton was entering Pittsburgh on his western reconnaissance. Only slightly less discomfited than that Federalist plotter, Thornton admitted to London that the reopening of the river was a Republican triumph that might well nullify plans for Anglo-American collaboration. He now urged that Louisiana be left to French ownership to make Americans more dependent on Britain.

One month later, on June 3, 1803, Rufus King arrived in New York with the stupendous news that the unpredictable First Consul of France barely a month before Britain's declaration of war against his government had offered to sell not only New Orleans but the whole of Louisiana to Jefferson's astounded commissioners. To America an empire was offered, and the lucrative neutrality in renewed European war was provided to pay for it. For Thornton the vision of Anglo-American alliance evaporated. For Federalists all hopes of recapturing the presidency crashed, since no man in America could now challenge the popularity of the Virginian.[24]

An era closed in 1803 with the resumption of war and the speedy ratification of the Louisiana Purchase, and Thornton knew it. Learning in April of his promotion to secretary of legation at The Hague, he utilized one of the frequent absences of the president and secretary of state from Washington to make a tour to Boston with his friend the Danish chargé Blicher Olsen. He then spent most of his hours in Philadelphia, preparing for the long-delayed arrival of the new minister.

The European war raised all the old neutrality questions, and Thornton urged on Madison mutual restitution of deserters and American acceptance of "the impressment of British seamen wherever found," protests over American arming of merchant ships, and a British "right" to use American ports against French cruisers. But Madison replied to his notes, the chargé said, with only "a little degree of humour," and with "a bitterness of tone and insinuation" that the secretary laid down doctrines "destructive of the well being of every civilized state," especially Britain. The United States, Thornton was informed, did not expect to receive in this war the cavalier treatment it had suffered in the past, and it utterly rejected the so-called right of impressment.

Although he now found few occasions for the gratifyingly frank talks he formerly enjoyed with the president, the chargé assured Hawkesbury that Madison's stiff tones did not reflect the milder position of the president. Thornton was unaware that Jefferson had been shown what Madison called the envoy's "very exceptional remarks" and had suggested a stronger reply than Madison actually delivered. To Hawkesbury, Thornton still suggested that Britain tacitly cease impressment in American waters to facilitate an agreement on the restitution of deserters. Also, for the only time, a British envoy supported an official Republican candidate—Jefferson, of all people—over the radical Thomas McKean, "a man," Thornton wrote, "of incomparably inferior talents" whose "bold wickedness" would be very unfortunate for the peace of Great Britain and the United States.[25]

In October, 1803, when Congress gathered early to ratify the purchase of an empire nearly as large as Europe, it convened in an American capital that was much the same as when Thornton took up Liston's work three years earlier. Some advances had been made: Jefferson was beloved by landowners for his interest in the town's development, and Congress had appropriated money to build offices for the departments of State and War and for furnishing the "Palace." The representatives now had a home in "the Oven," an elliptical brick building near the rest of the Capitol. Other money had been spent on the marine corps barracks and the navy yard. Land sales were still poor, but venturesome merchants were offering a wider selection of foodstuffs, dry goods, and jewelry, and local craftsmen produced clothing, furniture, and a little tinware and beer. A branch of the Bank of the United States had opened in 1801, and the start of the Valley of Virginia grain trade had enlivened a developing Georgetown-Alexandria rivalry. There were more inns and boardinghouses on Pennsylvania and New Jersey avenues, and despite the feebleness of the local government and the refusal of Congress to provide funds, streets were being cleared and in some cases topped with gravel between the larger clusters of buildings. Most streets, however, remained rutted, potholed, stump-filled, and dangerous for night travel.

The impatient diplomat, like most of Washington's officials, spent much time visiting, both for social reasons and as almost the sole means of gathering information. The Palace was the central gathering place, and there Thornton, like his colleagues, was the butt of the president's mildly malicious selection of dinner guests, one of whom was the despised Thomas Paine. Edward Thornton was a favorite and frequent guest of Mrs. William Thornton, wife of the district commissioner and Capitol designer, and he occasionally joined wealthy Col. John Tayloe in his beautiful new Octagon House, already a Washington landmark. Most of his time the homesick diplomat spent on routine reporting, sparring with Madison, and hoping for the arrival of a successor. Finally, on November 13, 1803, there burst upon the quiet little town the entourage of His Majesty's Envoy Extraordinary and Minister Plenipotentiary Anthony Merry, and his wife. The new arrival brought Hawkesbury's official approval of Thornton's tenure and permission for him to return to England before taking up his next post, but only when Merry judged it expedient to release him. Since a new secretary of legation did not arrive until December and the new minister proved to need extensive counsel, Thornton was compelled to spend eight more months in America, first as secretary and then as attaché.

The weary diplomat therefore took up for the second time the training of a senior minister. This time Thornton did so under multiple afflictions: he perforce spent less time in Philadelphia and more in Washington with Merry; he served under a man of intellect inferior to his own; and with growing anger he watched the Anglo-American relationship that had absorbed twelve years of his life deteriorate in dislike and increasing distrust.

A measure of this deterioration, and perhaps of Thornton's skill as a diplomat, lies in two reports. On November 25, 1803, shortly after Merry's arrival, a unique item appeared in the Philadelphia *Aurora*. "We may now speak of the chargé d'affaires Mr. Thornton without the suspicion of sinister views," wrote the editor. "Had all the Ambassadors which have preceded Mr. Thornton acted with the same decorum which has marked his deportment for upwards of twelve years, while he resided here, less jealousy and more good-will would have subsisted between the two nations." Yet eight months later, when Thornton on July 21, 1804, finally sailed from Philadelphia accompanied by a warm official commendation from Merry, he remarked bitterly that he left without having gained one friend in America in his thirteen years of residence.[26]

Thornton's later career was more erratic. He was sent from America to be secretary of legation at Berlin. From 1805 to 1807 Thornton rose to ministerial rank in several German courts, then was driven from the Continent by Napoleon's victories. In two subsequent tours in Sweden, Thornton did his best work, negotiating one treaty that brought Bernadotte into the alliance against Napoleon and another that united Norway and Sweden. Passed over as a proposed peace commissioner with America at Ghent in 1815, Thornton found his most difficult assignment in maintaining British interests in the tangled affairs of Portugal. He went to Brazil as minister to the Portuguese court in exile, and in 1822 he accompanied King John back to Portugal.

His successes everywhere were achieved without much personal regard from Britain's political leaders and with few supporters besides those Scots who kept Liston and him in office. He was too conciliatory to please his sovereign and the other Ultra-Tories or Malmesbury, whose protégé was Francis Jackson, his envious rival. Castlereagh used him, but neither he nor the duke of Portland liked Thornton's performance. After Thornton's Swedish career, Castlereagh refused him the title of Knight Commander of the Bath, usually accorded successful diplomats.

Made a privy councillor by virtue of his diplomatic appointments, Thornton was decorated by Portugal and later received the British Knight Grand Cross of the Bath. In 1812, when forty-five years old, Thornton married a Hanoverian woman in London, and of their six sons a namesake born in Stockholm achieved knighthood and an ambassadorial career that included the American post. After his assignment in Portugal ended in 1824, Thornton returned to England, where, at age fifty-seven, he lacked the political backers that sent Liston at seventy to Constantinople for six years. Hence he retired to Wembury House, Plymouth. Edward Thornton died in 1852 at the age of eighty-six, having never doubted the fallacies of American democratic premises or the personal frailties of Thomas Jefferson, to whom he attributed the republic's most glaring iniquities.

Anthony Merry

"He was a very good hater."
—Mrs. Piozzi, *Anecdotes of Samuel Johnson*

DIPLOMATIC relations between His Britannic Majesty's Foreign Office and the Court of Spain, whether active or passive, provided a training ground for young career hopefuls. Four of Britain's six ministers to the United States had served earlier in Spain. Hammond's brief stay there was little more than an opportunity to receive the valuable diamond gift customarily presented to a departing diplomat, but Liston's five years there had often involved him in commercial negotiations in which he used an assiduous consul at Málaga named Anthony Merry.

The son of a West Country wine and provisions merchant trading to Europe and Canada, Merry had begun his diplomatic career as consul at Majorca and at age thirty-one had already lived some thirteen years in Spain. To reward his assistance, Liston in 1787 helped Merry secure the consul generalship in Madrid. To this position, Liston wrote, Merry would bring activity and attention to business, a knowledge of commerce, and a valuable command of the Spanish language. He also possessed, Liston added, "singular moderation and candour" and "a degree of gravity and apparent reserve." Even his "extreme modesty which in some situations might be considered a disadvantage will not fail to operate here in his favour." In other words, Merry was a tradesman's son and therefore ineligible for a prestigious station, but he knew his place, was industrious, and maintained the usual network of useful commercial spies.[1]

Barely installed in 1787 as consul general, Merry received by chance the opening diplomatic barrage of the Anglo-Spanish Nootka Sound controversy, which, after a poor start, he reported accurately until relieved in 1790 by a more seasoned diplomat. He continued for ten years as consul general in Spain, after which he was consul general and (for six months) chargé at Copenhagen. In September, 1800, Grenville told Rufus King that "an agreeable man" named Merry would soon succeed Liston as minister to America, primarily for dealing (as a commercial specialist) with the Loyalist debt agreements that King was negotiating in London. The American suggested that he was expecting fresh instructions on the negotiations and that Merry might be detained in England until the new developments were known, a plan to which Grenville agreed.[2]

A new series of delays then developed, in part from the emergence of new administrations in both countries, and when preliminaries for an Anglo-French peace looked favorable, Merry was sent to Paris in July, 1801, as commissioner for prisoner exchange. Merry then served as secretary of a peace embassy with Earl Cornwallis at Amiens, where he mainly provided backstairs information; his personal contribution was little. His Lordship, himself not a notable wit, complained privately that "Mr. Merry lives with us; but although he is by no means an inefficient man in business and has good qualities he does not conduce much to our amusement."

After these negotiations, Merry returned to Paris to continue with prisoner exchange and to assist in treaty ratification. There, for eighteen months ensconced in the mansion of an ousted French marquis, the provisions merchant's son maintained an ambassador's state on a chargé's salary and coped with some five thousand Britons who flocked to Paris to stare at Napoleon and his court. Merry dined with the great and near-great, presented endless claims, stamped visas, provided passports, and assiduously reported suspicious French activities. He was presented to the First Consul, who gave him the usual snuffbox and reportedly relished the epithet "Toujours Gai" that was part of the totally humorless bureaucrat's family crest and was also his malicious nickname among his Foreign Office colleagues.[3]

Meanwhile, someone had to go to America. In the Foreign Office a plan had evolved for Liston's ministerial successor to be Francis Jackson, the fiery arch-Tory son of a Carmarthen protégé; however, Rufus King had made inquiries that confirmed earlier suspicions. In a letter curiously mingling accuracy and error about the two most disastrous British ministers in early Anglo-American diplomacy, King described a "positive, vain, and intolerant" Jackson, fully equipped with "English prejudices in respect to other countries" and looking upon an American assignment merely as a stepping-stone in his career. Merry, on the contrary, was said to be a "plain, unassuming and sensible man

... the reverse of Mr. Jackson," who wished to go to America for an "agreeable and permanent residence." King, therefore, urged Merry's appointment. Hawkesbury agreed, but as American relations seemed quiet, Merry was given another Spanish assignment and only sixteen months later did he prepare to depart to relieve the long-suffering Thornton.

Meanwhile, the nominee at the age of forty-six took a step that was to prove disastrous for "an agreeable and permanent residence" in America. On January 21, 1803, by special license in London he married Elizabeth Leathes, the well-to-do widow of John Leathes of Herringfleet Hall, Suffolk. The new Mrs. Merry was a large, overpowering woman, vain and vivacious. She was proud of her position in county society, her jewelry, and her portraits, and she was given to striking dress and fluctuating moods. Her passion was conversation, her hobby horticulture, and her ambition to receive the social deference due a salon hostess and minister's wife. "Her manner," said a snobbish but observant English guest at her salon, was "not quite correct." Merry was particularly aware of her financial advantages.[4]

A week after the marriage the *Gentleman's Magazine* noted Merry's promotion to be His Majesty's Envoy Extraordinary and Minister Plenipotentiary to the United States. The appointment was not universally applauded. William Cobbett, for one, argued for the appointment of a well-known figure: "'*Who* is Mr. Merry?' the Americans will ask and people in this country will put the same question ... without much chance of obtaining an answer.... Is he the sort of man to go to America as the representative of His Majesty?"[5] The editor deplored the practice of sending to America "consuls, secretaries, chargés d'affaires, the mere stop-gaps of the corps diplomatique ... men who follow diplomacy for bread" and concluded, "Poor Mr. Merry! What can he do? What use will he be of?" since there were "no crouching English nobility there whom he may serve as gentleman usher, and as to any other possible function, how can he be possibly fit for it?"

Cobbett was as usual unfair, but as usual he had a point. To Rufus King, Merry was preferable to a reputedly insufferable Jackson. To Hawkesbury he was a useful journeyman to be provided for and whom the Americans seemed to prefer over a well-connected gentleman. And, to his former employer, Liston, in retrospect Merry was "a most honourable, worthy, good man and of all those who were likely to accept of the Embassy he appeared to me the most fit for it and especially the least likely to *do harm*."[6]

Merry himself approached the mission with more than usual assets and liabilities. He recognized it as a reward of careful service, and as a position not usually given to a tradesman's son. He had gained his post by meticulous attention to the orders of his masters, most of whom like himself were hard-line Tories who were quick to destroy those diplomats who did not aggressively uphold Britain's positions—in their terms, "act like an Englishman." He had sunk his capital into preparing for a mission in which he carried not only his country's dignity but also the pretensions of a slightly faded society hostess of fragile emotional balance. In private correspondence his young secretary described the minister as "slow, indefatigable, clear sighted and vigilant. He does his business like clockwork, has a tenacious memory . . . and a quick observation. He knows everybody in Europe almost and in conversation about persons and characters is inexhaustible, but as to imagination I never saw a man who had so little concern about it. He is full of honor and integrity and without any levity but in [sic] his table."[7] But years of caution under pressure and his newly married state took their emotional toll. Before he left England he was "laboring under a distressing emotional disorder," and Merry carried with him to America an introduction to the famous Dr. Physick in Philadelphia. So a hardworking, businesslike, humorless, and intense bureaucrat of professional ability but limited perspective set forth under mental stress for the most trying post then in the British diplomatic service.

After a month spent in England accumulating the servants and necessities required by the status of His Majesty's ministers overseas, the Merrys departed from Spithead on September 25, 1803. On that voyage the British frigate *Phaeton* bore as remarkable a variety of sources of future ill will and national harassment as ever approached American shores in peacetime. In diplomacy, Minister Merry himself was to be the most wretched, and hence the most passionately critical, of Britain's early envoys. In war, Capt. George Cockburn of the *Phaeton* would as admiral assist in burning down the capital toward which the ship now headed. The young Irish poet Tom Moore was included in Merry's party because his family was known to the elder Merrys and he now sought relief from his debts by a clerkship in Bermuda; he was to reciprocate Merry's assistance by sympathy and some long-remembered literary caricatures of the republic and its leader. Another *Phaeton* passenger was Charles Williamson, brother of a protégé of First Lord of the Admiralty Melville and himself a friend of Melville. Williamson had already met Merry in London, and during the next year he was to invite the minister to participate with him and Aaron Burr in a seditious plot against the republic.

During a boisterous voyage the snobbish Moore helped keep up the passengers' spirits with wit, songs, and anecdotes. He admired the arrogant Cockburn as "a man of good fashion and rank" and conjectured with perhaps unconscious cruelty that Mrs. Merry "has been a fine woman." Merry himself, as usual, created no sharp impressions on anyone. The miseries of the six-week voyage did not end at Norfolk, for there Elizabeth Merry exchanged the wretchedness of seasickness for a two-week bout with malaria. Meanwhile, damages from the tumultuous voyage compelled Cockburn to bring his ship to the wharf for repair, whereupon fourteen sailors deserted. In Alexandria they encountered, in Elizabeth Merry's phrase, "six days' disputation with winds, tides, and ignorant navigators," so that it was November 25 before they met Thornton at Alexandria.

Edward Thornton provided the first lift to their spirits, and Mrs. Merry termed him "a *quiet*, sensible, well-informed man, without brilliancy or elocution, well educated and full of information which he details slowly from a natural impediment in his speech." He was, she added, "a great acquisition and I rejoice to hear he is not likely to leave us." Next day the entourage bounced in a coach over intolerable roads and were finally put down at the Union Tavern in Georgetown until they might find, she said, "a hovel of our own."[8]

The battered minister allowed himself but a Sunday's rest before meeting Secretary of State Madison. Then, on November 29, 1803, he donned the glittering regalia of ministerial formal dress and went with Madison to the Palace for his official presentation to the president. That now famous occasion began unfortunately with an accidental encounter in a narrow passageway from which Merry had to back out awkwardly, after which the resplendent minister faced a president in his usual informal clothes and indoor slippers. Although greatly surprised, Merry reported officially at the time only that he was received by the president in his "usual morning attire" and that he was pleased with Jefferson's personal and political criticisms of Bonaparte. In retrospect after social and political warfare, the encounter appeared sinister,

Anthony Merry

and Merry wrote arch-Federalist Josiah Quincy that the president was "not merely in an undress but actually *standing in slippers down at the heels*" and in clothes "indicative of utter slovenliness and indifference" in a negligence so studied that "I could not doubt that the whole scheme was prepared and intended as an insult not to me personally but to the sovereign I represented."[9]

Two of the most demoralizing months of his life followed. Merry had been fully briefed on Federalist protocol by Liston, who had received the first visits from all Americans except the president, vice-president, senators, and secretary of state and who with his wife had invariably received places of honor at the presidential table. The Merrys naturally anticipated the same deference. But in a series of interviews Madison informed the minister that, under Jeffersonian Republican canons, envoys would pay first calls on all cabinet members, that there would be no precedence in approaching or sitting at the president's table, and that the same rules would be observed at cabinet members' functions. Not only would foreign diplomats and their wives be treated like other guests but there would also be absolutely equal treatment of foreign envoys of all ranks below ambassadors (of whom there were none in Washington) and including chargés (who currently represented Denmark and France). "In a word," wrote Merry angrily, Jefferson would "put . . . diplomats on a level as to each other and as to the lowest American citizen."

Still worse were the presidential dinners. At one Elizabeth Merry was perforce taken in to dinner by her husband in the absence of any other escort. At another her husband sought a relatively high place of honor only to be outflanked by a swift but unknown congressman "without Mr. Jefferson using any means to prevent it." The president also repeated earlier whimsies by having France's Pichon at table with Merry and by paying marked attention to Spain's Yrujo and other diplomatic rivals.[10]

In the self-conscious and politics-ridden capital this diplomatic aversion produced an earthquake. Federalists were soon describing Jefferson's dress on receiving the minister as gown, slippers, and nightcap. Former secretary Pickering upheld Merry's claims, and the Federalist *Gazette of the United States* catalogued presidential barbarisms. Minister Yrujo's American wife assured Dolley Madison that war would ensue. Tom Moore, returning from an unsatisfactory Bermuda job, heard the minister's tales and after his own imagined slight by the president affirmed that only Britain's temporarily embarrassing military position saved Jefferson from chastisement for his "most pointed incivility" to Merry.

The minister himself was not the fool that later historians were to portray. But a formative twenty years near the ceremonious Spanish court had warped his frail sense of proportion. All British ministers to America as elsewhere were enjoined in their general instructions to insist on receiving the same "ceremonies and distinctions" that had been accorded their predecessors and to challenge anything in their reception "that may in any shape be derogatory to our royal dignity." Patrician envoys might interpret these routine instructions broadly, but a tradesman's son on his first independent ministerial mission would do so at his peril.

Moreover, easily as imperative as George III's royal dignity in London were the sensitivities of Elizabeth Merry in Washington. This formidable woman, "accustomed to adulation" according to Merry's secretary, was described with her husband by society leader Margaret Smith as "a large, tall, well-made woman, rather masculine, very free and affable in her manners but without being graceful. She is said to be a woman of fine understanding and she is so entirely the talker and actor in all companies that her good husband passes quite unnoticed; he is plain in appearance and called rather inferior in understanding."[11] The minister's inferior understanding could nevertheless perceive threats both to his professional career and to domestic peace. However, he chose a poor defense: a boycott of all social occasions where he and his wife "might be exposed to a repetition of the same want of distinction towards us." Merry also concluded a pact with Spain's Minister Yrujo (currently under presidential displeasure for foot-dragging over the delivery of Louisiana) to attend no presidential function unless their wives alternately received social precedence at the Palace. The ministers would also take their wives in to dinner first at embassy dinners for cabinet members. The women, meanwhile, decided to boycott all cabinet dinners in Washington and even declined to attend the New Year's reception at the Palace. The minister reported all this to London and awaited approval.[12] It was the wrong response.

Meanwhile, despite a changing scene, Washington remained overwhelmingly rustic. Bears and other beasts were displayed on the Palace grounds, which were surrounded by a mere wooden fence and were "apparently untouched by spade or pickaxe." Vast spaces still sep-

George Hammond, 1791–1795. Portrait by John Trumbull. (Courtesy Yale University Art Gallery, New Haven, Conn.)

Robert Liston, 1796–1800. Portrait by Gilbert Stuart. (Courtesy National Gallery of Art, Chester Dale Collection, Washington, D.C.)

Henrietta Liston, wife of Robert Liston. Portrait by Gilbert Stuart. (Courtesy National Gallery of Art, Chester Dale Collection, Washington, D.C.)

Anthony Merry, 1803–1806. (Courtesy Library of Congress)

Elizabeth Merry, wife of Anthony Merry. (Courtesy University Press of Virginia)

David Erskine, 1806–1809. (Reproduced from Beckles Willson, *Friendly Relations*. Boston: Little, Brown, 1934)

Augustus Foster, 1811–1812. From a portrait at Glyde Court, County Louth. (Reproduced from frontispiece, Augustus Foster, *Jeffersonian America*. San Marino, Calif.: Huntington Library, 1954)

Charles Bagot, 1816–1819. Portrait by John Hoppner.

Mary Bagot, wife of Charles Bagot. Portrait by John Hoppner.

Stratford Canning, 1820–1823. From a miniature by A. Robertson, 1816.

arated the small clusters of buildings, and water for both washing and drinking was brought by bucket from public wells. Gentlemen shot woodchuck near the Capitol and geese, ducks, and snipe along the stream called the Tiber. On the whole, Washington was, as Randolph commented, "like Mosco, very grand in some things, very mean in others, and very dull in all." In the fall, a week of Jockey Club racing emptied the halls of Congress. Public dinners at taverns honored prominent men or marked special occasions. Frequently a theater troupe more daring than talented made a brief appearance, and portraitists came and went. Plans for the first formal school were being made, and the principal religious services were still those conducted in denominational rotation in the House of Representatives chamber. In late spring Congress adjourned, most officials left for their homes, and silence and summer heat fell on the little town.

Since there were no permanent theater, social clubs, libraries, or gardens, few forms of entertainment existed outside of social affairs. They were both an end in themselves and an opportunity for transacting political and diplomatic business. Society itself was determined rather than brilliant. Paying and receiving calls was a major activity, and constant private evening parties provided refreshments, dancing, cards, chess, and conversation. The capital's outstanding hostess was the kind and charming Dolley Madison. Another favorite was Mrs. Margaret Bayard Smith, wife of the owner and editor of the *National Intelligencer*; her hospitality somewhat offset her husband's rampant Republicanism and his habit of printing embarrassing or derogatory items on Britain's food riots, military losses, political tyranny, and general shortcomings.

The Palace was of course the town's principal social focus, and although Jefferson limited formal receptions to those on New Year's and the Fourth of July, the Palace was the scene of frequent impromptu gatherings and regularly scheduled congressional dinners. The president, as Thornton had found, was far more available than his predecessors had been, and even the Federalists who jeered at "the charming and amiable democratic equality" dispensed by "the left-legged ruler of this ill-fated country" rarely declined the opportunity to enjoy the cuisine of his excellent French chef and to "wish that his French politics were as good as his French wines."

Cabinet members shared the social burdens with their chief and used their evening parties for conducting official business. In addition, while Republican economy was reducing the number of American embassies overseas, the capital's corps now included the Swedish consul, Richard Soderström, and R. G. Van Polanen, minister resident from the Batavian Republic. From time to time painted and shaven-headed Indian chiefs arrived seeking gifts, as did Tunisian and other Mediterranean diplomats.[13]

In this pervasive social activity, Merry's decision for defiance and boycott merely meant that he and Mrs. Merry had, in Jefferson's words, "put themselves into Coventry" and that he had lost "the best half of his usefulness to his nation." The president believed Merry to be "personally as desirable a character as could have been sent us" but "unluckily associated with one of the opposite character in every point." Jefferson sought to propitiate Mrs. Merry with a packet of "very valuable and scarce seeds" and abandoned his practice of having an official hostess so as to go in to dinner with the nearest lady. But when these and other overtures were ignored by the Merry-Yrujo coalition, the president concluded that Elizabeth Merry was a virago and a marplot and that "we shall endeavor to draw him into society as if she did not exist." Significantly, the president resented Merry's "display of diplomatic superstition" for the opportunity it presented his own political enemies, while the secretary of state feared it would fan endemic Americanophobia in London. The secretary therefore instructed American envoys to explain carefully that the new canons reflected no anti-British stance and also to gather information on diplomatic usages abroad. The Americans abroad replied that Merry received more attention than they did, and as to future repercussions, their predictions reflected their own political views. Monroe, King's replacement in London, watched the matchless arrogance of Tory society surpass itself when directed at a Jeffersonian Republican, and he merely suggested caution. Federalists were gloomier.

"Toujours Gai" himself, while waiting for the cabinet approval that never came, explained almost every event as part of a calculated Jeffersonian denigration of foreign diplomats. His imaginary adversaries ranged from the president to the clerks in Madison's office who presumed to speak to him before he addressed them. Thornton perforce followed his chief's lead and lost popularity; France's Pichon followed Jefferson's new canons faithfully.[14] The real importance of the prestige warfare was, as many contemporaries realized, that it reflected a new American attitude far eclipsing the gaucheries of the "pele mele system."

In the midst of the tempest, Merry frequently visited the new brick building close to the Palace that housed the departments of State and War. Ushered by a clerk into what he called Madison's "very indifferent little room," the Briton after an amiable greeting received, usually in good-tempered tones, some very firm assertions of American neutral rights. Encouraged, both Thornton and Merry knew, by the acquisition of Louisiana and the resumption of European war, Madison urgently proposed to end impressments and forcible visitations at sea; to define blockade and contraband more closely; to regulate seizures; and, in effect, to open British West Indian trade to American ships. Merry was left in no doubt, he told Hawkesbury, that the United States was prepared to press strongly for a "more convenient system of neutral navigation than the interests of the British Empire have hitherto allowed His Majesty to concur in."

Events emphasized Madison's sermons. In the peaceful interval of 1802–1803, Britain's navy had dismissed forty thousand seamen, many of whom were now employed on American vessels, and in the renewed war the Admiralty feared a desperate shortage of trained crews. Inevitably the rate of impressments rose, so that from 1803 to 1806 the number of men impressed exceeded that of the entire previous decade of Revolutionary and Napoleonic wars on the Continent. Therefore, as secretary and minister fenced, Congress called for lists of the impressed, and two bills were introduced to protect seamen and to legalize measures against British captains acting in American ports. Congress also passed the Mobile Act, allowing the administration a vague authority to annex territory in dispute with Spain, and the Senate refused to ratify the northwestern boundary article in Rufus King's Canadian boundary convention.

In less than three months and during the social precedence battle, America and Britain appeared to the excited Merry to be on a collision course toward war because of Jefferson's inflated self-image and Britain's desperate wartime situation. The minister's High Tory excitement also reanimated Thornton's suspicions. The former chargé wrote Hammond describing the American attitude as incredibly changed because the Louisiana Purchase had "elevated the President beyond imagination in his own opinion." Angry and perhaps uneasy over his former optimistic dispatches, Thornton urged that "everything as it relates to this country now depends upon our firmness; if we yield an iota without real and perfect equivalent . . . we are lost." Britain's policy must be "firm and indifferent" though nonprovocative, "since we have more than half the people on our side."[15] As his sailing date approached, Thornton grew steadily more bitter.

By the time of Thornton's departure in July, 1804, Merry had got his diplomatic feet under him. He sturdily told Madison that London would never accept American claims of neutral rights. He sweepingly defended the British captains who virtually blockaded New York to seek deserters and seize ships, even while he privately urged them to restrain themselves. Merry reported on the administration's quarrel with Yrujo over East Florida, and while loathing Jefferson he admitted the probability of Republican electoral success in 1804. Although he occasionally wrote home of the mild Madison's "temper and evil disposition" and "high language" "accompanied with some degree of menace," his personal relationships with the secretary were good, Madison in turn finding him "at bottom a very worthy man and easy to do business with."[16]

Unfortunately, Merry also began to indulge in the separation and disunity fantasy that had nearly destroyed Liston. He sought to fan anti-Republican anger in New England, to create it in the west (over West Florida diplomacy), and to encourage Creole anger over lack of civil rights in Louisiana. But in 1804 the most serious disunion potential centered on Burr's schemes, already known to Merry through Thornton. The vice-president's break with Jefferson, his defeat in the New York governor's race, and the death of Hamilton on the Weehawken dueling ground inevitably brought a Burr emissary to Merry's door. This was Charles Williamson, Merry's fellow traveler on the *Phaeton*. Williamson had met Burr through land speculation and was now en route to London with Burr's plan "to effect a separation of the western part of the United States from that which lies between the Atlantic and the mountains." To London Merry sent guarded approval, writing that Burr still had important connections, talents, and a hatred of Jefferson that would make him useful to his employers. The intrigue continued into the summer months.[17]

"Toujours Gai" argued with the secretary of state and hatched plots with the president's enemies in the midst of continuing personal frustrations. Legation files sent by sea from Philadelphia were shipwrecked and though rescued were indecipherable. Early in 1804 "at enormous expense," Merry purchased and combined the "mere shells" of two houses on K Street NW to make an embassy large enough for suitably lavish entertainment. The Merrys had brought an Italian maître d'hôtel, a French chef, an English valet, and a Scottish maid, among other servants, but they found the warnings of their predecessors fulfilled as their servants left them to become citizen-landowners. Replacements were hard to find in the small white population of the little town. In a slur at his tormentors, the minister explained to London that the difficulty lay in part in "the quality of the inhabitants which from their poverty and habits altogether (even those of the officers of the government) renders decent and able domestics unnecessary." Compelled to rely on free blacks and slaves, the minister was scandalized by having one of the latter seized from his embassy by "the inferior clerk to a merchant" acting as a peace officer. When appealed to, Merry said, Madison, "with his habitual resource of sophistry," denied redress "in language dictated by pique as well as by a jealous sensibility of the disadvantages of the seat of government." Worse still, the half-literate owner of the slave presumed to apologize to Merry as to an equal.

Meanwhile Elizabeth Merry carried on her social campaign, sometimes against unfair odds. A skirmish with Martha Jefferson Randolph over the "first visit" prerogative having ended in discomfiture, the minister's wife rolled in her heaviest artillery. She appeared at Secretary of the Navy Robert Smith's formal ball in a stunning dress of white and blue satin and crepe shimmering with spangles and setting off her diamond tiara, combs, and earrings, and with her considerable bosom ablaze with a diamond necklace. Alas, the beautiful young Betsy Smith Bonaparte, sister-in-law of Napoleon, appeared that evening in a gown so revealing her natural charms that "no one dared look at her but by stealth," and the administration ladies, including her aunt, decreed that in future she should wear more clothes or not appear in public.[18]

In London the Foreign Office took as little heed of Merry's precedence quarrels as of his wife's social defeats. In April, 1804, the feeble if well-intentioned Addington ministry crashed. Pitt came in to pursue war to the utmost, and the absence of Grenville and other more moderate Tories from his government foreshadowed stormy American relations. Pitt's ardent nationalism responded in kind to the fanatically mercantilistic pamphlets of John Holroyd, earl of Sheffield; the rigidity of George Rose at the Board of Trade; and the flamboyance of George Canning in the House of Commons. By mid-1804, the powerful combined lobby of British shipping and West Indian sugar interests called for the exclusion of Americans from the French and Spanish West Indian carrying trade to Europe. The new prime minister was soon committed to both economic warfare and a British shipping monopoly in the name of military victory.

The foreign secretary for this program was the second-string Dudley Ryder, Lord Harrowby, who found on his desk Merry's angry dispatches describing Jefferson's "high tone" in denouncing impressments, blockades, and the right of search and claiming the very trading privileges Pitt was soon pledged to destroy. Far more important to his masters than Merry's recital of social affronts were his reports of the Senate's rejection of King's convention and of new congressional bills to punish British captains for actions that the Admiralty regarded as essential for British maritime supremacy. In Henry Adams's words: "On one side Pitt and Lord Harrowby stood meditating the details of measures . . . for taking away from the United States most of the commercial advantages hitherto enjoyed by them; on the other side stood Monroe and Jefferson, equally confident, telling the Englishmen that very much greater advantages must be conceded."[19] Neither Monroe in London nor Merry in Washington would survive even the first clash of such protagonists.

In 1804 the new order opened spectacularly in America. Captain Bradley, of His Majesty's ship *Cambrian*, accompanied by another warship, ran amok in New York harbor, seized from the deck of a British merchant ship fourteen alleged American seamen he thought to be British deserters, insulted revenue and quarantine officers, and refused to heed Mayor De Witt Clinton's remonstrances. Enraged by an American attempt to arrest one of his officers, Bradley then dropped down to Sandy Hook, where he instituted a blockade lasting several weeks, holding French ships in port, stopping all traffic for search, and firing cannons while he boarded ships and seized cargoes and passengers. Even Consul Barclay was aghast, but Merry (though he despised this colleague) fully defended Bradley even while he vainly besought the fiery captain to cease his personal war with the Union. Madison, disgusted with Merry's "diplomatic pettifogging," finally removed the problem to London, but there Monroe, when he at last obtained an interview, found that Lord Harrowby refused even to discuss matters involving impressment, seizures, and neutral rights.

To Merry the foreign secretary was more explicit. In an instruction of November 7, he deplored America's "increasing acrimony" but asserted that Madison's "pretensions" against impressment were "too extravagant to require any serious refutation" since it was an age-old British right. The Jay treaty having expired, regulation of commerce was to be turned over to the Privy Council; the Americans had rejected the King convention by amending it; and Merry, without using "language of a hostile or menacing tendency," was to make all of this clear to the Americans. Neither Merry's social slights nor Pitt's plans for West Indian trade restrictions were mentioned. However, British positions for the next eight years were laid down in this November, 1804, instruction: immutability on impressment coupled with the transfer of trade regulations to a wartime Privy Council and its allied mercantilist Board of Trade. Even the stylistic tones of the future were present: mingled incredulity, patronization, patient reasonableness in the face of American obtuseness, and ultimate threat; the caustic Canning of 1809 and the blandly obdurate Castlereagh of 1811 both spoke through Lord Harrowby.[20]

As the foreign minister opened the British assault, Merry was away from the battleground. He had left Washington in July after writing a sober dispatch on American opinion, and he proposed to escape the capital's heat by staying at Baltimore and then Philadelphia. But months of anger and professional disappointment, his wife's illness and tears, and "high language" from Madison now plunged the minister into a half-psychosomatic illness described by a hopeful rival as "of the apoplectic kind," from which he had first suffered in England.

Merry fell ill in Baltimore but reached Philadelphia, only to suffer a serious relapse. Though feeble and nervous, he kept up his reports: on Yrujo's anti-administration antics, on Captain Bradley's dramatics, and on the arrival of the new French minister, Louis-Marie Turreau de Garambouville. During these months of illness and dejection, he also conferred with Burr's emissary of disunion, Williamson. In October, his mental depression eased, but he was then afflicted violently by hemorrhoids, and the barbarous surgery that ensued required a further two-month convalescence in Philadelphia. Meanwhile, the government had resumed business in Washington. It was only a few days before Christmas when the ailing minister and his unhappy wife overcame the wretched roads and their reluctance to return to the capital they despised.[21]

A few days later the embassy was brightened by the arrival of Augustus Foster, the new secretary of legation. He was the handsome, spoiled son of Elizabeth Foster, a well-connected young beauty separated from her husband and living in a celebrated ménage à trois with the duke and duchess of Devonshire. Not nobly born despite rumors inspired by his mother's beauty and partiality for the nobility, Augustus Foster combined an all-encompassing snobbishness with redeeming playfulness, observation, and good humor. To the ill and discouraged Merrys, he was a liaison with all they revered, and Foster's correspondents in England produced a stream of ridicule of Americans that supported their scorn and raised their spirits.

Despite his illness, Merry at once presented his new secretary to the president, who, Foster allowed, "behaved very civilly in general." Jefferson, he wrote, looked and dressed "like a very plain farmer, and wears his slippers down at the heel; only think what must have been Toujours Gai's embarrassment when at his first audience he went all bespeckled with all the spangles of our gaudy court dress." Years later Foster further remembered the president as "a tall man with a very red freckled face and gray neglected hair, his manners good natured, frank and rather friendly though he had somewhat of a cynical expression of countenance."[22]

In London Tory ministries were less interested in their envoy's personal impressions than with the emphasis with which British positions were put before American administrations. Their minister in America was therefore influential at home when he could (like Hammond) furnish useful secret information while a treaty was under negotiation or when (like Liston) he could influence the secretary of state in a critical period of American decision making. Neither condition prevailed for Merry in 1805–1806. In October, 1805, the publication of James Stephen's *War in Disguise* signaled the approaching triumph of mercantilist thinking in British leadership. More ominously for America, on October 21, 1805, at Trafalgar, Britain became the unchallengeable ruler of sea warfare. The British Order in Council of May 16, 1806, though intended as a compromise, began the policy of sweeping American overseas markets into British hands and interdicting all trade to Europe and European colonies save that which the cabinet might choose to allow. Impressments (essential for manpower), seizures (partly to enhance naval zeal by the prize system), and paper blockades (as a basis for seizures) implemented this policy. On the Continent the new emperor Napoleon I destroyed enemy coalitions and drew a new map. Beginning in November, 1806, the emperor responded to the British Orders in Council with successive decrees even surpassing the Orders in denials of neutral rights.

Across the ocean Jefferson's administration was no more prepared to enter such Anglo-French conflict than Washington's had been. But the Republicans now administered the affairs of a nation of more than twice the size and almost half again the population of the United States of 1794, and neither Jefferson nor his secretary of state would accept such limitations on national commerce as Washington and Jay had reluctantly conceded. In such an impasse ministers might debate and secretaries and clerks might numb their fingers with endless correspondence, but nothing would result save rebuff and resentment until surrender, war, or both. A ten-year Anglo-American modus vivendi began to collapse in the winter of 1805–1806 for reasons beyond the power of peaceful diplomacy. Merry's role, like Monroe's in London, was to bear the popular anger of his hosts and to present his government's position with what little guidance that government might provide.

At the Foreign Office in late 1804, Lord Harrowby closed his career by falling down a flight of stairs, and his successor, Henry Phipps, Lord Mulgrave, presided over the ministry from January, 1805, until the ministry collapsed with Pitt's death in 1806. Mulgrave, fully described as "a Tory gentleman of modest abilities," was like his colleagues absorbed with the fury of the war on the Continent. Merry was, therefore, seldom informed or effective; he had no prior warning in the winter of 1804–1805 when the Pittites began to draw the commerce of France and of her ally Spain into British hands through Parliamentary acts, Orders in Council, and licenses. In September, 1805, when news arrived in America of the *Essex* decision by which Britain reestablished the Rule of 1756 and thereby seemed to sweep away the foundations of America's reexport West Indian trade, Merry was as unprepared as the angriest American shipowner. Although he reported regularly on Jefferson's plans to acquire East Florida and Texas from Spain, he did not perceive that the choice of means to achieve these ends took precedence over Anglo-American relations. Hence, when the president inclined toward force against Spain, Merry was surprised to hear him talk of an Anglo-American alliance; later, when bribery of France seemed a more feasible means, Merry was shaken by sharp Madisonian lectures and newspaper attacks.[23]

On March 4, Merry and Foster witnessed at the Capitol the second Jefferson inaugural. They noted with approval that this time Jefferson came formally dressed and rode to the ceremony accompanied by groom and secretary. But, contradicting the fulsome descriptions in the *National Intelligencer*, Foster assured his mother "there was nothing dignified in the whole affair," especially in the ensuing reception when "blacks and dirty boys . . . drank his wines and lolled upon his couches before us all." A sort of parade consisted of "low persons, for the most part Irish labourers" and "the jingling of a few pipes and drums." The president was reportedly in high spirits, but his former vice-president nursed other emotions.

A few days after the installation of Vice-President George Clinton, Aaron Burr visited the British legation for the first of several long, intimate discussions. Burr now proposed a revision of the plan first proposed in 1804 by Charles Williamson, of whom nothing more had been heard. The New Yorker told Merry that the Louisianians, whose discontents the minister had fomented, awaited only the protection of a foreign power and coordination with their fellow westerners to strike for independence. He now laid before the enthralled Merry the same allurements that John Chisholm had less skillfully presented to Liston in 1796. Burr professed the details to be too incomplete to disclose, but a favorable response would bring an agent to London with particulars.

The requirements were much the same as Chisholm's had been: "two or three frigates and the same number of smaller vessels to be stationed at the mouth of the Mississippi" to prevent an American blockade and "the loan of about one hundred thousand pounds." In return Britain would receive the immense market of a vast territory and perhaps outright possession of strategic places like East Florida. Burr hoped that Britain would respond so that he would not have to turn to France, he said, and the immediate necessity was the dispatch of an intelligent, discreet, and French-speaking British consul to New Orleans. A month later the arch-conspirator headed west after assuring Merry that matters were "in the most prosperous train" and a liaison agent with Merry would soon appear. The dazzled minister assured London that Burr had all the talents, energy, intrepidity, and firmness necessary and was regaining all his American influence through Republican schisms.

Ill-omened silence and miscalculation then fell upon the Burr-Merry schemes. The liaison agent did not appear. When the newspapers in the summer of 1805 began to question Burr's motives and to raise ominous talk of British assistance to conspiracy, the spellbound Merry failed to see the danger and merely deplored the indiscretions of Colonel Burr's co-conspirators. As months wore on and Mulgrave succeeded Lord Harrowby at the Foreign Office, no acknowledgment or comment came from London. In fact, Burr's plan for New World revolution, like Miranda's, became less attractive to Pitt than did plans for direct military and economic assault on France itself. This assault, of course, meant further clashes with America over neutrality, and in 1805 Monroe wrote Madison that Pitt's new policy "breathed fire." And it was clear at the London embassy that "no American would be dealt with if he could be ignored."[24]

Pitt's new bellicosity was naturally most congenial to his minister in Washington. Merry's dispatches denounced American seamen's certificates of citizenship as fraudulent, stolidly reported rising American anger at seizures resulting from the *Essex* decision, and applauded arguments in Stephen's *War in Disguise*, bringing statistics to support the exclusion of American trade from the Indies. Elated by Admiral Nelson's great victory at Trafalgar, Merry counseled Downing Street that the best response to American anti-British legislation would be to send a reinforcement to the squadron on the American Station "sufficiently great to be noticed," which would "stop all the hostile proceedings of this government." In April, 1806, a shot from the British warship *Leander* patrolling off New York accidentally killed an American merchant seaman, producing a real crisis. Even Federalists demanded reprisals, Barclay was besieged in his home, and mobs sought British officers. "Toujours Gai" sagely advised his government that Americans were too avaricious to fight and that only force would "command from this government that respect which they have recently lost toward Great Britain."[25]

A most dangerous feature of Merry's advice to London was his reliance on John Randolph, a frequent guest at the embassy and by now a violent opponent of administration policies. Although he allegedly considered all diplomats to be "privileged spies," the eccentric aristocrat was welcomed by Merry, who, like most Englishmen visiting

America, considered Randolph to be one of the few gentlemen in the country. The minister reported the Virginian's vitriolic attacks on his cousin in the Palace, but he did not warn the Foreign Office that Randolph was merely the disaffected leader of a small band of malcontents. Therefore, London saw the congressman's diatribes as corroborating Merry's reports of grave and probably mortal Republican schisms. It was dangerously overstated support for a Tory hard-line policy.

In the routine of diplomatic business Merry was always knowledgeable and businesslike, but by 1806, his personal fury and prejudice made him dangerous to diplomacy and useful to his government only in confirming their misconceptions of American opinion. His reports now sounded much like Hammond's 1794 tirades on American "hatred of England," but this unimaginative "clockwork" minister, ill, slow, and bored, had none of young Hammond's fire. He merely clung doggedly to the despised post he considered both a patriotic duty and a personal financial necessity.

Even among the administration's opponents he had little support. His friend Randolph remarked scornfully of the psychologically insecure minister that "if anyone asked him 'what o'clock is it' he would be apt to reply, 'I will write to my government for instructions.'" Moderate Federalist William Plumer found Merry socially amiable and knowledgeable of men and business but "neither the scholar nor man of talents." Timothy Pickering, who could not shake off his habit of advising British ministers sympathetically on British policy, nevertheless wrote Liston that his successor was "without the qualities necessary in a public minister" and that his work included a "specimen of imbecility."

As for the administration, Madison found Merry pleasant but "exceedingly cautious" and maintained the peculiar illusion that Merry was "a medium of conciliatory and useful communication with his government." The secretary tried to soothe by an invitation to Montpelier, but relations with the Palace continued to be strained. At the 1806 New Year's reception the president after a brief greeting to the minister became absorbed in a band of Osage Indians. Most guests still managed to enjoy themselves, but "Toujours Gai" detected personal affront, and five minutes after arrival he and Secretary Foster made a well-noted departure.[26]

In the summer months the minister and official family escaped to Philadelphia where, as in Washington, Elizabeth Merry was often ill.

Merry himself, though chronically angry and fearful of a return of his maladies, was outwardly civil to Madison and unfailingly kind to young Foster, who lived in the legation. The young secretary was unofficially shown how to live well on a Foreign Office salary, allowed to compose dispatches, and in general instructed for the profession, for which purpose he had been placed with the veteran Merry. Foster appreciated these kindnesses and wrote sympathetically that "the desertion of the servants, climate, incivilities, and the ennui of Washington altogether have made great havoc with his health and I dare say he looks at least ten years older than when he left Europe." The secretary saw "a man of consummate integrity" who "sincerely loves his country" for which he "sacrificed here his health and every comfort for certainly he passes a miserable life here."[27]

Merry's personal misery was increased by the tears and anger of his wife. According to Foster the "spying, inquisitive, vulgar, and most ignorant race" of American women remarking on her dress or diamonds or walking on her gown reduced her to tears "at having to live in such a place." The ladies, though they were "the daughters of tavernkeepers, boardinghouse keepers and clerks' wives" yet were "as ceremonious as ambassadresses." Worse still, on attending receptions in her honor Elizabeth was apt to find that the company included her haberdasher and his wife. Her escape was her passion for botany, in which she had a real proficiency and a reasonable library. The pious Federalist Representative Manasseh Cutler, a fellow botanist, was a frequent visitor who talked books, compared plants, and deplored with her the frivolities of female Americans, whose private apartments, Elizabeth wrote, contained "not a flower, not a dried specimen of any kind."

Politician-pastor Cutler like the rest of Washington also savored official Merry hospitality at lavish teas or musicals or balls and dinners on royal birthdays, the peaks of society in the little capital. By virtue of the two houses converted into one, the guests were passed from servant to servant to the second floor, where the Merrys received them— he, reported as "agreeable" and she, "a tall and elegant woman . . . very social." From thence the fortunate (usually Federalist) guest passed into a ballroom where gleaming tables for two hundred stood decorated with roses and blazing with candles in silver candelabra. There was a massive six-by-four-foot silver centerpiece, Venuses and cupids on lofty pedestals, porcelain vases, elegant china plates, silver-handled forks and knives "in the French stile," and gold and silver flatware for desserts together with stemware and urns containing vintage wines. The food itself was somewhat exotic, for the new French chef (a handsome, well-educated emigré, himself a Palace guest), though still compelled at times to buy his vegetables from Baltimore and his butter from Philadelphia, invariably produced temples and towers of pastries interspersed with fruits and sweetmeats. After dinner came talk, chess, backgammon, and cards, after which the surfeited guests stumbled or bounced homeward over the cratered roads.[28]

Young Secretary Foster on arrival had immediately dubbed the capital "an absolute sepulcher," adding that it might drive him mad by its sheer "miserableness." To avoid this disaster he read *The Tempest* and *A Midsummer Night's Dream*, translated Cicero, rode, or shot birds near the Capitol. However, even for the bored young dandy the winter of 1805 was colorful enough to bring him and his colleagues out to struggle six or seven miles every night through atrocious streets to the crowded rooms of homes or hotels. Prestigious visitors were headed by the scarlet-and-gold-clad ambassador from Tunisia with an entourage that included Turks, Negroes, and an Italian band. Various Indian delegations included Creeks, Osages, Pawnees, Sac, Sioux, and Missouri and Mississippi natives sent by Lewis and Clark from their western explorations. French republican hero Gen. Victor Moreau fascinated Foster, as he did most Britons. The capital welcomed General Eaton from his North African adventures, along with the former Pasha of Tripoli and Jerome and Betsy Bonaparte, who had tried in vain to escape the British fleet to reach France, where an obdurate Napoleon refused to accept their marriage.

Some of the glamour lost by Yrujo's defiant retreat to Philadelphia was regained from France's Baron Louis-Marie Turreau de Garambouville, who kept the scandalmongers fully occupied. The new minister had ferocious expressions, an immense moustache, fiery eyes, a keen humor, and an unwanted harridan for a wife. The minister's flagrant dalliance with the more complaisant women of the town brought on marital warfare conducted with flatirons and bottles. On one celebrated occasion the baroness's screams during a beating were drowned out by musical numbers rendered by a quick-witted aide on an instrument variously reported as a violin, flute, cello, or French horn. Merry's sober entourage of course avoided when possible their enemy's envoy, whose glittering court dress, though not his carriage, outshone the Briton's.[29]

Among these colorful goldfish appeared the shadow of a shark. In November, 1805, Burr's promised agent—Senator Dayton of New Jersey—appeared, followed in March, 1806, by Burr himself, fresh from a western tour. With him the minister had three private interviews. Despite Merry's confession that he had heard nothing from London on the plan, Burr's superb persuasiveness never faltered as he talked of "more success than even he had looked for" in the west, "ten thousand stand of arms" at one deposit, and at New Orleans "a complete train of 52 pieces of artillery." The Floridas would be given to England in return for the money and ships to sail from New Orleans to Veracruz with a western army to "march thru Mexico, a fine high road throughout." Burr said New Orleans was the only part the westerners wished, and as an open port would present the west's trade to Britain. If the Union broke up as expected "a division would ensue" by treaty, and "the whole of the western Gulf would be open to Britain." The dazzled minister continued to be impressed, he said, with the "veracity of his [Burr's] statements as well as the practicability and great utility . . . to Great Britain of the enterprises." With sure skill Burr played on Merry's dearest hope—that, as he wrote London, "when once Louisiana and the western country become independent, the Eastern states will separate themselves immediately from the Southern; and the immense power which has risen up with so much rapidity in the Western Hemisphere will, by such a division, be rendered at once informidable."[30] A few days afterward Dayton was describing even wilder schemes to Yrujo, and seven months later, in June, 1806, Merry saw Burr briefly again and once more had to report lack of success. Yet Merry, before leaving America, conferred about the plan with Sir John Poo Beresford, the admiral commanding the North American Station in 1806. The minister's last dispatches from Washington mixed lingering hopes and resignation over the western enterprise, in which Merry never fully perceived the conspirator's double game nor his own less than percipient role.[31]

The last June meeting of the would-be disunionists had somewhat less importance for Merry since his American career had already crashed. In January the overworked Pitt died among the ruins of his last coalition, and the succeeding Ministry of All the Talents represented in both countries a hope for better Anglo-American relations. In the Foreign Office, Charles James Fox, critically ill, sought to cultivate America despite British restrictions on neutrality. However, he found in Merry's dispatches only disparagement of Jefferson and admonitions to ignore American resentments expressed lately in the Gregg and Nicholson Nonimportation resolutions. These unhelpful counsels had culminated in what appeared to be Minister Merry's unauthorized encouragement of treasonable schemes against the American government itself. The minister's Americanophobia and his widespread bipartisan unpopularity might well jeopardize Fox's whole American policy.

Hence, on March 7, 1806, in his first instruction to Merry, Fox informed him that "in consequence of your long continued ill state of health," His Majesty, while expressing the usual formula of "entire approbation" of his conduct, had been pleased to grant him a leave of absence to return to England. His intended replacement was Thomas Douglas, fifth earl of Selkirk, a speculating Scottish nobleman who was promoting emigration to Canada and in fact had already settled eight hundred of his countrymen there.

The official blow was accompanied by a private letter attributing the recall to Merry's state of health and offering to provide a more appropriate or less arduous position. Since April, when he had heard of Fox's arrival at the Foreign Office, Merry had known that his American career was in danger, but he had expected to be given a more honorific reason together with another, more elevated post. Hence, his private reply to Fox expressed a correct but bitter civility, admitting that the climate was bad for him but denying any interruption of his duties, "except for one very short interval," on account of health or age "not exceeding fifty." Merry reminded Fox that he had not gained the office from "connexion, interest, or influence" and asked only some new office "which should not imply disgrace." He added that he had been compelled to purchase one of his first appointments with practically all of his small private means and had further drained them for legation expenses in America; as his early recall prevented him from recouping his expenses he requested the "pecuniary reward which is usual, or which may, in your opinion, admit of for three and twenty years service in the Foreign Line."[32]

Merry's impending departure met with various emotions in various quarters. Madison regarded it as a favorable sign, but, in London, Monroe wrote that since the circumstances of Merry's return were "not a little mortifying to him" he hoped Merry's unfriendly feelings would not complicate matters further. Young Secretary Foster had been brought up in Fox's political circle and yearned to be chargé d'affaires, for it now appeared that a newly chosen replacement, David Erskine, might not arrive soon. In London, Foster's beautiful mother divided her attentions between the now widowed duke of Devonshire, to whom she hoped to be married, and Fox, from whom she sought office for her son. However, for some reason Foster was passed over, and, furious at being denied promotion after two years of drudgery "in this land of swamps and pawnbrokers," Foster wrote Lord Aberdeen requesting a leave of absence also, "for I believe it would be my near ruin to remain a year longer in this mean disgusting country, where you may have to dine with your footman."[33]

Merry, meanwhile, remained at his post writing grim dispatches. Everywhere Fox's attempt at rapprochement was thwarted. The announcement of a British blockade of German rivers that was intended to be conciliatory had the opposite effect, and the reports in London of Randolph's polemics in Congress further convinced hard-line Tories that a divided Republican administration in Washington was unpopular in America. Merry consistently attributed every factional dispute in the Congress of 1806 to "general weakness, predeliction [sic] for and submission to France, and duplicity of conduct."[34] The Jeffersonians, he insisted, were convinced that an exhausted and debt-ridden Britain would retreat before the new (weak) Nonimportation law, and both he and Foster insisted that only a small show of British naval power in American waters would win the day for Britain's whole position.

Finally, in November, Minister David Erskine and his family arrived and to the Merry's relief agreed to buy their furniture and equipment. After a month in Alexandria, Merry responded to Fox's order to return quickly by sailing for Liverpool on December 6, 1806. Elizabeth Merry's health was unequal to a winter voyage so she remained near Alexandria until, her servants having deserted her, she returned alone to England in the spring of 1807.

After less than a year in England the "very worthy but nervous man," as Malmesbury called Merry, was sent to Denmark for the quite impossible task of conciliating the Danes after a British seizure of their fleet. He did not even land in Denmark. In 1808, in London Merry conferred with Burr in an attempt to get George Canning interested in the western scheme but was turned down immediately by a Canning subordinate, probably Hammond. He then assumed a minor diplomatic role, was accepted with amused and slightly derisive tolerance by Canning and his new young circle of diplomats, and, in 1809, was briefly in Sweden until driven out by French troops. About America he persevered in poor judgment. Merry sent unnecessary and bad advice to Francis Jackson, his former colleague in France, who was a more spectacularly unsuccessful envoy to Washington than he himself had been, and by 1812 he was corresponding with the dangerous Timothy Pickering, who was inciting Federalist political paranoia on the eve of war.[35]

Retired by then, "Toujours Gai" became a country squire, holding the office of justice of the peace at Yarmouth. He lived at Herringfleet Hall, taking occasional trips to London to ferret out gossip at the Foreign Office. At times he traveled to Bath to take the waters and to provide some society for Elizabeth Merry, whose unceasing boredom in America had accompanied her home. After she died and Herringfleet Hall reverted to Elizabeth's family, Anthony Merry returned in 1824 to his native Dedham. There he lived with his sister until his death at Dedham House on June 14, 1835, in his seventy-ninth year. By a codicil to his will he left his medals and the snuffbox given him by Napoleon to his fellow Americanophobe George Hammond in appreciation for the arch-Tory's kindness to the tradesman-turned-diplomat.[36]

David Erskine

"The interest of America, and she ought to know it, is trade with all the world; an union with any particular nation will of course make enemies of the nation's opponents, confine her commerce, involve her in European politics, and lead her into schemes directly opposite to her interest. If America is suffered to remain at peace and to carry on her trade uninterruptedly she must be one of the great nations upon earth. . . ."

—David Erskine to Thomas Erskine, 1799

As the *Leonidas* sailed down the Potomac in December, 1806, bearing the ailing and discouraged Merry, the two English-speaking nations were ever more closely approaching a diplomatic impasse. On the British side, a nation and its leaders never doubted that the future of free men everywhere depended on an invincible British navy that would eventually paralyze Napoleon's armies. British commercial leadership was also becoming aware of the threat of the American carrying trade to British mercantile supremacy—a war in disguise. Thus, an alliance of patriotism and commercial rivalry was forged that was as unmoved by debates on neutral rights and impressment as it was unshaken by threats of reprisal. In a wartime turbulence of rumors, fears, and triumphs, British statesmen often rose above the passions of their frenzied countrymen, but though no foreign secretary from the well-disposed Grenville and the liberal Fox to the indolent Wellesley and the caustic Canning wished for an American war, none flinched at that possibility.

On the American side, Jefferson and Madison faced both French and British spoliations with minuscule forces, savagely divided parties, and an agrarian people who abhorred taxes. Peace therefore seemed a political and philosophical necessity. But nothing compelled the Virginians to accept the alleged moral superiority of the British cause over their own. Furthermore, playing one nation against another and using economic weapons were American tactics older than the republic itself. The president and his secretary of state, therefore, attempted a policy of economic reprisal that was acceptable to a majority of their countrymen and that they had every historical reason to trust. The collision of that policy and British war imperatives was to destroy Merry's three successors.

Whatever Americans thought of His Majesty's representatives in their midst, the Washington assignment suffered relentless disparagement in London. Because of Yankee bumptiousness and republicanism and the absence of European social amenities, the American appointment remained so unpopular that the few British diplomatic veterans peremptorily declined it. Even junior diplomats accepted a Washington post hoping it to be a brief interlude. Prominent nonprofessionals unanimously agreed with the peer who "would not for a dukedom and the Garter sacrifice my time and comfort in such a mission among the Yankees." But though the average tour of the first seven envoys from London was only two and a half years, foreign ministers before Canning tried to appoint seasoned candidates with professional experience that might be useful in America. Once—and only once—a friendly amateur was sent, with results that ruled out a repetition for decades to come.

David Montague Erskine's familiarity with the American scene began in 1789. His father, Thomas Erskine, was a Scottish Foxite lawyer of urbane manners and celebrated wit, invincible before a British jury and beloved of the public for his defense of free speech and such popular underdogs as Tom Paine, Horne Tooke, and Admiral Augustus Keppel. A philosophical liberal who maintained a steady reciprocal disdain for High Tories, Thomas Erskine was nevertheless a friend of his Ultra-Tory relative, Consul General Phineas Bond in Philadelphia. Since the Scot's personal heresies included an investment of some $300,000 in the best American securities, possibly "as a good second string to his bow whatever falls out in England," in the grim fall of 1798 he sent his eldest son, David Montague, to America to transfer the securities to Consul Bond through a power of attorney.[1]

Young Erskine at twenty-four was as typical a product of the Whig aristocracy as a successor, Charles Bagot, was of the Tory aristocracy. He had been educated first in Edinburgh and then at Westminster School and Christ Church, Oxford. His American errand was a substitute for the Continental Grand Tour then unavailable to Englishmen. Landing at Norfolk to avoid the yellow fever reported in the north, Erskine wrote his pro-American father that he was not entirely enchanted with this "last place I should think of coming to were I to change my country"; however, it was the "contempt which they seem to hold for what we call the polite and elegant" that bothered young Erskine more than the physical crudities of the country.

The son wrote his notoriously speculating father that the republic was "a nation of merchants . . . almost wholly engrossed with the . . . pursuit of wealth . . . which has a tendency to blunt their finer feelings. . . . The speculations in land have done more to corrupt the morals of the people than half a century of luxury will ever do." The American contrast of dreams and reality intrigued him, especially plans for the national capital: In Washington "piles of buildings" had been ordered "upon a scale larger than the world ever saw," though in 1798 there were not ten houses for the legislators and "the projected metropolis" was "an immense wood cut out in the form of a town," the streets of which "were marked for three miles in length and 100 yards wide."

Thomas Erskine wisely ordered his son not to travel with his countrymen, for he said "it is the vice of Englishmen that they herd together in all countries and come back with their old ideas." Consequently, David carefully included Republicans and Federalists as companions. Liston and Bond furnished introductions, and the Listons, pleased with his good nature, took him along on their 1799 Lake George junket.

Seeing America through the usual veils of homesickness but with a clarity not often possessed by the ministers of his king, young Erskine wrote his father that there would be no Anglo-American alliance for "between one party hating us and the other being at bottom jealous of us no great reliance ought to be placed upon their attachment" and "no alliance in my opinion can ever be of the slightest service." His view of the republic's leaders, too, was kinder than those of his countrymen. He wrote of Adams's "understanding and integrity and firmness," of Jefferson as a man traduced by political foes, and of a shrewd and hardworking Gallatin. Senators he saw as "quite what they ought to be" and in general his view of public men was "much more favourable than I had expected."[2]

The most important impressions on the young Scot were those of female Philadelphia society. Through friendship with John Cadwalader, son of a deceased merchant friend of Washington, the Scot found in the elegant homes of William Bingham and Alexander Baring "a great many pretty young girls" and though avowing "not the slightest particle of the 'tender passion'," he soon fell in love with Frances Cadwalader, daughter of his friend. Inevitably, in spite of a promise that his father would never have a daughter-in-law whom he had never seen, the Erskine-Cadwalader marriage took place in Philadelphia's Christ Church on December 16, 1799. The senior Erskine regretted the alliance as a possible cloud on his son's bright future in the Foreign Office, but the marriage was a happy one. Depending on the political eye of the beholder, Frances was "chunky" and given to deeply cut gowns, or "a beautiful woman," or "a good kind of young woman without sprightliness." An apolitical American lady described her in 1808 as "very pretty . . . short and fat, her eyes large and black, her nose aquiline, her teeth white and even."[3]

The marriage prolonged Erskine's first American visit, and in 1800 he asked Liston for a recommendation as a commissioner of arbitration under Jay's Treaty. But although the kindly minister wrote of him as "a young man of excellent talents, capable of great application . . . and . . . highly and delicately honorable," the application failed. The Erskines returned to England where he was called to the bar at Lincoln's Inn in 1802. That July the Peace of Amiens provided an opportunity for the two Erskine men to visit Paris, where the elder was presented to Napoleon by Anthony Merry. When the short peace ended and Pitt began his last ministry, the Erskines went into political exile until 1806 because of George III's unalterable opposition to Fox. However, Pitt's death brought Fox into the Foreign Office in the Ministry of All the Talents. Thomas Erskine then became lord chancellor—one of admittedly great integrity but of such reputed ignorance of equity jurisprudence that his decisions were known as "the Apocrypha."[4]

The lord chancellor and his critics were one, however, in the avid pursuit of employment for their offspring. David had no sooner replaced his father in the House of Commons as member from Portsmouth than Thomas was asking Fox "in a most anxious manner" to send his son to America. The foreign secretary was hesitant to send Federalist Bond's relative to Jefferson's capital, preferring the pro-American but eccentric speculator Thomas, earl of Selkirk, who accepted and then refused. Lord William Bentinck, able and more experienced, was the next choice, but refused out of hand. Meanwhile the chancellor's letters to Fox pleaded for his son: "He is thirty-two years of age, has been four years in America, is acquainted intimately with all the considerable persons there, and his wife's family are . . . extensively connected. . . . I can . . . *be sure* that it would be a most popular appointment."[5]

In May Fox was won over and credentials were prepared, but delays ensued, and only after spending some weeks with the Listons in their home outside Edinburgh did the minister with wife and mother-in-law leave for his post. Frances Erskine had meanwhile received a spiteful letter from Elizabeth Merry describing Washington chaos and Sally McKean Yrujo's tears during her husband's wars with Jefferson.

The entourage arrived at Annapolis on October 29, 1806, and Erskine was presented at Washington on November 3. After a sincere exchange of good wishes the minister visited Philadelphia and his wife's relatives for nearly a month, for there was a delay in receiving his instructions. Moreover, London was center stage, since Monroe and William Pinkney had been meeting there with Henry Richard Fox and William Eden, First Baron Auckland, to attempt a treaty on the overriding problems of impressment and neutral rights. When the packet boat arrived, however, it brought far graver news for Erskine personally. Fox's long illness had ended with his death on September 13, 1806, while Erskine was en route to America, and the envoy's position was thereby weakened.

By December the minister had established his family in the newly remodeled embassy, left his handsomely engraved calling cards, and joined the hectic round of social events. On December 4, he wrote his first dispatch, in which good and bad news alternated. Jefferson had issued a proclamation against Burr's western enterprise, and Erskine, impressed with the president's firmness and sure of his success, was relieved that his own denials of Burr's claims of promised British aid were readily accepted by the administration. The president also suspended again the operation of the weak Nonimportation Law of April, 1806. On the other hand, as Baron Auckland and Fox had maintained the traditional British stand on impressments, Madison showed equal firmness as well as "disappointment and vexation." Erskine told an unmoved Foreign Office that whatever the merits of either case, "I am persuaded that no cordiality can be expected from this country whilst it is deemed necessary by His Majesty to enforce that right."[6]

On February 6, 1807, dispatches from France brought grim news of Napoleon's decrees of November 21 from Berlin, creating a total paper blockade of the British Isles and announcing the future confiscation of any ship with British merchandise entering France from Britain or her colonies. The gratifying wave of anti-French feeling that subsequently swept the capital was heightened when a brief note from Monroe reported that a treaty had emerged from the negotiations in London; this supposedly meant that Britain had yielded on impressment to take advantage of the Berlin Decree of her adversary. Like most Britons, Erskine felt that most American decisions were made in fear of Napoleonic wrath; therefore, on March 2 as the Senate approached adjournment Erskine anxiously anticipated the treaty's arrival since it would have to be ratified quickly before senatorial courage failed. Next day the blow fell. Erskine's own copy of the treaty arrived before Madison's, and after a quick, startled reading the young envoy hastened with it to the secretary.

The interview was sobering. As Erskine wrote Lord Howick, successor to Fox in the Foreign Office, "The first question he [Madison] asked me was what had been determined on the point of impressment . . . and when I informed him that I had not perceived any thing that directly referred to that question . . . he expressed the greatest astonishment and disappointment." The secretary of state then emphasized that this omission and the note added by the British commissioners requiring that America refuse to be bound by the Berlin edict were fatal objections. The president had later remarked that as to the addendum, "the influence of Washington himself" would have been insufficient to secure that ratification, though he personally still hoped for an accommodation.[7]

Jefferson's immediate decision not even to submit the treaty to the Senate—because Britain was bound in no way while America gave up every major argument save war—placed him in the mainstream of American opinion. Although historians later criticized Jefferson for his decision, contemporary opposition was confined largely to Federalist editors, politicians, and shippers.[8] Erskine explained this to Downing Street along with the faint placatory addendum that Congress would not declare war over anything put in or left out of the treaty, and for English aristocratic sensibilities he added that because of the wide American franchise, "property has really no influence in . . . the government of this country" and "the passions of the people have been more attended to in the consideration of the treaty than the substantial interests of the country."[9]

Actually, Erskine's concern was unnecessary. In January, 1807, a British Order in Council had already struck back at the Berlin Decree by prohibiting from almost the whole coast of Europe the immensely important neutral carrying trade from European port to port. Quite apart from speculation into what might have been, the Berlin Decree and the British January Order had immediately outdated the Pinkney-Monroe effort, and the question of its utility was now moot. The more the leadership and people of England and America studied the treaty, the more they concluded, for different reasons, that it was a mistake or a stillborn nullity.

This debacle did not, however, disturb Erskine's popularity with the administration. The tall, gangly young minister was more affable than handsome, having a broad brow, large wide-set eyes, generous nose and pleasant mouth, fine reddish hair, and features thickened somewhat by a childhood acne. The easygoing, informal style of his own and his father's household and his ensured social position made him entirely indifferent to the ministerial dignity that had so occupied and bedeviled Merry. Foppish Secretary Foster wrote despairingly of his chief:

He is everything you please, in a way, but a man of business, with no strong feelings of any kind and never in my life did I know a man of so little vanity, or with less concern for dignity of behaviour. The situation of British ministers is a very eminent one from many circumstances in this country, but when it is frisked and jerked about upon the shoulders of a hail fellow well met sort of man I confess it gives me pain.[10]

Indifferent to his secretary's pain, the young Scot jolted over the dusty roads of the capital in a hack or in his family's coach bearing the family motto "Trial by Jury." Ironically, Merry's successor dressed with an informality that matched Jefferson's. "He would," wrote Foster, "have gone in boots to visit the President but for me and cares nothing about driving to his House or Palace (which it may be called for its size) in a dirty hack without a servant." As tyro diplomats, the Erskines did not know, as the veteran Merry had, how to keep up appearances at minimum expense, but they were kind to young Foster, who admitted "they [the Erskines] mean everything for the best, and were it not for national feelings I should be contented."

It was of course this very absence of oversensitive "national feelings" that made the new minister welcome with the administration. Neither the president nor his cabinet regarded Erskine as influential at home after Fox's death. Indeed, the very contrast between Britain's rigorous measures and the friendly goodwill of her envoy emphasized his lack of influence. But the administration members, recognizing his goodwill, talked freely with him, and Madison wrote Monroe (probably for transmittal to the Foreign Office) that "it would be difficult to find a successor who would give or feel more pleasure in the station than the present incumbent."

Federalists of course regarded Erskine with a disappointed and lofty disdain. Arch-Federalist Pickering believed that the "feebleness of Merry and Erskine" had helped preserve Jefferson's hated regime, and he longed for a "stronger" minister whose intransigence would bring down the administration. The pompous William Plumer disparaged Erskine's legal talents and saw him as "a young inexperienced man, of feeble intellect—and very ignorant. . . . His actions and conversation are puerile—there is no dignity in his person, manners, or observations." The American senator, however, recorded similar criticisms of Spain's Yrujo and France's Turreau, and noted with surprise that European nations sent such "feeble characters" because, he concluded bleakly, "they consider the United States of little consequence to them."[11] In the early summer of 1807, the British exemplar of European indifference took his entourage to a small villa near Philadelphia. There David Erskine learned from his visiting brother Henry of a development at home that was to be fatal to his career.

By March 1807, William Grenville's Ministry of All the Talents had displayed a striking lack of any talent in dealing with George III's semiparanoia on the subject of Ireland. The Ministry thereby gave the monarch an opportunity to oust Grenville in favor of William Bentinck, duke of Portland, and the Tories of the far right. The duke was little but a figurehead; the real leadership in American eyes was Chancellor of the Exchequer Spencer Perceval and Foreign Secretary George Canning, each of whom combined talents and deficiencies fatal to an already failing Anglo-American relationship. Both men were courageous, obstinate, egotistical, and friendlier to America than were many of their countrymen. Nevertheless, both agreed that the destruction of Napoleon by Britain was a moral obligation.

Spencer Perceval's contribution to the future Anglo-American war was based on the unshakable conviction that the exclusion of America's neutral carrying trade was a necessity for Britain's military triumph and national greatness. Relieved by special royal patronage from the necessity of supporting his large family by other means, Perceval, a close friend of mercantilist James Stephen, devoted his career after the age of forty-five to writing skillful appeals to his countrymen's combined patriotism and avarice. He thus developed a political influence at once unabashedly chauvinistic and widely popular.

George Canning's was a far more complex personality. The son of a widow who had perforce turned to the provincial stage to support her children, he was brought late by a noble kinsman into England's snobbish social and political establishment. By a shrewd marriage he brought himself wealth. Thereafter, Canning's career was a casebook in psychological overcompensation and his shifting course bore the occasional whiff of the perfidious. An admiring cousin, Stratford Canning, could say only that he was "in the main an honest man."

Canning was a devoted protégé and follower of Pitt; in the Commons his eloquence and skill in debate were marred only by a caustic wit and the use of ridicule. In foreign policy he pursued a clear-eyed realpolitik dedicated to military triumph, and his intelligence, driving energy, and confident egotism opened a new chapter in Britain's diplomatic service. Considerate of and at times playful with his undersecretaries and even clerks, the secretary built up an intense personal loyalty in the office. At the same time his vigorous, personally written instructions to British diplomats abroad ranged in tone from firmness to flagellation. Canning was inclined to rely on a studiously correct personal diplomacy when, as in America's case in 1807, a senior foreign diplomat resided in London. He therefore regarded the function of his Washington minister to be that of rigid adherence to and defense of instructions from London. To him, diplomacy was the traditional chess game played with an eye on domestic politics; to Erskine and Madison it was an attempt to accommodate positions.[12]

Reservations in England about the new foreign secretary were shared by young diplomats in Washington. The occasionally pretentious Foster thought Canning "all froth, smoke, and noise" and his wit inappropriate in a statesman. Erskine probably shared his father's view of the secretary as "utterly and totally unfit for the office."[13] For some time it appeared to the State Department that a new minister would be sent to Washington, but because of the pressure of European events and perhaps awareness of a shaky power base in the Commons, Erskine was not replaced. Given their antipathetic natures, a clash was inevitable between the young, inexperienced Scot and the aggressively egotistical Tory chauvinist. Though he continued to function competently, Erskine had little chance for success after the Portland ministry took office.

The forbidding stance of Britain's new ministry reflected mounting Continental disasters in 1807 and thereafter. Checked briefly at Eylau in February, Napoleonic armies swept to victories culminating on June 14 in the overwhelming triumph of Friedland. This victory was followed by French occupation of Europe from the Baltic to the Adriatic, and rumors circulated of a truce between the Emperor and the Tsar. British diplomats were driven headlong from Europe's capitals, British alliances crumbled, and the wealth and manpower of the Continent seemed to be at France's disposal.

The British siege mentality of earlier years was replaced by apprehension, fury, and defiance. While their government found the neutral pretensions of America irritating and irrelevant, the British people were caught up in a firestorm of fury at America and its people. An English pamphleteer expressed the national mood:

> Hatred of America seems a prevailing sentiment in this country. Whether it be that they have no crown and nobility, and are on this account not quite a *genteel* power; or that their manners are less polished than our own; or that we grudge their independence and hanker after our old monopoly of their trade; or that they closely resemble us in language and laws . . . the fact is undeniable that the bulk of the people would fain be at war with them.[14]

None of this of course compelled Jefferson to renounce national self-respect or to embark on a suicidal war. Although he and his administration were sensitive to the rudeness and sneers of British leaders, they never fully understood that this galling arrogance merely floated on the surface of a sea of popular animosity.

In June, 1807, against this backdrop Vice Adm. Sir George Cranfield Berkeley cast Anglo-American relations into new depths. Sir George owed his command in American waters to his brother's command of parliamentary votes, and, as an embodiment of British naval arrogance and Americanophobia, was most maladroitly stationed at Halifax. From there he had for a year carried on his vendetta by a stream of bellicose letters of advice sent directly to Grenville, Bathurst, and other ministers. In the spring of 1807, infuriated by the desertion of British seamen and their subsequent enrollment in American ships, the vice admiral ordered his captains to search for deserters on the United States warship *Chesapeake* if found outside territorial waters.

On June 22, Capt. S. P. Humphreys in the flagship *Leopard* encountered the *Chesapeake* as she left Norfolk. Humphreys hailed Capt. Samuel Barron, who unsuspectingly allowed the admiral's orders to be shown him and, unprepared for conflict, fired but one shot while the *Leopard* hulled his ship twenty-two times and inflicted twenty-one casualties before he surrendered. The British then boarded, refused Barron's surrender, and removed four alleged deserters.

When the *Chesapeake* returned to Norfolk, bipartisan fury shook the nation. Jefferson assembled his cabinet for marathon sessions and issued a proclamation excluding British warships from American waters unless in distress or on diplomatic business. The cabinet voted to bring American warships home from the Mediterranean, outlined diplomatic and military plans, and advised the president to call Congress into session in October. Jefferson began quiet but intensive military plans that included ordering gunboats readied, asking the governors to prepare for a call of one hundred thousand militia, and arming coastal forts. Across the nation editors urged violence, and mobs roughed up British landing parties, destroyed ships' equipment, and temporarily seized British seamen. Foster, traveling to Boston when the storm struck, wisely abandoned horse, curricle, and groom to travel incognito while a mob threatened to throw the equipage into the North River. Even Consul Barclay was alarmed, but British captains reacted by defying the president's proclamation, impressing seamen, and threatening to attack ports.[15]

In this excitement the administration rightly judged that Erskine was "much embarrassed between what is right and his fear of the naval officers and of his own government." Gallatin also expressed cabinet opinion that the young Whig envoy "having neither orders nor advice from his government . . . cannot be very easy and will not be very influential." Consequently he was treated "with more civility than cordiality."

Still, though without influence in either capital, Erskine acted with energy and intelligence. To Canning he sent "with the greatest concern" details of the encounter along with newspaper clippings on belligerent mass meetings and resolutions. When the senior officer of the Norfolk squadron threatened war and blockaded the coast in retaliation for the proclamation and the destruction of his water casks by irate citizens, Erskine urged him to cease his threats. Unable to obtain from Berkeley (who despised him) the reasons for the seizure of the four men, the minister suggested to the admiral that their home government might be a more appropriate judge than the admiral as to whether American enlistment of his sailors was a national insult. Meanwhile Erskine frankly told Canning that he hoped the British cabinet did not support Berkeley as the admiral claimed it did. While describing rising American anger to London and alerting Canadian officials to possible war, Erskine also told Canning that Jefferson could not get a declaration of war if Britain chose to offer an apology and renounce any claim to impress from American warships.

Although an accurate reporter, Erskine upheld his nation's position. His sympathy for Jefferson's philosophy did not prevent him from sharply criticizing presidential leadership. He protested a citizen's interruption of Berkeley's shore correspondence and attacked the president's proclamation as too hasty. He denounced interruption of the Norfolk consul's communication with the fleet there and defended Berkeley as well as he could with the information given him. To Madison he complained that while newspapers "exceeded the bounds of decency in their angry and insolent expressions of hostility towards Great Britain," they took no notice of Canning's acts of conciliation.

As had Liston and Thornton before him, Erskine suggested to Canning—had that minister cared to listen—that British naval commanders' insults within sight of land cost Britain more resentment than the most rigid enforcement of maritime claims elsewhere. He also shrewdly perceived that Jefferson was less interested in redress for the *Chesapeake* affair than in use of the incident to support general American claims against impressment under the Orders in Council. This was soon borne out when Madison instructed Monroe in London to link the abolition of impressment with any reparations for the *Chesapeake* affair. Canning was thus able to turn aside as irrelevant any question of apology or reparations for the *Chesapeake*, though he disavowed the right to search American warships and he recalled Berkeley. At the same time, he seized on an American suggestion of a special mission to Washington to deal with reparations. British prestige was safe at home and abroad, but American opinions of Canning sank still further in the long decline leading to 1812 and war.[16]

As the months passed without any real conciliation between the two capitals, there was little to cheer the young minister. For Erskine, the foreign minister's having dealt exclusively with Monroe in the crisis was ominous. Erskine was merely told to conform his language to that of correspondence sent to Washington. The special envoy for the *Chesapeake* negotiations might permanently supersede him, and meanwhile, his role was essentially that of a chargé. In both capitals lingering efforts to save the aborted Monroe treaty ceased. In late 1807 Anglo-American relations entered upon what was to be a three-year estrangement in which the major contention shifted from impressments to commercial warfare.[17]

In early October the *National Intelligencer* reported that Britain had reacted to rumors of a Franco-Russian alliance by a demand on neutral Denmark for the delivery of her fleet. Britain's demand was backed by overwhelming force and was brutally delivered by the same Francis Jackson once intended to be envoy to Washington. When Britain's demand was refused, Copenhagen was nearly destroyed and Denmark lost her fleet, merchant ships, and colonial possessions. The implications of this attack on a neutral were not lost on American leaders, especially since Jackson had told the Danes that England found it "impossible to distinguish any longer between a neutral and an enemy but by her becoming an ally or an open foe."

In the same dark fall, a House of Commons committee opened an all-out assault on American West Indies trade, the cabinet ordered an intensification of impressment, and a spate of Orders in Council appeared. The most important of these, issued on November 11, 1807, demanded essentially that countries that excluded Britain's trade be considered blockaded. Ships trading with them would be confiscated if caught. Exceptions made for neutrals merely provided that they might be allowed to trade through British ports and by paying British taxes. Britain had now abandoned her old hope of bringing America into an alliance. Her policy henceforth would be to keep America out of the war by a combination of slightly veiled threat, legalistic diplomatic dialectic, and various small concessions to entice American avarice. There would be no concession to American claims for a neutral's rights. Napoleon's predictable response was his Milan Decree of December 17, stating that every ship that obeyed Britain's Orders or traded with Britain or went to ports occupied by the British forces would be liable to French seizure. The logical conclusion of commercial warfare in Europe had been reached: no American ship could sail to a British- or a French-controlled port without possible seizure by one or the other of the belligerents.

This crisis in the European war of attrition produced two effects on President Jefferson. The first was that beginning in December, 1807, Jefferson shifted his perception of America's neutrality dilemma from one stemming primarily from Britain to one forced on the Republic by both the belligerents and the totally new dimensions of commercial warfare. The second effect was a conviction of the necessity of protecting America's ships—public and private—from the "madhouse of Europe." Such protection would be obtained by extending the nonimportation agreements of the Revolutionary period into a total prohibition of American exports to foreign ports, which would not only protect the American ships from seizures but also provide time for America to improve its military posture.

Accordingly, in response to a short presidential message on December 18, Congress passed the famous Embargo Act, prohibiting all American vessels except those directed by the president from sailing to foreign ports and requiring vessels in the coastal trade to post heavy bonds against European detours. The embargo measure passed swiftly and was signed into law on December 22 after little debate, little administrative machination, and no premonition of the problems it was to engender later.[18]

During this momentous step in American diplomacy, Erskine got short shrift when he sought to mitigate resentments, but his personal relations with the administration remained cordial. Madison assured him that the embargo did not presage war but was merely for the defense of American ships caught between the belligerents' economic weaponry. Erskine himself thought it represented a simple fear of further British impressments. Rather desperately, the young Whig sought some good news or amicable interpretation to place on every American decision.

Meanwhile, the professional threat to him personally loomed in the arrival in Norfolk on December 26 of George Henry Rose, the genial figure Canning chose to negotiate on the *Chesapeake* matter in what was later called "the weirdest mission in Anglo-American annals." Unable to obtain his first choice, Canning had settled on the eldest son of "Old George" Rose, currently treasurer of the navy and vice-president of the Board of Trade, a Pittite whose ceaseless pursuit of office for self and family was almost unrivaled even in that day.

Young George had little professional aptitude for the mission. However, he had been chargé and secretary of legation at The Hague and Berlin, he possessed a pleasant temper and good manners, and his

British condescension was clothed in more than usual courtesy. His negotiating skill mattered little since he was bound by instructions so rigid that Canning's first choice had refused the mission; these instructions involved so many layers of preconditions that the mission had not the slightest chance of success. Only Rose's lifelong passion for diplomatic employment or perhaps a provisional promise of succeeding Erskine—or a missionary impulse manifested in his later years—could have induced even this placid placehunter to accept such a hopeless assignment.[19]

Erskine's own insecurity made him doubly careful to avoid collisions with the new mission. When Rose followed his master's instructions to obtain written guarantees on his ship's freedom, even though such guarantees were unnecessary under the law, Erskine obtained them. Rose then proceeded to Washington to be warmly greeted on nearly all sides. Though Gallatin and others suspected that the mission was sent "to amuse and divide," Federalists were lyrical over the "fascinating manners," "splendid talents," and "inflexible integrity" of the "pleasing and instructive man," whose claim to thirteen years in Parliament covered what was in fact a total lack of distinction there. As they talked with the smiling and agreeable envoy and basked in his gentle condescension, Pickering and his fellow Federalists hoped that Rose would replace the more pro-Republican Erskine, and they all agreed that if the mission failed "it will be our own blame," since Pickering assured them that while he did not know Rose's instructions, "nothing in reality will be denied."[20]

As Madison proceeded through successive stages of negotiation with Rose (occasionally accompanied by Erskine), the new envoy's instructions compelled him to reject each arrangement as it was worked out. First he agreed to British reparations, to be simultaneous with the revocation of the president's proclamation excluding British warships; then he was forced to reveal Canning's absurd demands that America renounce its captains' alleged encouragement of British desertions and also disavow most of Commodore Barron's actions in the clash with the *Leopard*. Both Erskine and Rose knew that these requirements doomed the mission. Although Rose never fully revealed his shackles, his later very equivocal descriptions of the negotiations gave Federalists the means for blaming the failure of the mission on Madison and imploring British forbearance.

On February 19 Erskine reported Rose's failure, and the special envoy, after sending even more disingenuous reports to Canning, finally left on March 27, 1808, resuming thereafter, with his father's aid, an undistinguished career. Aside from a further decline in Canning's credibility in America, the principal effect of the mission was the mischievous publicity given Pickering's later correspondence with Rose. In it, the leader of the small arch-Federalist clique (who was presented in Britain as a major opinion maker) attacked his own government and implored his countrymen to disobey their nation's laws.[21]

As December brought official notifications of the recent Orders in Council and the Milan Decree, and in the spring, as Napoleon's Bayonne Decree cynically provided for further seizures, it became increasingly impossible to determine which belligerent was more indifferent to American claims to neutral rights. The impossibility of abject surrender to or simultaneous war with both European powers produced for Republican leadership a crisis inflamed by the violent rhetoric of the 1808 presidential campaign.

For Erskine, this American election, one certain to continue in office a congenial Republican leadership, ironically added to his frustrations. Nearly all public men knew that Madison was overwhelmingly likely to succeed his fellow Virginian. This prospect, however, produced a curious mutation in the perception of the secretary of state. To Federalists, Monroeites, and Clintonians, and hence to Englishmen with whom they corresponded, the formerly hapless "Little Jimmy" began to metamorphose into a cunning Machiavelli, who, as the chosen successor of a Francophile president, had rejected Monroe's treaty of 1806, defeated George Rose's pacific mission, misrepresented Canning's amiable efforts, and all the while dominated Britain's feeble amateur minister in Washington. Not merely followers of Madison's rivals but also such influential figures as Consul Thomas Barclay and Admiral Berkeley steadily projected back to Downing Street the image of a misled and too compliant Erskine. These reports were not offset by the favorable accounts of lesser figures such as John Howe, confidential agent of Sir George Prevost in Canada, and they undermined Erskine's none-too-strong position at Downing Street at a critical time.[22]

By contrast, the British minister was personally unusually popular in Washington society in the election winter of 1808–1809. The physical scene still presented challenges. The Palace was now improved in appearance and convenience by an encircling stone wall and flanking service buildings, but homes and buildings were so scattered that party goers still covered a circuit of four to six miles in an evening. Night travel still involved contending with rutted, rocky, and stump-filled roads on which, said one traveler, "every turn of your wagon wheel is for miles attended with danger." Augustus Foster wrote his mother in 1807 that he had "forgotten what a good road is or what the term 'street' means," and he and the minister's brother, Henry Erskine, were overturned in a gully "*going* to a party one night." John Randolph pictured himself "almost bruised to death, in a dark cold night," and though "*in the heart of the capital of the U.S.,*" he was "*out of sight, or hearing, of a human habitation.*" At the Palace the outgoing president's casually democratic manners and almost shabby dress continued to amaze diplomats, but his last New Year's reception, held on Monday in deference to the Sabbath, was as crowded as usual. There Erskine in court dress and sword was outshone by the splendid trappings of his rival, France's Minister Turreau, whose diplomatic skill, however, was hampered by an almost complete ignorance of English.

At balls, receptions, dinners in private homes, and somber little private conferences, David Erskine, realizing that the nations' relations were degenerating dangerously, talked attitudes and possibilities with Republican leaders. Jefferson appealed to his own record to disprove any pro-French bias, but he still spoke to Erskine of "eternal war" as long as the Orders in Council were in effect. Jefferson also referred bitterly both to Canning's failure to curb his high-handed naval officers and to his talent for caustic language "stinging to every American breast." On the other hand, as news from the states' elections made Madison's succession to the presidency ever more certain, he and some of his presumptive cabinet, especially Gallatin and Robert Smith, seemed to Erskine to be (though still anti-British) more diplomatically congenial than the plainspoken but occasionally bellicose Jefferson. The new administration's members shared their dilemma frankly with the anxious young Scot.

Each passing week showed that the embargo was causing unacceptable agrarian losses and creating more illicit shipping through the high profits it brought the lawbreaking shipowner. Thus the law was throwing rank-and-file Republicans into revolt, while in New England threats of disunion grew more violent. New legislation for more stringent enforcement was failing. England, though affected, was not suffering from the economic embargo, partly through American violations and partly from new markets opened in the West Indies. It was increasingly clear that though Jefferson still insisted that the embargo would have its intended effects if adhered to, and though Jefferson now saw the measure as a means of restoring an agrarian America and crushing High Federalism, the Embargo Act would have to be repealed, and soon. On the other hand, popular resentment at the November Orders, new impressments, and the virtual British blockade of the American coast made submission to the Orders impossible.

In talks with Erskine, the new administration seemed to be saying that America would give up its cherished trade with the French colonies in return for the repeal of the Orders. In reality the Jeffersonians were suggesting the renunciation of direct trade with France from the West Indies and not the more valuable "broken voyage" from the colonies through American ports to the mother country. But Erskine did not perceive or did not appreciate the difference. More important to him, the president-elect and his future cabinet reiterated for weeks that the choice for Britain lay between eventual war with America or a repeal of the Orders, but that if Britain chose repeal, a de facto American economic alliance would follow against France if that country persisted in her decrees.

Events seemed to bear out this assessment. On March 1, 1809, Congress replaced the Embargo Act with the Nonintercourse Act. This law forbade both British and French warships to enter American harbors except on urgent business and replaced the *Chesapeake* proclamation against British ships alone. The new law prohibited both nations' merchant ships from entering American ports after May 20 and refused entry to either nation's goods, but it allowed the president to revoke the ban against either belligerent that honored American neutrality claims.

On March 4, 1809, Erskine witnessed James Madison's crowded inaugural ceremony, escorted Mrs. Madison's sister in to dinner, and attended the nation's first inaugural ball, at all of which a smiling Jefferson impressed many observers as by far the happier of the two Virginians. The British minister was now convinced that a nearly desperate new administration must be rescued from its untenable economic warfare or it would inevitably turn the nation to open war against Britain or France or both, whereas a repeal of the Orders would surely mean Anglo-American collaboration against Napoleon. It was a belief carefully cultivated and repeated by Madison and shared by many Republicans and even some Federalists, but not, significantly, by Erskine's shrewd and experienced Tory relative Phineas Bond in Philadelphia or his colleague Thomas Barclay in New York.[23]

In London during that winter, George Canning read his minister's dispatches from America with unusual interest. His government's stringent economic policies and its military reverses were under fire in Parliament, but the foreign secretary knew from a variety of sources, including American ones, that Jefferson's plan for economic warfare through the embargo was about to be abandoned because of strong political discord. Discussions with William Pinkney, now the American minister in London, indicated in January that legislation proposed to replace the Embargo Act would favor any nation that accommodated itself to American claims. Canning therefore felt that he could drop the Orders without appearing to yield to the embargo, and he might use the change to bind the unstable republic in an economic alliance against France.

In January and February, 1809, therefore, the foreign secretary acknowledged with some sarcasm Erskine's assurances of a new and more sympathetic administration and then carefully authorized his American minister to make two agreements. First, to settle the *Chesapeake* matter, Erskine might by an exchange of notes offer the reparations suggested by Rose, though only after receiving explicit, formal revocation of Jefferson's *Chesapeake* proclamation closing American ports to British warships. Second, Erskine might propose that Britain, after receiving in London an official note agreeing to three conditions, would withdraw the Orders in Council. The three conditions were: (1) America would open its harbors to British warships and withdraw its trade embargoes against Britain but maintain these restrictions against France and her allies; (2) America would renounce wartime trade with the French colonies denied to her in peace (that is, she would accept the hitherto unacceptable Rule of 1756); and (3) Britain would be free to capture American vessels trading with France and her allies. If the American government accepted these three preconditions, London would send a special minister to America to conclude such a treaty. In short, the price of the repeal of the Orders was a de facto Anglo-American economic alliance to be enforced by the British navy.[24]

David Erskine was an imprecise and sometimes negligent diplomat, but he was by no means a fool. He was far more in touch with real American majority opinion than his Foreign Office had been for years. Regardless of whether he grasped Canning's intent to bind a baffled

America to Britain's war policies, he did know that Canning's three preconditions would be unacceptable in Washington. On the other hand, Canning's instructions had been written before Congress passed the Nonintercourse Act placing the belligerents on a more equal footing and offering either of them a legal trade with America in return for relief from its attacks on American trade. Further, the special envoy to be sent out to adjust details might then settle such matters as the French colonial trade. Most important to Erskine, Canning had at last offered a possibility of the all-important repeal of the Orders; from this, much might follow.

The foreign secretary had held up his January instructions so that they might be sent in February by Charles Oakeley, who was to relieve at last the impatient Augustus Foster as secretary of legation. Immediately after Oakeley arrived on April 7, 1809, Erskine informed Secretary of State Robert Smith that he was empowered to settle the major commercial differences between the nations. Negotiations began at once and proceeded quickly under the hope of a conclusion in time to release the spring merchant fleets. The negotiating teams were unequal: minds such as Madison's and Gallatin's directed a muddled Robert Smith against the most inexperienced minister ever sent from Britain to the United States who was, in addition, a young Scottish Whig as remote in philosophy as in distance from George Canning.

As Smith and Erskine turned first to *Chesapeake* reparations, Erskine had wit enough to reject an American demand for the punishment of Admiral Berkeley, but he carelessly allowed the inclusion of Madison's ill-natured reprimand of George III for not doing so. After this poor beginning they turned to Canning's preconditions and agreed that the first—removing barriers against British ships only—was already agreed to by the terms of the Nonintercourse Act in conjunction with the present agreement. They also agreed that the third—allowing British enforcement—was unacceptable to America. As to the second—American acceptance of the Rule of 1756—Robert Smith assured Erskine that there would be no trouble in settling it by a commercial treaty with the future special envoy, and Erskine agreed to waive it. However, through eagerness, ignorance, or a confusion from prior talks with Gallatin, Erskine allowed the matter to be defined in terms of the direct carrying trade between France and her colonies, leaving untouched the lucrative transshipment through American ports. Further, he did not report this damaging change to Canning. Worst of all, Erskine did not present the foreign minister's three essential preconditions as such, but only as "suggested modifications," and he discarded Canning's requirement for an explicit ratified agreement to arrive in London prior to the lifting of the Orders.

President Madison and his cabinet hesitated—probably as much over Erskine's influence in London and his understanding of technical matters as over Canning's good faith. But their latest information from Pinkney agreed with Erskine's description of the foreign secretary's encouraging stance. Hence on April 19, Madison acted under the Nonintercourse Act by issuing a proclamation revoking the trade barriers against Britain and providing for renewed American trade as of June 10, in consequence of David Erskine having "by the order and in the name of his Sovereign" removed the Orders in Council as of that June date.[25]

Elated by the apparent success of economic pressure, the Madison administration basked in unprecedented popularity and cherished several illusions. One was that the French would react with similar concessions, another that a British mission, headed by the fondly remembered Edward Thornton, would soon arrive to implement the agreement. Erskine himself was hopeful but understandably apprehensive.

Erskine's disobedience was based on more than stupidity or sentiment. He was convinced that removal of the Orders was essential for both nations because the administration by law and by its members' private assurances to him would in return retaliate against France. Above all he believed, or hoped, that the Portland government would agree with him on the importance of improved Anglo-American relations, and that therefore the future special envoy could work out mutually acceptable details. Hence he felt his agreements at least met the spirit of his instructions and could cause no harm. He therefore sent an explanatory and defensive account of his *"conditional agreement"* and waited with hope but probably no great conviction for his chief's reaction.[26]

The reaction was volcanic. Canning had little faith in the capacity of most of his ministers and especially that of Fox's Scottish Whig appointee. Moreover, he was faced with Parliamentary opposition that deeply feared "servile compliance" with "American pretensions" and especially so when the failure of the embargo would reveal American weakness. Furthermore, Canning, despite his arrogance, did not consistently court American enmity, and after sending Erskine's careful instructions he had turned to a slight modification of the Orders and to blockade as an alternative. Then on May 22 he received Erskine's account of the Washington agreement. In those dispatches Canning saw loss of face and national prestige along with collapse of a private strategy—all because of a disobedient Whig subordinate. His fury produced an explosion that became legendary among the clerks and secretaries of the Foreign Office.

Doubtless the raging foreign minister would have destroyed that "damned Scotch flunkey" at once had not the British cabinet chosen to discuss the flunkey's agreement for three days. Some members even favored accepting it. However, convinced that the collapse of the embargo destroyed economic coercion, the Portland government reaffirmed the now traditional Tory view that the ill will or belligerence of America was preferable to its economic competition.

Canning therefore had the congenial task of repudiating Erskine and the more intricate one of disavowing his agreement. The first was easily accomplished by showing that the envoy had clearly and repeatedly disobeyed his instructions and, in the *Chesapeake* matter, had allowed foreigners to speak disrespectfully of his king—a disrespect, to be sure, less offensive in tone than Canning himself habitually used in addressing foreign governments. On May 30, 1809, he summarily informed Erskine of his replacement.

When he came to why the agreement itself was disavowed along with Erskine's disgrace, the foreign secretary was necessarily more disingenuous. Aside from personal pique and an improvement in England's position in the war, the secretary's real objection was that the agreement conceded good faith to American leaders and failed to bind the republic into an economic alliance against France. Erskine was not told to explain the disavowal. To Parliament and in the press Canning merely charged him with disobedience. To Pinkney, the foreign minister admitted that the mere renewal of American commerce with Britain was insufficient cause for the removal of the Orders.[27] His rationalization convinced a Britain mainly concerned with war prospects, and Erskine was quickly forgotten. But when the rejection and disavowal arrived in America on July 21, suspicions of Canning's bad faith were confirmed from New York to New Orleans: the hapless Erskine became a hero in the wrong country.[28]

Ostensibly as a friendly gesture, Canning promised an immediate replacement for Erskine. But through his same fatal hubris he chose from the ranks of British diplomats the worst possible replacement.

Francis James Jackson was notorious even in Britain for a ruthless ambition and for his obvious relish of his unadmirable performance in the 1807 bombardment of Copenhagen. From the arrival of the news of Jackson's appointment in July until Jackson's arrival in September, Erskine played the miserable role of the discredited envoy abroad.

These months could not have been placid, and inevitable disappointments made them even less so. Citing British refusal to withdraw the Orders in Council, Madison by proclamation suspended British trade. But the president and his administration were thoroughly at a loss to understand Canning's actions because of their ignorance of the foreign secretary's actual instructions to Erskine, which neither Madison nor Gallatin, the real negotiators, had seen. In the beginning at least, no American leader could be entirely angry with an envoy who had in effect given up his career in an attempt at accommodation. To Madison it was clear that Erskine must have "taken liberties" with Canning's instructions, which were probably absurd to begin with—the whole performance a "mixture of fraud and folly." Jefferson had more confidence that Erskine could justify himself, having "a belief of his integrity, and in the unprincipled rascality of Canning." There was agreement that Canning "was as much determined that there should be no adjustment as . . . [Erskine] was that there should be one." The minister himself assured the administration that he had intended no fraud.

Nevertheless, as time passed and he wrote further dispatches home (and the British government published them), they showed that he did not always agree with the American cabinet members' recollections of the negotiations leading to the agreement. Questions arose over his conversations with Gallatin on the colonial trade. No sooner had Erskine made his peace with the secretary of the treasury over this than he was called on to clear the same officer of having said that Madison was more friendly to Britain than was Jefferson. On August 1, he wrote to his scornful successor a defense and explanation of his agreement, and on August 6, 7, and 10 he wrote very able dispatches to Canning that were deferential in tone and totally ignored, partly perhaps because they exposed the unreality of his instructions as to practicality if not legality.[29]

At last, on September 11, Erskine introduced newly arrived Francis Jackson to Secretary of State Robert Smith, but since the president did not return to Washington from his Virginia home until fall, Erskine's farewell audience was delayed until October 2. That month he lingered at the capital and then on October 30 left on the warship *L'Africaine*, which had brought Jackson. On his arrival at Spithead a month later he wrote the Foreign Office asking if further explanation or a visit was desired. Before the disgraced diplomat had left America, Canning's egotism and intrigue had plunged him into the political wilderness, but Tory ranks were unbroken against the Whig diplomat. When he requested the usual privilege of attending a royal levee to greet his king and "offer further explanations," the new foreign secretary, Lord Wellesley, carefully explained to both the king and the diplomat that "while he could not be completely denied access to His Majesty's presence," "he was not to infer from that indulgence any diminution of the disapprobation which has been signified to him respecting . . . his conduct in America."

For fifteen years Tory disapprobation meant conspicuous diplomatic unemployment. Thomas Erskine's American investments collapsed in 1815 under the economic and military warfare that closed in, and family finances suffered accordingly. Both Erskine men nevertheless enjoyed the company of John Quincy Adams, John Tayloe, Benjamin Rush, and other well-disposed Americans. In 1823, on Thomas's death, David succeeded to the peerage. His American wife, Frances, presented him with fifteen children, and after her death in 1843, he married twice more.

Meanwhile Canning, restored to the Foreign Office, sent his miscreant minister in 1824 first to Stuttgart and then to Munich, where he remained until 1843. The Whig offender was thus an accredited diplomat under George III, George IV, William IV, and Victoria, although the simple-minded William was enamored of his prejudices and regarded the then elderly Erskine as a radical *bête noire*. Despite this disapproval by Ultra-Tory monarchs and their like-minded subjects, Erskine outlived Canning, Wellesley, and all his contemporaries on the American scene. He died at his Sussex home at the age of seventy-eight, six years before the Civil War shook the American republic, for which his admiration, however costly, never wavered.[30]

Francis Jackson

"An undisguised personal and national haughtiness (with a sweet sauce of studied, unremitting, ceremonious condescending politeness and attention) is much more advantageous than is supposed or guessed."
—John James, first Marquis Abercorn, to Earl Aberdeen

THE appointment of Francis Jackson to succeed David Erskine has the fascination of the irrational. Canning, having brutally disgraced the most agreeable minister yet sent to America, then replaced him with the most obnoxious professional then available among British diplomats. The predictable result was a collapse of Anglo-American relations and a major step toward war.

Francis Jackson, like George Hammond, was an able, if flawed, product of the diplomatic patronage system. His middle-class father, Thomas Jackson, was a good classical scholar at Christ Church, Oxford, who in 1767 became tutor to a distinguished first-year student, Francis Osborne, later marquis of Carmarthen and duke of Leeds. Thomas became the young nobleman's "bear leader" or traveling tutor on the Grand Tour and, like Liston's, the lives of Jackson and his family were shaped by this chance but strong relationship. As Pitt's secretary of state for foreign affairs from 1783 to 1791, Carmarthen rained favors on his old tutor. After marrying an obscure vicar's daughter, Thomas Jackson ministered to successively more important churches and became chaplain to the king, prebendary of Westminster, and a canon of St. Paul's.[1] When his first son was born in December, 1770, the father naturally chose the given name of the marquis, who with the bishop of Worcester (Jackson's great-uncle), stood as godfather.

Probably because of the bad health that dogged him, young Jackson was first educated at home. In his early teens Francis entered the University of Erlangen. However, with Carmarthen in the Foreign Office, Francis Jackson's formal education was soon replaced by diplomacy. In

1786, at fifteen, he was appointed a clerk and in the next year he joined the embassy at The Hague. In 1788 he was for a time secretary of legation to the ministers of the states general; he held the same post at Berlin from 1789 to 1791. His chief there was often ill, and Jackson acted occasionally as a somewhat otherwise-minded chargé d'affaires.

The young auburn-haired diplomat with fair skin and blue eyes above his high-bridged nose displayed polished manners or high arrogance, according to his audience. He constantly pressed for advancement—on one occasion it was for extra pay, on another for the embassy at Warsaw. Using the name of his patron duke as a "near relation," Francis Jackson became the suitor of a favored court functionary's daughter in order to secure King Frederick William II's application to London to give him an embassy. Although the suitor allegedly "went to such lengths as to render a marriage necessary in order to re-establish the reputation of the young lady," according to one detractor, no marriage occurred, and ill health sent Jackson back to London, from whence he explained to the lady by letter that his friends deemed their marriage unsuitable for him.[2] His next post was secretary of mission at Madrid under Lord St. Helens, and in his chief's absence he held several interim chargé appointments and did his best work. In 1795 he carried out special ministerial assignments in Vienna to strengthen the Austrian emperor's resolve against Napoleon Bonaparte, and in the next year he went to Constantinople.

By 1796 the able and ambitious young Ultra-Tory had two important qualifications as a diplomat: the backing of powerful reactionaries and a record of success in several medium-level posts. An American diplomat described him as "an impetuous young man full of English prejudices . . . who cannot do his nation much service." His professional colleagues did not all like him, probably for his ruthless ambition and mercurial temper. Nevertheless, he impressed Pitt, who even proposed to entrust him with the delicate task of talking peace with Bonaparte in late 1796, until Wilberforce and other moderates succeeded in substituting James Harris, earl of Malmesbury.

Jackson then suffered two difficult years while being driven with various pro-British governments from Turin, Genoa, and other Italian cities by the victorious French armies. By 1800 he was again in England awaiting assignment. When Merry went with Cornwallis to Amiens, the American post was open, but Hawkesbury was amenable to Rufus King's preference for Merry.[3] Meanwhile, the Christ Church–

Westminster axis turned again for Jackson. A fellow alumnus, Charles Abbott, sat in Parliament and became speaker when Addington succeeded Pitt as prime minister in 1801. While Merry accompanied Cornwallis for the peace effort, Addington at Abbott's request awarded Jackson the pleasant duty of representing George III in Paris until the peace terms were made final.

Jackson lived in considerable state in the French capital while developing his acute Francophobia. In the French people he found "deep duplicity," and their society was "an uninterrupted picture of vulgarity and profligacy," characterized by a "rooted hatred of Britain." Bonaparte, he wrote, was totally untrustworthy, "sarcastic, vulgar, and impertinent," and his ministers were "base." Like his mentor the earl of Malmesbury, Jackson was deeply opposed to a peace, and he regularly bypassed the more moderate Foreign Secretary Hawkesbury to report to his reactionary patron. Jackson, like Anthony Merry, was outraged that French ministers took precedence over foreign envoys; he himself kept all ministers at a distance and proudly admitted to a personal unpopularity that was due, he said, to his refusal to be "servile and subservient."[4]

After the Amiens treaty was concluded, Jackson returned to London in April, 1802. America, which he felt was "so much out of the way," had again been talked of, but Speaker Abbott provided the Berlin post again. There, on December 12, 1803, just as Merry was reaching America, Jackson married the daughter of a Hanoverian baron and master of ceremonies of the court. Elizabeth Jackson was later criticized for "liberal conduct," but whether or not she had been Francis's earlier light-of-love, the marriage was a happy one and rapidly produced three fair-skinned, auburn-haired young Jacksons.

As the fragile peace began to collapse in mutual distrust, Jackson's mission was to secure Prussia's adherence to a developing British alliance. But when Fox succeeded briefly to the Foreign Office in 1806 he brought home both Merry and Jackson. Neither was to return to the post he sought to retain, and Jackson's failure to do so was explained in the earl of Malmesbury's complaint that while the young Ultra "certainly had a fair and just claim" to it, there existed "strong prejudices against him at the Office."[5]

The "prejudices" soon found a wider audience. British overseas intelligence began reporting that following his victory at Friedland and meeting with Tsar Alexander II on the raft at Tilsit, Napoleon would force neutral Denmark into a northern alliance in which their fleet might prove to be decisive against Britain. The Portland cabinet therefore sent twenty ships of the line, forty frigates, and twenty-seven thousand troops to demand the surrender of the Danish fleet. An agent to perform such international bullying would need either supreme tact or arrogant insensibility, and for the latter, neither the earl of Malmesbury nor Secretary Canning lacked the candidate. On July 18, 1807, Jackson was summoned to Downing Street and instructed to accompany the fleet and demand the surrender of the Danish ships for £100,000 yearly. The demand, if refused, was to be enforced by a systematic destruction of Copenhagen by the overwhelming forces of Lords Gambier and Cathcart.

The envoy sailed with the fleet and in August went ashore for stormy interviews with the Danish prince royal and foreign minister. With apparent relish Jackson informed them that the world no longer held neutrals, that the weak must bow to the strong, and that Britain's patience with unfriendly Danish neutrality was at an end. When his hosts sought to protest the demands, Jackson begged them not to talk unacceptable nonsense. Then, after personal reconnaissance, he reported to his admiral that the negotiations were over and that inferior numbers and water shortages made the Danes helpless. A three-day bombardment of the city followed, killing two thousand noncombatant civilians. Jackson, watching from the flagship, wrote to his family, comparing the invading troops to eager foxhounds on the scent and assuring them that "we live admirably here." When approximately half the city was destroyed, brother George Jackson carried home the Danish capitulation.

Some days later Francis followed his brother to London. To his astonishment Jackson found his errand, and particularly his performance, under attack in Parliament and his personal browbeating of the Danish leaders under discussion at private gatherings. George III, who hated him as a bully, a garrulous diplomat, and "one of the toadeaters of the late Duke of Leeds," received Jackson at court but told him the Danish prince royal should have kicked him downstairs for his arrogance. Jackson reported to his family that Canning was pleased with him and he felt the Danes were responsible for "incurring" the war. He wrote that the widespread commiseration for the Danes arose because "the magnitude of our achievement startled the public."[6] The epithet

"Copenhagen Jackson," applied to him for the rest of his life, he probably regarded as complimentary.

The day after Jackson had sailed for Denmark, news of the *Chesapeake-Leopard* affair arrived in London. Canning, after striking down the neutral Danes in mid-1807, then dallied with the neutral Americans in 1808 through George Rose's delaying action. But Erskine's disobedience to Canning's instructions was another matter, and the foreign secretary in May, 1809, reached for his diplomatic whip.

Canning probably did so for a number of reasons. One was sheer personal anger over the minister's disruption of the foreign secretary's highly personal diplomatic strategy. Another was the English public's blood lust, now at fever pitch and calling for more "firmness," that is, for the kind of high-handed arrogance at which Jackson excelled. Another was Canning's continual underestimation of Madison's character and ability. Still another, at least in part, was the sheer lack of able men willing to go on the mission after the Erskine debacle.

Jackson himself shared his colleagues' reluctance. An intelligent man despite arrogance and temper, Jackson knew that he was again being sent to bring a government to heel, this time from the miscalculations or malfeasance of Erskine's tenure, but that this time his armament was thin. Although this eldest son usually described his assignments glowingly to his admiring and close family, on this occasion Francis wrote his brother that he was "entering upon a most delicate— I hope not desperate—enterprise." Canning, he wrote, was insistent on his going, and a refusal of the mission would have been disastrous "for I plainly saw that he was resolved to set me aside altogether if I refused." Typically, he also was careful to secure good terms: a considerable increase in salary, a promise of at least a year's tenure, an enlarged entourage of eighteen servants, and a promise that brother George would replace Charles Oakeley as his secretary of legation. In turn he was cautioned to tone down his manner.

Many participated in Jackson's unease. Pinkney wrote from London that America's friends there "felt this gentleman's conduct will not and cannot be what we all wish, and that a better choice might have been made." He could only hope that Canning wanted an accommodation and that by ability, Jackson, "with some small occasional allowances," would "do very well." John Trumbull expressed similar reservations. In America, Republicans prepared for the worst. Caesar Rodney urged Madison not to receive the new minister, citing his Copenhagen performance as one of a long list of "mischievous errands" he had allegedly performed "which from character he is suited." Others wrote of the faithless maneuvers of the court and of Canning. Gallatin thought Jackson, like Rose, was sent "to amuse and to avoid," and he hoped for a speedy end to it.

The president noted the tales of Jackson's diplomatic enormities, but was inclined to blame Canning's "general slipperiness," and he urged that since Jackson might have been named just to be rejected, to refuse him would give both the minister and his mission too much significance. He knew all about Jackson, though, and cautioned his administration members that to extend Jackson anything beyond mere politeness would be more likely to "foster insolence than to excite liberality or good will." The crucial question of course was Jackson's instructions, which the administration expected would contain an explanation of Erskine's disavowal and would propose some initiative.[7]

The object of all this apprehension was meanwhile delayed a month in England and did not arrive at Annapolis until September 5, 1809, on the frigate *L'Africaine*, after a fifty-three-day voyage. Both by his fever season custom and by diplomatic tactics, Madison took care to be at his home, Montpelier, when the Jackson ménage—wife, three children, servants, carriage and coachman, and mountainous baggage—arrived at the capital. The minister declined to follow the president; he was, he wrote, "accredited to the President of the United States and not to a farmer." Having neither reason nor authority to press matters, Jackson presented Erskine's letter of recall to Secretary of State Smith and with the experience of an old campaigner, settled down in the city's best inn to prepare for a bearable tenure.

Through Consuls Bond at Baltimore and Wood at Norfolk, the minister acquired a chef, subscribed to an Ultra-Federalist newspaper, and purchased saddle horses. In the pleasant, cool October, the adult Jacksons took long rides into the neighborhood, which they found to be "of great beauty." The city itself, he wrote home, "resembles more nearly Hampstead Heath than any other place I ever saw . . . the appellation of streets being bestowed on six or seven houses . . . [and] only two contain half a dozen houses adjoining each other." Between stood "wood, heath, gravel pits, etc." The general air was "wild and desolate from few people and poor cultivation and the city . . . as they call it, is, from the first house to the last, five miles in length." Jackson also created the most often quoted image of early Washington when he wrote his brother that he "put up a covey of partridges the other day about three hundred yards from the House of Congress, yclep'd the Capitol." Georgetown reminded him of Tunbridge Wells in its "beautiful prospect." In these early days he found American travel accommodations "not much worse than I have met with before in my life" and the prices comparable to England's and exorbitant only in relation to the poor quality of products.

In spite of Consul Wood's warnings of the "evils and inconveniences these would-be gentry bring upon us," Jackson was tolerant of American gaucheries. When they asked "impertinent questions" he reflected that it was "in their nature as much to be inquisitive as to be sallow in their complexions." The tavern loungers gratified his pride by gawking at his servants' livery, at his gleaming carriage and horses, and at the glowingly rosy-cheeked young Jacksons. An astonished Elizabeth Jackson received a call from the innkeeper's wife, who shook her by the hand, so the Jacksons gamely followed the Erskine precedent and returned the visit to the woman's home next door. But the new minister was pleased that his guests were usually "a different set from Erskine's," since "many of the Democrats who were his intimates do not come to me." He admitted receiving from officials only "the utmost civility and . . . none of those hardships and difficulties of which the Merrys so bitterly complained."[8]

Both of his immediate predecessors, in fact, incurred his scorn. Merry, he said, had not learned America, having never got a mile out of Washington except when traveling to Philadelphia, and had apparently mishandled the protocol matter. Jackson planned to use the "common, three-windowed houses built together" that Merry had bought and the Erskines refurbished, but Jackson wrote his mother that "a Scotsman with an American wife who would be a fine lady are not the best people to succeed," and the house was in "such a state of ruin and dirt" that the necessary cleaning and redecoration would require that the Jacksons stay for several weeks at the Union Tavern. They were never to inhabit the embassy that he so elaborately reconstituted.

Before leaving London, Jackson had received what he called "a foolish but very good natured letter" from Erskine, whom he at first regarded as "a very amiable creature in private life, but somewhat weak withal." However, as Jackson waded through the embassy files, the chasm between the philosophies of the two men appeared and he found that the Scot had been "playing the devil." The "Conqueror of Copenhagen" found his predecessor's letters to be "a mass of folly and stupidity," whose author was, charitably speaking, "really a greater fool than I could have thought it possible to be," making Britain "the instrument of these people's cunning" and accepting from Madison language in which "every third word was a declaration of war." The new envoy wondered how the old one could have been suffered to remain in America for two years, and he assured Canning that he himself would give America "blow for blow" and make the administration leave him "in peace."[9]

During the weeks while Jackson awaited the president's return from Montpelier, other experiences ensured that the minister would not be left "in peace." Like his predecessors, Jackson was unprepared by his former assignments to European courts for the democratic rowdyism and lower-class Anglophobia that was especially widespread in the coastal cities. Thus, when some British officers at Norfolk asked for the local "price of chickens," they were accused of soliciting "respectable females" and a near riot ensued. When runaway seamen from the frigate *L'Africaine* who had been allegedly impressed were jailed on application of Consul Wood at Baltimore, a mob produced a habeas corpus in the form of a threat to tear down the jail. In these melees of democracy Jackson first encountered the virulent editorials of the Republican press, whose violence, he wrote "could not be exceeded if the two countries were at war." From this rowdy press he deduced for his superiors in London an American partiality to France and "undissembled aversion to our national character and national institutions and regret at our national prosperity." On a personal level he found that the performances in his own career, notably at Copenhagen, had been scrutinized to support "unqualified and scurrilous abuse" and the "grossest falsehoods used for the purpose of traducing" him.

Like his predecessors, Francis Jackson retaliated briskly. Almost immediately he secured a channel of information into the administration. Richard Soderström, an elderly Swedish count, had long been in America as Swedish consul general, but generally without pay except for recoveries of commercial debts and covert stipends for information rendered the British embassy. A courtly man and good table companion, Soderström was recommended by Merry as being necessitous for passing out propaganda as desired by the British minister. Jackson also established communications with an Englishman, living in personal disgrace in New York, who was able to insert anonymous propaganda in Federalist William Coleman's New York *Evening Post*. This "J. R." came to Washington on an allowance from the minister and set up a channel for receiving attacks on the administration and claims of bad faith in leading a gullible Erskine to disobey his instructions. Plans for an embassy-financed newspaper failed, but these and other agents provided Jackson with valuable personal and official service.

Equally useful were the Federalist politicians who dined with the Jacksons and served up spicy political gossip and interpretations of administration perfidy and incompetence. Since 1807 Timothy Pickering had longed for a strong British minister to replace the "feeble" Merry and Erskine and to humble the loathed Republican leadership. Robert Knox, a homesick Englishman in Philadelphia, wrote Jackson in September warning of the "bigotry so predominant in this rabble government and whole country," where American liberty consisted of "scurrility, tar, and feathering." Erskine, Knox wrote, had "shamefully prostrated our dearest rights by conceding to America what she had no right to expect."[10] From these and other British sympathizers of both nationalities, Jackson gleefully reported to London such Federalist malice as that the secretary of state as a lawyer had taken illegal bribes and that the president's wife had been a barmaid in her father's tavern. More dangerously he also repeated that American policy reacted mainly to French success and was aimed largely at the election of key Republicans. He became personally convinced that—as Canning's instructions had already conveyed to him—the American administration knew of the three preconditions for agreement given to Erskine and had knowingly and deceitfully misled the young Scot into abandoning them, thereby justifying his disavowal and recall.[11]

Jackson hugged this dangerous weapon the more closely because he had known since before leaving London that he was vulnerable. America had every right to demand an explanation for the disavowal of Erskine's agreement and might reasonably expect another British initiative. Instead, Canning told Jackson: (1) to offer no explanation for the disavowal, (2) to suggest closing the *Chesapeake* affair on the same terms Rose had unsuccessfully proposed, (3) to take no initiative, and (4) to accept for transmittal to London American proposals for the repeal of the Orders only if they conformed to Canning's three famous preconditions. The worst suspicions of Madison and his advisors were well founded, and the only real question was whether as in Denmark—but without troops and ships—Jackson would by his personality transform an objectionable performance into a national insult. As the date approached for the president's return from his Virginia estate, a slight unease crept into the British minister's dispatches to Downing Street.[12]

Promptly on October 1, the president arrived in the capital. Next day Erskine had his farewell audience and Secretary of State Smith informed the new envoy that the president would receive him at the Palace at noon on October 3. Mindful of Merry's debacle, Jackson inquired as to the appropriate dress and probable ceremony and was assured that Madison, "a plain, simple man," was opposed to ceremony and would receive the minister in ordinary dress "as one gentleman to another."

The next day Smith "in dusty boots" walked with Jackson to the mansion, presented him to the president, and retired. According to Jackson the "plain and rather mean-looking little man" upon receiving the minister's letter of credence and remarks on Britain's desire for an accommodation asked him to be seated and then carefully read the letter. He then obliquely invited suggestions as to how this accommodation might be attained, but the minister turned the question aside and the remainder of the interview involved only cakes, sweet wine, and desultory talk.

The next day Jackson had his first conference with the secretary of state. In that position Robert Smith represented a political appeasement of the powerful Baltimore Republican family but was disastrously incompetent. Affable and handsome but quite probably the dullest man to hold the office in the history of the republic, Smith had yearned to open negotiations before Madison's return but had been restrained by the president. Now he was to be used primarily to verify suspicions that Jackson had nothing to offer in negotiation.

During the following two days' discussions both diplomats sustained shocks. Following his instructions, Jackson offered the same reparation for the *Chesapeake* attack that Rose had; it was refused again. Pressed for the reason behind the disavowal of Erskine's agreement, Jackson first equivocated, then refused to put it in writing, then, still equivocating, unwittingly revealed that he had no power to make proposals for the repeal of the Orders and could only provisionally accept any if they were in accordance with Canning's three preconditions. Meanwhile, Smith managed to imply obscurely that he had known something of Canning's preconditions (thereby confirming Jackson's suspicions) but then denied that the administration knew of Erskine's instructions.

The impasse in the negotiations was now clear. The next day's talk was postponed for three days, ostensibly for American consultations but in reality for Madison to take over the actual drafting of the American notes over Smith's signature. Francis Jackson never divined this change, and it destroyed him.[13]

Madison's first note over Smith's signature threw the Briton off balance. "Smith" expressed the president's regret that Jackson inexplicably had no explanations and no powers of initiative. The note then said that "to avoid misconceptions incident to oral proceedings" future negotiations would be conducted in writing. Jackson's precarious composure immediately shattered.

Not knowing that this was Madison's means of harnessing Smith and directing negotiations, he resolved [he wrote home] to prevent at once "the idea that every species of indirect obloquy was to be submitted to." Hence he wrote Smith that there was no precedent "in the annals of diplomacy" for such a decision between friendly countries. Worse, "Smith's" note had pressed him again for the cause of the disavowal, though Smith himself had earlier implied to the minister that he had known Canning's requirements. Furthermore, both Canning and the Federalists had said the administration knew of the preconditions, and Erskine had written to London that he had "shown" the administration members his instructions. Jackson raged to Canning that the Americans "must have known"; then in his reply to Smith he challenged him with the charge that the administration had known Canning's preconditions and therefore His Majesty had every right to disavow an agreement known by both parties to violate Erskine's instructions. Secretary of Legation Oakeley labored fourteen hours making copies of this masterpiece of confusion, after which it went to the secretary of state.

A week of silence then fell, attributed by Jackson to his last note, written "in a style that brought them in some degree to their senses." Smith assured him that the stipulation for written negotiations was merely to aid his own poor memory, and the two had a friendly visit, despite what Jackson called the American's "disposition to be very sulky and, if opportunity offers, very insolent." Britain's representative also spent the week hiring newspaper and pamphlet writers for the British cause and advising Canadian officials to maintain military preparedness since Madison's prestige was deeply involved in the Erskine agreement. Jackson also suggested that the Foreign Office send brother George to Louisiana to thwart Bonapartist designs there, meanwhile counseling his brother to hold out for £1,000 and expenses but to remember that posts were scarce and "most things are better than whistling in the market place at Newcastle."[14]

Best of all in the interim week was American social capitulation. Experienced, perhaps by her father's profession in protocol, Elizabeth Jackson had performed the difficult feat of holding court in a tavern, and soon after Jackson's presentation had paid her first call on the First Lady. Of course she found Dolley Madison deficient in social stature, but surprisingly likable: a handsome fat woman of bourgeois class "without distinction in manners or appearance, but, to be just, . . . also without pretensions," and "very fit to grace the President's table." The minister found that Madison had abandoned Jefferson's "pele mele system" so troublesome to the Merrys. At a presidential dinner Elizabeth Jackson was conducted to the table by President Madison while Francis Jackson escorted Mrs. Madison, who was, in his words, "fat and forty but not fair." The gratified minister wrote both Canning and his brother, "I do not know that I ever had more civility and attention shown me," and "I was treated with a distinction not lately shown to His Majesty's Ministers in this country," a distinction he attributed to his last chastening note.[15]

Immediately thereafter his world shook again. On October 19, he received another note signed by Secretary Smith (but far beyond that amiable gentleman's skill) demolishing the Briton's position. It began by reminding him that only a year earlier Canning had required Pinkney in London to put his communications in writing; so much for the "unprecedented" violation of diplomatic rights. "Smith" then continued that the President still required a formal satisfactory explanation of the disavowal of Erskine's agreement and provided a reference to Vattel on the rules of such a disavowal. The note then expressed surprise at Jackson's statement that Erskine's instructions had been known in America and denied that this was so.

Jackson was now totally confused by his conviction of American connivance in Erskine's violation of instructions and by his failure to perceive the real author of the State Department notes. In his confusion his natural combativeness rose. "If we give them any satisfaction at all," he wrote his brother, "we had better send it wrapped up in a British ensign and desire them to make what use of it they please." To Smith he replied by admitting for the first time that Erskine had been disavowed simply for disobeying his instructions. Then, made inept by anger, he repeated a second time that the Americans had known that Erskine violated his instructions in making his offer and hence had acted in bad faith in signing the agreement.

A lull then followed during which Jackson followed London's orders in trying to secure American recognition for Chevalier Onís, representative of the anti-Napoleonic Spanish Junta. The best he could manage was an informal introduction to the president at the Georgetown racetrack, and the chevalier, he wrote home, "might as well have stayed in Seville."[16] But the Conqueror of Copenhagen was not to be left "in peace."

On November 1, in a brief message again written over Smith's signature, Madison noted that the true cause of the disavowal—disobedience—had at last surfaced, and now he requested as an "indispensable preliminary" to further talks that Jackson make known his full powers. Most ominously the president noted Jackson's repetition of the charge of American bad faith with Erskine. "Such insinuations," the note warned, "are inadmissible in the intercourse of a foreign minister with a government that understands what it owes itself."

The arrogance of Francis Jackson, triumphant at Copenhagen, now brought ruin upon him in—of all places—Washington, and at the hands of—of all people—"Little Jimmy" Madison. Told to place the blame for Erskine's debacle on the Americans, he had done so by following Canning's intimations of American bad faith. These grounds were deeply resented and unprovable, but to abandon them now would be a national retreat and a personal embarrassment he could not accept. Madison's last warning was to Jackson merely such a note "as no minister of His Majesty ought to receive without remonstrance," and he privately wrote Canning "there is nothing to be got here by concession. I say more; concession would now be giving up every pretence to character."

On November 4, therefore, Francis Jackson responded to "Smith's" note with a reply that was to end his diplomatic career. Reasserting that the administration was responsible for Erskine's violations of instructions and therefore for his disavowal, the minister murkily responded to Madison's warning on "insinuations" of bad faith:

Least of all should I think of uttering an insinuation where I was unable to substantiate a fact. To facts . . . I have scrupulously adhered and in so doing I must continue whenever the good faith of His Majesty's Government is called in question, to vindicate its honour and dignity in the manner that appears to me best calculated for that purpose.[17]

To vindicate George III's honor as interpreted by Canning, Jackson had thrice called the Madison administration dishonest, and now Canning's bomb in the famous instructions to Erskine claimed its second victim. This time it was not a "damned Scotch flunkey" who was destroyed but the foreign secretary's own chosen agent, to whom on November 8, 1809, Madison through Smith applied the scalpel:

Finding that . . . you have used a language that cannot be understood but as reiterating and even aggravating the same gross insinuations, it only remains, in order to preclude opportunities that are this abused, to inform you that no further communications will be received from you, and that the necessity for this determination will, without delay, be made known to your Government.[18]

A pause followed. Jackson could not appear penitent to anyone, let alone Madison, but he remembered that Jefferson had removed Spain's Minister Yrujo's effectiveness by a "state of excommunication." Jackson was so shaken that he astonished "Smith" by requesting passports for protection of himself, family, and complete official entourage. So as to give Madison "a chance to retract," as he explained to Canning, he sent Oakeley to the secretary of state's office to say that Jackson "could not imagine that offense would be taken" by his notes and none was intended. But when Madison suggested a verbal amendment to remove the offense, the minister repeated demands for a retraction from the administration, and as instructed, Smith merely remarked that the matter seemed settled.

Then at that crucial moment in his career and as he prepared to quit Washington, Jackson learned from the *National Intelligencer* that Canning had fought a duel with Castlereagh and that the British cabinet would be re-formed without either. Like his despised predecessor, the minister had lost his sponsor at a critical moment; moreover, he was detested and excommunicated by the administration to which he had been sent.

Yet like Hammond, Jackson was extricated and his mission transformed by circumstances outside of himself—in Hammond's case by Grenville and in Jackson's by the violence of American partisan politics. His personal defense far exceeded in skill his professional diplomacy.

To brother George he wrote for propaganda use that England would have to support him for "taking high ground" necessary for maintaining "certain principles of our supremacy," and that he had been expelled because (1) he did not show "an equal facility with Erskine to be duped by them," and (2) America had a prearranged plan not to come to terms. To the Foreign Office professionals he wrote that Madison would not negotiate because the administration expected that George III's recurring madness would bring in the Prince of Wales and a Whig government, and also the president expected France to triumph in the war. To Canning, Jackson shrewdly pointed out that their positions were mutually dependent: the instructions Canning gave him made accommodation impossible, and, if he had withdrawn his charge of American bad faith, he would have destroyed Canning's arguments. By bringing his family to America he showed his zeal for his mission, and he had twelve years of successful service to demonstrate his competence. To avoid other insults, he did not leave a chargé in Washington, and he would wait first in Philadelphia and then in Baltimore to learn the wishes of his government. On December 2, he sent Oakeley to London with this defense.

Meanwhile, Jackson further infuriated the administration by sending to the British consuls in America a circular letter designed for public consumption. In it he repeated the "fact" of American dishonesty and the necessity of defending this "fact." He insisted that he had no intention of offending, and he blamed the whole matter on the administration. At the same time, private letters to Americans were tempered to the recipients: to moderates he deplored the fate of Erskine, who "did as well as he could" but had unfortunate ideas and still more unfortunate intimacy with "Whigs and Jacobins." To Ultra-Federalists he attacked Madison, and to American-haters like Lieutenant Governor Craig and Admiral Warren he wrote of Americans' cowardice and jeered at their ignorance.[19]

The officially discredited minister spent December in Philadelphia gathering information through Soderström, Bond, and various other agents and sympathizers and opening new propaganda channels through Jacob Wagner's virulent Baltimore *Federal Republican*. Like most of his predecessors, Jackson, as he denounced the American style of democracy, turned to congenial Ultra-Federalist sympathizers. He inevitably exaggerated their political influence because they defended his positions and soothed the raw wound of his intolerable dismissal.

So, as Ultras like Pickering, Josiah Quincy, and James Lloyd rushed to his defense and became his propagandists, the minister gained confidence and moved from defense to offense.

To London, Jackson suggested that Americans were in fear of British retaliation by war, or at least the dismissal of Pinkney. In December he assured the Foreign Office that "a great and respectable part of the community" saw nothing wrong in his conduct and knew of Madison's predetermination not to negotiate. Nervous about the daring publication of the circulars, Jackson assured London that they were influencing American opinion further in his favor. By December the minister's confidence had risen sharply and so had the number of his suggestions to London. He urged that no new minister be sent, no new negotiations be begun, that the Orders in Council be reaffirmed, and that American trade be excluded from Britain. He enclosed supportive letters from Federalist leaders and drew £500 more from London to bribe the secrets of the cabinet from Federalist clerks and to support his own newspaper propaganda as Republican editors mounted furious attacks on him.[20]

The president, having long since given up on Jackson as a useful channel of conciliation, after his dismissal merely gave the *National Intelligencer* material in support of his position. Madison's real problems were more serious than Jackson. In the cabinet, the incompetent Robert Smith, upheld by his powerful senatorial brother, quarreled with Gallatin; in Congress, anti-Madisonites led by John Randolph and Nathaniel Macon promoted Monroe and the Smiths. Worse, the Nonintercourse Act of March 1, 1809, had failed to bribe either Britain or France to acknowledge America's neutral rights in return for its trade. Throughout the congressional session, therefore, the divided Republicans were faced with the dark alternatives of war or submission, and they wrangled bitterly among themselves while Federalists belabored them from without. Jackson's dismissal merely underlined the problem of hammering out a new policy to bring the belligerents to American terms.

This bitter session saved Jackson. He was closely advised of political wrangles by Pickering, Bayard, and his paid spies. Far more highly regarded in Federalist circles than in London, Jackson was pictured by the Ultra-Federalists as a martyr to a confused, divided, pro-French, and untruthful administration. By letters, pamphlets, and editorials sent to London he could show that he was upheld by the party that was traditionally Britain's best friend in America. "If the ministers will not tell my brother's story and support him, . . ." wrote George Jackson in London, "the American people it seems are determined to do it for them . . . five pamphlets were received by the last mail." Such identification of the Ultra-Federalists and "the American people" was typical, and, as it turned out, crucial for Jackson.[21]

In England the intrigues of Canning against his colleague Castlereagh had finally brought disaster to the already shaky Portland government. In 1809, after much maneuvering, it was reconstituted under Spencer Perceval, although damaged by the absence of the best political minds in Britain. A measure of its weakness was that the one new political figure of any importance in it was the new foreign secretary, Richard Colley Wellesley, Marquis Wellesley, whose brother was conducting the desperate British campaigns in Spain against Napoleonic marshals. On November 27, Pinkney received notice of the administration's dismissal of Jackson. After waiting for the arrival of British dispatches from America, on December 27 Pinkney went to the Foreign Office and was courteously received and told that Jackson would be replaced. On January 2, 1810, he followed up with a note asking for the recall.

Thereafter immense complications arose. Wellesley was a pathologically dilatory minister, who cared nothing for Jackson and had no desire to insult America. On the other hand he loved office, the new government was weak, and the majority in Parliament was violently and contemptuously anti-American. Jackson was a zealous and efficient diplomat of considerable service, who had probably intended no personal insult to the president, and he had been promised a year's service abroad. There were also wartime problems of a new administration and details of face-saving in America. Then there was the wave of letters and pamphlets from America supporting the minister. Could Britain's staunchest friends in America be rebuffed?

Wellesley therefore waited two months before answering Pinkney's January request, then told him that Jackson would be recalled but without any mark of the king's displeasure with his American service. The foreign secretary even managed a reproof to Madison for the abrupt dismissal and as a further snub announced that Jackson would not be replaced by a minister but by a mere chargé d'affaires. Accordingly, but only after another month, the foreign secretary on April 14 wrote Jackson the traditional formula expressing the king's "undiminished sense of the zeal, fidelity, and ability which you have manifested in a long course of public service," but explaining that under the circumstances a return to Washington would satisfy neither Jackson nor His Majesty's honor. Therefore, Jackson could return to England when he desired, after turning the mission over to John Philip Morier, who was being sent as chargé.

Pinkney was deeply disappointed by the delays, the expression of approbation, and the decision not to name a ministerial successor. He knew Wellesley had but "a mean opinion of that most clumsy and ill-conditioned minister" in America, but felt Wellesley's dilatoriness and Federalist expressions from America had changed the foreign secretary's original plans. Madison also attributed the eventual British response to Federalist advocates for Jackson, but observed that the spring elections had now shown that most Americans upheld the administration's performance.[22]

The widespread anti-Jackson outrage of ordinary citizens was in fact often if inelegantly expressed beyond furious editorials and resolutions by grand juries. One angry crowd mistook an English traveler for Jackson in Lebanon, New Hampshire, and threatened mayhem. In Kentucky one Isham Talbot was charged with profanity by a grand jury for yelling "God damn Mr. Jackson. The president ought to . . . have him kicked from town to town until he is kicked out of the country." William Cook was similarly charged for yelling "God damn Timothy Pickering—he ought to be hung."

Statesmen equivocated, Congress quarreled, and ordinary Americans swore because Jackson now personified diplomatic stalemate and American national frustration. Political analyses in his own dispatches continued to be strange mixtures of tactical perception and strategic misconception. Jackson shrewdly described Republican frustration, ineptitude, and factionalism, and he perceived that many Federalists were more anti-Madisonian than pro-British. "At bottom they are all alike except that some few are less knaves than others," he wrote, and he found some of the "new-fledged" Federalists "very tenacious" about American national interests. On the other hand, he insisted that the success of British policy depended heavily on the ministry's support of his position, and he described Republicans as a not only divided but also diminishing minority of Americans. When the spring elections of 1810 belied his political estimates, he simply attributed Republican success to Erskine's folly and saw every occasional Federalist success as a personal vindication of himself.[23]

Socially he found events far more gratifying when the entourage moved north of the capital. At Baltimore, Elizabeth Jackson wrote that she was "very popular" at balls and dinners even though the cuisine was "detestable," the table linen coarse, and the wines limited in variety and indifferent in quality. Philadelphia was also Republican and disappointing, though Federalists there were hospitable despite mob threats. New York, however, where the family arrived in early February, was a triumph. It was always social and currently anti-Madisonian, so the Britons were both an embellishment and a political reproach to the Virginians. There was, Francis wrote, "as much life and bustle" as in "Liverpool or any other of our great commercial towns." For four months their social calendar was filled with balls, dinners, and receptions: the Jacksons were "well stuffed with turkey and Madeira," the citizens' "two staple articles in the eating and drinking way." A wealthy Mr. Hogan lent the minister his estate on the Hudson, eight miles from town, and there Jacksons young and old enjoyed flowering gardens, orchards, swings, and "other ruralities." Steamboats passing up the Hudson "at four miles an hour against wind and tide" produced astonishment and fear in the servants, but Francis predicted "great and beneficial changes" in water travel because of the new invention.

The minister's anger at the administration naturally continued, and even Federalists astonished him by believing their country soon would "take a conspicuous and influential part in the affairs of the world" in spite of probable continued Republican rule. But inevitably the good treatment from middle- and upper-class Americans softened Jackson's perceptions of Americans as a nation. He wrote to his family that he and Elizabeth had encountered many people of good (European) taste, friendliness, and good humor, and he admitted that Americans "laying themselves out to give pleasure to the best of their ability" did not "justify the ridicule and contempt" that some "over fastidious persons have not scrupled to heap upon their well-meaning entertainers."[24]

The curious spectacle of Americans competing to honor a foreign official who had repeatedly insulted their government reached a climax in Boston, to which Federalist governor Christopher Gore officially invited the Jacksons in February, 1810. During this time the Federalist legislature passed by a large majority a resolution stating that they could perceive "no just or adequate cause" for Madison's treatment of Jackson. However, in the following April, Massachusetts voters, following examples set elsewhere, replaced Gore with Republican Elbridge Gerry and gave the Republicans a twenty-vote majority in the legislature. Nevertheless, the Jacksons decided to go, and when they arrived in Boston in early June, Federalist sentiment and British social éclat produced welcoming ovations and nine days of feasting and receptions. At one splendid official banquet Jackson pointedly ignored the Republican governor and offered a provocative toast; at another Pickering, amid songs and cheers, electrified the ecstatic Federalists with his toast to "the world's last hope—Britain's fast-anchored isle." Escorted from the city by a guard of honor, the Jacksons completed their triumphal three-week tour.[25]

Despite the flattering attentions of such luminaries as Massachusetts' senate speaker, its chief justice, and Harvard's representative, not all was serene. Some public meetings (Jackson called them mobs) passed resolutions considerably less gratifying than those of elegant, upper-class Boston. In "that dirty nest of philosophy, Philadelphia," there was a "disgraceful outrage" in which bullets were fired during a diplomatic celebration of the Russian emperor's birthday. In Albany, Jackson saw himself burned in effigy. His servants created the usual problems after exposure to republicanism: one footman, according to the minister, "had a fit of American independence" and was summarily fired.

Much worse was the absolute silence of the Foreign Office, from which Jackson by the end of February, 1810, had had no reaction to the events of the past November. In March the mail packet brought a private letter from Pinkney to Robert Smith written when Wellesley had been talking of recalling Jackson. While the *Intelligencer* proclaimed that the minister would leave in disgrace, Federalists were in near despair that Britain would either avenge her minister's treatment by devastating war or that it would disavow him and thereby destroy their party.

The beleaguered Jackson rallied his followers by sheer bravado. When in London his friends managed to find that no immediate recall was imminent, Jackson wrote his family that from this thin encouragement he could put a good face on the matter and "make it clear that my conduct has been generally and loudly applauded." Throughout April,

1810, he raged privately to his family and political mentors over lack of ministerial support. To the earl of Malmesbury he wrote that if he did not receive a public and distinguished mark of approval or if any minister was sent as a replacement, it would be the worst blow to Britain since American independence, and Britain's American friends (Federalists) would "never venture to hold up their heads again." In letters to brother George, Francis insisted he was indifferent to the cabinet's reaction since he had only followed instructions, but "they ought to insist on my being reinstated."[26]

At last on June 7, Wellesley's April instructions arrived in Philadelphia. In these, the first Jackson had received since December, the British cabinet had apparently devised a plan to infuriate all protagonists equally. Jackson's services would be approved in general but not the American experience, and a replacement would be sent, but merely a chargé. Pinkney's criticisms of Jackson's circular letter to the consuls had also been made public in England. The furious minister defended his circular, thanked Wellesley for the formal approbation, and assured the foreign secretary of the pleasure with which the minister would leave America. As an added thrust, he described his triumph in Boston, where he had received such attention from public men "as had never before been shown to any publick minister."[27] He then asked for a frigate for the trip home, rather than an American mercantile vessel, because of both the size of his entourage and his unpopularity.

Like most Britons he yearned to see Niagara Falls, so after a few routine dispatches he rented a house "in the pretty village of Haarlem," where he left children and servants while he and Elizabeth spent three weeks visiting Niagara, western New York, Quebec, and Montreal. However, Canadian hospitality was more restrained than Boston's, and the Jacksons returned home in mid-August.

Meanwhile, in London, after preparing Jackson's April dispatch Wellesley lapsed into his normal lassitude and weeks went by, to the common frustration of Americans, George Jackson, and Charles Oakeley, the latter two both hoping to be the chargé at Washington. Finally in July the instructions were complete for Morier, the young diplomatic handyman chosen to relieve Jackson. Morier endured a stormy voyage on the *Venus* and arrived in early September bearing his credentials and instructions for Jackson to turn the embassy over to him. In New York on September 15, 1810, Francis Jackson composed his last dispatch—a mammoth, comprehensive view of the society, economic prospects, and political structure of the United States. The Jacksons departed the nation next day on the *Venus*.[28]

On arriving at Portsmouth the former minister went up to London at once, hoping for a notable official reception that would signify approval. He found that Princess Charlotte was dying at Ramsgate and that the king and most other notables were absent from the capital. British policy, conforming to a bad wartime situation, required a conciliatory tone with America, so official approval of Jackson's American mission was never given. No longer the darling of a Malmesbury or the sword of a Canning, Jackson wrote notes to Wellesley on unimportant details and sought to delay the naming of a successor. His status still commanded some anti-American attention, and London merchants tendered him a dinner with some 150 guests, "none," he informed his family, "but the heads of the most respectable houses"; but this was small change for the man sent to bring a president to heel.

The political wheel turned further against him when George III's madness necessitated a regency under his detested son. Although the Perceval Tories remained in office, the "extremely idle" Wellesley refused Jackson recognition or reward, either from consideration of Erskine family connections or from other uncertainties of regency politics. In March, 1811, he obtained a fifteen-minute interview with the regent, who, he reported, behaved handsomely "both in form and substance," but a year later Jackson's accounts from the American mission were still enmeshed in red tape. In society he was called a "disagreeable coxcomb" and "presumptuous and vulgar," and Elizabeth, who now acted as his secretary, was referred to as his "German has-been demi-rep of a wife." In 1811 precarious finances necessitated a move from Bath to Brighton, which, though disagreeable, was cheap and allowed him to rent his home in Bath to tenants.

As Jackson's private affairs and Anglo-American relations grew worse, brother George observed cheerfully that Morier in Washington was "as deep in the mire as Francis was" and that the Yankees said he had "out-Jacksoned Jackson." Francis himself kept up a patronizing correspondence with former American friends and propagandists, including Timothy Pickering, whose screeds by 1811 even Consul Bond called "for the most part too vapid to command public attention" for long. Francis deplored the eventual dispatch of a full minister to America but consoled himself by reflecting that the post was "a bed of roses on a dunghill."[29] When war came, both Jackson brothers were dismayed by British naval performance.

In April, 1813, Francis fell victim to a wasting and persistent illness, probably cancer. Weak and dim-sighted, he put on a gallant front lest he be "at once laid on the shelf as an invalid," but trips to Bath and Brighton doctors were fruitless. In November, 1813, he wrote George, whose professional career was rising, that there was "little more left of your brother than a skeleton." In June, 1814, the sinking man was promised a privy councillorship, but the next month he was writing pathetic letters to the foreign secretary, Viscount Castlereagh, beseeching "the usual bounty," since it had "pleased God to prolong" a life now "only attended with increasing suffering and increased anxiety for his family's future." A few days later Francis Jackson said farewell to his brother, urging him to leave on a French assignment.[30] On August 5, 1814, death finally relieved the sufferings of George Canning's second professional victim to America and the third successive minister whose career had been destroyed in Yankeeland.

Augustus John Foster

"It is by no means a country pleasant for a gentleman to live in; indeed there are very few gentlemen to be found in it."
—Augustus John Foster to his mother, 1807

OF the curious procession of British envoys to pre-Jacksonian America, Augustus Foster was among the most good-tempered. He was also unquestionably the most trivial and the most useless. Mentally shallower than both Erskine and Jackson, Foster failed not through disobedience or quick-tempered arrogance but rather from a combination of helpless adherence to Foreign Office instructions and the complexities of American politics in the prewar year.

His father, John Thomas Foster, was a clergyman's son who became a dull Irish M.P.; the elder Foster had, however, married one of the most colorful women in the lurid chronicle of Georgian morals. Elizabeth Hervey, daughter of the earl bishop of Bristol, was neither superlatively beautiful nor strikingly intellectual, but her compelling charm drew friends and lovers from the highest British and Continental society. Edward Gibbon once declared in a celebrated tribute that "if she chose to beckon the Lord Chancellor from his woolsack in sight of all the world he could not resist obedience." For such an enchantress, life with an ill-natured Irish politician was inconceivable: after the birth of her sons Augustus John on December 4, 1780, and of his brother George, the couple separated. The children were left in the care of the Foster grandfather, a miserly if noble churchman in Ireland. Elizabeth traveled over the European continent as the governess of two illegitimate children (one perhaps her own) of the dreary but amorous duke of Devonshire, maintaining meanwhile a long and highly successful ménage à trois with the duke and duchess.[1]

In 1796 John Foster died and Augustus and his brother George immediately and joyously ended a fourteen-year separation from their mother. Augustus was reported to be a "very fine boy with only a slight

Irish accent," who matriculated the next year at Christ Church, Oxford. He also attended classes at Weimar and Drogheda, knew—without comprehending—Goethe, Schiller, and other intellectuals, and traveled in Sweden, Greece, and the Ottoman Empire. After two years he joined the Horse Guards, but abandoned the army for diplomacy, for which he was suited less by intellect than by his mother's close relationships at ducal Chatsworth and by his aunt's marriage to a cabinet member. During the Peace of Amiens he visited Paris with his mother, met Napoleon and Talleyrand, and dined with Madame de Staël. He then became secretary of legation at Naples, after which he was sent to America for further training under Anthony Merry.

Augustus Foster arrived in late 1804 at the capital he found "an absolute sepulcher" and "a sad distance from all the civilized world." To Americans he was "an agreeable rather than a handsome man, of very pleasing conversation and politeness," and he cheered the lugubrious household of "Toujours Gai." In 1806 the duchess of Devonshire died and Elizabeth's prospects—with Augustus's—flourished. In the rural American capital he aped the English aristocracy he hoped to join, and in spite of saving money by living at the embassy and possessing £800 in private income and £300 of actual salary, he was astonished at "how trifles run away with it." The trifles included fine horses and a smart mulatto groom with whom he rode daily until noon. He hunted, translated classics, sat for Gilbert Stuart, and wrote chatty, homesick letters. Though kindly and tactful he despised republicanism and particularly American society—"the most motley vulgars the world has ever known"—and jeered at "the descendant of Montezuma" at the presidential palace.[2]

When Merry left America in 1806, Foster remained. He was too young himself and too honest not to admit liking the well-meaning Erskines, however distressed by that minister's dress and informality. He disliked Canning but admired Francis Jackson's Copenhagen episode. Fox's death and Erskine's mounting troubles convinced the young dandy that he must escape America at all costs, and he obtained a leave of absence, while his mother campaigned ceaselessly on his behalf for a better post. George Rose's useless mission provided an escape, and Augustus Foster left America with that gentle nonentity on March 8, 1808. He then served briefly in Sweden because of a spy's report that an important Swedish general and admirer of Elizabeth Foster believed himself to be Augustus's father. When his mother achieved the long-expected marriage to the widowed duke of Devonshire and the Swedes subsequently joined Napoleon's empire, Foster returned to Britain.[3]

In the spring of 1810, the beleaguered Perceval ministry looked out upon a bleak wartime landscape. In Austria Napoleon's marriage to Marie Louise had brought him a powerful military ally; in Holland Napoleon's brother Louis faced the choice of joining the Continental System or abdicating; in Portugal the British army was threatened by Masséna in the north and Soult in the south. Only in the minor American theater did dogged resistance seem successful. There, though Minister Jackson had been dismissed from relations with Madison's administration, he was showing impressive evidence that the republic's population included a strong "British interest." And in May a contentious Congress apparently conceded the failure of economic weaponry by passing the so-called Macon's Bill. This threw American ports open to both European belligerents with a threat to reimpose restrictions on one if the other rescinded its coercion of American trade—apparently an unlikely contingency.

In June, 1810, even the Jackson difficulty was solved by a compromise, the sending to America of a chargé d'affaires, John Philip Morier, whose lowly rank was meant as a reprimand to the Yankees for their treatment of Minister Jackson. Morier, born in the Ottoman Empire, was the thirty-three-year-old son of a British diplomat and a famous Dutch beauty. His family and political connections with the Wellesleys and other personages together with minor diplomatic experience had been sufficient to garner him the American post over the ambitions of Charles Oakeley, George Jackson, and others. He was described by George Jackson as "a very gentleman-like and intelligent man" with "a very favourable impression" of Francis Jackson's proceedings in America and a preference for more "spirited conduct" of the same kind. In other words, he was a High Tory with all the arrogant prejudice that had nullified Jackson's higher ability.

When this chargé went to America, Britain had for five years by Orders in Council, licensing systems, and sea power made all neutral shipping subservient to her own prosperity and war aims and controlled not only the destiny of American shippers but also the livelihood of American farmers. It was Morier's misfortune that, despite the flounderings of the lame-duck Eleventh Congress, the days of a Francis Jackson or a Marquis Wellesley were passing. As Morier approached American shores, a four-year diplomatic logjam began to break up and the current of American nationalism gained momentum.[4]

Succeeding events and Morier's reaction to them would not be helpful to the next British minister. The chargé's arrival in September, 1810, almost coincided with the news that France's foreign minister, the duke of Cadore, had written American minister John Armstrong that because Macon's Bill of the previous May had removed American restrictions on French commerce, the Berlin and Milan decrees would be revoked as of November, "it being understood" that if Britain did not also revoke her Orders in Council and renounce the paper blockade, America would enforce its rights against her. Deep fogs of terminology and interpretation followed Cadore's letter, and the long list of French seizures continued to grow.

Still, it became clear in the next few months that despite rising American resentment, no full minister was likely to replace Jackson, that the *Chesapeake* outrage of 1807 would not be redressed, and that Britain would insist that the Cadore letter was fraudulent and would amend neither Orders nor blockade. Future historians would debate whether Madison was duped by Napoleon or whether he instead seized an opportunity to end an impasse. In any case, Pinkney on instruction warned Wellesley that America would assume the Cadore letter to be valid and therefore, by the Macon law, Congress in three months would reimpose restrictions on British shipping to America. The American minister was given authority to negotiate in London on impressment, or, in the absence of favorable prospects, to come home. After further British inaction, the president in early November, 1810, issued a proclamation accepting Cadore's letter as genuine and setting the stage for Congressional action against Britain.

In another unwelcome development, Morier learned a few days before Congress met that in response to an administration-sponsored "rebellion" in the Spanish territory of West Florida (from New Orleans to the Perdido), a convention of rebels there had petitioned for annexation by the United States.[5]

Morier met these reverses with sturdy misjudgments worthy of his most obtuse predecessor. Told of Madison's impending proclamation on the Cadore letter, the chargé followed Federalist dogma in assuring London that the warning should be ignored because Congress and not the Francophile president determined foreign policy. He suggested that Britain reply by a trade embargo to "bring these people to a just sense of the true station they hold in relation to her."[6] When Madison informed Congress on December 5 that he had authorized the governor of the New Orleans Territory to administer West Florida, Morier wrote an officious and slightly threatening note of protest.

The American response should have enlightened him. Despite continued French seizures of American ships, Congress supported the president's acceptance of Cadore's letter, and at 5:00 A.M. on February 28, 1811, an act barring imports on British ships passed the House, Morier reported, "amidst the drunken shouts of the majority." Senate agreement followed on March 2. The British could now import from America in American ships but could not ship to America. Meanwhile, to Morier's protest over the West Florida seizure, Madison replied chillingly through Secretary Robert Smith that the matter was between Spain and America and that the latter would make such explanations as it chose in London.

Significant American initiatives continued. In Washington on April 6, 1811, Madison replaced the garrulous and incompetent Secretary of State Smith with James Monroe, thereby acquiring a secretary who could write his own notes and at the same time detaching Monroe from the Randolph schism. In London, when Pinkney's continued pressure on Wellesley brought only renewed refusals to accept the Cadore letter as bona fide, the American minister intimated his plans to leave and a month later did so after a final chilling audience with the prince regent. Like all abrupt actions, this flustered Wellesley; within forty-eight hours he produced a semi-apology for the delay and announced that Augustus Foster would go to America as minister and envoy.[7] The appointment did not mean that Britain was prepared for a new approach to mutual problems, but it did indicate that the Perceval ministry felt toward America less hostility than petulance; America was thought to be flattered by being sent a nobleman as minister, and Foster's somewhat tenuous relationship to the peerage was considered at least as important as his prior service in America.

At the time of the new appointment, Augustus Foster was thirty-three, good-humored, vain, indolent, and self-assured in his main interest, which was society. His snobbishness was derived from an adoring mother and aristocratic relations, but like Thornton he escaped arrogance by a whimsical humor, and like Erskine's, his politeness was disarming. Both in America and later he kept a social journal and uncommonly amiable notes. He represented the triumph of natural shallowness over privilege, education, travel, and experience. The usually fair-minded High Anglican had gained little maturity or shrewdness since his carefree days as secretary of legation. Because his current aims in life were to marry Anne Isabella Milbanke (who later chose Lord Byron instead) and to enter Parliament, his mother needed strong arguments to promote the American appointment in his mind. "As to Parliament," she wrote, "pray . . . consider how few people rise to any eminence in it," whereas American service would likely bring "flattering marks of approbation." Furthermore, absence might make the undemonstrative Miss Milbanke grow fonder. Elizabeth won, as usual, and in May, 1811, the new minister with little enthusiasm sailed on the *Minerva*.[8]

Others shared his misgivings. Francis Jackson naturally viewed his successor lightly: "a very gentlemanlike young man quite equal to doing nothing . . . which is now the best possible policy." For Republicans the appointment presented a mild hope that Foster's Whig family connections might promote a slight thaw in the current freeze. Most Federalists knew that "Lord Wellington campaigning in Spain is by far a more important agent in the negotiations than Mr. Foster can be." Some writers thought his mother's new position as a duchess instead of a duke's mistress might be helpful. The administration's *National Intelligencer* editorialized that although Wellesley had already ruled out any favorable change, Foster's conduct would not, as had Jackson's, disgrace the British nation and that he would be a gentleman "as far as he consistently can with the letter of his Instructions."[9]

These instructions, in fact, conveyed perfectly how the Perceval administration's contempt for America blinded it to the ending of an era. When Wellesley wrote them, Britain's problems were grave, as were her military reverses. Britain's formerly flourishing commerce was in shambles. As a rising industrial nation Britain required not Stephen's dream of a carrying monopoly, but access to European and American markets. Yet war in Europe and American legislation threatened both. Britain's warehouses had few foreign customers, her merchants were increasingly falling into bankruptcy, the Exchequer had stopped specie payment, and the normal flow of trade was choked by her Orders or, as in the Indies, was satiated. In the political arena, the king was clearly insane, and a regency act (with all its uncertainties) was a necessity;

yet, when the act passed in February, 1811, the prince regent amazed the country by retaining the Perceval ministry, whose remedy was a grim maintenance of the status quo.

Consequently, in the face of all the Anglo-American problems, Foster carried ten instructions, none of any value. He was ordered to settle the *Chesapeake* affair without recriminations by either side and to protest cautiously against the Florida seizure and French prize violations. The principal instruction was a mammoth composition by Ultra-Mercantilist Perceval that guaranteed the failure of Foster's mission. It again pronounced the Cadore letter invalid and asserted that Britain would neither repeal her Orders nor relax her blockades until the president denounced his own proclamation, Congress repealed the trade restrictions, or France explicitly withdrew her commercial restrictions against Britain. If America refused to repeal her own restrictions, the Perceval government would retaliate by raising customs duties or denying America the East Indies ports. In general, the ministry merely reiterated its indifferent dislike of America when, in Henry Adams's words, it "sent out Foster, powerless either for defence or attack, to waste his time at Washington, where for ten years his predecessors had found the grave of their ambitions." [10]

The new and not very hopeful minister had a long voyage of more than seven weeks, including a stop at Bermuda. There he learned that on May 16, the American frigate *President* under Commodore John Rodgers had clashed with the British sloop of war *Little Belt*. The latter was badly damaged, and thirty-two of her men were killed or wounded. At Annapolis Foster witnessed what he called "the usual danger incident to the arrival of HM's ships in American ports" when a young seaman leaped overboard for a four-mile swim to American shores. After exchanging ceremonial messages with William Pinkney, who had arrived from England the same day, Foster disembarked with Secretary Anthony St. John Baker and seven servants. At sundown on June 30, he entered the capital and took over from an angry and contentious Morier. [11]

The next day he wrote Monroe asking for a meeting with the president. Accordingly, on July 2, 1811, Foster, Morier, and Baker went to the Palace for official presentation. They were accompanied by Secretary of State Monroe, who was, Foster remarked pointedly, "rather more dressed than has been customary at his department." The president was also formally dressed in black coat, stockings, and buckle shoes, his powdered hair gathered in a small pigtail. He was, Foster wrote his mother, "a little man with small features," his face "rather wizened . . . but occasionally lit up with a good natured smile." After brief conversation and an introduction to Dolley Madison—whom he found to be "perfectly good tempered and good humored"—the minister returned to the State Department to open official conversations.

Britons and Federalists had hoped that since Jefferson's rejection of his 1806 treaty, Monroe would be more pro-British than either of the other Virginia leaders. But much had happened since 1806, and Foster found that the new secretary of state, while maintaining "the most mild and conciliatory" tone and manner, was yet remarkably firm. Such bumbling comments as the inept Smith had let fall to both Jackson and Morier were notably absent. Moreover, the president, who worked closely and harmoniously with his secretary, was both too simple and too complex for the minister's shallow gauge. In the same year that Foster had angrily resigned the legation secretaryship, James Madison had achieved the presidency. Since then, successive Republican efforts to forge effective economic weapons had produced dangerous political enemies at home, and abroad, the indifferent contempt of Napoleon and the British cabinets. Persistent, meticulous, and courteous, this president had by mid-1811 arrived at a crossroads: significant British easement on neutral rights or war.

Foster's strategic problem, which he never perceived, was that the Republican effort for neutral rights by economic coercion was by 1811 no longer—if it ever had been—a retreat from war, but was a substitute, and one that was wearing thin. A national consensus was slowly forming to the effect that British ship seizures, Orders in Council, paper blockades, impressments, and suspicious activities on the northwest frontier were becoming unacceptable to the point that war, though still urgently to be avoided, was now no longer unthinkable. Macon's Act, regarded by many as the ultimate submission, had instead proven to be a trap for someone, and the Cadore letter, valid or not, could not now be relinquished as a leverage against a British position hitherto unalterable. Even the *Chesapeake* insult of 1807 had by 1811 become merely another in a line of affronts, this one happily avenged by the crushing, if one-sided, defeat of the *Little Belt*.[12]

Faced with these attitudes, Foster in the weeks following his arrival found the traditional British combination of threat and condescension to be a paper sword. First he chose to defer his one concession—the *Chesapeake* reparation—in order to attack the secretary on the *Little Belt* matter. Monroe calmly denied there had been any aggressive orders to Rodgers and regarded the whole matter as a mere clash of high-spirited officers. Foster then raised the West Florida seizure, using, he reported, "as much force as temperate language would admit." The secretary's replies were jolting. "It was with real pain, My Lord," Foster wrote Wellesley, "that I was forced to listen to arguments of the most profligate nature," such as that the United States had shown remarkable forbearance in not urging other Spanish colonial revolts. Fearful for East Florida, the minister asked how far the United States might carry their seizures; Monroe merely laughed. The shaken young diplomat suggested to London that he be allowed to threaten Britain's serious displeasure.[13]

Subsequently, Foster turned to commercial problems and showed Monroe his instructions, which not only affirmed traditional British positions but also—in a probably crucial escalation—insisted that the Orders would be maintained until France opened her ports to British, as well as to neutral, shipping. The minister then formally requested the suspension of the prohibition against Britain, convinced that Madison's "known character for indecision" would scarcely deny recent French seizures of American ships, coupling this with threats of retaliation if refused.

In reply, the administration, which now regarded him as an angler for American public opinion rather than as a sincere negotiator, took its official ultimate position: that in the international area the French decrees were officially repealed and that hence, any French seizures were made by municipal regulations with which Britain had no concern. To counter Foster's threat, Madison merely called Congress into session for November, a month earlier than usual. Just then, on July 22, official news arrived that as of the previous May, Napoleon had opened his ports to American ships and restored vessels seized since the president's proclamation that restored French trade. This enabled the president to order the new minister to France, Joel Barlow, to sail at once and to replace chargé Jonathan Russell (transferred to London in the same capacity). Foster was told that no new minister would be sent to Britain until Congress approved. By the end of June, 1811, perceptive men in both countries knew that an impasse had been reached, though in Parliament the Orders were just then coming under attack from the pressure of merchants made frantic by losses.[14]

As an essentially social being without political shrewdness, Foster to the end read diplomatic and political situations in social terms. In addition, his youth, foppishness, and obvious pleasure in society made his essential but perhaps overly elaborate rounds of entertainments seem a part of his character. They reduced his personal stature instead of enhancing Britain's prestige, as had the social affairs of veterans like Liston or Merry. On his arrival he found Russia's Count Pahlen ensconced in the double house enlarged by Merry and decorated by Jackson, so he chose as his embassy a house at the corner of Pennsylvania Avenue and Nineteenth Street, destined to be occupied in wartime by Madison after the failure of the mission. Here the good-tempered young envoy conducted a ceaseless and lavish round of entertainments whose success, like those of most ministers', colored his dispatches. Immediately after his arrival he wrote London that "it would seem as if members of the government vied with each other in paying me attention, which I . . . attribute to . . . a necessity of conciliating Great Britain." Later he wrote that negotiations would be fruitless until the Orders were repealed and at the same time that he had received "as great attentions . . . as I believe have been paid to any foreign minister who has been sent to this country." In view of the "high tone" he had been "compelled" to use officially, he was very gratified by the precedence invariably given him. He could not know that Francis Jackson had been similarly gratified a week before Madison banished him.[15]

As did his predecessors, the minister contracted a dangerously distorted myopia from Federalist partisanship. By 1811 this party was a national and Congressional minority, but with Randolph's allied "tertium quid" they contained an able, often wealthy, and educated leadership unlike the somewhat bucolic and surly Republican members. Politically and philosophically congenial to Britain, they soothed and misled Foster as they had his predecessors, advising his course and assuaging his bruises while their newspapers anesthetized the light-minded young diplomat from the painful realities of public opinion. Tutored by them, he wrote Downing Street that Madison was indecisive and dominated by Jefferson, that more newspapers were becoming pro-British, that France was steadily losing to Britain in American goodwill, and that an Anglo-American "good understanding" could be obtained by year's end if only Britain would maintain her "decisive language."

In August the president left Washington for Montpelier, and the usual summer exodus began. Foster moved to Liston and Erskine's retreat, the small cottage called "Solitude" outside of Philadelphia. There he spent six weeks in the constant entertaining he found relaxing. His hosts and guests included Sweden's Soderström, Spain's Onís, and Russia's Pahlen, along with American Federalists Charles Pinckney, the Middletons, Joseph Hopkinson, Judges Chew and Peters, editor Robert Walsh, and the bishop of Baltimore. Talk ranged on famous social beauties, the corruption of the South, Republican gaucheries, America's commercial losses, striking social personalities, and good carriagemakers. In late September, 1811, newspapers brought Augustus Foster dark personal news: his stepfather the duke had died, and Elizabeth Foster, no longer the reigning duchess, now faced the open hostility of the new ducal family.

In the midst of the social pleasantries, Foster heard the alarming rumor that the Federalist leadership planned to support a declaration of war against Britain so that the inevitable military defeat would ensure a Federalist president. Suspicions of American designs on East Florida also troubled him, and he warned Vice Admiral Sawyer in the West Indies to keep watch on the machinations of Georgia's Governor Mathews. The young envoy was spared the awareness that in the late summer Madison and Monroe had concluded that unless the Orders were soon repealed, Congress would have to be asked for war.[16]

In late October, officialdom, including the British diplomat, returned to the peculiar combination of architectural grandeur and rural discomforts of the American capital. Foster now found that his decision to defer *Chesapeake* reparations until after America atoned for the *Little Belt* affair was a mistake since there would be no such atonement. Thus, while the administration prepared for the opening of the Twelfth Congress, Foster hastened to settle the *Chesapeake* matter. On November 12, both nations accepted an agreement that was virtually identical—except for the absence of reference to George III's honor—to that negotiated by Erskine in 1809 and repudiated by Canning: indemnities to the families and return of the surviving impressed seamen. Foster's delay in proposing the agreement had destroyed most of its usefulness, and it did little to cool rising anger over more British offshore patrolling and the inevitable seizures and impressments.[17]

On November 4, 1811, Congress gathered in its two ornate chambers connected by a long, unpainted wooden shed to hear a grim presidential message. Madison indicted both Britain and France, but Britain, he said, bore the heavier onus for increasing her demands while threatening retaliation for the new Nonimportation Act. Responsibility for the *Little Belt* affair was laid squarely on the British captain. The most specific stern proposals were recommendations for more military and naval preparations. Already, gunboats had been recommissioned, frigates were cruising the coasts, and some regular troops and militia had been called up. The president now asked Congress to raise and fill army quotas, to prepare the militia for national service, to develop the service academies, to increase supplies, and to encourage the permanent development of manufactures. In all of this, Federalists and Republicans alike read something resembling a war message. So did France's Minister Louis Serrurier and so, briefly, did Augustus Foster.

He had no need to interpret, for Madison took pains to make America's position clear to him, repeatedly, both through Monroe and in a personal interview on November 29. Repeal of the Orders, said the president, was an indispensable preliminary because France had revoked her decrees by the Cadore letter insofar as they affected international neutral commerce, and illegal seizures by French privateers were irrelevant to the main issue. Britain might reopen negotiations either by repealing the Orders or by tacitly abandoning them. The president admitted the risk of war in arming merchant ships, but was prepared to take such risk if Congress concurred. In short, the issue was abandonment of the Orders or war. America, said the president, would not act until Foster reported this position and received the Foreign Office response by the American packet *Hornet* in the spring of 1812.

A few hours after this sobering conference on November 29, Chairman Peter Porter reported the House Foreign Affairs Committee's response to the president's stern message: the report was a yet louder call for the nation to defend its rights by force. In the ensuing debate the House majority and the president seemed to be agreed that if British commercial restrictions continued into the following May, war would follow.[18]

Unwillingly, Foster began to be convinced. Since neither the *Chesapeake* settlement nor threats of retaliation had cooled the president, as expected, it began to dawn on the minister that "it is also possible that this government may really be in earnest" and might bring on war by seizing East Florida or establishing convoys for its merchantmen. Foster therefore urged Admiral Sawyer to avoid searching convoyed ships, and he suggested to London that it might be well to enforce the Orders only on the coast of Europe to avoid incidents off American shores. "War appears to be wished by a considerable party," he wrote, and in December, 1811, he saw a real danger of it "in spite of the palpable and absolute want of means in this country to make war on us." Noting Harrison's victory over the Shawnees at Tippecanoe, Foster vigorously denied to Americans the widespread charges of British meddling in the northwest. When new instructions from Wellesley again reaffirmed Britain's refusal to alter the Orders, the young minister replied that the foreign secretary would have seen from his American dispatches that "the ground taken by America almost precludes the hope of any good resulting from further negotiations."[19]

Unfortunately for Foster, matters now rested with the new Twelfth Congress. There, such imponderables arose as to baffle everyone and not least the British diplomat, whose dispatches on the American scene became an explorer's journal through alternating patches of faint sunlight and dense fog. The origin of the dilemma was that the dominant Republican party had been created and become successful on a program of peace combined with cheap and limited centralized government whereas a spirited response to national insult denied both these dogmas. The president sought a larger army, a strong navy, and, worst of all, higher taxes. Meanwhile, supposedly friendly France was still seizing ships, or at least her privateers were. Britain was the traditional Republican enemy from history, by the more flagrant and visible use of her power, and, to some expansionists, by the enticements of her own Canada and her ally's Florida. But New England ships under British convoy profitably carried flour to her armies in Portugal, and Federalists everywhere regarded war with Britain as both philosophically and politically insane. At the end of 1811, most Americans were intensely irritated by repeated national insult, but neither the people nor their representatives desired war with either European belligerent, let alone both. War presented a fearful prospect demanding a national unity that did not exist; inevitably, therefore, Congress's moves toward it were slow and contradictory.

This Twelfth Congress, Foster reported, "certainly brought with it an accession to both houses of men of talents and respectability," including bellicose Henry Clay as speaker. On the whole there was not, however, a radically changed membership. In the Senate, Timothy Pickering was replaced by Joseph Varnum, called by a colleague "an ass in talent and information." George Bibb of Kentucky was no leader, and worst of all, the anti-Gallatin clique of Robert Smith, William B. Giles, and Michael Leib controlled the committees that received the president's program. The new House was more friendly, but there, too, a three-to-one majority of Republicans was weakened by indecision and rivalry manipulated by Edmund Randolph and the "Invisibles."

The result of all this was four months of wrangling, indecision, and maneuver that totally confused Foster. Henry Clay and James Monroe worked closely together, supported by Peter Porter, David Williams, Langdon Cheves, John Calhoun, and others, but it was an uphill fight. In January, 1812, a compromise bill provided for twenty-five thousand new troops and the regular army to be filled to its ten thousand-man quota, but many scoffed at these expectations. In February a bill to raise fifty thousand volunteers had to be made vague as to their use abroad. The nation was supposedly preparing to fight the world's mightiest navy, but a bill to increase its own minuscule naval power failed by a vote of 62 to 59, and even funds proposed for repairing existing ships were cut by one-third. To Secretary Gallatin's chagrin a bill to recharter the Bank of the United States failed, and in mid-February recommendations of the Ways and Means Committee chilled war fever by urging that customs duties be tripled, a direct tax of $3 million be placed on the states along with other direct taxes, and a loan of $11 million be sought, though Federalists prophesied no takers in the northeast.

Still, in March, 1812, the appropriations bill did pass. By this time it was apparent that an angry and divided Congress was slowly accepting the idea of war with one or both European nations while denying the means of waging it with either. In late February Foster reported that preparations "as if for war with England are in progress," and that "if no concessions be made on the part of Great Britain, war may ensue in the course of a fortnight."[20]

But in the exclusively political little city, the shifting alliances of Federalists, War Hawks, philosophical Republicans, schismatics, and administration supporters confounded predictions. The baffled minister wrote Wellesley that he "felt it impossible . . . to explain on paper in any satisfactory manner the situation of our affair in this country," whereupon he committed the fatal blunder of his predecessors by choosing the least creditable of all guides—a Federalist clique, who for twelve years had misunderstood and minimized the national will.

As so often before, Anglophile dinner guests assured a British minister they would guide him in the American wilderness. Again a minister was advised that his nation should not alter the Orders "in any manner" for the Republicans would soon be hurled from power by a people made furious by ruined trade or ruinous war. Again Madison was portrayed to a foreign diplomat by his fellow Americans as a weakling who "cannot retract with credit nor advance without probable ruin" and would therefore seize at a mere change of names in the Orders as a way out of his troubles. The minister, like his predecessors, heard and reported that Federalists were gaining ground in several states while schisms rent the Republicans, and Britain's role might be to send more warships to the Halifax Station along with a few veiled threats, to send fifty or one hundred impressed American seamen home with "a little money in their pockets and some civil words," and perhaps to put a check on some contemptuous language about Americans commonly used by the London *Courier*. Above all, Britain should not strike first lest it unite Americans. With such advisors, Foster, less than a month after foreseeing war in a fortnight, predicted no war but that "after a great deal of noise" an American delegation might be sent to London or letters of marque issued.[21]

These confused assessments reached a British government absorbed by the slowly improving aspects of the war in Spain but also with Napoleon's ominous preparations in eastern Europe, and Foster himself carried little weight. Nevertheless, these dispatches were among the most unfortunate ever sent from the Washington embassy, for their arrival in late 1811 and early 1812 coincided with the strongest Parliamentary assault on the Orders in three years. Relentlessly deepening depression produced from Opposition members the most serious calls for repeal yet, but Foster's confusion, equaled by that of chargé Jonathan Russell in London, played a tragic part in blunting the attack.

On March 9, Madison, as determined to maintain the nation's war ardor as Foster was to decry it, sent Congress a brief message promising a revelation that while the administration in 1809 was negotiating in good faith with David Erskine, a secret agent named Capt. John Henry had been engaged by Governor Craig in Canada to stir up secession in New England. Henry had instructions to find out whether the British might count on active New England secession and perhaps an alliance in case of war with America. Henry's reports, from February through May, 1809, were purchased from him by the administration and were said to depict a New England ripe for secession. Like the Federalists, Foster was "deeply embarrassed" and hastened to deny any complicity. But when the administration did not indict as traitors the Federalists as a whole nor release the names of individuals, the party rallied with ridicule and invective, and the sensation died. The relieved minister did not notice that the affair, though overblown by the administration, still left Britain the villain and helped to unite the Republicans.[22]

Instead, Foster was, as usual, absorbed in the personalities of society and in the almost incessant festivities of the last winter of peace. Politicians, diplomats, and visitors gossiped and feasted at receptions, card parties, balls, and dinners; the minister's social preeminence made him the most lavish host in the capital. His weekly dinners included fourteen to sixteen guests, Republicans and Federalists, and he held smaller "choice" parties every Saturday or Sunday. At the height of the acrimonious war debates, he claimed visits from "upwards of seventy members of both houses." Occasionally he recorded a "dinner of malcontents," that is, Federalists and schismatics. Randolph, deposed from his Foreign Affairs Committee chairmanship, was a Foster favorite who proclaimed the superiority of Foster's wines and dinners over those of France's Serrurier—whom Foster carefully ignored.

Other frequent guests were aristocratic John Tayloe, Charles Carroll, Vice-President Clinton, Gouverneur Morris, Speaker Clay ("very war-like"), Chief Justice Marshall, Treasury Secretary Gallatin, and Republican warhawks Cheves, Lowndes, and Porter, along with Senator James Bayard, also a favored hunting companion. Occasionally the minister dined with congressmen, and he cultivated the politically wavering and bibulous Senator Brent of Virginia. With Secretary of Legation Anthony Baker he regularly attended the races, himself on a fine animal and attended by a resplendent groom. On January 12, 1812, he outdid himself with a lavish ball and supper on the queen's birthday, gathering two hundred guests from three hundred invitations. The young snob privately recorded gaffes and absurdities of bucolic guests but in honesty also noted "many sensible worthy men in Congress" of both parties. He played chess with Monroe who, the minister was convinced, was more pro-British than the administration that he now repented joining. The secretary of state was, however, "very poor" and lived "with Mrs. Monroe in too great seclusion entertaining very sparingly which does not fail to be commented on in a place where good dinners produce as much effect as in any other part of the world." Foster himself claimed to have spent more than £9,000 on entertainment and in his first six months petitioned the Foreign Office for relief.

Of course there were bad moments. He boycotted the presidential levees during the Henry affair, which aligned him with absent Federalists. Occasionally Republicans denounced him and his entertainments as an "opiate," while for some Federalist tastes he spent too much time with Monroe, who was, they said, "playing the Erskine game" with him. One grouchy Ultra saw Foster as a "very pretty young gentleman" but in appearance "too much that of a boy for Minister Plenipotentiary," and who "looks as if he was better calculated for a ball room or drawing room than for a Foreign Minister." More painful to Foster was gossip about his romances, which he feared might reach Anne Isabella Milbanke in London. On the other hand, flatterers told him he could determine the next American president by his diplomacy, and he was convinced that the British minister "really plays a great part and he should have a larger house . . . than is allowed and he should be married."[23]

Shock waves rolled throughout March, 1812. After the Henry episode, Madison desired an embargo on shipping to allow American merchantmen to get home safely, probably followed by a declaration of war if the Orders remained unchanged. On March 19, the British ketch *Gleaner* brought dispatches from London and caused such excitement that Congressional committees adjourned to get the news. A chastened Foster took bleak tidings to Monroe. Writing on January 28, after receiving Foster's warnings about the possibility of armed merchant ships, Wellesley strongly reprimanded his minister for even hinting at a possible compromise and ordered him to repeat that the British position would not change regardless of consequences. Monroe listened intently but said only that he had hoped for better news.

France then became the villain when her frigates burned two American grain ships bound for Portugal, and Congress erupted in an uproar. Foster took the occasion to twice request written proofs of French repeal of her decrees, but Monroe merely told him that the administration saw no use in debating a position it had adopted and to which it remained committed. The president's request for a brief embargo went to Congress, and while it was debated newspapers reported the resignation of Wellesley as foreign secretary and his replacement by the equally High Tory and personally icy Robert Stewart, Viscount Castlereagh. The House then passed the embargo and, after delay by a captious Senate, it was signed into law on April 4, three days after it had been requested.[24]

Whether the new law was intended to deny food to Wellington's armies in Portugal—to which Foster was consigning huge quantities of flour under licenses of protection against British seizure—or whether as a substitute for or preliminary to war was unclear. When the minister pressed for clarification, both president and secretary were polite and indirect. With Wellesley's latest obduracy on his desk, Foster might have seen the situation as hopeless; however, his Federalist friends explained the law as merely another trick to reelect a desperate president. Thus assured, the minister fatuously told London that "it is not unlikely that the session may terminate favourably to our interests after all."

April and May were frustrating to both president and minister. The embargo left worried farmers with unsold crops, and angry New England shippers refused to support government loans and elected some Federalists to office. De Witt Clinton's candidacy threatened in the approaching presidential election, war preparations slowed in Congress, and France refused to affirm unequivocally that her decrees were in fact repealed. Meanwhile, the homesick minister heard from Monroe in "very decided language" that America would not recede, and since private letters from England told him that Prime Minister Spencer Perceval was "as fixed in his place as in his purpose," the minister began almost reluctantly to collect information for Castlereagh on state militias, the navy, military posts, and America's scattered efforts at manufacturing.[25]

Meanwhile, the confused minister tried to influence American events as best he could. First, he asked Monroe for the names of allegedly impressed Americans so that he might secure their release. Then, at a Sunday dinner "grand council," he schemed with all Congressional Federalists to delay possible war votes by calling for recesses or adjournment or by absenteeism. Foster then asked these guests to promise the president reelection votes in return for abandoning the War Hawks. Later there were rumors of British bank notes dropped on the floor of Congress.

On May 18, 1812, the Republican caucus met in the Senate chamber and renominated Madison by a vote of 82–0. Elbridge Gerry of Massachusetts was nominated for vice-president. The failure of the schismatics to break Republican ranks was a blow to Britain's minister, though he had little opinion of De Witt Clinton, and he now became almost a nuisance to an administration absorbed in the realities of war preparations. His efforts to obtain recognition of the British-controlled Spanish Junta quickly failed. His protests that American warships were not carefully restrained received no notice, nor did his reiterated demands for proof of the legal status of the Cadore letter. In mid-May he wrote Castlereagh of his "disagreeable situation," citing that the impeccably polite Monroe had not answered one of the minister's six or seven notes written since February 16, and adding that only an awareness of the prince regent's desire for peace prevented his representative from "insisting upon an explanation from the American government."

The personal and social scenes were similarly frustrating. Invitations to functions continued, along with compliments on his taste and manners, but Secretary Baker, while listening to House debates, was denounced from the floor as a privileged spy in collusion with Randolph. The president told him that "in the present state of things," he could not attend the minister's social functions, and cabinet members followed suit, sometimes without explanation.

Personally Foster was both priggish and highly sexed, and he yearned for Anne Isabella. "I long very much to get back to England," he wrote his mother. "It is now a year since I was appointed . . . and I am already quite weary of the situation tho if I were married I think I would like it better." On April 2 he suggested to the Foreign Office that his remaining in America would be of no use to anyone as matters were at an impasse, whereas bringing him home might "alarm" the administration into sending a minister to London. Three weeks later he applied for a leave of absence and besought his mother to "tell Lady Liverpool how much my affairs in Ireland suffer from my absence and lay great stress upon the sacrifice I make pro bono publico. It is all true." Frustrated for home and Anne Isabella, Foster wrote three weeks before the declaration of war that "no minister ever had such temptations to break up a negotiation. I would give the world to go back for six months."[26]

The "negotiation" Foster liked to think existed had in fact long ceased, and the last steps to war were not so indirect as they appeared. On May 13 Congressional Republicans directed the return of absent colleagues "forthwith," and Madison and his House leaders met apparently to synchronize actions on a possible declaration. Six days later the long anticipated *Hornet* arrived. Tragically for the Anglo-American world, the packet, though delayed, had still left England too soon to bring the real news—that Britain's long adherence to the Orders in Council was collapsing in Parliament under attacks by journalists, Opposition members, and failing merchants. Neither could the ship bring the equally vital information that on May 11 Prime Minister Perceval, pillar of the restrictive system, had been assassinated at Westminster.

Instead of such dynamics, the *Hornet* brought instructions for Foster that constituted a blueprint for disaster. These reached Washington on May 22, 1812. The British cabinet, absorbed primarily with Napoleon's imminent assault on Russia, had issued a policy statement totally reaffirming cabinet support for the Orders. Also, in a long instruction dated April 10, Castlereagh unwittingly ensured war. He reasserted that the French repeal was fraudulent, defended the whole British position, and raised new barriers by asserting that even if France repealed her decrees against America, unless the repeal also applied to Britain and her allies, then the Orders would remain in force. In a separate instruction, Foster was again severely cautioned against any suggestion that the Orders would be removed.

So intransigent was the new foreign secretary that Foster for his own protection showed the statesman's long defense to Madison and Monroe, but refused to let them copy it, since he knew it would go at once to Congress. Oblivious to irony, he explained to Castlereagh that through the necessity for countering American "trick, falsehood, and artifice," he had sent the secretary of state a "copy" that omitted the new demand against France and delayed even this in hopes of slowing a war vote.

Foster then played Britain's last cards. First, he offered to divide with America the license trade with the French West Indies that America had long protested. This offer rejected, he made his final offer: that Britain would give up this trade altogether in return for a restoration of American trade and acceptance of a rigorous blockade of the French empire. Both president and secretary of state refused to bargain away their nation's neutral rights.[27]

Ignorant, of course, of the panicky flight in Whitehall, the Republican leadership read once more the chilling phrases rejecting the American position. Madison then sent the weary Congress accounts of Foster interviews and Castlereagh's instructions, together with a long message. In this message Madison reviewed the dreary history of Anglo-American conflict over the Orders, ship seizures, impressment, blockades, and Indian incitements. He noted that the French had repealed their decrees affecting America and discussed the Henry affair and the recent British escalations of demand in the face of repeated American attempts to negotiate.

The Foreign Relations Committee replied in a manifesto, and on June 4 the House voted 79–49 in favor of war. In the Senate the matter was far more in doubt, and substitute motions multiplied. In the end, after agonizingly close votes on some of these, a reluctant majority came to feel that open conflict or national disgrace with party disintegration were the only alternatives, and on June 17, by a 19–13 vote the Senate also chose war. The next day the House accepted minor Senate changes, and the president on June 18, 1812, signed a declaration that signified the close of the long struggle in diplomacy.[28]

During the debates Foster tried to raise old arguments on the Cadore letter, vigorously denied British agitation of Indians, and attempted to delay the war vote by means ranging from diplomatic notes to assigning an aide to keep Virginia's Senator Brent too drunk to attend Congress. The administration countered by using his notes against him with individual congressmen, and Brent outdrank the aide. The minister knew the vote would be close, but although he understood American reluctance to go to war, he underestimated resentments and interpreted public ignorance of events as opposition to fighting.

On June 20 he transmitted the declaration to London with comments on "this extra-ordinary measure that seems to have been unexpected by nearly the whole nation and to have been carried in opposition to the declared sentiments of many of those who voted for it." To Madison he offered to carry American proposals to London during an armistice and made other efforts to halt hostilities, especially after news almost immediately arrived from captured ships that in Parliament the ministry had given notice first of the discontinuance of the Orders and then of their repeal on June 23. But the president was too aware of potential political attacks for ending war by negotiation, too sure of the advantages of military initiative, too distrustful of Britain, and perhaps too scarred by his experience with Erskine's agreement to accept any armistice.

The civilized amenities of an earlier age together with Augustus Foster's social *sang-froid* were notable during his last American days. Citizens offered to buy his horses and party furnishings. He drove about to show himself unafraid, went to the theater as usual, and received sympathetic and curious visitors. On the evening of the declaration of war he attended a presidential levee unaware of the vote and reported Madison "ghastly pale" and socially "discomforted." After the vote he and Monroe, he wrote, "endeavored to frighten one another for a whole hour by descanting on the horrors of war" and then went off to drink tea together at the secretary's house. At the president's invitation the minister had a final amicable and regretful visit with him on June 23, the very day on which Castlereagh admitted to Parliament that the Orders in Council had been repealed by the ministry.[29]

After sending the war news to England by private traveler, directing circulars to his consuls, and warning the West Indian fleet and other ships, Foster entered his chariot with two pet dogs and Vice-Consul Wood and left Washington on June 25, 1812. Secretary Baker remained to transmit messages and later to exchange prisoners. The minister passed through Baltimore by day purposely to show himself unafraid, not knowing that Monroe had charged Republican hotheads there to maintain decorum, and he spent several days in New York visiting and sightseeing. On July 17 he arrived by ship in Halifax and there awaited favorable winds, evaluated rumors, and after some indecision decided to return home. Later the Parliamentary Opposition excoriated him for this; Castlereagh had hoped he would stay with Admiral Sawyer and await developments. Foster later explained that he left so as to hasten the departure of a large British fleet to bring the war home to America (as the Federalists urged) or to expedite peace by transmitting Madison's terms (as the president had suggested). His reasoning satisfied Castlereagh when, after some mildly exciting alarms at sea, he arrived home on August 22, 1812.[30]

Foster's post-American career was long and mediocre. He and the earl of Liverpool (Perceval's successor as prime minister) were understandably anxious to escape blame for yet another war, and though the country was absorbed by the stupendous drama of Napoleon's Russian campaign, the ministry made much of him. He received £3,000 more for American expenses and was kindly received by the king. A copy of the British declaration of war was sent him for his comments.

Foster later entered Parliament and attempted to defend the American policy against the Opposition's Baring and Whitbread. In an obviously nervous maiden speech, he stressed the illogicality, unpopularity, and unexpectedness of the American declaration; he also managed to exonerate American Federalists and blame the war on the Republicans. The latter consisted, he said, of the lower orders of society, who were directed by hotheads who were kept in power by "creating new states from the desert districts of the South." Whitbread's brief reply was telling, and an Opposition member felt "he must be a person of little penetration who does not see through the pomposity of Augustus and the shallowness of his mind."[31]

In 1814 Foster was in Paris to see the Allies' triumphant entry and was presented to various royalty. From there he was sent as minister to Copenhagen, where he spent ten uneventful years in the placid Danish capital he approvingly called "an easy, idle Court, scarcely affording material for one dispatch a week." Having escaped what friends called the "horror of an American Mrs. Foster" and though Anne Isabella chose another, Foster found other loves and, in 1815, married Albinia Jane Hobart, daughter of a member of Parliament and sister of an earl. The couple had three sons. For six years, his adored mother, Elizabeth, lived in Rome as a brilliant salon hostess until her death in 1824, after which Foster began nineteen years of service as minister plenipotentiary to the king of Sardinia. Turin, called "the dullest town in Europe," was a congenial post; visitors admired the views from his villa and found him a gracious host who had become "quite a Piedmontese in his tastes." His long service was recognized by his admission to the Privy Council, knighthood in 1825, and receipt of minor orders of European and British chivalry.

Foster's not unfriendly *American Notes*, made during and after his Washington residence, were excerpted and mentioned at some length in the *Quarterly Review*. With Bayard, Josiah Quincy, and other Federalists, he kept up a correspondence that lacked the venom of Francis Jackson's post-American letters. Toward the American capital's barbarisms, however, he never relented, and he wrote Bayard in 1815 that the war would produce one good "if your government should find themselves obliged to quit Washington forever." The next year he wrote his successor in America a pleasant note urging him good-humoredly to get Congress to "give up capitol hill and that eternal avenue with frogs on one side and snipes on the other."[32]

When Foster retired from Sardinia in 1840, the good-natured young fop that Americans had known was a sixty-year-old veteran diplomat afflicted at times by depression. Eight years later he chose a death more dramatic than anything in his life had been. On August 1, 1848, at Branksea Castle in Dorset he suddenly slashed his own throat, influenced perhaps by the example of his fellow Irishman Castlereagh, with whom he shared the diplomatic failure of the last Anglo-American war.

Interlude

"No government in the world understood better than the British how to accommodate their pride to their interests."
—John Quincy Adams, 1818

"I consider the mission to America as the best, at this moment, in the whole circle of our diplomacy for a person wishing to rise in the profession.
—Charles Ellis to Charles Bagot, 1815

THE War of 1812 suffered—and still suffers—a bad press. Britain never gracefully accepted a declaration of war against her, especially by a minor power, and ever since the Senate's reluctant six-vote margin for war on June 17, 1812, Tories and American Federalists and Neo-Federalists have assailed the decision as unnecessary, foolish, wicked, or all three. To many then and now, America's war performance demonstrated by its very incompetence the frailties of the republic and the incapacity of the Republican leadership.

Yet just as transatlantic events had been intimately connected with the outbreak of the American war, so that war and contemporary European developments crucially shaped both American nationality and the structure of Anglo-American diplomacy that followed. From the acquisition of Louisiana in 1803 to the outbreak of war in 1812, Republican America wrestled—under the handicap of her unprecedented neutrality claims in a world at war—to redefine the Anglo-American relationship of the Federalist era. The years from 1812 through 1818 constitute a holding pattern until the nineteenth century had time to readjust Anglo-American positions of the earlier eras, a readjustment substantially defined by 1824.

No matter that Britain had repealed the detested Orders in Council even before the war to obtain that repeal had begun; no matter that American diplomatic *sine quae non* such as impressment were abandoned at Ghent or that the republic gained neither Canada nor Florida. The distracted and badly directed American war effort was sustained except in New England by local sentiment that paradoxically reflected a sporadic but stubborn national spirit, and the real losers of 1815 were the only groups that might seriously frustrate the republic's national future: British Ultra-Tories, American Ultra-Federalists, and Indians. In January, 1815, the barbecues, bonfires, speeches, church bells, and banquets across America did not really celebrate the victorious war described by orators, but rather a coming of age that was even then noted by the observant Gallatin: "They are more Americans; they act and feel more as a nation."

In Britain that same year the jubilation that followed Waterloo closed a war of not three years but twenty. Britons cherished visions of peace with low taxes, cheap bread, and prewar normalcy. These were not to be. The next two years saw the worst depression the kingdom had known. Overstocked merchants found few Continental buyers with money or credit, and the goods dumped in Britain from her colonies merely brought glut and stagnation. The £56 million formerly spent each year for military supplies had to seek new channels, while more than four hundred thousand demobilized men produced a labor surplus. From 1816 to 1818 the price of iron dropped from £20 to £8 per ton. Factories closed and inflation, successive bad harvests, and a new wheat tariff combined to drive up the price of bread. Paper money fluctuated wildly, and Continental trade chilled under new political clouds.

Traditional European diplomacy, too, soured in the postwar years. At Vienna Castlereagh had structured a settlement of redrawn boundaries and "legitimate" monarchs and committed a reluctant British cabinet to a Concert of Europe to maintain a Continental peace. But France's restored Bourbons "learned nothing and forgot nothing," and Russia's mystic Alexander, Prussia's weak Frederick William, and Austria's colorless Francis nowhere raised enthusiasm. Monarchs and ministers were in fact united only in their aim to stamp out the liberalism and popular nationalism destined to be the main forces in nineteenth-century Europe. While revolutions in Spain and Italy transformed Castlereagh's Congresses from guarantors of peace into political jailers, reaction reached overseas. The restored monarchs listened sympathetically to Spain's call for the compulsory return of her revolted colonies and the old exclusion of outside commercial interests, often British.

Victory, then, should have confirmed Tory Britain's twenty-year system; instead, Lord Liverpool's government looked from London upon a discontented countryside and a continent in ferment. Under these circumstances the prince regent might assure brother monarchs of his sympathy with their absolutist principles and might venture what Richard Rush called "cautious incivilities" to that new American envoy, but His Royal Highness's ministers viewed the situation somewhat differently. Traditional disgust for Yankees sharpened by disappointments in war and commercial rivalry permeated popular opinion and literature, but the cabinet could not afford the luxury of mere hatred, and Whitehall began to experience a change of mind if not of heart. The American republic, it appeared, was peopled with poor soldiers but good customers. Their manners were rude and their society coarse, but their economy was often complementary to Britain's and their thirst for English goods unslakable. American political views were absurd, but Americans were largely Anglo-Saxon and their governments representative. As an alternative to a reactionary and autarchic Europe, their nation represented not a friend but a relation, a potential competitor, but above all a customer. With a customer-competitor a "nation of shopkeepers" could do business.

And so the Malmesburys and the Eldons of an essentially eighteenth-century Britain moved from the political stage to the picture gallery. A Castlereagh supplanted a far dimmer Wellesley, to be in turn replaced by a reeducated Canning, a Huskisson, and a Grey. Mutual animosities and suspicions persisted, yet Britain remained by all odds the world's most powerful nation and sensible Americans knew that her trade was as essential to their prosperity as her peace was to their tranquillity. But Anglo-American relations now turned not on what Britain would allow but on what Americans would accept. The difference, a vast one, opened a new era for both countries.[1]

Charles Bagot

"The truth is that your mission is at this moment by far the most important of any in our diplomacy."
—William Wellesley-Pole to Charles Bagot, 1818

"No man who has ever once been at Washington can ever forget it."
—Stratford Canning to Charles Bagot, 1820

"No human being who has not experienced it can conceive or ever hereafter be made to understand, what an English minister in America really goes through. It is wretchedness of a kind to which there is nothing similar."
—Charles Bagot to Lord Binning, 1816

THE first postwar British minister to Republican America proved that success in his office, however rare, did not require superlative qualifications. A realistic foreign secretary was essential; manners, tact, and personal connections with Britain's powerful were equally so; unusual intelligence was dispensable. To these requirements Charles Bagot conformed so precisely that while his patron the duke of Wellington "raised common sense to the level of genius," Bagot was translating discretion into triumph.

He was born on September 23, 1781, at Blithfield House, Staffordshire, the second son of Sir William, first Baron Bagot, newly raised to the peerage in recognition of twenty-six years of undistinguished Ultra-Tory service in the House of Commons. Sickly and unscholarly, handsome and playful, young Bagot was considered "good natured" and "not quite fashioned," and he proceeded somewhat slowly through Rugby and Christ Church, Oxford, to find himself in 1801 possessing a bachelor's degree and an uncertain future.[1]

His most promising assets were well-placed friends and relatives. Cousin John Sneyd was a rector whose political influence derived from friendship with George Canning's brother-in-law (later a duke) and with others on the fringes of wealth and power, such as Charles Ellis, who had been close to Canning since Eton days and sat in Parliament. Bagot's sister Louisa had married Walter Sneyd, a personal friend of the prince regent, and she was herself cherished by the royal princesses. A career in politics or diplomacy was therefore indicated; Charles was admitted to Lincoln's Inn to study law while he followed John Sneyd's advice to "labour to find grace in Canning's sight." Unfortunately when Pitt resigned as first minister in 1801, Canning followed his chief into political exile.

This relegated Bagot to months of social life and mere availability. Men saw him as "good natured and good tempered," but as a "coxcomb in dress and manner,"[2] ostentatiously taking snuff and declaiming in the style of an earlier age. Among the females of society, however, the handsome socialite had more admirers, and on July 1, 1806, after a whirlwind courtship he married Mary Charlotte Anne Wellesley-Pole. Her father had taken the additional surname of the Irish godfather whose estate he had inherited and thereafter was to sit in Parliament from 1763 to 1821, when he entered the peerage. Her uncles were foreign secretary Richard Wellesley and Gen. Arthur Wellesley, the nation's new military hero in Spain. The marriage was for both a love match and for Charles an alliance with an already powerful house soon to be the most famous in Britain. Family influence in the spring of 1807 prevailed when an uncle presented Bagot with a Commons seat from a family pocket borough, but he was not to serve in Westminster. In March of that year George III called the infirm duke of Portland to preside over an administration in which George Canning took the Foreign Office.

British fortunes were then sinking. In June Napoleon crushed the Russians at Friedland and by July 9 had met the Tsar on the famous raft at Tilsit to form an alliance that was to give Copenhagen Jackson employment. In the western hemisphere Admiral Sir George Berkeley roused America to fury by the attack on the *Chesapeake*. As Canning organized the Foreign Office, the northern undersecretaryship fell vacant. The new secretary, with an eye to Bagot's powerful relations, wrote him a letter in August, 1807, that illustrates the twenty-six-year-old's reputation as something less than a workhorse: "I intreat you not to decide without weighing well *all* the chances of inconvenience . . . uncomfortableness and possibly . . . final disappointment . . . French is . . . indispensable . . . The labour is very hard; and it is daily and constant. It requires entire devotion to it."³ Father-in-law Wellesley-Pole also relayed warnings about the potential employment. The position was said to demand "fagging without cessation or relaxation," so an offer should not be accepted if Bagot was "either afraid or unwilling to fag," and he would be dismissed at once if found unfit from "indolence, ill-health, insufficiency, or . . . *Mary*." But, Mary's father continued, "it is a mistake to suppose that what is called business is injurious to health."⁴

Despite the somber admonitions on fagging and French, Bagot accepted the undersecretaryship immediately. The association thus cautiously formed was the most important of Bagot's professional life, for in the following two grim years the two men formed a very close personal and professional relationship that lasted until Canning's death. Canning, eleven years his senior, taught Bagot the tactics of forceful diplomacy, exemplified when he disgraced Erskine and sent Jackson's unlovely arrogance to both Denmark and America. However, in 1809 his intrigue against Robert Castlereagh in the War Office brought a duel, and when both men left the cabinet, Bagot followed his chief.

He then endured five years out of office, during which time diplomatic posts abroad successively vanished before Napoleonic victories. By 1812 only six of Britain's Continental missions existed, five of these to courts whose monarchs were in exile or prison or had lost significant territory. At home when the Portland government fell in 1809, Spencer Perceval and his colleagues subordinated everything to the prosecution of a victorious war, including the fluctuating campaigns of Mary Bagot's uncle, Gen. Arthur Wellesley, in Portugal and Spain. Following the emperor's Russian defeat in 1812, the wars of liberation broke his empire throughout Europe, and in March, 1814, the Allies entered Paris, Napoleon abdicating on April 11. During these cyclonic events the diplomatic impasse in America became almost irrelevant, and neither Francis Jackson's arrogance nor Augustus Foster's elegance could arrest the slide into Anglo-American war in June, 1812. That same year Bagot's hopes sank when Castlereagh succeeded Richard Wellesley in the Foreign Office. Castlereagh remained there after the assassination of Perceval brought in the administration of Robert Banks Jenkinson, who, as Lord Liverpool, was to confound predictions by remaining as first minister for fifteen years.

On Napoleon's abdication, Castlereagh sent Arthur Wellesley, now the duke of Wellington, to Paris as ambassador, but the duke preferred his own secretary over Bagot's application. Still, the claims of the former undersecretary, or rather of his family, were now in fact undeniable. In July, 1814, he was sent to Paris as special envoy for war claims, but Napoleon's return from Elba drove him home, and when Wellesley-Pole joined the cabinet a more prestigious post was now in order for the unemployed relative of three powerful figures, two of them peers. The plums—Vienna, St. Petersburg, and The Hague—were reserved for the more experienced envoys, but on December 24, 1814, a peace treaty had been signed at Ghent with the surprisingly durable and now more important (if still turbulent) American republic, which therefore required a new minister plenipotentiary.

This post had been usually thought of as requiring less acumen than endurance, but what one peer called "that most obstinate and ill disposed set of people" now had a capital in ruins from British arson that seemed to require a tactful, socially prestigious envoy. Castlereagh therefore made the offer to Bagot, who immediately accepted. On June 8, 1815, the prince regent held audience both to install Charles Bagot as His Majesty's minister to the United States and to receive John Quincy Adams, the new minister from the republic. From London, Charles wrote letters to Wellington in Paris, to various relatives, and to Mary, who was vastly unenthused and nursing a sick child in Dover. Bagot emphasized to her the augmented perquisites as showing the enlarged importance of the mission, which would be a better "means of erecting a reputation" than "more convenient but less important posts."[4]

Several correspondents congratulated him, but most illuminating was the reaction of George Canning, now minister to Portugal, to whom his protégé had explained his plan to conquer American contentiousness by kind treatment. The statesman noted for supercilious lectures to the Yankees replied that American "disagreeableness" was immaterial and "amply overbalanced by the peculiar importance of the station." "I am afraid, indeed," the American-baiter continued, "that the question is not so much how you will treat them as how they will treat you, and the hardest lesson which a British minister has to learn in America is not what to do but what to bear." The recent success at Waterloo would be helpful, he added, "after the (to say the least) unbalanced successes and failures of the American war."[5] In August, during Castlereagh's absence, Lord Bathurst prepared Bagot's formal instructions. But although Americans were pressing for a minister to settle postwar problems, delays ensued because Bagot's intended ship was shorthanded and because Mary was expecting another child who Bagot was determined should be born in England. The interim, however, was highly important.

Foreign Secretary Robert, Viscount Castlereagh was only rarely concerned about American matters, and he disdained republicanism about as keenly as any of his predecessors. But while by no means generally receptive to innovation, this handsome, cold, verbally incoherent but courageous aristocrat was a realist. He understood clearly that with a "restored" nationalistic absolutism on the Continent, the frantic anti-American mercantilism of the Stephens-Perceval era with all its political insensitivity was no longer either practical for Britain or acceptable to America. Dominating the British cabinet's foreign policy to a degree unknown since Pitt or Grenville in the 1790s, Castlereagh simultaneously created a new diplomatic roster for the Foreign Office and began to rewrite Anglo-American diplomacy.

Thus, in Paris Ambassador Wellington broke precedent by calling first on America's Minister William Crawford. In London the foreign minister himself undertook the instruction of his new appointee. In written form the substance of these conversations appears best in his instructions to Bagot's successor. Like him, Bagot was told to cultivate American opinion carefully, "always holding in mind that there are no two states whose friendly relations are of more practical value to each other or whose hostility so inevitably and immediately entails upon both the most serious mischiefs." The new minister was told to conduct routine business in person so as to avoid Jackson's debacle, and to keep clear even of the appearance of "desiring to mix in the parties of the country," for, Castlereagh wrote, "we have never derived any advantage . . . but rather the reverse from building . . . on such a foundation."[6] Such instructions given ten years earlier might well have changed the course of Anglo-American diplomacy.

Finally, in December the new minister was sworn a member of the Privy Council to enhance his stature and to please his hosts. In early January, 1816, at Portsmouth, Charles and Mary Bagot and their younger children embarked together with a coachman, groom, maître d'hôtel, French cook, undercook, valet, three footmen, and two housemaids, "(the ugliest I could find)." After seven weeks of rough weather and an earthquake at the Madeira Islands, in March the frigate entered

Chesapeake Bay, "the grandest thing imaginable," Bagot wrote, admiring the vast rivers and large flocks of swans. On March 16 the ship arrived at Annapolis, and when seven British seamen followed invariable custom by leaping from the minister's landing boat to find a career in the republic, Bagot shrewdly broke tradition by attributing this to their own initiative and not to American instigation. Two days later the entourage reached Washington and took up residence at Crawford's Hotel while a mansion at the present Twenty-fourth and L streets was prepared.

Bagot immediately took over from chargé Anthony St. John Baker, whose course since Foster had left him at the capital in 1812 as commissioner of prisoners had shown little of the new conciliation. For illegally using safe-conduct passes left by Foster, the commissioner had been summarily deported, barely saved by Madison from grand jury indictment. At Ghent he had been secretary for the British commissioners and then had languidly brought the peace treaty to America, where he served again as chargé while engaging in active if mild skirmishing with the administration. He was now to become consul general.

On March 20, 1816, Bagot met Monroe at the secretary's office and on the next afternoon was presented to the president. To Bagot, Madison had a yellow and "not a prepossessing countenance" and wore his hair in a pigtail "which I thought had been obsolete." The occasion was mildly pleasant, but if the president's coiffure was obsolete his social canons were novel. Three days after the presentation, a State Department clerk delivered to the embassy new rules of official etiquette differing significantly from the earlier ones in which Bagot had been instructed in England. The new canons "as a matter of hospitality" allowed the British minister and his wife precedence at dinners in their honor, but otherwise both senators and cabinet members would take precedence. When the minister mildly inquired the reasons for the change, Secretary Monroe—a scarred victim of London's matchless official rudeness—merely asked how the rules differed from British practice.[7]

Unlike a famous predecessor, Bagot reported the change with little comment, partly from common sense and partly because sterner tests awaited his professional skill. Rarely had a British diplomat been directed to seek harmony in a capital of such stark public ruins so recently the work of British troops. Smoke-stained and roofless, the Palace and the two capitol wings (particularly the House) were mere gutted walls. Their plastering was streaked and often fallen, their glass chandeliers had collapsed and melted into lumps, their cracked and broken columns had fallen and burned to lime. Formerly beautiful drapes, furniture, and ornaments lay in ashes along with several thousand books from the Congressional library. Offices of the Treasury, State, and Navy departments were gone, as were the arsenal and rope walk. The navy yard and two warships had been burned to prevent capture; three bridges over the Potomac were also destroyed. Five libraries had perished. The pleas of Commissioner William Thornton had saved the Patent Office, but the *National Intelligencer* had paid for its Jeffersonianism with the destruction of its offices, along with a few private homes. The whole scene of ruin, wrote one patriot, was "enough to make one cut his throat if that were a remedy."[8]

Yet the minister found that a sturdy affirmative reaction had occurred even before his arrival. In March, 1815, commissioners for redesigning the capitol had been appointed, and after remarkably short debate the little town's embattled claim to be the national capital had emerged triumphant from the ruins, reaffirmed by both president and Congress. In 1814 Congress had met first in a hotel then in the remodeled post office building. In December it had moved to a privately financed brick building erected for the purpose, where it was to remain for four years until the capitol reconstruction was finished. Meanwhile, the members appropriated rather generously for the restoration of the public buildings on a more elaborate scale than before. Madison had already summoned Benjamin Latrobe, architect of the first capitol, to begin plans for a more ornate structure, and his work was carried on by Charles Bulfinch. The original designer of the Palace, James Hoban, lived in Washington and was commissioned to restore his work, soon to be more generally known as the White House because of its newly whitewashed walls. Meanwhile, the president, in October, 1815, had moved from Tayloe's Octagon House to the corner of the Seven Buildings at Pennsylvania Avenue and Nineteenth Street. Cabinet members worked in various private homes while plans went forward for their new offices.

In the spring of 1816 the capital's social scene reflected the national euphoria. American naval commanders such as Bainbridge, Chauncey, and Rodgers took the lead in smoothing wartime resentments, and Stephen Decatur became a particular friend of both Bagots.

The mild natures of the president and secretary of state helped. Dolley Madison's famous charm enveloped the newcomers, and of this first lady about whom former British envoys had waxed sarcastic, Bagot was careful to be heard saying that "she looked every inch a queen."[9] The president's dinners were simple but elegant, for the French chef, John Sioussa—inherited from Minister Merry—did not allow his alcoholism to affect his excellent cuisine. Other notable hostesses included publisher William Seaton's wife, Mrs. Gallatin, and the wives of Richard Rush and Alexander MacComb. Mornings were spent in rounds of calling, and at two or three in the afternoon most government offices closed. Teas were at six and at private evening parties a profusion of meats, patés, sweetmeats, cakes, punch, and "every species of luxury" appeared. Some members of Congress were encouraged by a salary increase from six dollars a day to fifteen hundred dollars a year and mileage to forsake boardinghouses to purchase or rent houses for their families during the sessions.[10]

Diplomats were traditionally the most sought-after guests, as the Bagots soon discovered. During the war the five members of the corps had spent most of their time in Philadelphia, and some still did. Napoleonic France's Louis Serrurier was now in the capital but was soon to be replaced. Russia's Andre de Daschkoff battled the administration from Philadelphia over the diplomatic immunity of his consul there who was accused of the rape of a twelve-year-old servant. From there also Spain's unglamorous but wily Chevalier Luis d'Onís, whose former Washington residence was to be Bagot's embassy, continued a tradition of complaints to the administration.

Among this feeble competition, blond, handsome Charles Bagot and his dark-haired, beautiful Mary created unrivaled impressions. "Determined to be pleased with everything," they learned names and faces, complimented widely, made innumerable visits, left a stream of cards, and appeared impeccably courteous at every occasion.[11] Mary was both the most beautiful of British diplomats' wives to visit America thus far and also the only wealthy aristocrat. Her flowers, jewels, elaborate costumes, and golden ornaments accentuated her charm. In the Washington of 1816, an Elizabeth Merry or even an Elizabeth Jackson would have been an anachronism; Mary Bagot complemented her husband as the perfect instrument of Castlereagh's rapprochement.

So in his early days Bagot found Washington "a much better city than I expected," and his position "much greater than I conceived when I was in England," though it was "a very arduous and . . . responsible one." He found everyone "uncommonly civil to us" and predicted that "I shall get on here very well . . . it is a grand post, I promise you."[12] His entourage had arrived at the "grand post" during the turmoil of a congressional session, and he summarized for his British correspondents the exotic scene: "Credentials, Congress, Visits, Senators, Consuls, Vice Consuls—[mail] Packets and their agents, Federalists and Madeira, Democrats and Segars, Slaves smelling like cats, Atheists, Methodists, and Cobbetts." Through it all the Bagots moved carefully, "never indulging," he wrote, "in any of the sarcasms of which the people are in constant expectation from every European, and especially from every Englishman." His main target was the anti-British *"malus animus"* that was "the food upon which the . . . predominant party in the country is nourished; but it is much better than it was."

But the postwar winding down was not easy for the Tory sophisticate nor the bumptious exuberant republic. Not only to the ever-suspicious Adamses or the former War Hawk Clay, but also to Jefferson, A. J. Dallas, Gallatin, and many other leaders "the settlement of 1814 was an intermission in the Anglo-American quarrel, not adjournment *sine die*." Prominent men took care to avoid excessive proximity to the British minister, and Bagot admitted that if traveling alone as a minister, he would be "exposed to have many disagreeable things said to him in public."[13] Nor was the *malus animus* entirely one-sided. To Whitehall, Jefferson never ceased to be the revolutionary Jacobin philosopher whose frantic Anglophobia produced most of the evils of American republicanism.

Bagot, warned by Castlereagh, was less acerbic, but he had all of the prejudices of his class. Partly from the hyperbole in which he and his friends wrote, partly from a shrewd desire to have his sacrifices and discomforts reach official London, and partly from sheer exasperation, the publicly urbane and gracious minister privately sent home a torrent of ridicule and disconsolate complaint along with subtle evidence of his successes in acquiring personal popularity and national goodwill. "I hope," he wrote soon after arrival, "that I have more '*nous*' than not to see how fortunate I am in having been placed in this situation, but I have neither society or pleasure—my business is my only amusement and of that I promise you that there is plenty."

As to the war, he wrote to his friend Thomas Hamilton, Lord Binning, the Americans "have certainly gained reputation . . . but they have lost nearly everything else, and I verily believe that they could not have maintained it six months longer." It *was* annoying to Wellington's nephew to hear "now and then a sly, sneaking, side face hint that Wellington is inferior in the military art to General Jackson, and that Nelson, Rodney, and St. Vincent were mere bunglers and drivellers in naval tactics when compared with Rodgers, Decatur and the *handsome* Porter."

American society, the minister privately confided to his cousin John Sneyd, was "abominable—a vulgarity . . . which we have not now the species in England . . . made of jealousy, vanity, suspicion, formality, dullness, gossip, pride, and sneakroot . . . I . . . had no idea til I came here how painful it is to live continually with rousing vulgars . . . The men are better than the women, they are all tolerably well informed . . . but the women are dolefully uncultivated."[14] Mary Bagot in a sarcastic journal and biting private letters also chastised her hosts for everything from their idioms to their addiction to charades and their use of knives for eating jellies or sherbets. In London her grandmother told drawing-room guests (including embarrassed American strangers) that Mary had written it was "worse and worse there . . . She never saw such unreasonable, ill-bred people as those Americans." This and other contretemps by Princess Charlotte frightened Bagot, and both he and Mary warned their friends not to repeat what they received in letters lest the consequences be fatal.

A major cause of the Bagots' private unhappiness was sheer physical discomfort, crowned by that *bête noire* of all British envoys, the American summer. In June they had moved to their new house and Charles wrote to Sneyd "if you had got into it you would hang yourself or die of dust and baldness and red brick . . . Recollect that it is stark new, and built with unseasoned wood, that it rings like a vault—that the doors won't shut and the windows won't open, and that it stands in a wilderness of brick kilns." Then summer descended. "A pint of American summer," the minister wrote, "would thaw all Europe in ten minutes. Sir, it is dreadful—it is deleterious—it leads to madness. Ice houses take fire and scream because they cannot bear it." Three days later he added, "I am dissolved. Shadrach was no such great fellow after all . . . The President, who is gone into Virginia for the summer, has left me the use of his ice house, a thousand blessings attend him." When the thermometer went to 90 degrees for two days he felt he would die, but was "saved" by a thunderstorm; "Your thunderstorms in Europe are squibs and crackers to them here."

The sweltering minister found no compensating pleasures. "There is nothing to eat in this place," he wrote Binning. "My cook is in despair—has run through all the changes of which bad necks of mutton are capable and is now stranded." He also found the cost of living, of which Foster had warned him, appalling, as did his predecessors. "Almost everything is almost twice as dear as in London except bread and butcher's meat. I am as stingy as a weasel and determined not to be ruined, but I am sometimes terrified." Escape by travel was ruled out because Bagot unlike the Listons found that "travelling is detestable in this country unless one travels in a gig or on horseback by oneself and can learn to dispense with separate bed and board, which the English Minister cannot do if he were inclined. . . . Moreover, [the urbanite added] when one has seen the principal cities, one great river, and one great forest, an accurate idea can be formed of all the rest. It is impossible to travel in winter, and in summer it is too hot to walk across the room."[15]

All his private frustrations failed to affect the minister's public poise. Moreover, he was no mere Augustus Foster, and after Congress adjourned at the end of April, he began a series of able dispatches to Castlereagh on significant congressional legislation. He also described William H. Crawford's presidential ambitions as ended by Monroe's endorsement by Congressional Republicans "in what is called a caucus" and defined this for His Lordship with accurate succinctness as "a meeting of such members of both Houses of Congress as may choose to assemble for the discussion and promotion of any particular measure."[16]

It was Bagot's supreme good fortune that in 1816 the Anglo-American world had little to quarrel about. Instead of his predecessors' flaming exchanges with American statesmen over impressment, ship seizures, and blockades, Bagot usually had only to deliberate with successive secretaries of state over implementations of agreements made in principle at Ghent or to deal with subjects on which British and American interests largely coincided. During his tenure only a few matters generated heat, and the few important problems unwound slowly over his three years in America.

Grounds for the most immediate of his achievements were laid even before his arrival. In November, 1815, President Madison, faced with Congressional reluctance to continue warship building on the Great Lakes, proposed through Minister John Quincy Adams in London that both nations reduce their armed vessels there to a fixed number, using these only for revenue patrol. Castlereagh's favorable if languid reply roused Adams's ready pessimism, but he subsequently raised the matter again and received a warmer response, since the foreign secretary recognized the burden of a naval construction race in the American wilderness. Adams lacked specific powers to conclude an agreement, so somewhat to Castlereagh's relief the matter was shifted to Washington, where Madison had already opened the subject with a then uninstructed Bagot. In July his instructions arrived, less sweeping in degree than the president and Secretary Monroe had wanted; however, the minister used the discretion given him to make further reductions, and in August, 1816, agreement was reached in three letters exchanged between Bagot and Monroe. After the usual delays, the Foreign Office concurred in January, 1817. In April of that year Bagot and Acting Secretary Richard Rush signed the convention, to which the Senate gave unanimous approval in April, 1818. It limited ships of both nations on Lake Ontario and the upper lakes and Lake Champlain, ended construction, and engaged both nations to use ships only in revenue law enforcement. It was a significant step in better attitudes and the relaxation of tensions. Castlereagh complimented his envoy warmly on his role, which was professionally minor but personally soothing.[17]

Since nearly all the other important diplomatic decisions of the next few years were made in London, Bagot's dispatches of his first year in America were primarily efforts to conciliate. Bagot dealt with the return of deserting seamen and of prisoners and of slaves carried off in the war; he defended America from charges of abetting West Indian privateering; and he dismissed the constant rumors of plots hatched in America to rescue Napoleon as "but the history of the reveries with which the exiled officers of France may naturally be supposed to beguile their time." More seriously, since Americans took a keen interest in the success of the rebellions in Spain's Latin American colonies, Bagot warily watched filibusters organized to aid the rebels. Of these momentous revolts he privately admitted to Canning that "I cannot make head or tail of the whole business, all I know is that the Patriots are all rascals"; but he pressed his friend privately and Castlereagh officially to define Britain's policy on Latin American independence—a "political problem," he wrote, "of no easy solution."

In other gestures of goodwill, Bagot shattered a cherished British dream by telling border Indian tribes not to expect British aid in the north during conflicts over Americans' encroachment. He restored to America lands along the Canadian border and hastened the demolition of Canadian forts in American territory. He refused to protest with Portugal's minister about the American reception of an envoy from rebellious Brazil or to Daschkoff over the Russian consul's arrest in Philadelphia. He reviewed sympathetically the petitions of allegedly impressed American seamen. And he made numerous inquiries and requests of London on behalf of Americans for favors to relatives, inventions, or literary recognition. Travelers to Britain were received at the embassy with marked attention and flattered with letters of introduction. These predictably resulted in high praises for the Bagots in London along with stories of Charles and Mary's immense popularity and influence in Washington.[18]

Meanwhile, the round of balls, teas, visits, and presidential levees continued. Charles relaxed his opposition to travel, and they visited Judge Bushrod Washington at Mount Vernon. Mary's journal described the scenery en route as wild but the roads more so, and though commanding a magnificent view, the mansion was in bad repair and admitted rats and winds. They visited the general's tomb, which she described as looking "exactly like an ice house, with a wooden door and key hold," and then spent "a *long* evening" featured by children, talk, and music.

In September the Bagots went to Philadelphia despite Foster's warning that if they did so they would lose their servants to "a set" of democrats "who delight to debauch newcomers and tempt them to become gentlemen at large." The Bagots braved this danger in order to meet their new and capable Secretary of Legation Crawfurd Antrobus, just out from England, whom Bagot immediately liked. Before moving on to New York they stayed a week in the Quaker City, where the social and official entertainment was so lavish that Bagot wrote a friend that he "never went through so severe a duty in my life, though it was very flattering." Then came a visit to the nearby home of the new French minister Baron Guillaume-Jean Hyde de Neuville. This large, usually genial Ultra-Royalist and his wife liked America and society, and the splendor of their equipage rivaled that of the Bagots. In New York, Bagot visited the much-respected Rufus King. Then, on learning from the newspapers of the death of Mary's sister, the family returned to the capital. A sad winter followed, for Charles's brother William died in England, and their own older children were there in school. "It is now," the minister wrote, "that I feel the immense distance which separates me from all I love . . . Remember me to all that care about me and recollect that I exist."

In that subdued winter in "my great comfortless house," his relief was in hopeful words from home. Father-in-law Wellesley-Pole wrote "We learn from all quarters that you have succeeded in being most popular . . . your dispatches are very much approved." Castlereagh was flattering, and at the Foreign Office Bagot was called the most promising of the younger diplomats. Canning also wrote approvingly, and American visitors in London gave Bagot's friends "such an account as never was heard of yours and Mrs. Bagot's popularity and influence."[19]

Spurred on by such reports, the naturally indolent Bagot entered upon "a prodigious winter, the busiest, the coldest, the ball-est, the tea-est, the dinner-est I ever passed . . . I have worked harder and done more disagreeable things in the past four months than I ever did in my whole preceding life." On March 4, 1817, Monroe's inaugural committee planned the first outdoor inaugural since Washington's. It was held in a portico outside Congress's temporary meeting hall and produced the largest crowd of civilian spectators yet to view an inaugural. However, a disagreement had arisen over Speaker Clay's desire to preside and his refusal to use the Senate's red plush chairs rather than the House's "plain democratic" ones. As a result, until a half hour before the president reached the Capitol, no seats had been prepared for the diplomatic corps, and when a "tribune" was hastily erected the diplomats were not informed of it. They therefore did not attend, which, Bagot reported, gave rise to "conjectures" and "some uneasiness." After the president returned to his home, however, the diplomats went "in state" to pay their respects and they attended the evening ball in his honor.[20]

Monroe named probably the most able cabinet since Washington's first one. Richard Rush headed the State Department until John Quincy Adams should return from London, when they would exchange positions. William Crawford, able if artful, was at the Treasury. John C. Calhoun, whom Bagot reported as a "young man of superior abilities and of considerable distinction as a public speaker," presided over the War Department, and William Wirt, "an eminent lawyer," was attorney general. Of Monroe himself the young Tory minister had a curious view. In the erect, gray-haired, fifty-nine-year-old veteran of the Revolution clad in old-fashioned small clothes, knee britches, and silk hose, Bagot perceived "a man 'altogether of a foxy appearance'" with "fingers itching to play king."

In his political strategy as well as in his own personality, the last of the Virginia Dynasty eluded the minister's full comprehension. President Monroe sought to introduce more social formality and administrative system to the executive office and to co-opt or compel the Federalists into a slightly modified Madisonian republicanism that would be acceptable to the vast majority of his countrymen. As a symbol of this unity, in May he began a tour of the northern and eastern states patterned after the first president's, and Bagot saw the unexpected success of the tour not as a change of sentiment in the Federalists but in Monroe himself. The president, the minister reported to Castlereagh, had become aware of "the evils to which the Executive government of the country has been exposed by the license of Democratic principles" and was trying "to put the whole system of the government upon a different and higher footing and to restore it to that strength and dignity of which it was so entirely divested by the doctrines and examples of Mr. Jefferson and his successor."

In short, the Boston *Columbian Centinel*'s famous "Era of Good Feelings" was, according to the minister, to be an era of Neo-Federalism. The Federalists were willing to help, but Henry Clay and many new western members of Congress "chosen from an inferior class of citizens" (as a reaction to a recently voted salary raise) were raising a western party to chastise him for his apostasy to Old Republicanism. Thus, the Tory envoy, like his predecessors, confused nationalism with Federalism. More understandably he could not foresee the role of the new secretary of state. Nor could he imagine that from the forests, canebrakes, and muddy rivers of the Florida frontier a shock-haired, impetuous brigadier general would soon burst upon the international scene to undermine political unity and to destroy his own peace of mind.

In late March, 1817, a relieved Bagot wrote to his cousin John Sneyd:

> The Congress and the frost are both broke up. Mr. Monroe . . . has been made king of these parts. The diplomatic body (D— their souls) is gone to Phiddledelphia, and I begin to have mine ease . . . In England as far as I recollect you have a small sort of summer consisting chiefly of roses, swallows, trouts, bees, peas, buttermilk, and things of that kind. Here we have the frog, the fever, the locust, lizard, blackamoor, thunderstorm, and all the sublimer features of that charming season of which I shall in about six months have the full enjoyment.[21]

Despite these gloomy features and the usual summer departure of most officials from the capital, the minister continued his social and professional rounds, broken only by a visit to the Madisons in the "Blue Mountains of Virginia." His mail carried the usual reports of American plots to free Napoleon, but other matters were more serious and persistent. One was the very complex question of the "right" or "liberty" of Americans to fish in the waters of the Gulf of St. Lawrence and to dry and cure fish on the shores of Ontario and Newfoundland provinces and various islands. Complicated by American politics, pre-1812 bellicosity, and smuggling operations, the problem at Ghent had been referred for further discussion. Castlereagh was determined to find an amicable solution and in 1816 sent Bagot "instructions four miles long" and full powers to make a convention, which the nervous minister privately confessed "frightens me to death." His three separate proposals had been refused by the administration and were now stalled awaiting the president's return.

Technical questions also arose through American shippers who already dominated the direct trade to Britain but now sniffed at the closed West Indian routes. "My opinion upon commercial matters is a very poor one," Bagot confessed privately to his friend Undersecretary Joseph Planta, and he further admitted that he could not answer Castlereagh's inquiries on the West Indies trade "in any satisfactory manner." Furthermore, the controversy over recognizing the governments of Spain's rebellious South American subjects was warming up. An American commission was preparing to examine the strength of the new governments, and Bagot had no instructions as to Downing Street's policy. Mishandling any of these touchy matters could imperil his reputation, of which favorable reports were now reaching London in gratifying numbers.[22]

The long, scorching summer was closing when on September 20, 1817, Secretary of State John Quincy Adams arrived at the capital to take up his new office in a large brick building on the present Seventeenth Street opposite G Street NW. The new secretary—short, plump, and bald—combined rigid independence, courage, and immense capacity for labor with a puritan pessimism and censoriousness that did not spare himself. His fiercely republican nationalism, his family history, and perhaps a subconscious envy made him predisposed against Britain, and he immediately perceived British Minister Bagot's intellectual limitations. Yet, despite an occasional clash, the secretary (called "Squintz" by Bagot and his friends because of an eye weakness caused by excessive reading) never subjected the minister to the violent verbal assaults he inflicted on Hyde de Neuville, Onís, and even Bagot's successor. For his part, Bagot entirely agreed with his friend W. H. Lyttleton's picture of Adams when both were diplomats at St. Petersburg: ". . . doggedly and systematically repulsive. With a vinegar aspect, cotten in his leathern ears, and hatred to England in his heart . . . I tried in vain to mitigate his venom."[23] The uniquely amicable relationship of Adams and Bagot, concealing a disdain on one side and on the other a tolerance of lesser talents, is a tribute to both men. In September when Adams arrived, the president had already returned from his tour in the East, but since the White House still reeked of plaster he left immediately for a month in Virginia. Adams gave up a visit to Madison on learning that the Bagots were at Montpelier, for, Adams explained, "I think it will be better to avoid a meeting at your house with the British minister."

On his own return to the capital Bagot began his most acrimonious exchanges with the secretary of state. On Monroe's order, but without informing the Englishman, Adams had sent Capt. James Biddle in the American warship *Ontario* to the remote Oregon coast to receive the return of a fort at the mouth of the Columbia River. Founded as Astoria by John Jacob Astor in 1811, sold to British traders, and then during the war placed under the British flag as Fort George by the captain of a British sloop of war, the fort was now to be returned by terms of the Treaty of Ghent. Biddle and a civil commissioner were also to assert American claims to sovereignty over the territory. Bagot was infuriated both by Adams's failure to inform him and by the American claim to the area; heated interviews followed, marked by sarcasm on Adams's part, outrage on Bagot's, and some ignorance of past events on the part of both. Fortunately, Castlereagh, as Adams dryly predicted, wanted no serious quarrel "on account of the occupation of so remote a territory," and after instructing Bagot to make some protest over Adams's secrecy and on American claims, the foreign secretary ordered the fort restored to the Americans, which was done in October, 1818.[24]

By that time events in London had laid the Oregon matter temporarily to rest. In July, 1818, Minister Richard Rush's suggestion of a broad negotiation was accepted by Castlereagh. Rush (in Bagot's summary "civil, shallow, prig, lawyer") was joined from the Paris embassy by Albert Gallatin, a particular *bête noire* of Bagot's, to whom he was "that sly Genevan" and "the Talleyrand of this country and the greatest rogue (always excepting Mr. Thomas Jefferson.)" These able representatives, together with Britain's Frederick J. Robinson and Henry Goulburn, under Castlereagh's benign auspices, produced the highly important Convention of 1818. Among other matters discussed were the Canadian boundary and Oregon sovereignty problems, Atlantic commercial relations, a compromise on the fishing controversy, and the long-festering impressment controversy. The Convention was signed in London in October, 1818, and ratified in Washington the next January. The Convention, together with the Great Lakes agreement, was a diplomatic peak in Bagot's tour, even though Bagot had a limited role in the former and almost nothing to do with the latter.[25]

The long session of the Fifteenth Congress met in December, 1817 and was not to adjourn until May, 1818. As always, the session brought a large increase in the capital's population. The Supreme Court also met, and foreign diplomats (now nine) were told by the administration that they were expected to live in Washington. Cheaper passenger rates on the steamboats together with profits from the land and cotton boom produced a migration of businessmen, families of congressmen, and casual travelers and curiosity seekers from every part of the Union. Bagot felt compelled "to receive in some way or other every man of consequence" whom the session drew. In addition he accepted most invitations, and in three months said he had returned "over 400 visits."

To most diplomats' relief, James Monroe ended the social informality of his predecessors. All members of the corps were treated equally, but there were no more casual drop-in visits to the White House. Envoys were received along with other guests on alternate Wednesdays, on national holidays, and at the usual twice-weekly presidential dinners. Protocol, including that for arriving and departing diplomats, was modeled on the prince regent's; other professional business was conducted more strictly through the secretary of state.

Meanwhile, balls, parties, teas, and receptions occurred almost nightly in private homes or hotels. Mrs. Monroe was usually in frail health and, caring little for society, relegated most duties to her married daughter, but her own ornate costumes and the beautiful new imported furniture and accessories in the restored White House drew large crowds. Mrs. Adams gave well-attended Tuesday evening receptions, and every leading minister gave more than one glittering ball that featured a lavish supper. At less ornate affairs the hosts were the vice-president, cabinet members, and the speaker of the House. Many evening parties, including balls, had rooms set aside for whist and chess players. Mary Bagot's beauty, dress, and manners continued to be a favorite subject; with Secretary Antrobus, Christopher Hughes, and others she danced the new and daring waltz Senator Otis reported, "to the dismay of all mothers." Such constant entertaining necessarily extended the social reason from the prewar six weeks to ten, from early December to late February.

From this social hubbub Bagot wrote Canning "I continue to be very civil . . . but . . . I have been so long so very polite that I think that if I ever get home again I shall be stark rude for several years in order to ease myself." One testimony to this civility was a note sent to the *Intelligencer* by "Diplomaticus Observatus" praising the "native urbanity of manners which eminently distinguishes you" and assuring him that "you are by far the most popular of your predecessors." At the same time the object of this admiration was writing to Canning "I am worn out and quite exhausted . . . and I am bilious and worried, and I wish Columbus was damned, and Dr. Franklin, and Pocahuntas [*sic*], and Sir Walter Raleigh, and Jackson and Liston and General Washington." But to Binning he vowed to go "sufferingly and doggedly on through the nuisances of a long Congress and till it is over and till the wild and hairy delegates of which it is composed are gone back into their woods and wigwams." With all his private grumbling that "I lead a horrible life," Bagot knew that "I have done and am doing essential service to the State" and hoped to leave Anglo-American relations "in a more favorable state than they have been for several years."[26]

Meanwhile Congress's "wild and hairy delegates" were not according to Britain the same courtesies that "Observatus" gave to its minister. They refused to license British traders in the northwest, and both houses passed further trade restrictions. As usual, Bagot was bored with commercial diplomacy: "Imports be damned and exports be damned. May the two tonnages, foreign and domestic, be both damned. Damn the coasting trade and the colonial system. Damn the codfish on the great bank of Newfoundland. Damn the sea island cottons, neutral bottoms, and the three Secretaries of State." Onís and Hyde de Neuville still harried him with plots supposedly to seize pirate-infested Galveston Island off the Texas coast or Amelia Island off Florida, or to place a Bonaparte on a throne in one of the Latin American colonies. At least, Bagot was relieved to find, the administration in spite of Clay's congressional rhetoric was still cool to a quick recognition of the former colonies as sovereign states.[27]

Spanish East Florida was a more serious matter. There an almost total deterioration of Spanish authority had made it a haven for runaway slaves as well as a base of operations for Seminoles and Creeks in the wilderness warfare of the Alabama-Georgia-Florida frontier. Through the business of furnishing supplies to the Indians or through general adventuring, various British subjects, usually from the Bahamas, had become advisors to the Indians. One of them, Col. Edward Nicholls, had actually made a treaty with the Creeks on behalf of Britain after the war, and the government's disavowal had not been so well publicized as the official reception of the Indians in London. Later, two other Britons, George Woodbine and Lt. Robert Ambrister, continued encouraging Indian resistance to American exploitation. A more humane and honest figure, Scottish trader Alexander Arbuthnot, meanwhile sought assistance for the Indians as early as January, 1817, and again in April, 1818, from both Consul Moodie at Charleston and Minister Bagot in Washington. The latter had promptly refused to meddle, for, he wrote, despite the Indians' "just complaint," "any interference on my part in behalf of the Indians within the United States but more especially those engaged in the operations of Colonel Nicholls in 1814" would antagonize the administration contrary to his instructions. The situation was further complicated by widespread American suspicion of British activity and fear that Spain might transfer the province to Britain before America could obtain it as part of the Louisiana Purchase or by other means. Minister Onís's strategy had therefore been to embroil Britain and America over Florida, and he sought a British mediation between America and Spain. Through such a diplomatic thicket Bagot had moved with great caution. Neither he nor Castlereagh really

Charles Bagot

wanted British mediation, and both were clearly relieved when Adams courteously declined their offer.[28]

Into this delicate situation burst the figure of Brig. Gen. Andrew Jackson with some twenty-five hundred various troops and a gunboat. In December, 1817, he had been ordered (by an administration that probably guessed but did not want to know his intentions) to proceed to the Georgia-Spanish frontier to avenge the Indians' slaughter of thirty-four ill soldiers and seven women. After some preliminary operations in deep southwestern Georgia, the general in March, 1818, crossed the frontier and built Fort Gadsden in Spanish West Florida. From there he dispersed the Seminoles, and moving deeper into Spanish Florida, captured the Spanish fort of St. Mark's, over which he raised the American flag. There Jackson also found and imprisoned trader Arbuthnot.

In the course of further penetration into the Florida wilderness, where he hanged some hostile Indian chiefs, Jackson by chance captured the fatally adventurous Lieutenant Ambrister. With him were his servants and some papers; these incriminated Arbuthnot in warning the Indians of his approach, as did some papers found on the trader's schooner. Jackson promptly tried British subjects Arbuthnot and Ambrister by courts martial, the former for acting as a spy and inciting the Indians and the latter for aiding the enemy and levying war against the United States. The two were found guilty and Arbuthnot was hanged and Ambrister shot on April 29, 1818. The general, after acrimonious exchanges with the Spanish governor at Pensacola, then captured two forts there, seized the archives, established American tax collection, and appointed a governor. Then Jackson returned to Tennessee.

The first news of this irruption reached Washington by June 18, 1818. Although personally infuriated, Minister Bagot made enough sense out of it to know that the matter was "of so grave a character" and involved "so many questions of such a serious nature" that he acted with the greatest care. Whereas his dispatches described Jackson's "unjust and sanguinary proceedings" as "perhaps totally unparalleled in the history of warfare" and while in private he denounced the "crying outrage" of the general's "flagrant injustice, duplicity, and savage cruelty," nevertheless he declined to join Hyde de Neuville and Onís in an angry protest over the invasion and merely pressed Adams for records of the court martial proceedings. Meanwhile he reported that Monroe's cabinet was divided on what to do about Jackson and that the whole matter had become embroiled in domestic politics, from which he predicted accurately that Jackson would be exonerated.

The wisdom of his restraint was soon evident. Some of the papers found by Jackson disclosed the activities of Woodbine and Nicholls and strongly implied a certain amount of knowledge of, if not connivance in, Indian affairs by the British government. As newspapers took up the old cry of "British perfidy," the minister found himself increasingly on the defensive. Although supported from London by evidence of British innocence, the minister found it expedient not to attend the House debates on Jackson.

In London, popular opinion was divided, and the slow arrival of full information on the episode helped dampen excitement. Most important, Castlereagh had no intention of endangering the Convention of 1818 and was deep in preparation for the congress to be held at Aix-la-Chapelle. So while London buzzed with some anti-American tirades, the foreign secretary merely chided Rush gently, bragged of his own self-restrained reaction, and in November, 1818, to Bagot's immense relief, approved fully of his cautious course. Following Adams's bristling defense of Jackson written in reply to Spain's protest, the Spanish ceded Florida to America in the Adams-Onís Treaty (signed in Washington on February 22, 1819), which closed the diplomatic importance of the matter though it did not dampen Bagot's enduring fury at the general.[29]

The Jackson episode from the spring to the close of 1818 was the last of Bagot's diplomatic tempests but not of his informative dispatches. His last American months brought Bagot both personal tribulations and triumphs. Two years of complaints to his friends over the labor and tedium of his work and his own deteriorating health added to private petitions for a return to England had produced some praise from his father-in-law mixed with dire warnings of disaster to his career if he left his post too soon. Friendly hints of the same dangers came from his friend Undersecretary Planta, and Wellington had earlier cautioned Mary, so in May, 1818, Bagot had backed off.

To Planta he denied excessive "wear and tear and expenditure of constitution," blaming a solicitous wife for those reports. "She sees me thin and often suffering from bilious headaches and looking the colour of a kite's foot," Bagot wrote, mixing apology and evidence, "and she very naturally thinks that I am more seriously unwell than I am. I do not believe that I am radically unwell; that is, that my liver is affected." He assured the undersecretary that he was "aware of the great trust that is in my hands" and that his performance with it would determine his professional future. However, this letter crossed with one from Planta who, personally concerned for him and perhaps under pressure from Bagot relatives, enclosed a conditional leave of absence.

This was the usual signal for release, but when Bagot received it in July, 1818, the Jackson affair was in full cry and Washington sweltered in a tremendously hot summer, "thermometers up at 100," he wrote, "men and horses (the latter I know to my cost) dropping down dead at every corner with it." Late in that summer Mary and the children came down with fevers, and later Bagot himself succumbed to one for the first time. It left him shaken and "taught me to dread this climate in a way that I had never done before." In December, still convalescing, he determined to leave the following spring.[30]

Still, neither Jackson nor illness could darken the winter's social season. On September 3 Mary presented him with their fifth daughter, their seventh child. In anticipation Charles had triumphantly obtained the prince regent's consent to be Georgiana Bagot's sponsor in baptism. Secretary Adams had agreed to attend the baptism, but when Monroe became uneasy at the rumor that his secretary would be proxy for royalty, Adams declined to attend, considerably annoyed at the president's timidity. An elaborate ball followed the ceremony, complete with the heraldic insignia of the prince, and gleaming plate and exotic dishes were ranged on a three-tiered table described by a Protestant senator as "producing somewhat the effect of a handsome Roman Catholic altar." Mary as always was striking, in a low-cut dress of silk, muslin, and lamé with diamonds and feathers. Even Bagot pronounced the affair "prodigious fine" although he had been dreading last-minute news of the queen's death and "my tarts and jellies stood trembling in the larder lest they should have to turn into funeral baked meats."[31]

All winter Bagot was sustained by visions of spring when he could "gladden my eyes once again with the sight of gentlemen and a good warm monarchy." Meanwhile he basked in reports of praise like that which had sustained him throughout his "pilgrimage." Planta wrote of Castlereagh's gratification "with your prudence and with the whole of your conduct in the affair of Arbuthnot and Ambrister." Undersecretary William Hamilton commended him for recognition "in a country where our countrymen have never before gained civic or I might almost say military honor before." The lord lieutenant of Ireland, a personal friend, sent congratulations on his reputation for success. At a Wellesley-Pole dinner party that included Wellington, Rush spoke of the satisfaction that Bagot's career there had given Americans and was directed by Monroe to say so to Castlereagh. The admiralty arranged for a fifty-gun frigate to bring his family home. In Philadelphia he was asked to sit for a portrait for a citizen's gallery of notables. As his departure day approached, Adams gave a dinner honoring three departing ministers, Bagot, Hyde de Neuville, and Onís, and in his final interview with the Englishman spoke handsomely of his accomplishments.[32]

Bagot's triumph in "exile" was a staggering civic compliment: a public ball in his honor, arranged by a bipartisan Congressional committee. He was immensely gratified by the notification, but "knowing the country as I do now," feared "at least a very disagreeable newspaper discussion and perhaps worse effects." But the invitation committee membership and the subscribers showed him that the event was obviously to be "no party affair." The occasion was a success, though Adams—ever envious of another's honors—wrote in his diary that "unpleasant circumstances" occurred. The guests were impressive in number and quality: the secretaries of state, war, and navy; all the Supreme Court; the army's commanding general; Commodores Rodgers and Decatur; the French, Prussian, and Dutch ministers; and many members of both houses of Congress. The Bagots' names were in transparencies, and entwined American and British flags decorated the tables. Upon the toast to the honorees the band played "God Save the King" and all rose, whereupon Bagot quickly asked a manager to have it immediately followed by "Yankee Doodle," so that "not a murmer [sic] was heard." His own brief acknowledgments were sanitarily nonpolitical. All the details he proudly and privately described to Planta as "symptomatic" and with a request to pass them on to Castlereagh or destroy the letter according to the underscretary's judgment. Bagot had earned his triumph, for the honor was unthinkable for any predecessor and especially gratifying but five years after the war and not quite three after his arrival.[33]

The ensuing weeks slipped away in preparations for departure and sales of embassy equipment. On April 14, the president being on his southern tour, Bagot called on Secretary Adams to take formal leave and to present Crawfurd Antrobus as chargé. The next day Charles and Mary with a secretary and four servants left for Annapolis to await the

Charles Bagot 195

frigate *Forth*. The children remained with Antrobus, which was wise for not until May 4 was the ship ready to sail. The *Intelligencer* editorialized that the departing minister was "the most popular and therefore the most useful minister that his government has ever sent to this country." Perhaps that article was written by Secretary Adams, for in his diary he provided with some chagrin the most apt summary of Bagot:

> The principal feature of his character is discretion . . . but neither his intellectual powers nor his acquisitions are in any degree striking. He has no depth of dissimulation, though enough to suppress his feelings when it is for his interest to conceal them . . . He has made himself universally acceptable. No English minister has ever been so popular; and the mediocrity of his talents has been one of the principal causes of his success. This is so obvious that it has staggered my belief in the universality of the maxim that men of the greatest talents ought to be sought out for diplomatic missions. Bagot has been a better Minister than a much abler man would have been: better for the interest of England better for the tranquility of this country—better for the harmony between the two nations, for his own quiet, and for the comfort of those with whom he has had official intercourse here.[34]

Unfortunately for Bagot, his career after the American success required more talent than charm. After a triumphant return to Britain he was created a Knight Grand Cross of the Order of the Bath and was later awarded the St. Petersburg embassy. Well received and a lavish host, Bagot did good work in the arbitration over slaves carried off during the 1812 war. But his heart was set on The Hague as closer to home, healthier, more prestigious, and pleasanter; when he was disavowed in 1824 for a diplomatic misstep in Russia, Canning, again the foreign secretary, gave Bagot the Dutch post. There he remained in a close, playful relationship with his idol until Canning's death in 1827.

After the separation of Holland and Belgium in 1832, Bagot accepted a brief errand to Vienna, then declined an appointment in India for reasons of climate. In 1841 he went to Canada as governor general, a position he had formerly deprecated. By now he had become temperamentally more imperious, and after a brief tenure marked by some controversy, he was rebuked by the colonial secretary. Bagot requested recall in March, 1843, but he died in Kingston, Ontario, in May of that year at the age of sixty-two.[35] Long before then, Bagot's successor in America had demonstrated John Quincy Adams's pained conclusion that for the British minister to America at least, intelligence was no substitute for civility.

Stratford Canning

"He is a proud, high-tempered Englishman, of good but not extraordinary parts; stubborn and punctillious, with a disposition to be overbearing, which I have often been compelled to check in its own way."
—John Q. Adams Diary, June 24, 1823

"The real truth is, even setting aside the climate, and local annoyances, that habits, principles, opinions, and interests such as ours are all fundamentally at variance with those which prevail on this side of the ocean."
—Stratford Canning to Charles Bagot, July 28, 1821

BEYOND a common willingness to accept discomfort, each of the eight British ministers to pre-Jacksonian America owed his appointment to individual specifics. Hammond was a personal favorite of William Grenville, Merry was a bureaucrat chosen to do a journeyman's job, and Erskine's appointment arose from a rare policy and party change. The choices of Foster and of Bagot rested primarily on powerful family connections, and Liston and Jackson were sent for opposite qualities already displayed in action. Of the eight, only Canning represented a combination of family connections, diplomatic success, and the high regard of two foreign secretaries. Also, for him alone the American experience was a minor episode in a long and very distinguished career overseas, and he alone rose to the peerage. On the other hand, his American tour illustrated that even when animosities were reduced, the divergence of national interests defied the high intellect of dedicated men.

Although Stratford Canning was the quintessential English Tory, his ancestors, like those of Foster, Castlereagh, Wellington, and George Canning, were Irish. The grandfather for whom he was named was nicknamed Counselor Canning for his reputed legal knowledge and was called by a biographer "not sociable," with a character of "extreme austerity." His children long recalled the terror inspired by his squeaking shoes as he walked about the house. He later demonstrated the authenticity of their fears by disinheriting and banishing two of his three sons. The eldest, George, suffered from Whig views and marriage to a penniless girl, went to England, and there died destitute in 1771, a year after the birth of his namesake son, the future foreign secretary and prime minister.

The Counselor's youngest son, Stratford, married an able and admirable woman, Mehitabel Patrick. She also failed to suit the senior Stratford, whose ready fury extended not only to disinheriting this son but also to persuading kinfolk to do likewise. Young Stratford, like his brother, went to London, but he prospered modestly in a mercantile firm and fathered a daughter and four sons and rescued his nephew George from a miserable life with his widowed actress mother. The merchant's kindnesses to his nephew before his own early death were amply repaid in later years by George's assistance to his cousin Stratford, seventeen years his junior.

Stratford Canning the diplomat was born on November 4, 1786, in St. Clement's Lane. His first formal education was in a small school in the Essex village to which his mother had retired after his father's death. His real training began in 1795, when his cousin George entered him in the lower school at Eton. Here he formed the essential aristocratic personal associations and on trips to London dined with George and political friends, heard Pitt and Burke in the Commons, and began his lifetime ambition for a career in Parliament. At Eton his personality took shape. In his first biographer's words he was "chary of his friendships," "not indiscriminately sociable," and "fond of his own thoughts." The idealistic, rigidly moral boy had little in common with most of his roistering schoolmates and spent his time in solitary walks and reading. Strikingly handsome, impatient, and fastidious, with an intellectual conceit fed by a small coterie of admirers, young Canning was, as he later admitted, "something of a prig," and he remained one.

In July, 1806, he was admitted to King's College, Cambridge, but the following year George Canning became foreign secretary in the Portland government and immediately gave his cousin the humble but instructive job of précis writer. Shortly thereafter, in mid-1807, he was appointed second secretary to Anthony Merry. At that time Merry's foredoomed effort was an alliance with Denmark, whose capital had just been destroyed by the British fleet after declining Francis Jackson's ultimatum. The Danes refused even to observe, in Stratford's words, "the gentle manners of the gentlest of plenipotentiaries," so Merry sailed to Sweden. There the mischievous fates that had already contrived to render "Toujours Gai" mildly ridiculous in his opening audiences with both Napoleon in Paris and Jefferson in Washington intervened again in an interview with Gustavus IV in Helsinborg; soon thereafter the mission returned home.[1]

Six months later Stratford Canning was sent by his cousin to the Ottoman Empire as secretary of embassy under Sir Robert Adair, who was to bring peace to an inconvenient state of war between Britain and the Empire and did so by the Treaty of Dardanelles in early January, 1809. Adair was then meant to go to Vienna as ambassador when Austria felt it safe to consider a British alliance. The foreign secretary seized the opportunity to appoint young Stratford in July, 1809, to be ad interim minister to the Ottoman Empire after his chief's departure. Though the Vienna plan was aborted by Napoleon's victory at Wagram, illness forced Adair's return to England, and at age twenty-three Stratford was an ad interim minister plenipotentiary with high salary, handsome plate, and financial allowances. He still had no appetite for diplomacy, and for two years he fought boredom and homesickness in a city "not fit for a gentleman to live in" while the new foreign secretary Wellesley left him uninstructed, the Porte kept him at a discreet distance, and England's desperate struggles excited his fierce chauvinism.

Impatient and spoiled by rapid advancement, Stratford reacted to boredom by arrogance and high-handedness more impressive to Turks than to Europeans. Once he ordered an attaché from the room for laughing at a guest's ribald jokes. In August, 1811, however, he was routed by the redoubtable Lady Hester Stanhope (eccentric and beloved niece of William Pitt then living in Constantinople) whose home he had forbidden his staff to enter when she disregarded his orders to stop visiting the French envoy. Lady Hester's deadly riposte was a letter to Wellesley (with a copy to Stratford) that provides a revealing glimpse of the young diplomat. "Mr. Canning," Lady Hester wrote, "is . . . both a religious and political methodist, and having appeared to doubt my love for my country, he will next presume to teach me my duty to my God!" Asking Wellesley not to chastise mere youthful zeal, the Lady continued "The best reward for his services would be to appoint him commander-in-chief at home and ambassador extraordinary abroad to the various societies for the suppression of vice and cultivation of patriotism. The latter consists of putting one's self into greater convulsions than the dervishes at the mention of Buonaparte's name."

Nothing could have shaken Canning more than this revealing sketch from a member of the class he admired and the sardonic amusement it might raise in Downing Street. He implored cousin George in London to contain the damage, but Lady Hester remained his friend, and the following year he triumphed professionally by helping to bring peace between Russia and the Empire in the face of Napoleon's threatened invasion of Russia. Robert Liston shortly thereafter relieved Stratford, and he returned home at once.

On his arrival Canning found all eyes on the Russian battlefields, and for two years during the Wars of Liberation he, like Charles Bagot, pursued society in London and Paris. He also toured the Lake District with his Eton schoolfellow Joseph Planta, fell in love with the same Anne Isabella Milbanke for whom Augustus Foster had yearned, and had a hand in founding the Tory *Quarterly Review*. Viscount Castlereagh, having succeeded Wellesley in the Foreign Office and made peace with George Canning, was complimentary to Stratford and promised employment soon. The young diplomat criticized His Lordship's lack of a proper education for high position and his "habit of using the first word that comes to hand without much regard for its signification," but admitted that in the foreign secretary "a clear judgment cropped out from under the rubbish," and concluded that his senior by seventeen years was "at heart a good-natured, high-minded, generous man" whose "courage never faltered." Castlereagh for his part valued young Canning's highly unusual penchant for hard work, and in 1814 sent him as envoy extraordinary and minister plenipotentiary to Switzerland, temporarily combining two ranks to create a promotion.[2]

Canning remained in Switzerland from 1814 to 1819, acquiring two experiences that would be helpful in America: he observed the operation of a federal system of government, and Castlereagh ("whose dispatches," he wrote, "form one long panegyric of non-intervention") taught him that there was "much to learn" and "much to leave alone." On the other hand, as the representative of the principal supporter of Swiss independence, he was treated with a deference, which, like the spectacular scenery, was not to be found in the raw and irreverent American capital.

In October, 1814, he was summoned briefly to the Congress of Vienna, and on August 3, 1816, while on leave in England he married Harriet Raikes, an heiress who died a year later after the birth of a stillborn child. The tragedy destroyed the last of Switzerland's waning charms, and Stratford drove even Planta and George Canning to impatience with his urgent pleas for a political post leading to Parliament or else for a diplomatic promotion. Again, Castlereagh acted. Moved by Stratford's ability, political connections, and friendship with the recently successful Charles Bagot, the foreign secretary rather suddenly offered him in September, 1819, the position of ambassador extraordinary and minister plenipotentiary to the United States, a slight but distinct promotion over Switzerland.[3]

Like Bagot's friends earlier, Canning's friends urged him to accept the challenge of "keeping those schoolboy Yankees quiet." His old chief Adair called the post "difficult beyond that of any other mission," and his able Swiss secretary, Henry U. Addington, described it as "the most important, difficult, and dangerous of all on the list . . . though bearing high rewards for success." Most important, in George Canning's judgment it was "precisely the most advantageous in . . . credit as well as . . . interest that could have been proposed." Worst of all for the nominee it was far away from Parliament, and he accepted it as the "bitterest cup that ever I raised to my lips" for this reason, not its "considerable risk and very great discomfort." Most compelling were the recent honors and promotion of Bagot, illustrating the rewards of success; so, he wrote, "if I do not die either of impatience or the yellow fever I shall be all the better for it a few years hence."[4]

No minister to America was ever briefed more carefully. The September appointment meant a postponed voyage to avoid storms, providing time for long conferences with Castlereagh, Bagot, and Rush. Having questioned his predecessor on every possible physical requirement, the bachelor minister was "nearly ruined" by the expense of transporting furniture, draperies, a billiard table, and immense stores of food, wine, kitchen and stable equipment, books, and ornaments. Two secretaries and eleven servants accompanied him, including a maître d'hôtel, French cook, valet, coachman, groom, footman, and "a clean, ugly, and monarchical housemaid"—all chosen by his predecessor's steward. Since Bagot advised that "your great difficulty will be to keep your servants," Canning spent additional money on wages and such comforts as an expensive brew of half-porter–half-ale which they "drank like dragons," but they "had to be kept comfortable and in good humour upon almost any terms." Altogether the seventy tons of baggage required four days to load on the frigate *Spartan*.[5]

In July, 1820, Canning attended the king's levee to be invested and he was sworn to the Privy Council. On August 11, the *Spartan* sailed from Spithead. Captain Wise was induced to stop at the Madeira Islands to take on quantities of wine since Bagot reported "Americans drink scarcely any other." Then followed a boring five weeks. Seasickness having afflicted the minister, his beloved books were neglected, and even the ship's band provided little distraction, since he admitted to a musical ear that could only barely identify "God Save the King." Ship routine, he wrote, induced a sort of "temporary idiocy" with little to do except reread Castlereagh's instructions.

Wisdom gained from the days of Hammond and Jackson—and conveyed in Castlereagh's instructions—directed Stratford to substitute personal interviews for written notes since "the tendency of the American government is rather to contentious discussion." Canning was to avoid even "the appearance of desiring to mix in the parties of the country" and to look "exclusively to the Government of the time being, in whatever hands it may be placed"—a cardinal rule in Bagot's success in avoiding "unbecoming acrimony." Commercial relations, fisheries, and boundaries were on the whole in satisfactory if unsettled condition, and the abolition of the slave trade by international patrol and trials was to be his major goal.

On September 20, 1820, the *Spartan* arrived at Hampton Roads, and after Antrobus and Consul Gray came on board, the ship proceeded to Annapolis. The new minister's first appraisal was approving: English-looking red brick houses, a clear atmosphere, and a passing steamboat. Salutes were exchanged with the fort, and he reported that his ship had lost not a soul through desertion. Canning was less cheerful as he approached the capital city through sun-scorched fields where "no scenes of picturesque beauty atone for the roughness of the roads." On the evening of September 28, he took up residence at a hotel near the Capitol, for after rejecting Merry's old house as too dilapidated and others as too small, Antrobus had authorized a month-long renovation of Minister Onís's former embassy.[6] The following morning Canning sent his letters of credence and Bagot's recall to Secretary of State

Adams, and asked for an appointment, which was set for that afternoon. There, in the secretary's little office near the presidential mansion, Adams seemed to Canning to display "every appearance of a conciliatory frame of mind." Unlike his predecessor Jackson, Canning offered to present himself to the president at his farm in Virginia, but Adams deemed this unnecessary, and the two agreed to meet again in three days to open discussions.

Surveying the Federal City, Canning, like his predecessors, found the scene highly depressing. The general perspective, he later replied, was "a low, flat space of considerable extent" bounded on the south by the Potomac and on the north by "a low dwarf range of hills surmounted with a row of detached villas. The greater part of this platform was occupied by brushwood and swamps, with here and there a sprinkling of shabby trees and intersected by two or three roads with several tracings of future streets." Householders and speculators had cut trees widely, leaving "naked, undulating common" and "marshes covered with coppice wood and inhabited by frogs, snipes, and woodcocks."

Over this rolling heath some twenty-five thousand people now lived in five or six separate settlements. Georgetown to the west had about nine thousand inhabitants; around the White House and toward the Capitol were about ten thousand more. Some two or three thousand people lived around the Capitol itself, and other groups clustered around the navy yard on the Eastern Branch. Along Pennsylvania Avenue stood about a mile of three-story buildings—hotels, stores, and homes. Most streets were still dirt, baked in summer, muddy in winter, and potholed all the time. On some parts of Pennsylvania Avenue and elsewhere, however, gravel was being laid down, and in 1819 Congress had begun appropriating money for oil for the streetlights erected in 1803.[7]

Canning nevertheless approached his task of maintaining the Castlereagh goodwill policy with the same care with which in England he had prepared himself for his tour. He arranged his household, read American newspapers teeming with "angry and blackguardly" letters against everything British or royal, and went to the racetrack at Georgetown. He wrote to Bagot thanking him for his advice and vowing to "keep your example in view" and "summon sufficient fortitude to bear for a time what you and Lady Bagot endured for three years." Antrobus had collapsed with a fever soon after the minister's arrival and wrote privately to Bagot

Canning is disposed as yet to see everything in its best light, but under it all I can perceive a great deal of constraint and a strong tendency to restiveness.

I am sorry to say that amidst his other fancies he has taken one to my staying with him the first session of Congress. As I feel not the slightest interest in anything that is going on in this infernal place I grudge very much passing another winter in Washington.[8]

One of the new minister's priorities in fact was to refurbish the somewhat tarnished image of his predecessor. After their return to England, both Bagots had been indiscreetly indulging their humor on American gaucheries, and reports of this, relayed home by Rush, were gleefully picked up by Consul Baker, not a Bagot admirer. Hence, on October 10, when Adams presented Canning and his staff to President Monroe, Canning took the occasion of Monroe's pleasant remarks on Bagot to make a short speech "high charged" according to Adams "both with compliments and with professions" in which he emphasized Bagot's continued admiration of America.

Well before this, however, Canning had opened conversations with the secretary of state on the most important matter of his mission: to secure American participation in an international patrol to search ships suspected of engaging in the slave trade and participation likewise in an international tribunal to try the slavers. Toward this end Castlereagh had worked since 1807, partly to appease English humanitarianism, partly to protect British merchants barred from the trade, and partly to champion liberalism in European eyes. After small successes with Portugal, Spain, and the Netherlands in outlawing the trade, he had been stopped at the congresses at Paris and Vienna, which did nothing about it. American response had also been lukewarm, for though Congress had outlawed the trade in 1807 and declared participation to be piracy punishable by death, Castlereagh's suggestion to Rush in 1818 that America participate had been rapidly turned down by Adams. Stratford Canning had therefore been directed either to secure American cooperation or to obtain an American alternative "on this subject which your court regards as of the very highest importance."

In their first two-hour debate Adams rejected the British proposal on several grounds: lack of constitutional authority for mixed courts, the unwisdom of American collaboration with the Concert of Europe, and above all, the relationship of granting a right of search for slaves with the long-contested British claim to search American vessels and impress seamen. Canning denied any similarity between the two types of search and though Adams in turn belittled the Portuguese and Spanish acquiescence to the plan, the meeting ended amicably.[9]

Two weeks later the minister appeared at the State Department for a three-hour argument over the same ground, still amicable, and when Canning asked for a counterproposal, Adams promised one. A week later the minister brought a long written précis of their conversations, and again the secretary descanted on constitutional objections and the long, bitter story of impressment of seamen. By now Canning knew something of a tenacity equal to his own. He wrote the foreign secretary that the proposals for search and mixed courts were dead issues, asked for proper replies to American counterproposals, and decided to defer future discussions until Congress met, at which time Adams had promised to sound out Congressional sentiment. Meanwhile, the secretary of state shifted the subject to his own passionate if unilateral interest in his forthcoming report on weights and measures.

This detour might have been useful had not Adams followed up with "the general state of European politics," that is, the recent popular uprisings in Italy and Sicily. His remarks became, as he admitted in his diary, "free" as he launched on a favorite topic—the ultimate destruction of the Continental monarchs, whose scepters were "turning to ashes in their hands" and whose "crowns were dropping from their heads." And how, then, would England face the choice of supporting her absolutist allies against "free and liberal institutions"? Under this republican homily Canning held his temper with mild rejoinders and a sardonic thrust (which Adams appreciated and recorded) "that he should always receive any observations that I may make to him with a just deference to my advance of years—over his . . . one of those equivocal compliments which . . . a Frenchman always returns with a bow."[10]

Nevertheless, pressure was building between the two men—both intelligent, stiff, contentious to the point of arrogance, and poles apart in their views of their governments to which they were passionately devoted. They were too alike, and an explosion was inevitable.

On November 13, 1820, the second session of the Sixteenth Congress began with only a bleak prospect for Canning's major diplomatic hopes. Members were still much disgruntled over the continuing economic decline that had begun between the Bagot and Canning tenures, and they were sore from the bruising rhetoric of their first session's savage debates over slavery in the proposed new state of Missouri. In the Senate a bill was introduced containing the new state's constitution, which barred the admission of free Negroes and mulattoes, thereby ensuring a second bitter debate. Reflecting this sectional bitterness, the House attempted to elect its speaker during two days with twenty-two ballots.

This hiatus gave Canning his first view of the House, which he reported in his usual ironic lines to a friend in London. The chamber was "stoved, carpeted, desked and sofaed in the most luxurious style," and "the independent representatives of Kentucky and Tennessee have the very best Brussels carpeting to spit upon." The wigless and gownless speaker sat under a gilt canopy, the galleries had curtains of silk and gold, and the foreign minister who was "admitted to survey these splendors reposes meanwhile on a setee [sic] of real damask."

Of the members Canning generally was tolerant, except for those from the western states, who "may be capable of making the very best laws, but I should not like to meet them in a lone place." Yet he remembered former War Hawk Clay as "an intelligent, useful, and well-disposed man, friendly to the English connexion." The House at length elected its speaker, John Taylor of New York. As there was nothing for Canning to do until Congress's sentiments on the slave trade were known, he occupied himself with visits, moved into his permanent embassy, and started to work on a new consular pay scale that had been referred to him.

In December Charles Mercer offered a resolution calling for papers on the state of the slave trade negotiation, and Canning reminded Adams of his promise to obtain Congressional opinion on the subject. In an economic depression and faced with a possible tariff fight and a certain battle over the Missouri constitution, Monroe decided on a cabinet meeting to form an administration position. At the session that took place on December 23, opinion was unanimous against mixed tribunals to try suspected slavers. On the right of search Thompson of the navy saw possible compromise, but both Calhoun and Adams were opposed and the president was decisively against it. The American counterproposal was determined to be an offer of collaboration by American ships patrolling the African coast. This was all confirmed by a second cabinet meeting and transmitted to the disappointed minister on January 2, 1821.[11]

By this time Canning's patience—"unfortunately that virtue which I have always found it most difficult to practice"—was depleted and his disappointment sharpened by Adams's self-confessed habits of "free remarks" on England and "opinions given with little restraint and in a dogmatical tone." Obedient to instructions, the minister maintained caution, but Adams's steady refusal to join systematic international efforts convinced him that the secretary of state, contrary to Congressional opinion, personally opposed effective control. In fact, Adams and Monroe's opposition arose, like many of their countrymen's, from the dismal history of British searches, seizures, impressments, and immoral prize court decisions from 1803 to 1812; like Castlereagh and George Canning, Stratford Canning never realized the severity of these wounds, which, along with sectional politics, were fatal to his diplomatic efforts.[12]

These frustrations led in January, 1821, to a storm as famous in State Department annals as George Canning's anti-Erskine tantrums had been at the Foreign Office. The Adams-Canning relations plunged to new depths. After Congressman John Floyd's committee had sweepingly denied any European state's claims to the American Pacific Northwest below 60° north (approximately the site of present Anchorage, Alaska), Floyd introduced a bill for American settlement of the Columbia River Basin. Canning knew of Bagot's clash with Adams over the *Ontario* voyage, heard some House debate on Floyd's bill, and read the commentary in the semi-official *Intelligencer*. He therefore suddenly presented himself at the State Department and in excitement unlike his usual casual approach began to question Adams sharply on American intentions in the northwest. Adams found the minister "more peremptory than I was disposed to endure," and his subject, American versus British territorial rights, roused his ready fury. Both men abandoned diplomatic language in furious sarcasm, demands, interruptions, and contradictions. The secretary refused to answer questions based on Congressional debate and newspaper account and directed Canning—as Madison had Jackson in 1809—to submit his communications on the subject in writing. Regarding this as a threat to both himself and Castlereagh's instructions, Canning responded in furious rejoinder. Such substantive debate as did occur over the rights of the nations was confused by ignorance: Adams forgot the details of Bagot's protests and Canning was unaware both of Bagot's professional mistakes and of the exact terms of the Convention of 1818.

The angry men broke off the meeting to recover themselves, but the next day Adams rebuffed Canning's half effort to resume the amenities. A second afternoon was spent in caustic recrimination. Adams was at his most brutal in bringing the "proud Englishman" to heel, and the latter was aware that his mission was in danger, but, he wrote, he "deemed it indispensable for the maintenance of my public character not to let myself be beat down by mere violence of tone and assertion." Between and after the disputations Adams carefully reported the details to the president, who was far more relaxed about it than the secretary. Both diplomats were shaken by the sudden discovery of such latent hostility and each reacted characteristically: Adams wrote in his diary about and obliquely deplored to Canning the matter of his bad temper; the Briton reported the episode in two dispatches (one of eighteen pages) and several private letters castigating Adams's "coarseness and rancorous enmity to England." He privately warned his friend Undersecretary Planta that if his antagonist "persists in the same line of coarseness and violence I question whether I have the requisite humility and patience for enduring it."[13] His next approach to Secretary Adams, not made until March, was much more formal, and their future conversations, though civil and occasionally bantering, were far less casual.

The diplomatic battlefield was of course not allowed to impinge on the winter's social events. The White House restoration having been essentially completed, the Monroes' New Year's reception was the largest and most lavish in memory. The president's style was formal, and his dinners were pronounced to be mediocre; the president received guests at his door and passed them on to be greeted by the beautifully gowned and bejeweled Elizabeth Monroe and her daughters. Parties in private homes were hot and crowded and formal dinners were rare. Consequently, the diplomats' entertainments were cherished. In February an admiring American described Canning's ball as unique: "The English are a half century before us in style. Handsome pictures, books, and all sorts of 'elegant litter' distinguish his rooms, the mansion being decorated with peculiar taste and propriety." Others praised the minister himself in terms that would have pleased Castlereagh and brought grim smiles from Adams: "Mr. Canning himself is a most unpretending man in appearance and manners; modesty appears to be his peculiar characteristic, which for a foreign minister is no negative praise." And another American reported: "Canning is a different character from his predecessor. His manner is mild, unostentatious, and apparently quite simple. His countenance wears an air of pensiveness which is interesting, but in tête à tête he shews himself to be a scholar and a gentleman."

Whatever his other contrasts with his predecessor, Canning found little pleasure in the social scene he was said to ornament. He paid the expected morning or afternoon calls, sat down unhappily to dinners at four or five in the afternoon, and most unwillingly of all attended balls and other evening parties beginning at eight. By custom he entertained all members of Congress "by scores at a time at the risk of overcrowding my table." Another risk was an addled head from answering the numerous toasts from various guests throughout dinner, so that "to shelter my brains" he had a glass of amber water set at his place. Also, since the "unguarded impulsiveness" and "outspoken freedom" of his Republican guests' conversation might produce "inconvenience," the minister had placed opposite him at table a large basket of flowers, thus reducing conversation to his immediate neighbors right and left. A fastidious diner, Canning was appalled at the speed and voraciousness of native trenchermen, agreeing that "no country ever contained so many dyspeptic cases as America." He despised dancing, and contrary to other observers, he reported that "to the immortal honour of the Americans cards have no ascendancy in the United States." His only real pleasures were reading (especially Scott's novels) and the company of wealthy conservative gentlemen, notably John Marshall, Rufus King, William Lowndes, and John Randolph, the last of whom displayed eccentricities more striking than those of the backwoods congressmen, but of a comfortably aristocratic nature.

In February, Adams's Florida Treaty arrived ratified by Spain, and the American Senate acted likewise, whereupon Clay secured a mild resolution allowing recognition of the rebellious South and Central American Spanish colonies. To Canning's relief, Floyd's Columbia River bill failed, and on March 3 Congress adjourned with little done in the preoccupation over Missouri. A House committee gave guarded approval to a mixed commission to try slavers, but the proposal never came to a vote. When in March Canning again visited Adams to seek further American proposals, the secretary told him he had none and requested not to be pressed further on the matter. The minister's intensive efforts against the slave trade had failed.[14]

On March 5, 1821, Canning and Antrobus in full diplomatic finery sallied forth in mud and cold to witness Monroe's second inaugural, this time in the House of Representatives. Though the diplomats had been notified of their special seats, the crowd was so great that even the president could scarcely attain the door and the official party was crushed and shoved. "We are all equal here, Sir," the minister wrote home caustically, though nearly everyone expressed regrets "always with the exception of Adams." Monroe as usual appeared with queue and powdered hair, old-fashioned coat, and shoe and knee buckles. Canning admitted him to be "really a good sort of man, and certainly respected with astonishing unanimity"; in fact, the minister expressed the unusual wish to see more of the president than "the strictness of republican etiquette permitted."

After Congress adjourned, Washington emptied as always, and Stratford was moved to admit that "things go on more smoothly than I had expected," with "a fair quantity of goodwill and civility, earned indeed with the sweat of one's brow, but still not to be despised." His servants had "behaved uniformly well" and "the accomplishment of chewing tobacco has not yet been fatal to my carpets." Unlike the active Bagots, Canning was "seldom incommoded with visits," and once wrote his brother "I have now sat down to dinner day after day for more than a month with my two secretaries, who, I take it for granted, have found the task to the full as painful as myself."

Daily he rose between six and seven, passed the morning alone, dined at five or six, and spent an occasional hour at talk and tea in the evening with a friend, then went to bed by half-past ten, while the majordomo locked up. On Sunday the entourage attended the Episcopal church, "whose rector," he wrote, "assures us in his sermons that the devil (with his horns and tail) is really and truly . . . at our elbows." The clergy generally were "Wesleyan Methodists, more remarkable for their whining tone and the *severity* of their creed than for any very formidable deviation from the doctrines of the Church of England." Some formal society of course persisted, and Canning marveled to "think of the good people having the courage to persevere in giving parties with the temperature nearly at 90. Madame de Neuville . . . and Mrs. Adams are the leaders of this madness." As did all his predecessors, Canning complained ceaselessly of the heat and swift, violent changes of temperature; he adopted a summer costume that included white cotton jacket, umbrella, and broad-brimmed straw hat.[15]

In April, 1821, Crawfurd Antrobus joyfully returned to England, by which time Canning found that "the miseries of the place are beginning to soak into me," and he warned Planta that he would not tolerate the mission beyond a third session of Congress. From heat, lack of important business, American society, and Secretary Adams he had lost his earlier optimism, or as he described it "the iron had . . . entered my soul . . . I had ceased to be in a state of innocence and like our first parents with an increase of knowledge I received an increase of misery." In June he went by steamboat to Mount Vernon to drink the king's health with Judge Washington. He also endured a sixteen-mile battering over a turnpike to the Great Falls of the Potomac and enjoyed visits with the venerable Charles Carroll of Carrollton at his home.

In June he learned that Adams had been invited to deliver the Fourth of July oration in the House of Representatives, so he opted for a diplomatic absence and hired a coach for a tour to Harper's Ferry, Virginia. Like the majority of His Majesty's early ministers to America, he found Republican Virginia objectionable. "Americans," he wrote home, "differ from the Scotch in having no pretensions to wit," and "vanity and ignorant self-importance *generally* prevail." To him the American yeomen beloved of Jefferson displayed "an air of affected independence, which being unnatural is very offensive." As for the Sage of Monticello, his *Notes on Virginia* "seems to do more credit to the author's fancy than to his accuracy." The minister kept his own careful travel notes, especially on the depressed economy.[16]

On his return to the capital he found that his premonitions of Adams's Fourth of July oration were accurate. The secretary of state had donned a professor's gown and from the House rostrum delivered what Russian Minister Poletica called "from one end to another . . . a violent diatribe against England." The rhetoric was lurid and the chauvinism extreme. Like Poletica, who had also avoided the occasion, Canning sent home a copy of the "extraordinary effusion" together with a scathingly ironic dispatch and private letters describing the secretary practicing his fire and brimstone before a captive household audience.

To Castlereagh, now the second marquis of Londonderry, Canning deplored the "contemptible appeal to the less enlightened feelings of the people" through a furious indictment of British tyranny and a "vulgar and indecent reference to the venerable name" of the late George III. Worse still, "the most anti-British part of Mr. Adams' harangue . . . ha[s] been hailed . . . as a strictly national declaration worthy of proceeding from the Department of State" and "a fair return for all the unwelcome remarks which have been made upon this country . . . by the writers and orators of Great Britain."[17] Officially Canning suggested that the speech was worth noting for Adams's present position and ambitions for the presidency. Privately he wrote to Bagot that whether "this . . . effusion" was "mere black vomit" or a first bid for the presidency, it was well designed to revive Anglo-American animosities.

Other events of the summer did little for Canning's fraying nerves. In March and April he had again tried unavailingly to get Adams's support for an international patrol or another American proposal, but he was now told again to resume the effort. Londonderry also sharply criticized Canning's January explosion with Adams over the Columbia River settlement, told him he was in error, and ordered him not to discuss the matter again without further instructions. Stratford replied with deference, but to Planta as usual he vigorously defended his legal interpretation as well as his personal response to the secretary of state's "overwhelmingly offensive tone and language."[18]

Since Congress was not to assemble until December, Canning had as little hard work to do in the autumn months as he had faced in the spring. His occupations, he wrote cousin George, were much like those of a college except for the monthly arrival of the diplomatic mail bag and "the daily perusal of six abusive newspapers." Administration members had departed, and although he knew Bagot had lost a chance for more popularity by not traveling, Canning delayed his own excursions, alleging a need to keep the staff from idleness.

Meanwhile, a spate of British and Continental criticism of America created local reaction, and once Canning wrote a newspaper article under a pseudonym in defense of some of Londonderry's remarks in Parliament. Stratford Canning was always intensely sensitive to threats to his professional reputation, and the volatility of American opinion, which had only amazed his predecessors, worried him.

> There is no concealing that while here one's character is at the mercy of accidents . . . in official transactions but also in the daily intercourse of society. By great patience, great circumspection, and great good fortune one may get on with tolerable success for a time, but a slight oversight could at any moment suffice to cancel every previous advantage. All that you have heard of the vanity, the suspicion, and the irritability of this people—or rather of these peoples—is with some exceptions but too true.

As to the capital, he wrote, "it would take a century to carry its population up to thirty or forty thousand souls—black and white." Magnificent buildings rose from a rubble where "the luxuries of paving and lighting are still only in prospect." The economic doldrums that Americans found distressing were seen by the minister as beneficial beyond mere economic welfare. It would, he wrote, "sober down" some of the citizens' "brilliant fancies . . . since the pleasant days of neutral trade and the glories of Perry and Jackson. Jonathan is still on horseback, but not quite so 'high in the saddle' as of yore." The newspapers' tones he found "decidedly softened," and "I have met with fewer instances of impertinences and more general civility than I had been led to expect." Even "chewing and smoking appear on the decline" and "indoor spitting is less common," while "breeches and silk stockings are not infrequently worn of an evening."

Perhaps in response to this perception of an emerging, depression-induced civilization, Canning himself became more mellow than many of his predecessors had been toward prominent Americans—always excepting Jefferson, Jackson, and Adams, the last "a grievous aggravation of the difficulties with which I have to struggle." Naval officers such as Chauncey, Rodgers, Bainbridge, and Hull he found especially courteous, and his personal attentions to Decatur's widow were long and intense enough to arouse wide comment.

If social amenities improved in the autumn and winter of 1821, diplomatic progress did not. In September a note from Adams again rejected British proposals for cooperation against the slave trade, suggesting merely informal collaboration between existing patrols. Repercussions then arose over a French ship captured by an American ship and later recaptured by its crew. Canning found himself engaged in such weighty matters as refuting rumors that the British had poisoned Napoleon at St. Helena, and as the time approached for Congress to assemble, he wrote sarcastically of preparing "for the important duties of giving dinners and attending the debates of Congress." In London the Foreign Office was currently more interested in restraining higher American tariffs and warding off American shippers' assaults on British West Indian colonial restrictions.[19]

To politically minded Americans, the 1820 session of Congress marked the opening battles for the presidency in 1825. Skirmishing had begun early between the followers of Clay and Adams, but the open candidacies of first Calhoun and then Jackson created hot Congressional warfare between the administration forces supporting Adams or Calhoun and their rivals, the Crawfordites and Jacksonians. In October Canning reported the anger of the "Old Republicans"—

Crawford men now known as Radicals—and their demands that the administration return to traditional Jeffersonian doctrines of economy and decentralized government. In public the minister kept discreetly silent, hoping intently for the success of any rival of Adams.[20]

Stratford Canning meanwhile found himself engaged in warfare of his own. He had always blamed part of his boredom on the absence of professional colleagues from other European capitals, but he disliked those who were in Washington. Thus he found Russia's Poletica "at times barely civil," and he felt the Hyde de Neuvilles would be more agreeable "in the more roomy circles of a real capital," particularly since the French couple "took it into their heads that I am *bound* to attend *all* their weekly parties" and "unconscionable dinners." Aware of his reputation for general unsociability, Stratford assured his cousin George that he was anxious to attain a friendly footing with his colleagues, "but I do not feel as if I had succeeded," and to Bagot he admitted that "from first to last I have suffered more arrogance from my diplomatic colleagues than from any or all of the natives."

The French diplomat, who was a particular trial, on December 19 gave a splendid supper ball of the kind that Canning felt "no display of beauty and no charms of conversation can metamorphose into a pleasure." With relations already strained over an incident involving a British admiral and the French slave trade, Canning chose to leave the ball early. When the host asked the reason, Canning replied to the effect that he attended some social affairs from pleasure and others, more briefly, from duty. Two days later at a presidential dinner for the diplomatic corps, Hyde de Neuville raised the matter with Canning at the president's table, and later, on leaving, in the mansion vestibule. As usual, the Frenchman's manner was the more excited and the Briton's words the more obnoxious—so offensive as to invite a duel. That scandal was only averted by the Russian and Swedish diplomats, and eventually, to Canning's relief, the two shook hands at the house of Russia's Poletica. As when tilting with Lady Hester at Constantinople and Secretary Adams in Washington, Stratford wrote disingenuous explanations to Londonderry and somewhat more honest ones to his cousin George Canning and to Undersecretary Planta. The only significance of this fracas was that, for reasons ranging from his health and own irascible temperament to republican society and Washington's weather, the minister had both opened and closed the year 1821 with violent and detrimental explosions. In January, 1822, he wrote Bagot that "we are all vastly civil again, but there are impressions that do not easily wear out, and I want but little more to make the place not only odious but intolerable to me."[21]

Fortunately the year 1822 was to be both personally and professionally calmer. Efforts to complete the Treaty of Ghent went on amicably but always slowly. Congress refused to pass a higher tariff bill, but denied the British request to differentiate between rolled and hammered iron. In June Parliament recognized that American purchase of British goods was more vital to Britain than the West Indian shipping monopoly, and by the American Trade Act opened most British West Indian colonies to American shipping. American shippers were to pay the same duties and charges as British shippers paid, provided that America would give Britain equal and reciprocal advantages. Both Cannings were infuriated at this retreat before economic nationalism, but Monroe and Adams were later to throw away the advantage.

On what Stratford Canning called "the interminable subject of the slave trade," the president and secretary of state maintained unyielding objection to the British proposals for international search and trial. As before, a House committee recommended restricted rights of search and Canning lobbied with like-minded Congressmen in both the long and short sessions, but the House never acted. The minister was told, probably by Crawford, that Adams's adamancy did not represent the cabinet's views, but that the secretary of state dominated the president. For a time the Englishman even suspected that Adams had a financial interest in the trade, and he was sure that presidential politics were involved. He appealed to the obdurate secretary as "a Christian as well as a statesman" with "the character of his country at heart," but had to confess to Londonderry that "I have no reason to flatter myself with the hope of having made a satisfactory impression on Mr. Adams's mind," and predicted that only a congressional mandate would achieve that miracle.

More important, Canning reported in detail the administration's moves toward recognition of Spain's former colonies as independent states. By the close of 1821 most of South America as well as Central America and Mexico were breaking or had broken from their mother country, and in March, 1822, Monroe's message to Congress recommended recognition of Chile, the United Provinces of the Plata, Peru, Colombia, and Mexico. Congress responded with an appropriation for American missions. With traditional friendship for the Spanish government, Britain was restrained from similar recognition of the rebels, whose final success was in any case still in doubt. But Canning—unwisely—attempted some levity with Adams on the subject: "So, Mr. Adams, you are going to make honest people of them," to which the acid reply was "Yes, sir, we proposed to your government to join us some time ago, but they would not, and now we shall see whether you will be content to *follow us*."[22] The minister's only retaliations were to beat the secretary at chess and (with Adams's assent) to decline attending a presidential dinner for the new minister from Mexico, who by long unofficial residence would outrank the Englishman.[23]

In the spring Canning's health was better and his personal life more tranquil. Still solitary when compared with the convivial Bagot and still impatient and caustic, he had by now adjusted to the undramatic agenda of current Anglo-American diplomacy. Moreover his intelligence now recognized that unlike the situations in his tours of Switzerland and the Ottoman Empire, the diplomatic and political initiatives of 1822 America rested with his host country.

Unlike George Hammond in the 1790s, he also perceived that despite his personal antipathy to the secretary of state, a government including such men as Monroe, Adams, Clay, Calhoun, and Crawford was quite capable (even in the midst of democracy's hubbub) of forming and administering national policy without the guidance of His Majesty's government or its minister in Washington. For example, he was uneasily aware that however difficult he found Adams to deal with, the secretary and able Richard Rush in London constituted an alternative and effective diplomatic bypass to Lord Liverpool and Viscount Londonderry. There were still decades of problems to be resolved by the imperial proconsular diplomacy in which Canning was so effective, but the scene for it was henceforth to be more often the Eastern, not the Western, Hemisphere.

Stratford Canning's activities therefore became yet more routine. He advised and directed consuls, contributed to the artistic and literary causes in Washington, and endured the capital's banquets and balls. In these social hothouses, gossips continued to be titillated by his marked attentions to the beautiful Widow Decatur, though more cynical Republicans predicted that he would never destroy his future, as they were convinced Erskine had done, by an American marriage.[24]

After two unfruitful sessions with Adams over a variety of matters, Canning determined to escape the summer heat in Washington. He, along with attaché Wilmot and two servants, set out on July 18 "in two smart hired hacks" instead of his own carriage, "a postillion being an unknown creature in a land of republicans." After two days with his friend Charles Carroll, he and his party in a week moved through Maryland, Pennsylvania, New Jersey, and on to New York. Stratford was pleasantly surprised by the countryside, better roads, and the accommodations, being "never required to dine at the table d'hôte" and given a separate sitting room. He was also provided with two bedrooms—"a really great stretch of accommodation in America," where two guests to a bed was still the norm in many places. He found New York manners "strikingly different" from those in Washington, for he "made acquaintance in person with the genuine tone of Yankee independence." A growing perceptiveness is evident in the comment (in Americanese) that "by taking things as they come and paying all that is asked, a traveller may get on, I *guess*, as well in this country as in any other. The great difficulty is to bear constantly in mind that what we call rudeness and impertinence in England is not meant to be any such thing in the United States."[25]

After a ninety-mile steamboat tour to Albany, Canning found himself at Ballston and at Saratoga "in the full vortex of an American watering place," which he was delighted both to have seen and to be unlikely to see again. Saratoga featured monastic but clean rooms, huge and hasty public means, crowds, heat, and little amusement. Shortly afterward, the party moved up the Mohawk Valley where Canning observed the passage of successive frontiers and their role in transforming dense forests into thriving towns. This minister, like his predecessors who traveled in America, was beginning to grasp something of the size and human resources of the republic, and like his fellows he felt that a "firm and systematic government" (meaning Tory England's) would produce "an empire of great, perhaps unexampled strength and prosperity" if sectional disunion did not prevail over centralism.

Corduroy roads and wild American hack drivers were torments, but "the worst that happened to us . . . was to eat occasionally with a blunt knife and a two-pronged straddling fork of no very clean appearance, to mumble a beefsteak of impregnable toughness and to sleep on featherbeds evacuated but one reeking instant before by the landlord or some one of his relations."[26]

From Niagara they sailed by steamboat and galley to Montreal and Quebec, where the field of Wolfe's victory moved this passionate Englishman almost as profoundly as had Wellington's at Waterloo. His party then returned for ten days at Boston—"far superior to what I had expected," its environs beautiful and its citizens hospitable. Here he heard the news of Foreign Secretary Londonderry's suicide. In some of his finest writing Stratford Canning eulogized a skillful and kind statesman whose personal consideration and kindness to him had extended over ten years. Despite their differences of method Canning recognized Londonderry as one of England's "ablest statesmen" and one "who was particularly friendly to the maintenance of a good understanding with the United States." On October 23 Canning and his party were back in the capital, and the next day he reviewed with Adams unsettled trade problems and the slave trade impasse—blocked only, he told the secretary boldly, by the latter's personal opinions. They also touched briefly on the revived fortunes of George Canning as Londonderry's probable successor.[27]

The Congress that began its short session in December, 1822, with a yellow fever epidemic still lingering was less belligerent toward the administration, since the Crawfordites were forced onto the defense on behalf of the Treasury secretary. In early January, 1823, Canning's former attaché, Henry U. Addington, "half frozen after ten weeks of sickness and starvation at sea," joined the embassy. The arrival of this capable subordinate, who, Canning wrote, "enjoys the advantage of having come out with a constitution already broken," heightened the minister's keen anticipation of his own release. So did the news in December of his cousin George's assumption of the Foreign Office, and confident that "the term of this nauseous portion of my life cannot now be very remote," he lost no time in applying formally and informally for the traditional "leave of absence" that meant permanent departure. Meanwhile, he plunged into the despised social routine. In February one of his guests testified to the minister's social magnificence and perhaps unconsciously to the diplomat's impatience to be gone when he wrote that there was "a great display of servants in white and purple liveries—of whom there were five and two or three others not in livery" as well as an elaborate silver service and a variety of wines "but I don't think the dinner was as good or the entertainment as agreeable as Poletica's where, however I felt more at home, which maybe made the difference."[28]

After careful investigation, Canning concluded that, contrary to British rumor, the Americans had no designs on Cuba, just as in London, Lord Liverpool was delivering to Rush the same renunciation. In March the Congress, which Stratford described as "generally admitted to have been the dullest body that ever met together," adjourned, but a few days previous the House by a vote of 131 to 9 had called on the administration to negotiate for the suppression of the slave trade. For some weeks George Canning had been pressing Stratford to revive negotiations—in writing—with Adams on the slave trade, and "though feeling that sickness of heart which arises from the consciousness of being engaged in a hopeless task," Stratford now did so. He found that the House vote had created such pressure on the administration that the secretary, though still defending his former position, now agreed to a convention to be held in London on slave trading, blockade, impressment, and commercial matters.

Other business also required the minister to call on the secretary despite what he called "the natural repugnance which I feel to seek occasions of conversation with a man so eminently disagreeable." Responding ungraciously to Parliament's American Trade Act of June, 1822, which partially opened West Indian colonies, Monroe's proclamation (despite the Briton's protests) had not removed anti-British duties. Now in its last days of the 1823 session and regardless of his arguments with Adams and Rufus King, Congress had enacted in effect a demand that Britain admit American vessels and goods to her colonial ports on the same basis as that of her own vessels from any part of her Empire. When Stratford Canning learned from an unyielding Adams and reported that the new American economic nationalism was in fact aimed at destroying the British imperial preference policy, his government's predictable response was first to tax and then to exclude American vessels from the colonial ports.

In fact, Stratford Canning's last American months once again illustrated an irony of early Anglo-American diplomacy: that in critical moments of change, British envoys to Washington were either eagerly awaiting departure (like Canning and Liston), or were of little influence (like Thornton and Erskine), or were quite politically ineffective (like Merry or Foster). Homesick, impatient, and suspicious of Adams's sincerity in several matters and "stupefied with the parish business of this pettifogging hemisphere," Stratford Canning was as ambivalent and uncertain a channel of communication as Thornton or Liston had been in observing converging Anglo-American policies.

In 1822, on assuming the Foreign Office, George Canning had begun Britain's withdrawal from an increasingly reactionary Holy Alliance and its military adventures, and later warned against a French occupation of Spain to free the odious Ferdinand VII from his popular government. In March, 1823, in the same letter that granted Stratford's release from America, the foreign secretary admitted that his warning to France had been rejected. As the Spanish constitutionalists fell back before the French armies, both British and American shippers saw an imminent restoration of absolutism in Spain with accompanying interdiction of outside trade with the colonies in the New World. Canning, in April, 1823, had wished success to the constitutionalists from the floor of the Commons, held Britain to be neutral in Spain's quarrel with her colonies, and handsomely praised historic United States neutrality, including the Jeffersonian variety of which he had once conspicuously failed to see the virtues. Taken together, all this clearly meant a British approach to an American administration that had already recognized the new republics and was soon to name the first ministers to the United Provinces and to Colombia.

On May 3, 1823, Stratford wrote George Canning that Adams had approached him on the possibility of joint action in resisting Russian claims to the northwestern American coast. Three days later he wrote ironically of the new South American states and of Adams's failings, but added that George Canning's liberal course

in the great politics of Europe has had the effect of making the English almost popular in the United States. The improved state of public feeling is very perceptible; and even Adams has caught something of the soft infection . . . On the whole I question whether for a long time there has been so favourable an opportunity—as far as disposition and general good will are concerned—to bring the two countries nearer together . . . It may be possibly worth your while to give this hint a turn in your thoughts.

Yet later in the same month in which he wrote this widely quoted letter, Stratford Canning learned from Adams of American insistence on equal shipping privileges with Britain in the latter's West Indian ports, and also that the proposed London Convention would deal with several matters beyond the slave trade. He further knew that George Canning's public praise for American neutrality was a Parliamentary ploy to cause problems for the Opposition. Therefore only five weeks after he had written of Adams's "soft infection," he wrote to George Canning one of the longest dispatches of his American tour, detailing his deep suspicions of Adams's sincerity in the West Indian commerce and slave trade matters, and emphasizing the secretary of state's presidential ambitions. Stratford Canning's American tour did not end in cadences of reconciliation.

On June 17, 1823, the minister formally bade farewell to the president, and a week later presented Addington to Adams as chargé. The next day he wrote his final dispatch from the capital he despised, and leaving his secretary Henry Parish as Addington's attaché, he departed for New York to await the arrival of George Jackson as commissioner for a Ghent treaty arbitration. Hezekiah Niles marked his departure with a friendly and perhaps shrewd comment: "He appears to have been much esteemed by the people of Washington and others who knew him best."

The secretary of state confided to his diary an appraisal both friendly and measured, testifying to their resemblances:

He is, of all the foreign ministers with whom I have had occasion to treat, the man who has most severely tried my temper . . . He has, however, a great respect for his word, and there is nothing false about him . . . Mr. Canning is a man of forms, studious of courtesy, and tenacious of private morals. As a diplomatic man his great want is suppleness, and his great virtue is sincerity.[29]

Unfortunately for the minister, George Jackson did not appear for six weeks, and the fuming Canning waited until August 9 before leaving on a packet boat, after a spate of letters to Planta and the foreign secretary explaining the change of plans. He arrived in England on September 9, 1823, and a few days later was with his cousin in Downing Street. It was an intriguing moment. He had been immobilized in New York when his cousin had begun what George called his "great flirtation" with the United States for a joint pronouncement against Holy Alliance adventures in the Western Hemisphere. In July he asked Rush to be sure his praises of neutrality reached America, and in August he pressed attentions on the snobbish and silly Christopher Hughes, now American attaché at Stockholm.

On August 16, when Stratford was at last at sea, the foreign secretary opened with Rush the possibility of an open statement of collaboration. Rush interposed the requirement that Britain, like America, should first recognize the new governments, but on September 18, a few days after Stratford's first conference with him in London, George Canning pursued the collaboration idea and made his final offer to Rush of a *future* British recognition of the former colonies. Meanwhile, in

Washington, Canning's "beast" in the State Department and President Monroe—having led both Cannings one step into the world of the future by recognition of the republics—were now preparing the president's famous "Doctrine," contained in his December, 1823, message to Congress.

The next year Stratford Canning found himself "still a Yankee in point of occupation though not of position" as he and William Huskisson began their negotiations in London with Rush on the slave trade, and later West Indies commerce, impressment, and other problems directed to them by their governments. Stratford Canning was not hopeful, and his doubts were realized. George Canning managed to separate the desired slave trade subject from the rest of the agenda, and a convention was signed in March, 1824, providing for international search of suspected slave ships and national trials of their crews. The foreign secretary hailed this as "a triumph of sheer straightforwardness" over that "scoundrel Adams." Nevertheless, the convention's ratification was defeated in the Senate by a combination of Crawfordites and other Adams enemies, and perhaps also by the long memories in America of such worthies as Admirals Sir Hyde Parker and Sir George Berkeley. Through Addington's letters Stratford kept up with affairs in America, hoping for a time that "Squintz has got into a scrape that may cost him the presidency by his counfounded duplicity," but later "very much afraid" that the secretary "will finally succeed in carrying" that office.

In September, 1824, Stratford Canning met and after a determined courtship married Elizabeth Alexander, much his junior, and then served a brief mission to Russia. Stratford could never, however, curb his impatient intolerance, and although George Canning and his own ability kept him employed in diplomacy, more than one senior diplomat sometimes found that "two Cannings at a time are too much for a peaceable man." By 1833 Stratford's incivilities had infuriated the Tsar of All the Russias as they had the American secretary of state, and the government of Tsar Nicholas I, denouncing him as "captious, distrustful, and suspicious," refused to receive him as ambassador.

After George Canning's death, Stratford again found his real effectiveness in Constantinople, where Britain's might and his keen mind could impose for a time a form of rationality. He served a total of seven tours there, once for sixteen years, holding the crumbling Ottoman

Empire together despite half-mad sultans, protecting Greek minorities when possible, and bringing as much order as possible from the Crimean War tragedy.

In 1852 Stratford Canning was made Viscount Stratford de Redcliffe. He attained the highest orders of British chivalry, serving briefly in most of the European courts. During a brief hiatus in his diplomatic career caused by some political infighting, he achieved his early ambition, reaching the House of Commons via a rotten borough. But, as his cousin George had suspected, the majestic tones of the proconsular diplomat did not sound good in the rowdy Commons, and he resigned his seat when he went on his fourth tour to the Ottoman Empire. He was more effective later in the House of Lords.

He retired from diplomacy in 1858 and spent the last twenty years of his long life with his wife and surviving daughters at his home near Tunbridge Wells and in London. He wrote poetry, political and religious papers, historical plays, and his memoirs. He died at age ninety-three on August 14, 1880, and his memorial statue stands in Westminster Abbey.[30] Representing both the best and the worst of nineteenth-century British diplomacy, he devoted more than fifty years to intense and intelligent public service, almost none of which was of significance in or to the American republic. In their maturer years, both he and the republic came to greater mutual respect, if never to a full comprehension.

Postlude:
Pride and Prejudice

WHEN Stratford Canning boarded the *Francis Freeling* for a wretched voyage home and a brilliant career half a world away, an Anglo-American period in mutual perception—and hence in diplomatic relations—had begun to close. This period opened when the dour realism of William Grenville sent George Hammond as first minister to the new republic, and then over Hammond's head the foreign secretary forged the two countries' first international stance in Jay's Treaty of 1794.

Unfortunately, that frail rapprochement was overtaken almost immediately by war in Europe. For twenty-two years, ten British foreign secretaries and their colleagues were desperately engaged in the destruction of French hegemony in Europe and the preservation of the British nation. In such cataclysms, American nationality occupied little British attention save as it might hamper or assist their central effort. In those twenty-two years the seven British envoys who were in America for any significant time were naturally directed toward the goal of achieving American assistance in Britain's cause, and only one, hapless David Erskine, dimly perceived during his American mission any real, deep current of American nationality.

These twenty-two war years brought painful experiences to the American psyche. Still, well-emphasized military and naval weaknesses did not drive this people to repudiate their nationality in behalf of either belligerent; instead, contention and war strengthened that conviction of separateness and unique purpose enjoined on them by their five presidents. The European belligerents' disregard for American ports and territorial waters, their denial of America's claims for neutrality, and their violation of basic rights of citizenship simply hardened convictions that the republic could not maintain by force. Neither the national purposes of Britain nor those of France were identical to America's, and most Americans knew it. And so a nationalism nurtured in frustration and insult somehow sustained its own war and was consummated at Ghent.

Yet while it was a contentious political nationalism that often annoyed the foreign secretaries, it was the frustrating American community itself with which British envoys to America grappled. This aggregation of peoples concurred on little but in a rejection of the "natural orders of society," in an absence of accustomed deferences, in an unabashed pursuit of gain and advantage, in accepted violence of invective in party and press, and above all (among the great majority) in a widespread, visceral dislike of British society, politics, and values. To the unhappy British representatives after 1800, the capital's two marble edifices rising ostentatiously amid wretched mud and unceasing discomforts daily epitomized the irrational pretensions of a volatile and hostile people—a people whose surface similarities to Britain's only briefly concealed the chasms that lay between the two.

In 1815 an inconclusive war and a capital laid to waste had only strengthened American nationalism and accentuated societal differences. The relentless logic of economic advantages and the adamant obtuseness of European reaction would inevitably alter Anglo-American mutual perceptions. The success of Bagot's shallow charm demonstrated how easily the two peoples could be brought to accept at least a surface amenity, whereas the sterility of the more intellectual Stratford Canning's tenure revealed the absence of any real friction in the basic concerns of the two nations.

Neither John Q. Adams's nor Andrew Jackson's administrations would see fraternity arise between the republic and the Empire. While chargé Addington and then Minister Charles Vaughan presided at the embassy in the 1820s and 1830s, the protective tariffs and commercial discriminations that Grenville had apprehended in the 1790s were enacted. Nor did the social amenities of the American capital startlingly improve. Much that "Toujours Gai" and Copenhagen Jackson had complained of remained. As Andrew Jackson approached his inaugural in the spring of 1829, conditions in the capital inspired the text of the Reverend Robert Little's sermon: "When Christ drew near the City, he wept over it." Years of recrimination and ridicule lay ahead from transatlantic travelers private and official, but a mutual recognition and a wry acceptance had been achieved. In the face of these, pride and prejudice would not long survive.

Notes

Prelude

1. Sir Edward Hertslet, *Recollections of the Old Foreign Office*; Frank T. Ashton-Gwatkin, *The British Foreign Service*, pp. 7–10; Ray Jones, *The Nineteenth Century Foreign Office*, pp. 11–12; Sir John Tilley and Stephen Gaselee, *The Foreign Office*; P. L. Bulwer, "The Diplomatic Service," *New Monthly Magazine and Literary Journal* 1 (1833): 418–29; Thomas H. S. Escott, *The Story of British Diplomacy—Its Makers and Movements.*

2. Hertslet, *Recollections*, pp. 165–74; Ashton-Gwatkin, *British Foreign Service*, pp. 11–12, 15, 16–18; H. W. V. Temperley, *The Foreign Policy of George Canning, 1822–1827*, pp. 259–60.

3. Hertslet, *Recollections*, pp. 1, 2, 7, 17, 20–23, 28, 29, 36, 140, 144; Ashton-Gwatkin, *British Foreign Service*, pp. 10–11; Jones, *Nineteenth Century*, p. 11. Official letters were headed "Downing Street" until 1807 and "Foreign Office" thereafter (Algernon Cecil, "The Foreign Office," in Sir A. W. Ward and G. P. Gooch, eds., *The Cambridge History of British Foreign Policy* III, 546–47).

4. Ashton-Gwatkin, *British Foreign Service*, pp. 7ff; Jones, *Nineteenth Century*, p. 39.

5. S. T. Bindoff, "The Unreformed Diplomatic Service, 1812–1860," *Transactions of the Royal Historical Society*, 4th ser., 18 (1935): 164; Temperley, *Foreign Policy of Canning*, pp. 260–61.

6. E. L. Woodward, *The Age of Reform, 1815–1870*, p. 188; Henry Adams, *History of the United States of America in the Administrations of Jefferson and Madison* IV, 56–57, 69–70.

7. Joanne Loewe Neel, *Phineas Bond: A Study in Anglo-American Relations, 1786–1812*, 162; C. K. Webster, *The Art and Practice of Diplomacy*, p. 39; Bindoff, "Unreformed Diplomatic Service," p. 155. See also E. Jones-Parry, "Undersecretaries of State for Foreign Affairs, 1782–1855," *English Historical Review* 49: 308–20.

8. C. K. Webster, *The Foreign Policy of Castlereagh, 1815–1822*, p. 41; Jones, *Nineteenth Century*, p. 136; Bernard Mayo, ed., "Instructions to the British Ministers to the United States, 1791–1812," *American Historical Association Annual Report, 1936* III, 1; Webster, *Art and Practice*, pp. 39–40; D. C. M. Platt, *Finance, Trade, and Politics in British Foreign Policy, 1815–1914*, pp. xxv–xxvii.

9. Ward and Gooch, *Cambridge History* I, 158, 221; R. M. Keith, *Memoirs and Correspondence . . . of Sir Robert Murray Keith*, ed. Mrs. Gillespie Smythe, II, 219; Woodward, *Age of Reform*, p. 190; Josceline Bagot, *George Canning and His Friends* II, 332, 349.

10. John Quincy Adams to John Adams Smith, May 17, 1819, in *The Writings of John Quincy Adams*, ed. Worthington Chauncey Ford, VI, 551.

11. Henry Adams, *The Education of Henry Adams*, p. 196.

George Hammond

1. For background on the decision to send a minister to America, see Frederick Jackson Turner, "English Policy toward America in 1790–1791," *American Historical Review* 7 (1901): 707–708; Francis S. Philbrick, *The Rise of the West, 1754–1830*, pp. 83–84; Samuel F. Bemis, *Jay's Treaty: A Study in Commerce and Diplomacy*, pp. 116–17, 119; Charles R. Ritcheson, *Aftermath of Revolution: British Policy toward the United States, 1783–1795*, pp. 91–140, 147–84; Mayo, "Instructions," pp. xi, 1; Dumas Malone, *Jefferson and the Rights of Man*, p. 398; P. Colquhoun-Grenville correspondence, 1791, in *Report on the Manuscripts of J. B. Fortesque, Esq., Preserved at Dropmore*, ed. Walter Fitzpatrick, II; J. Leitch Wright, Jr., *Britain and the American Frontier, 1783–1815*, pp. 13–31.

2. Joshua Johnson to Thomas Jefferson, July 7, 1791 (transcript), John Franklin Jameson Papers, Library of Congress; Helen J. Cowan, "Selkirk's Work in Canada," *Canadian Historical Review* 9 (1928): 299; Alexander Hamilton to George Washington, April 11 and October 6, 1791, in Alexander Hamilton, *The Papers of Alexander Hamilton*, ed. Harold C. Syrett et al., VIII, 277–78, IX, 289; Gouverneur Morris to Thomas Jefferson, December 28, 1790, in Gouverneur Morris, *Life and Correspondence of Gouverneur Morris*, ed. Jared Sparks, II, 55–56; Frank H. Hill, "Pitt and Peel," *Transactions of the Royal Historical Society* 4th ser., 13 (1937): 206–11; W. A. Miles to Buckingham, December 13, 1790, in W. A. Miles, *The Correspondence of W. A. Miles on the French Revolution, 1789–1817*, ed. Charles Popham Miles, I, 182; Bemis, *Jay's Treaty*, p. 171; Ritcheson, *Aftermath of Revolution*, pp. 139–40; J. G. Simcoe to Evan Nepean, March 16, 1791 (transcript), Jameson Papers; Turner, "English Policy," p. 719; Neel, *Phineas Bond*, pp. 83–84; Bond to Grenville, October 8, 1791, in Phineas Bond, "Letters of Phineas Bond," ed. John Franklin Jameson, *American Historical Association Annual Report*, 1897, I, 491.

3. Beckles Willson, *Friendly Relations: A Narrative of Britain's Ministers and Ambassadors to America, 1791–1930*, pp. 3, 4; John Tickell, *The History of the Town and County of Kingston-upon-Hull*, p. 735; S. T. Bindoff, E. F. Malcolm-Smith, and C. K. Webster, eds., *British Diplomatic Representatives, 1789–1852*, 3rd ser., 50 (1934): 9, 40, 98, 184; *Diary and Autobiography of John Adams*, ed. L. H. Butterfield, II, 303, III, 117, IV, 65; Keith, *Memoirs and Correspondence* II, 236, 237–38, 247, 260; Sidney Lee, "George Hammond," *A Dictionary of National Biography*, ed. Leslie Stephen and Sidney Lee, VIII, 1125–26; Grenville to Hammond, May 24, 1791 (transcript), Jameson Papers; Edward Thornton Memoir, Thornton Papers, Library of Congress; Grenville to Hammond, May 24, 1791, in Fitzpatrick, *Manuscripts of Fortesque*, II, 80.

4. Bindoff, Malcolm-Smith, and Webster, *Diplomatic Representatives*, p. 184; Thornton Memoir, Thornton Papers. The appointment of secretaries of embassies was made by the Foreign Office until the end of 1815 (Charles Webster, *The Foreign Policy of Castlereagh, 1812–1815*, p. 48).

5. Bond to Grenville, October 8, 1791, in Bond, "Letters," p. 491.

6. Douglas Southall Freeman, *George Washington: A Biography* VI, 334; William Gordon to John Adams, September 15, 1791, in "Letters of William Gordon," ed. W. C. Ford, *Massachusetts Historical Society Proceedings* 63 (1940): 563–66; Jean de Ternant to Montmorin, November 13, 1791, in "Correspondence of the French Ministers to the United States, 1790–1797," ed. Frederick Jackson Turner, *American Historical Associa-*

tion Annual Report, 1903, II, 69; John Todd to James Madison, October 30, 1791, in *The Writings of James Madison*, ed. Gaillard Hunt, VI, 59; Joshua Johnson to Thomas Jefferson, July 2, 1791 (transcript), Jameson Papers; Willson, *Friendly Relations*, p. 6.

7. Hammond to Grenville, November 1, 1791, in Fitzpatrick, *Manuscripts of Fortesque* II, 223.

8. See note 7.

9. Kenneth Roberts and Anna M. Roberts, trans. and ed., *Moreau de St. Mery's American Journey, 1793–1798*, pp. 267–68.

10. Mayo, "Instructions," p. 20; Ternant to Montmorin, October 24, November 13, 1791, in "Correspondence of French Ministers," pp. 62–63, 68–69; Willson, *Friendly Relations*, p. 5; Hammond to Grenville, November 16, 1791 (no. 4), to George Aust, November 16, 1791 (pvt.), both in Henry Adams, "Transcripts of the Dispatches of the British Ministers to the United States," Library of Congress. Unless otherwise cited, all of Hammond's dispatches and letters are from this source; Thornton Memoir.

11. Hammond to Aust, November 16, 1791 (pvt.), in Adams, "Transcripts of Dispatches."

12. Malone, *Jefferson*, pp. 396–98; Jefferson to Hammond, December 15, 1791, Hammond to Jefferson, December 14, 1791, January 20, 1792, June 20, 1793, in William R. Manning, ed., *The Diplomatic Correspondence of the United States, Canadian Relations* I, 46–48, 387–88, 389–90, 403; George Beckwith to Lord Dorchester, December 2, 1791, in Turner, "English Policy," p. 734; Hammond to Grenville, March 6 (no. 11), April 5 (no. 16), June 8 (no. 22), 1792; Jefferson to Madison, June 4, 1792, Madison Papers, Library of Congress; Ritcheson, *Aftermath of Revolution*, chapter 12; Neel, *Phineas Bond*, pp. 87–93; Bemis, *Jay's Treaty*, p. 17; Willson, *Friendly Relations*, p. 6; Merrill D. Peterson, *Thomas Jefferson and the New Nation: A Biography*, pp. 451–54; A. L. Burt, *The United States, Great Britain, and British North America from the Revolution to the Establishment of Peace after the War of 1812*, pp. 127–29, 134, 136, 143; Thornton Memoir.

13. Hammond to Grenville, December 6 (no. 8), 1796, in Manning, *Diplomatic Correspondence*.

14. Hammond to Grenville, December 19 (no. 13), 1791, January 9 (no. 3), April 5 (no. 16), June 8 (no. 22), October 3 (no. 35), November 6, 12, 1792, March 7 (nos. 6, 7), April 2 (no. 11), 1793, in Manning, ed., *Diplomatic Correspondence*.

15. Jefferson, "Anas," March 11, 1792, in *The Writings of Thomas Jefferson*, ed. Paul L. Ford, I, 186–87; Arthur Burr Darling, *Our Rising Empire, 1763–1803*, pp. 142–43; Marshall Smelser, "The Federalist Period as an Age of Passion," *American Quarterly* 10, no. 4, (1958): 391–419, and "The Jacobin Phrenzy: The Menace of Monarchy, Plutocracy, and Anglophilia, 1789–1798," *Review of Politics*, 21: 239–58; David Erskine to his father, December 8, 1798, January 1, 1799, in "D. M. Erskine: Letters from America, 1798–1799," ed. Patricia Holbert Menk, *William and Mary Quarterly*, 3rd ser. 6 (1949): 257, 277–78; Willson, *Friendly Relations*, pp. 12, 24; Hawkins to Jefferson, March 26, 1792, "Letters of Benjamin Hawkins," *North Carolina Historical Review* 12: 259.

16. Thornton Memoir, Thornton Papers; Hammond to Grenville, September 5, 1792, March 7 (no. 5), 1793, in Manning, *Diplomatic Correspondence*; Thornton to Bland Burges, June 11, 1792, Thornton Memoir, Thornton Papers.

17. Grenville to Hammond, March 12, May 2, July 5, January (n.d.), January 10, 1794, in Mayo, "Instructions," pp. 38–39, 40–42, 44–47, 47–49.

18. Bradford Perkins, *The First Rapprochement: England and the United States, 1795–1805*, p. 186.

19. Jack L. Cross, *London Mission: The First Critical Years* pp. 60, 64–65; Free-

man, *George Washington* VII, 53, 62–63, 65–67, 89; Fauchet to the Commission on Foreign Relations, September 5, 1794, in "Correspondence of French Ministers," 417; Manning, *Diplomatic Correspondence* I, 58–60, 400–401, 402, 403, 404–406; Hammond to Grenville, September 17, 1793; (no. 19) and to Bland Burges, November 10, 1793 (Pvt.), Adams Transcripts.

20. Alexander De Conde, *Entangling Alliance: Politics and Diplomacy under George Washington*, p. 278; Hammond to Grenville, October 3, 1792 (no. 39), May 17 (no. 14), June 10, July 7, October 12 (no. 20), November 10 (no. 22), 1793; Bemis, *Jay's Treaty*, p. 202.

21. Grenville to Hammond, May 28, 1792, Hammond to Grenville, January 1, 1793, Bishop White Certificate, May 20, 1793, Phineas Bond to William Hammond, February 5, 1793, all transcripts in Jameson Papers; Willson, *Friendly Relations*, pp. 8, 9, 13; Leslie Reade, "George III to the United States Sendeth Greetings," *History Today* 3, no. 11, (1958): 770–80; Neel, *Phineas Bond*, p. 110.

22. Hammond to Grenville, October 12 (no. 20), 1793.

23. Fitzpatrick, *Manuscripts of Fortesque* II, 443–44; Benjamin Rush, *Letters of Benjamin Rush*, ed. L. H. Butterfield, pp. 655, 657; Grenville to Hammond, January (n.d.), 1794, in Mayo, "Instructions," pp. 49–50; Reade, "George III," p. 778; Ritcheson, *Aftermath of Revolution*, pp. 294–95.

24. Hammond to Grenville, April 17 (no. 15), 1794; Grenville to Hammond, August 8, 1794, in Mayo, "Instructions," pp. 60–62; Bond to Grenville, April 17, 1794, in Bond, "Letters," p. 546.

25. Hammond to Grenville, October 12 (no. 20), 1793, in Fitzpatrick, *Manuscripts of Fortesque*, pp. 443–44.

26. Stuart Gerry Brown, *The First Republicans*, pp. 103–104; Cross, *London Mission*, p. 101; Bemis, *Jay's Treaty*, pp. 218–19, 233, 238–40; Philbrick, *Rise of the West*, pp. 150, 152, 156; Burt, *United States*, pp. 133–36.

27. Hammond to Grenville, February 22 (no. 2), 1794; Randolph to Hammond, February 21, April 29, 1794, in Manning, *Diplomatic Correspondence* I, 61, 62–63. Hammond to Grenville, February 22 (no. 2), March 7 (no. 4), September 27, 1794, Adams Transcripts; Hammond to Randolph, March 10, May 22, June 7, 1794, in Manning, *Diplomatic Correspondence* I, 409–10, 411–12, 413–17; Minute to Rufus King, April 7, 1793 [1794], in Rufus King, *The Life and Correspondence of Rufus King*, ed. Charles R. King, I, 523–24; Willson, *Friendly Relations*, p. 14; Fauchet to Commission on Foreign Relations, September 3, 1794, in "Correspondence of French Ministers," pp. 407–409.

28. Neel, *Phineas Bond*, p. 130; Roberts and Roberts, *Moreau de St. Mery*, p. 268; Coxe to Jefferson, May 31, 1794, Jefferson Papers, Library of Congress; Randolph to Washington, June 20, 1794, in Freeman, *George Washington* VII, 177; Margaret Hammond to her father (n.d.), 1795, in Willson, *Friendly Relations*, p. 17.

29. Wolcott to Wolcott, Sr., April 14, 1794, in George Gibbs, *Memoirs of the Administrations of Washington and Adams* I, 133; Fisher Ames to Christopher Gore, March 5, 1794, in *The Works of Fisher Ames, with a Selection from His Speeches and Correspondence* I, 137.

30. John Quincy Adams, *Memoirs of John Quincy Adams, Comprising Portions of This Diary from 1795 to 1848* I, 38–39.

31. Hammond to Grenville, April 17 (no. 15), May 8, 25 (no. 20), 1794, in Mayo, "Instructions," pp. 54–57, 67; Freeman, *George Washington* VII, 163, 167–68; Bemis, *Jay's Treaty*, pp. 254, 256, 264, 267, 268; Hammond to Bland Burges, April 28, 1794 (transcript), Jameson Papers; Hamilton, *Papers of Hamilton* XVI, 130, 132, 348–49, 405, XXX, 381–84.

Notes   229

32. Bemis, *Jay's Treaty,* pp. 265–66; Grenville to Hammond, May 10, August 8, November 20, 1794, in Mayo, "Instructions," pp. 36, 60–63, 64–66, 73–75.

33. Hammond to Grenville, April 15 (no. 10), May 27, June 9, August 3, 16, September 5, 28, 1794, January 5, 1795; Fitzpatrick, *Manuscripts of Fortesque* III, 520–28; Fauchet to the Committee on Public Safety, April 24, 1795, in "Correspondence of French Ministers," p. 662; William Cobbett to Hammond, August 8, 1800 (transcript) and Joseph Priestley letter, January 13, 1797 (transcript), both in Jameson Papers.

34. Hammond to Grenville, April 17 (no. 15), August 3, 1794, January 5, 1795; Grenville to Hammond, May 10, October 2, 1794, in Mayo, "Instructions," pp. 54–57, 67; Albert H. Bowman, *The Struggle for Neutrality: Franco-American Diplomacy during the Federalist Era,* pp. 182–84, 198–99, 204–205; Bemis, *Jay's Treaty,* pp. xii, 229, 246–48, 273–77, 337–44, 358–59, 370. Contrary views of Hamilton's role are in Burt, *United States,* p. 155; Ritcheson, *Aftermath of Revolution,* pp. 415–20; Perkins, *First Rapprochement,* pp. 85–86; Forrest McDonald, *The Presidency of George Washington,* pp. 142–43, 152. See also Hamilton, *Papers of Hamilton* XVII, 459.

35. Grenville to Jay, November 21, 1794, F. O. 5/15.

36. Jay to Grenville, November 22, 1794, in John Jay, *The Correspondence and Public Papers of John Jay,* ed. Henry P. Johnston, IV, 145–47; Fitzpatrick, *Manuscripts of Fortesque* III, 534–36; Grenville to Hammond, August 8, 1794, in Mayo, "Instructions," p. 61; Burt, *United States,* pp. 156–57.

37. Grenville to Hammond, December 9, 1794, in Fitzpatrick, *Manuscripts of Fortesque* II, 651; Grenville to Hammond, December 10, 1794, in Mayo, "Instructions," p. 77.

38. Grenville to Hammond, April 15, May 9, June 5, 1794, in Mayo, "Instructions," pp. 80, 83, 85; Hammond to Grenville, April 28 (no. 8), June 25 (no. 17), July 18 (no. 23), 27 (no. 29), 1795, F.O., 1795; Burt, *United States,* pp. 157–58; John Bach McMaster, *A History of the People of the United States from the Revolution to the Civil War* II, 246–50; Raymond Walters, Jr., *Albert Gallatin, Jeffersonian Financier and Diplomat,* pp. 96–97; William Vans Murray to James McHenry, December 24, 1795, in Bernard C. Steiner, *The Life and Correspondence of James McHenry,* pp. 160–61; Mayo, "Instructions," pp. 88, 99–100; Freeman, *George Washington* VII, 260–62; McDonald, *Presidency of Washington,* pp. 164, 165.

39. Margaret Hammond to her father, September (n.d.), 1795, in Willson, *Friendly Relations,* p. 17; Grenville to Hammond, May 9, June 5, 1795, in Mayo, "Instructions," pp. 83, 85; Hammond to Grenville, July 27 (no. 28), August 14 (nos. 32, 33, 34), 1795; Freeman, *George Washington* VII, 279–95; Moncure D. Conway, *Omitted Chapters of History Disclosed in the Life and Papers of Edmund Randolph,* pp. 270–357; Gibbs, *Washington and Adams* I, 232–33; Peterson, *Thomas Jefferson,* p. 549; Edmund Berkeley and Dorothy Smith, *John Beckley, Zealous Partisan in a Nation Divided,* pp. 112, 113, 115; Neel, *Phineas Bond,* pp. 134ff.; McDonald, *Presidency of Washington,* p. 165; Hamilton, *Papers of Hamilton* XVII, 527–30; De Conde, *Entangling Alliance.* Almost alone among historians, De Conde considers Hammond a rousing success as minister to America; Adams, *Memoirs of John Quincy Adams* I, 152, 160, 163, 164; Mayo, "Instructions," pp. 89–90, 116.

40. Adams, *Memoirs of John Quincy Adams* I, 139–46, 167, II, 590; Neel, *Phineas Bond,* p. 132; Fitzpatrick, *Manuscripts of Fortesque* III, 141; Willson, *Friendly Relations,* pp. 18ff.; Liston to Foreign Office, May 6, 1800 (draft no. 18), Liston Papers, University of Edinburgh. For Hammond's continued malice, see Sylvester Douglas, *The Diaries of Sylvester Douglas,* ed. Frances Bickley, I, 285–87; Gabrielle Festing, *John Hookham Frere and His Friends,* p. 47; H. W. V. Temperley, *Life of Canning,* p. 56; Temperley, *Foreign Policy of Canning,* pp. 260–61; James Harris Malmesbury, *Diaries and*

Correspondence of James Harris, First Earl of Malmesbury, Edited by His Grandson, the Third Earl III, 595; Berkeley to Bathurst, August 13, 1807, in Francis Bickley, comp., *Report on the Manuscripts of Earl Bathurst Preserved at Cirencester Park* 76, 63; Planta to Bagot, July 12, 1816, Ellis to Bagot, July 4, 1817, in Bagot, *George Canning* II, 28, 54; Adams, *Memoirs of John Quincy Adams* I, 139–46, 167.

41. Adams, *History of the United States* V, 45; Hammond to William Hamilton, April 30, 1814, manuscript in possession of Colonel Barnes, Cobham, England.

Robert Liston

1. Gouverneur Morris, *The Diary and Letters of Gouverneur Morris*, ed. Anne Cary Morris, II, 101.

2. Liston to Henry Cunningham, March, 1796, in Willson, *Friendly Relations*, p. 19.

3. Mrs. Liston to James Jackson, April 25, May 6, 8, 1796, Mrs. Liston Diary, all in Liston Papers.

4. Liston to Hammond (draft), May 4, 1796, Lady Bute to Mrs. Liston, March 18, April 2, 6, 1796, Mrs. Liston to James Jackson, May 28, 1796, all in Liston Papers.

5. William Pinkney to Secretary of State Pickering, March 7, 1796, in Manning, *Diplomatic Correspondence* I, 465–66; Chauncey Goodrich to Oliver Wolcott, Sr., May 27, 1796, in Gibbs, *Washington and Adams* I, 340.

6. Liston to Hammond, May 31, 1796. Unless otherwise cited, all Liston dispatches and other communications to and from the Foreign Office are from drafts or originals in the Liston Papers.

7. Mayo, "Instructions," pp. 99–100, 105; Gerard Clarfield, "Postscript to the Jay Treaty: Timothy Pickering and Anglo-American Relations, 1795–1797," *William and Mary Quarterly*, 3rd ser., 23 (1966): 106–12; Liston to Grenville, August 30, 1797, July 3 (no. 4), 1796, Liston Papers.

8. Mowat to Liston, March 27, 1797, in Mayo, "Instructions," p. 119; Grenville to Liston, October 7, 1796, in Mayo, "Instructions," pp. 122–23; Clarfield, "Postscript to Jay Treaty," pp. 112–70.

9. George W. M. Kyte, "Robert Liston and Anglo-American Cooperation, 1796–1800," *Proceedings of the American Philosophical Society* 93, no.3 (1949): 261; Liston to Rufus King, June 20, 1796, Liston Papers; Liston to Hammond, June 20, 1796, Liston Papers.

10. William Spohn Baker, *Washington after the Revolution, 1784–1799* II, 244–45; Rush to Adams, December 15, 1807, in Rush, *Letters of Rush* II, 958.

11. Mrs. Liston to James Jackson, May 26, 1796, and Mrs. Liston Diary, both in Liston Papers.

12. Letters to Henrietta Liston, and Liston-Coutts correspondence, Liston Papers; Priestley to T. Lindsay, January 13, 1797 (transcript), Jameson Papers; Adet to the Foreign Ministry, March 31, 1797, in "Correspondence of French Ministers," p. 1005; Grenville to Liston, January 27, 1797, in Mayo, "Instructions," p. 130; Liston to Grenville, April 18 (no. 17), 1797, Liston Papers.

13. Mrs. Liston to James Jackson, September 6, 1796, Liston Papers; Georgetown *Museum*, July 19, 1796.

14. Liston to Grenville, October 13 (no. 14), November 19 (no. 25), 25 (no. 29), December 20 (no. 31), 1796, March 18 (no. 10), April 18 (no. 15), 1797, Liston Papers.

15. Adet to Foreign Ministry, June 3, 1796, and instructions of the ministry to chargé Mangourit, in "Correspondence of French Ministers," pp. 909, 942.

16. Mrs. Liston to James Jackson, December 9, 1796, February 24, 1797, Liston Diary, March 3, 1797, all in Liston Papers; Liston to Grenville, November 18 (no. 26),

1796, January 25 (no. 2), February 13 (no. 3), March 16, 1797, February 6 (no. 3), 1798, Liston Papers; Liston to Hammond, March 16, 19, April 8, 1797, Liston Papers; William H. Masterson, *William Blount*, pp. 304–305, 307, 309; Memorandum to Chisholm, May 17, 1797, deposition of Chisholm, November 29, 1797, Collot to Yrujo (n.d.), in "Documents on the Blount Conspiracy, 1795–1797," ed. Frederick J. Turner, *American Historical Review* 10 (1905): 584–86, 601–605; Liston to J. H. Goverts, March 16, 1797, in King, *Life and Correspondence* II, 198.

17. Masterson, *William Blount*, pp. 312–13, 316–19; Liston to Hammond, September 7, 1797, Liston Papers; Liston to Grenville, June 24, 1797, Liston Papers; Darling, *Our Rising Empire*, pp. 271–72.

18. Liston to Grenville, June 24, July 8, 1797, Liston Papers.

19. Liston to Pickering, June 19, July 2, 1797, in Manning, *Diplomatic Correspondence* I, 482, 483–84; Pickering to Liston, July 1, 1797, Pickering Papers, Massachusetts Historical Society (hereafter cited as Pickering Papers); Pickering to King, July 5, August 8, 1797, and King-Grenville correspondence of August, 1797, in King, *Life and Correspondence* II, 196–97, 209–10, 216, 218–19.

20. Liston to Grenville, July 8, August 30 (no. 36), 1797, Liston Papers; Thornton to Grenville, December 5, 1797, Francis Moore to Liston, November 30, 1797, Liston to Hammond, July 18, September 7, 1797, all in Liston Papers.

21. Mrs. Liston to James Jackson, July 12, 14, 1797, Liston Papers.

22. Liston to Hammond, April 19, 1797 (Pvt.).

23. Mrs. Liston to James Jackson, April 8, 1797, Liston Papers.

24. Liston to Grenville, July 13, 1797, Liston Papers.

25. Mrs. Liston's Diary. Grenville approved the embassy site, but because of Congress's refusal to ratify the offer, it came to nothing. Liston to Grenville, March 20 (no. 9), 1798, Liston Papers; Grenville to Liston, June 8, 1798, in Mayo, "Instructions," p. 153.

26. Pickering-Liston correspondence, July, 1798, Pickering Papers; Liston to ship captains, June 29, October 15, 1798, Jameson Papers.

27. Louis-Guillaume Otto, "Considerations sur la conduite du gouvernement des Etats Unis, envers la France . . ." in Bowman, *Struggle for Neutrality*, p. 298.

28. David Erskine to his father, January 1, 1799, in Erskine, "Erskine's Letters," pp. 279–80.

29. Liston to Grenville, May 2 (no. 20), 1798, January 29, February 18 (no. 12), 1799, Liston Papers.

30. Liston to Grenville, May 2 (nos. 20, 21), 20, August 31 (no. 52), September 27 (no. 55), 1798, Liston Papers.

31. Darling, *Our Rising Empire*, p. 314–15, 329–33.

32. Liston to Grenville, February 22, March 4, 1799, Liston Papers; Hamilton, *Papers of Hamilton* XXII, 489–90, 504; Liston to Grenville, November 7 (no. 63), 1798, January 31 (no. 7), March 4 (no. 17), November 4 (nos. 60, 61), 1799, November 28 (no. 44), 1800, Liston Papers.

33. Mrs. Adams to her sister, December 30, 1799, in Abigail Adams, *New Letters of Abigail Adams, 1788–1801, with an Introduction by Stewart Mitchell*, ed. Stewart Mitchell, p. 224; Page Smith, *John Adams* II, 1015–16.

34. Liston to Grenville, June 8 (no. 40), September 5, December 31 (no. 67), 1799, October 8 (no. 36), November 28 (no. 46), 1800, Liston Papers; Pickering-Liston correspondence, August–December, 1799, especially August 9, Pickering Papers.

35. Thomas Blount to John G. Blount, June 28, 1798, in William H. Masterson, ed., *The John Gray Blount Papers* III, 243; Liston to Grenville, September 5, 1799, Liston Papers; New York *Argus*, November 8, 1799, in Hamilton, *Papers of Hamilton*

XXIV, 7; Philadelphia *Aurora*, July 15, 25, 26, August 3, October 24, 1799, April 15, May 10, 1800; Berkeley and Smith, *Beckley*, p. 237.

36. Beckley to Gallatin, February 4, 1801, in Berkeley and Smith, *Beckley*, p. 214; Jefferson, "Anas," January 2, 1800, in *Thomas Jefferson* I, 281–82; Liston to Grenville, July 11, 1799, February 5, 1800, Liston Papers; Pickering-Liston correspondence, July 13, 15, 26, August 3, 1799, Pickering Papers; Philadelphia *Aurora*, July 15, 26, August 3, October 24, 1799, April 15, May 10, 1800; William Cobbett, *Porcupine's Works* XI, 11–17.

37. Rufus King to Pickering (with extract), March 4, September 2, 1800, James McHenry to Pickering, June 24, 1800, Pickering to King, June 26, 1800, in King, *Life and Correspondence* III, 212–13, 260, 261; Pickering to Jacob Wagner, June 12, 1800, Pickering Papers; Liston to Grenville, May 6 (no. 18), 1800, Liston to Hammond, March 30, April 3, May 9, November 7, 1799, and Liston to Grenville, April 5 (Pvt.), 1800, all in Liston Papers; Neel, *Phineas Bond*, pp. 143–44.

38. Alexander De Conde, *The Quasi-War: The Politics and Diplomacy of the Undeclared War with France, 1797–1801*, pp. 270–72; Liston to Grenville, May 27, 29, July 5, November 4 (no. 41), 1800, all in Liston Papers; Albert Beveridge, *The Life of John Marshall* II, 497–99.

39. Mrs. Liston's Diary.

40. Mrs. Liston to James Jackson, November 29, December 18, 1799, Liston Papers.

41. Liston to Grenville, December 21, 1799, December 26, 1799, Liston Papers; Baker, *Washington* II, 382.

42. Liston to Hammond, summer, 1799 (n.d.), February 14, August 26, 1800, Liston to Grenville, October 7 (no. 57), 1799, February 6 (Pvt.), May 6 (no. 19), 7 (Pvt.), 1800, Liston to Nathaniel Marchant, July 28, 1800, all in Liston Papers; William Cobbett, *Letters from William Cobbett to Edward Thornton Written in the Years 1797 to 1800*, ed. G. D. H. Cole, pp. 3–4.

43. Grenville to Liston, February 28 (Pvt.), 1800, Liston Papers; Grenville to Liston, February 28, 1800, in Mayo, "Instructions," p. 183.

44. Liston to Grenville, May 7 (Pvt.), 1800, F.O. 5/29A.

45. Liston to Grenville, May 7 (Pvt.), 1800, Liston to Hammond, August 26 (private), November 7, 1800, Henry Stuart to Liston, November 20, 1800, Captain Laurie to Liston, November 13, 1800, Latrobe to Liston, June 18, 1800, Abigail Adams to Liston, April 3, 1800, all in Liston Papers; Liston to McHenry, May 24, 1800, McHenry Papers, Library of Congress; Charles C. Paullin, "Early British Diplomats in Washington," *Records of the Columbia Historical Society* 44–45 (1942–43): 243; Liston to Grenville, May 28, July 5, 1800, Liston Papers.

46. Liston to Pickering, December 10, 1800, Pickering to Mrs. Liston, April 7, 1812, both in Pickering Papers; *National Intelligencer*, November 19, December 29, 1800, March 16, July 13, 1801.

47. William Cobbett, *Cobbett's Political Register* 8, no. 15 (October 12, 1805): 547–48; Ernest Hartley Coleridge, *The Life and Times of Thomas Coutts, Banker* II, 355–56, 357; Pickering to Liston, May 19, 1805, Liston Papers; Theodore Lyman, Jr., to Timothy Pickering, June 15, 1819, Pickering to Mrs. Liston, April 7, 1812, both in Pickering Papers; Giovanni Costigan, *Sir Robert Wilson: A Soldier of Fortune in the Napoleonic Wars*, pp. 105–106; Robert Wilson, *General Wilson's Journal, 1812–1814*, ed., Anthony Brett James, I, 2, 23, 29, 113, 124, 268; Selections from the Wilson Private Diary, Jameson Transcripts; Walter Scott, *The Journal of Sir Walter Scott*, ed., W. E. K. Anderson, p. 493; Adams, *Memoirs of John Quincy Adams* III, 364, 470, 474; George Jackson, *The Bath Archives: A Further Selection from the Diaries and Letters of Sir*

George Jackson . . . from 1809 to 1816, ed., Lady Jackson, 2 vols. I, 287, 347; Webster, *Foreign Policy, 1812–1815,* pp. 48, 86, 89, 430; Webster, *Foreign Policy, 1815–1822,* p. 40; John Goldworth Alger, *Napoleon's Visitors and Captives, 1801–1815,* p. 78; Willson, *Friendly Relations,* p. 37; Fitzpatrick, *Manuscripts of Fortesque* VII, 140; Douglas, *Diaries of Sylvester Douglas* I, 393; *Gentleman's Magazine* 160 November, 1836: 539.

Edward Thornton

1. Thornton Memoir, Thornton Papers.

2. Burges to Bond, August 3, 1791, in Neel, *Phineas Bond,* pp. 97, 99, 116; Thornton Memoir, Thornton Papers; Steiner, *Life of McHenry,* p. 143; Hammond to Grenville, April 17 (no. 15), August 16, December 1, 1794, Adams Transcripts.

3. Thornton to Burges, September 1, November 3, 1793, Thornton Papers; Thornton to Burges, May 27, 1794, in James Bland Burges, *Selections from the Letters and Correspondence of Sir James Bland Burges, Bart. . . . ,* ed. James Hutton, pp. 248–49; Conway, *Omitted Chapters,* pp. 270, 271; Bond to Grenville, April 17, 1794, in Bond, "Letters," p. 546.

4. Thornton to Burges, November 3, 1793, Thornton Papers; Cobbett, *Letters,* pp. xxiv–xxxvi, 2, 20, 22, 50, 71; Burges, *Selections from Letters,* p. 314.

5. Henrietta Liston to Nathaniel Marchant, April 10, 1798, Hammond to Liston, June 8, 1798, both in Liston Papers; Cobbett, *Letters,* pp. xxxvii, 1, 2; Thornton to Burges, June 11, 1792, in Burges, *Selections from Letters,* pp. 222–24.

6. Thornton to Burges, June 11, 1792, in Burges, *Selections from Letters,* pp. 222–24.

7. Thornton to Burges, April 2, June 11, 1792, March 5, 1793, in Burges, *Selections from Letters,* pp. 201–202, 222–24, 231–32. Thornton mellowed somewhat in later years (Perkins, *First Rapprochement,* p. 24; Thornton Memoir, Thornton Papers; Willson, *Friendly Relations,* p. 34; Thornton to Hawkesbury, February 15, 1801, F.O. 5/32).

8. Thornton to Grenville, December 24 (no. 4), 1800, F.O. 5/29; Gallatin to his wife, January 15, 1801, in Henry Adams, *The Life of Albert Gallatin,* pp. 252–55. A brief but colorful summary of early nineteenth-century criticism of the capital is in James Sterling Young, *The Washington Community, 1800–1828,* pp. 41–48.

9. Oliver Wolcott to his wife, July 4, 1800, in Gibbs, *Washington and Adams* II, 377–78.

10. Morris, *Diary and Letters* II, 394–95. Wolcott to his wife, July 4, 1800, in Gibbs, *Washington and Adams* II, 377–78; Gallatin to his wife, January 15, 1801, in Adams, *Albert Gallatin,* p. 252; Robert J. Hubbard, "Political and Social Life in Washington during the Administration of President Monroe," *Transactions of the Oneida Historical Society* 9 (1903): 59.

11. Abigail Adams to Thomas B. Adams, November 13, 1800, Abigail Adams to Mrs. Smith, November 21, 27, 1800, in Abigail Adams, *Letters of Mrs. Adams, the Wife of John Adams, with an Introductory Memoir by Her Grandson, Charles Francis Adams,* pp. 380–85.

12. Thornton to Hawkesbury, March 9, 1801, F.O. 5/32; Young, *Washington Community,* p. 22; Wolcott to his wife, July 4, 1800, in Gibbs, *Washington and Adams* II, 378; Anne Hollingsworth Wharton, *Social Life in the Early Republic,* p. 73.

13. Gallatin to his wife, January 22, 1801, in Adams, *Albert Gallatin,* p. 255; Thornton to Hawkesbury, December 13, 26, 27, 1800, F.O. 5/29, January 16 (no. 4), February 15, 17.

14. Thornton to Hawkesbury, February 28 (no. 13), March 4 (no. 15), 5, December 8 (no. 57), 1801, F.O. 5/32.

15. Thornton to Hawkesbury, March 4, 1801 (no. 55), F.O. 5/32.
16. Thornton to Hawkesbury, March 4, 7, December 8 (nos. 55, 56), 9, 1801, F.O. 5/32; Willson, *Friendly Relations*, pp. 30–33; Adams, *History of the United States* II, 342–44; Darling, *Our Rising Empire*, p. 529.
17. Thornton to Hawkesbury, June 2 (no. 32), August 9 (no. 33), 1801, F.O. 5/32, August 4, 1802, F.O. 5/35.
18. Thornton to Hawkesbury, March 12, October 1 (nos. 47, 48), December 8 (no. 57), 1801, F.O. 5/32, January 29, February 1 (no. 6), 20, April 3 (no. 15), May 1 (no. 21), 1802, F.O. 5/35, January 3 (no. 3), 1803, F.O. 5/38.
19. Thornton to Hawkesbury, February 5 (no. 7), 28 (no. 14), March 28 (no. 21), June 2 (no. 30), August 10 (no. 40), December 18, 26, (no. 60), 27, 1801, F.O. 5/32; April 3 (no. 16), November 26 (no. 47), 1802, F.O. 5/35; Thornton to Madison, March 7, 1802, Madison Papers; De Conde, *Quasi-War*, p. 291; Perkins, *First Rapprochement*, pp. 152–56; Irving Brant, *James Madison, Secretary of State, 1800–1809*, pp. 59, 61–62, 68–69, 87–88, 89; Hammond to Thornton, June 6, 1801, Hawkesbury to Thornton, January 12, 1802, both in Mayo, "Instructions," pp. 189, 191.
20. Thornton to Hawkesbury, January 26 (no. 3), February 1 (no. 7), March 6, July 3, September 27 (no. 41), 1802, F.O. 5/35; Brant, *James Madison*, pp. 44, 79; Perkins, *First Rapprochement*, pp. 160–61; Adams, *History of the United States* II, 346–48; Dumas Malone, *Jefferson the President, First Term, 1801–1805*, p. 254.
21. Brant, *James Madison*, pp. 98–99; Perkins, *First Rapprochement*, p. 163; Malone, *Jefferson, First Term*, p. 167; Thornton to Hawkesbury, February 24, March 6, August 4, November 30 (no. 50), December 28 (no. 55), 1802, F.O. 5/35; Thornton to Hawkesbury, January 3 (no. 2), 31 (no. 8), February 17, March 9 (no. 14), 11 (Separate), 1803, F.O. 5/38.
22. Thornton to Hawkesbury, January 26 (nos. 3, 4), 1802, F.O. 5/35; January 31 (no. 8), February 17, March 9 (nos. 14, 16), 1803, F.O. 5/38; Wilson Cary Nicholas to Samuel Smith (n.d.), 1803, Smith Papers, Alderman Library, University of Virginia.
23. Thornton to Hawkesbury, March 11 (Sep.), 1803, F.O. 5/38.
24. Perkins, *First Rapprochement*, pp. 164–67; Adams, *History of the United States* II, 347; Ward and Gooch, *Cambridge History* I, 315–23.
25. Thornton to Hawkesbury, April 5, 7 (no. 21), May 3, 5, July 2 (Sep.), 4 (no. 31), August 26, September 10 (Sep.), 30, November 1 (no. 52), 1803, F.O. 5/38; *Gentleman's Magazine and Historical Chronicle* 63, pt. 1 (1803): 375; Brant, *James Madison*, pp. 160–62.
26. Philadelphia *Aurora*, November 25, 1803, in Willson, *Friendly Relations*, p. 40; Merry to Hawkesbury, July 13 (Sep.), 1804, F.O. 5/42; Thornton to Hawkesbury, July 16, 1804, F.O. 5/42; Mayo, "Instructions," p. 196; Augustus Foster to his mother, July 20, 1806, Augustus Foster Papers, Library of Congress.

Anthony Merry

1. St. Helens to Grenville, June 15, 1791, in Fitzpatrick, *Manuscripts of Fortesque* II, 99; Malcolm Lester, *Anthony Merry Redivivus: A Reappraisal of the British Minister to the United States, 1803–1806*, p. 4; Notes on Merry from the British Museum, George Merry to W. Da Costa, June 5, 1774 (transcript), Liston to Carmarthen, June 10, 1787 (transcript), all in Jameson Papers; *Gentleman's Magazine and Historical Chronicle* 54, pt. 1 (1784): 239.
2. Parliamentary Reports, 1715–1801: Report of Expences of Civil List, March 15, 1802, pp. xi, 208 (transcript), Jameson Papers; William Ray Manning, "The Nootka Sound Controversy," *American Historical Association Annual Report* (1904): 364–65,

366, 371–72, 378, 399; Mayo, "Instructions," p. 22, no. 11; Extract of note of Baron Jacob Kloest, August 1, 1800 (transcript), Jameson Papers; Ward and Gooch, *Cambridge History* I, pp. 197–98; St. Helens to Grenville, June 15, 1791, in Fitzpatrick, *Manuscripts of Fortesque* II, 99; Bindoff, Malcolm-Smith, and Webster, *Diplomatic Representatives*, p. 41; *National Intelligencer*, October 18, 1800; Rufus King to the secretary of state, September 30, October 31, 1800, November 30, 1801, in King, *Life and Correspondence* III, 315, 325–26, IV, 26.

3. King to the secretary of state, November 5, 30, 1801, May 8, 1803, in King, *Life and Correspondence* IV, 11, 26, 253; Charles Duke Yonge, *The Life and Administration of Robert Banks, Second Earl of Liverpool* I, 61, 66, 79, 80; *The Journal of a British Chaplain in Paris during the Peace Negotiations of 1801–1802*, ed. A. M. Broadley, pp. xlii, 55, 247; Alger, *Napoleon's Visitors*, pp. 21–22, 24, 25, 28, 31, 71, 75–76, 106; Ward and Gooch, *Cambridge History* I, 307; Douglas, *Diaries of Sylvester Douglas* I, 310, 341, 342; Jackson correspondence, in Malmesbury, *Diaries* IV, 203, 204; Catherine Wilmot, *An Irish Peer on the Continent, 1801–1803*, ed. Thomas U. Sadleir, p. 68; Charles Ross, *Correspondence of Charles, First Marquis Cornwallis* III, 384, 418, 489; Arthur Paget, *The Paget Papers: Diplomatic and Other Correspondence of the Rt. Hon. Sir Arthur Paget, GCB, 1794–1807*, ed. Augustus B. Paget, II, 15, 50, 56, 58, 61; Goddard to Grenville, August 11, 1806, in Fitzpatrick, *Manuscripts of Fortesque* VIII, 268–69; Castalia Granville, *Lord Granville Leveson Gower (First Earl of Granville), Private Correspondence, 1781 to 1821* I, 329, 366.

4. *Journal of a British Chaplain* p. 247; Malmesbury, *Diaries* IV, 203; King to Madison, April 10, 30, 1802, to Pickering, December 25, 1809, in King, *Life and Correspondence* IV, 100–101, 113, V, 177–78; Bindoff, Malcolm-Smith, and Webster, *Diplomatic Representatives*, p. 185; Lester, *Anthony Merry*, pp. 11–12.

5. *Gentleman's Magazine and Historical Chronicle* 73, pt. 1 (1803): 83, 375; G. H. Rendall to John F. Jameson, August 28, 1921, in Jameson Papers; William Johnstone Temple, *Diaries of William Johnstone Temple, 1780–1796*, ed. Lewis Bettany, pp. 128, 142, 143, 144, 145, 157; Cobbett, *Political Register* III, 571–72, 628–29.

6. Liston to Pickering, May 2, 1806, Pickering Papers.

7. Augustus Foster to his mother, July 20, 1806, "Notes and Recollections Respecting the States in the Years 1805–06–07 and 1811–1812," Library of Congress; Thomas W. Moore to Canning, September 30, 1822, Stratford Canning Papers, F.O. 353/8.

8. Lester, *Anthony Merry*, p. 18; Thomas Moore, *Memoirs, Journal, and Correspondence of Thomas Moore*, ed. Lord John Russell, I, 132–33, 134, 137, 138, 141, 143; Thomas Moore, *The Letters of Thomas Moore*, ed. Wilfred S. Dowden, I, 46, 47, 49, 50; James Scott, *Recollections of a Naval Life* I, 24, 25, 26, 28, 30, 46; Thomas Barclay, *Selections from the Correspondence of Thomas Barclay*, ed. George Lockhart Rives, pp. 153, 154; Thomas Robson Hay, "Charles Williamson and the Burr Conspiracy," *Journal of Southern History* 2 (1935): 185, 186; Moore to his mother, November 28, 1803, Mrs. Merry to Moore, Sunday 1804 (1803), in Moore, *Memoirs* I, 143, VIII, 50–51; Thornton to Hawkesbury, December 6, 1803, (no. 55) F.O. 5/38; *Records of the Columbia Historical Society*, vol. 33–34, p. 244.

9. Merry to Hawkesbury, December 6 (no. 1), 1803, F.O. 5/41; Merry to Josiah Quincy (n.d.), in Esther Singleton, *The Story of the White House* I, 34.

10. Merry to Hawkesbury, December 6 (Sep.), 21 (Sep.), 1803, F.O. 5/41, January 30 (Sep.), 1804, F.O. 5/41; Merry to Hammond, December 7 (Pvt.), 1803, F.O. 5/41; Lester, *Anthony Merry*, pp. 30–36; Malone, *Jefferson, First Term*, pp. 378–92; Brant, *James Madison*, pp. 163–65; Adams, *History of the United States* II, 368ff. Merry's social warfare had obscured for some historians his considerable ability in professional routine,

especially in the earlier part of his tenure. Cf. Nathan Schachner, *Aaron Burr*, pp. 286, 308 and Lester, *Anthony Merry*; Willson, *Friendly Relations*, p. 44.

11. Mrs. Samuel Harrison Smith, *The First Forty Years of Washington Society Portrayed by the Family Letters of Mrs. Samuel Harrison Smith*, ed. Gaillard Hunt, p. 45; Samuel Taggart to John Taylor, January 13, 1804, "Letters of Samuel Taggart, Representative in Congress, 1804–14, Introduction by George Henry Haynes," *Proceedings of the American Antiquarian Society* 33, pt. 1 (1923): 125; Brant, *James Madison*, pp. 163–64; Moore to his mother, June 13, 1804, in Moore, *Letters* I, 161; Benjamin Ogle Tayloe, *In Memoriam: Benjamin Tayloe*, p. 137; Mayo, "Instructions," p. 3.

12. Brant, *James Madison*, pp. 164–65; Willson, *Friendly Relations*, pp. 44f.; Pichon to Talleyrand, February 5, 1804, in Adams, *History of the United States* II, 373–74; Jefferson to William Short, January 23, 1804, in *American Historical Review* 33 (1928): 834; Madison to Monroe, February 16, 1804, in Madison, *Letters of James Madison* VII, 121; Nathaniel Macon to John Steele, February 12, 1804, in "Letters of Nathaniel Macon, John Steele, and William Barry Grove," ed. Kemp P. Battle, *James Sprunt Historical Monographs* 3 (1902): 49.

13. Smith, *First Forty Years*; Anne Hollingsworth Wharton, *Salons, Colonial and Republican*, pp. 188–90; Young, *Washington Community*, pp. 216–18; Constance McLaughlin Green, *Washington, Village and Capital*, pp. 37–38, 42–43, 45–49; *National Intelligencer*, July 1, August 21, 1801; John Cotton Smith to Rev. William Andrews, January 6, 1802, in John Cotton Smith, *The Correspondence and Miscellanies of John Cotton Smith*, ed. Rev. William Andrews, p. 59; William Plumer, Jr., *Life of William Plumer*, p. 245; Augustus Foster, *Jeffersonian America: Notes on the United States of America Collected in the Years 1805–6–7 and 11–12*, ed. Richard Beale Davis, pp. 8, 9, 10, 12, 18; Augustus Foster to his mother, December 30, 1804, in (Cavendish), *The Two Duchesses . . . Family Correspondence, 1777–1859*, ed. Vere Foster, p. 197; Randolph to Gallatin, July 8, 1804, June 28, 1805, Mrs. Gallatin to Gallatin, June 5, 1804, all in Gallatin Papers, Library of Congress.

14. Jefferson to Short, January 23, 1804, in *American Historical Review* 33 (1928): 834; Brant, *James Madison*, pp. 165–66, 168; Madison to King, December 18, 1804; Christopher Gore to King, February 8–9, 1804, in King, *Life and Correspondence* IV, 332–33, 341–42; Jefferson to Monroe, January 8, 1804, in Adams, *History of the United States* II, 375–76; Malone, *Jefferson, First Term*, pp. 384–85, 387, 391–92, 499–500; Madison to Monroe, February 16, 1804, in Madison, *Writings of James Madison* VII, 119–23; Merry to Hawkesbury, January 30 (Sep.), 1804, F.O. 5/41; Monroe to Madison, April 26, June 28, July 1, 1804, in James Monroe, *The Writings of James Monroe*, ed. Stanislaus Murray Hamilton, IV, 170–72, 208–209, 221–22; Lester, *Anthony Merry*, pp. 40–44.

15. Brant, *James Madison*, pp. 170–76, 254–58; Adams, *History of the United States* II, 380, 381, 383–86, 396–99; Perkins, *First Rapprochement*, pp. 173, 174, 177–79, 181–83; Reginald Horsman, *The Causes of the War of 1812*, p. 27; Merry to Hawkesbury, December 6 (no. 1), 31 (no. 6), 1803, F.O. 5/41; Thornton to Hammond, January 29 (Pvt.), 1804, F.O. 5/41; Foster to his mother, July 20, 1806, Augustus John Foster Papers, Library of Congress.

16. Merry to Hawkesbury, December 31 (no. 8), 1803, F.O. 5/41, January 2 (no. 10), April 29, July 18 (no. 40), September 4 (no. 45), October 1 (no. 52), 1804, F.O. 5/41 and 5/42; Barclay, *Correspondence of Barclay*, pp. 162, 178–79, 189, 191, 193; Malone, *Jefferson, First Term*, p. 144; Brant, *James Madison*, pp. 207–255; Marshall Smelser, *The Democratic Republic, 1801–1815*, p. 151; Madison to Monroe, February 16, 1804, in Dolley Madison, *Memoirs and Letters of Dolley Madison, Edited by her Grand-Niece*, p. 62.

17. Merry to Hawkesbury, March 1 (no. 19), 13, April 29, May 7, to Harrowby, July 18 (no. 41), August 6 (no. 44), September 4 (no. 47), 1804, F.O. 5/41 and 5/42; Merry to Hammond, March 4 (Pvt.), 1804, F.O. 5/41; Adams, *History of the United States* II, 390–92, 395; Schachner, *Aaron Burr*, pp. 285–86; Hay, "Charles Williamson," pp. 178–80, 185–86.

18. Foster, *Jeffersonian America*, p. 17; Foster Journal, April 29, 1812, Library of Congress; Morier to Wellesley, October 7, 1810, F.O. 5/70; Merry to Hammond, December 7 (Pvt.), 1803, March 4 (Pvt.), 1804, F.O. 5/41; Paullin, "Early British Diplomats," p. 247; Brant, *James Madison*, p. 169; Merry to Hawkesbury, June 1 (Sep.), 1804, F.O. 5/41; Mrs. William Thornton Diary; Malone, *Jefferson, First Term*, p. 383; Wharton, *Social Life*, p. 114; Smith, *First Forty Years*, p. 45.

19. Perkins, *First Rapprochement*, p. 175; Horsman, *Causes of the War*, pp. 28–29; Adams, *History of the United States* II, 412–20, 421–22; Brant, *James Madison*, p. 169.

20. Brant, *James Madison*, pp. 254–56; Basil Hall, *Fragments of Voyages and Travels*, pp. 47–48; Merry to Harrowby, July 18 (no. 40), August 6 (no. 42), September 4 (no. 45), October 1 (no. 51), 1804, F.O. 5/42; Barclay to Vice Admiral Mitchell, August 25, 1804, in Barclay, *Correspondence of Barclay*, pp. 191, 203–206; Harrowby to Merry, November 7, 1807, in Mayo, "Instructions," pp. 208–11 and in Adams, *History of the United States* II, 422–25.

21. Merry to Hawkesbury, June 3, to Harrowby, July 18 (nos. 39, 40), August 6 (nos. 42, 44), October 1 (no. 50), October 1 (Pvt.), 18 (no. 53), 24 (nos. 55, 56), November 10 (no. 57), December 4 (nos. 62, 63), 26 (no. 64), 1804, F.O. 5/42; Barclay to Vice Admiral Mitchell, August 14, 25, to Hammond, August 23, to Merry, August 24, 1804, all in Barclay, *Correspondence of Barclay*, pp. 187, 188, 190, 191; Foster to his mother, December 6, 1804, Foster Papers.

22. Augustus Foster to his mother, December 6, 30, 1804, in (Cavendish), *Two Duchesses*, p. 197; Foster, *Jeffersonian America*, p. 10; Merry to Harrowby, December 27, 1804, F.O. 5/42.

23. Merry to Mulgrave, June 30 (no. 26), September 30 (no. 40), November 3 (nos. 44, 45), December 2 (no. 50), 3, 1805, F.O. 5/45 and March 19 (no. 15), May 4 (no. 22), August 31, November 2 (no. 51), 1806, F.O. 5/49; Bradford Perkins, *Prologue to War: England and the United States, 1805–1812*, pp. 77–95; Adams, *History of the United States* III, 44–48, 97–102, 108–10; Brant, *James Madison*, pp. 287–88; Horsman, *Causes of the War*, pp. 55–57, 79–81; Dumas Malone, *Jefferson the President, Second Term, 1805–1809*, pp. 57–59, 97–98; Perkins, *First Rapprochement*, pp. 79–84, 181; Lester, *Anthony Merry*, pp. 26–28.

24. Foster to his mother, July 1, 1805, in (Cavendish), *Two Duchesses*, p. 229; Foster, *Jeffersonian America*, p. 15; Merry to Harrowby, March 29 (Most Secret), to Mulgrave, April 29 (no. 22, Most Secret and Confidential), August 4 (no. 34, Most Secret), 1805, F.O. 5/45; Thomas P. Abernethy, *The Burr Conspiracy*, p. 23; Adams, *History of the United States* II, 401–403, III, 220, 226; Schachner, *Aaron Burr*, pp. 308–309; Smelser, *Democratic Republic*, pp. 106, 154.

25. Merry to Mulgrave, September 30 (no. 40), 1805, F.O. 5/45; January 3 (no. 1), February 2 (no. 7), 24, March 2 (no. 10), 6, 19 (no. 15), 25, 1806, F.O. 5/48 and to Fox, April 16, May 4 (no. 23), August 31 (no. 42), 1806, F.O. 5/48, 5/49; Barclay to Merry, April 16, 26, 27, May 3, 13, June 29, 1806, in Barclay, *Correspondence of Barclay*, pp. 218–20, 230, 232, 237–38, 240–41; Brant, *James Madison*, pp. 368–69, 370.

26. Merry to Fox, August 31, 1806, F.O. 5/49; Brant, *James Madison*, pp. 162, 168, 206–207, 368, 370–71; Foster, *Jeffersonian America*, p. 22; Foster to his mother, September 22, 29, November 3, 7, December 1, 1805, March 25, July 20, 1806, Foster Papers, and February 8, July 1, September 2, December 27, 1805, March 10, 1806, in

(Cavendish), *Two Duchesses*, pp. 204–205, 229–30, 238, 259, 274–75; Dorothy Margaret Stuart, *Dearest Bess: The Life and Times of Lady Elizabeth Foster*, p. 135; William Plumer, *Memorandum of Proceedings in the United States Senate, 1803–1807*, ed. Everett Somerville Brown, pp. 338, 348, 364, 448; Pickering to Liston, March 19, 1805 and to Merry, January 1, 1806, Pickering Papers; Tayloe, *In Memoriam*, p. 240.

27. Foster to his mother, June 2, September 2, 22, 29, November 7, 1805, March 25, 1806, Foster Papers; Foster to his mother, March 10, 1806, in (Cavendish), *Two Duchesses*, p. 275.

28. Foster to his mother, June 2, 1805, Foster Papers; Foster, *Jeffersonian America*, p. 55; Brant, *James Madison*, p. 169; Manasseh Cutler, *Life, Journals, and Correspondence of Reverend Manasseh Cutler*, ed. William P. Cutler and Julia Cutler, II, 181–85, 190, 280, 325; Timothy Pitkin to Elizabeth Pitkin, February 16, 25, 1806, Baldwin Papers, Library of Congress; Singleton, *White House* I, 59; Merry note of July 3, 1805 (transcript), Jameson Papers.

29. Foster to his mother, June 23, 1805, March 25, 1806, Foster Papers; Foster to his mother, February 8, 15, June 30, December 27, 1805, March 10, 1806, in (Cavendish), *Two Duchesses*, pp. 205, 206, 227–29, 257–59, 275–76; Mrs. Foster to Foster, October 29, 1805, in (Cavendish), *Two Duchesses*, p. 245; Brant, *James Madison*, pp. 266–69, 305–10, Foster, *Jeffersonian America*, pp. 22–42, 47ff., 58–59.

30. Sir John Poo Beresford's notes on conference with Merry, Beresford Manuscripts, North Riding, York County Records Office, Northallerton; Merry to Mulgrave, November 25 (cipher), 1805. Beresford's notes are sometimes more specific than Merry's dispatches. The Mexico project, according to Dayton, was added after Burr's western trip, March–November, 1805. Abernethy, *Burr Conspiracy*, p. 39.

31. Beresford Notes; Merry to Fox, November 2 (nos. 51, 52 cipher), 1806; Abernethy, *Burr Conspiracy*, pp. 36–37, 56; Brant, *James Madison*, pp. 340–41, 343; Adams, *History of the United States* III, 228–32, 250.

32. Fox to Merry, March 7 (Pvt.), 1806, in Mayo, "Instructions," p. 220; Harrowby to Merry, August 21, 1804, F.O. 5/41; Merry to Mulgrave, March 19 (no. 15), 1806, F.O. 5/52; Foster to his mother, May 3, 1806, Foster Papers; Mrs. Merry to Manasseh Cutler, May 17, 1806, in Cutler, *Life of Manasseh Cutler* II, 280. Merry to Fox, April 16, June 1 (Pvt.), 1806, F.O. 5/52; Mayo, "Instructions," p. 220.

33. Foster to his mother, March 25, 27, May 3, 28, September 8, October 28, 1806, and Aberdeen to Foster, January 21, 1806, all in Foster Papers; Elizabeth to Augustus Foster, February 3, July 3, 9, in (Cavendish), *Two Duchesses*, pp. 272, 286, 289; Brant, *James Madison*, p. 371; Foster to Fox, November 4, 1806, F.O. 5/49.

34. Merry to Fox, May 4 (no. 22), 1806, F.O. 5/52.

35. Malmesbury, *Diaries* IV, 399–404; Schachner, *Aaron Burr*, p. 455; Bagot, *George Canning* I, 283, 296, 301–302; Jackson, *Bath Archives* I, 80; Pickering to Mrs. Merry, April 9, 1812, Pickering Papers. A recent and more favorable view of Merry, particularly as a professional diplomat, can be found in Lester, *Anthony Merry*.

36. Jackson, *Bath Archives* I, 317–20; G. H. Rendall to J. F. Jameson, August 28, 1921, Jameson Papers; *Journal of a British Chaplain*, p. 27; Lester, *Anthony Merry*, pp. 121–25; MS, codicil in possession of Colonel A. C. Barnes, Cobham, England.

David Erskine

1. Lloyd Paul Stryker, *For the Defense: Thomas Erskine . . . The Most Enlightened Liberal of His Times*, p. 5; Adams, *Memoirs of John Quincy Adams* III, 440, 478; Richard Rush, *A Residence at the Court of London* II, 352–53; Christopher Hobhouse, *Fox*, pp. 94–95, 218–19; Foster to his mother, November 1, 1807, Foster Papers; Erskine, "Erskine's Letters."

2. Mrs. Liston's Diary, June 22, August 5, 1799, Liston Papers; Henry Morse Stephens, "David Erskine," in *Dictionary of National Biography*, ed. Leslie Stephen and Sidney Lee, VI, 819–20; Adams, *Memoirs of John Quincy Adams* III, 440; David to Thomas Erskine, October 18, 1798, January 1, 1799, in Erskine, "Erskine's Letters," pp. 252–84; Stryker, *Thomas Erskine*, pp. 494–95.

3. David to Thomas Erskine, January 1, 1799, in Erskine, "Erskine's Letters," pp. 274–75; Neel, *Phineas Bond*, p. 143; Wharton, *Social Life*, pp. 115, 195; William Lee, *A Yankee Jeffersonian: Selections from the Diary and Letters of William Lee of Massachusetts*, ed. Mary Lee Mann, pp. 200, 290; Stephens, "David Erskine," p. 820; Perkins, *Prologue to War*, p. 103; Foster to his mother, November 1, 1807, Foster Papers; Francis Few, "The Diary of Francis Few, 1808–1809," *Journal of Southern History*, ed. Noble Cunningham, Jr., 29 (1963): 355.

4. Liston to Grenville, April 5, 1800, Liston Papers; Stephens, "David Erskine," p. 819; Alger, *Napoleon's Visitors*, p. 28; Granville, *Correspondence* I, 366; John Cam Hobhouse [pseud. Baron Broughton], *Recollections of a Long Life by Lord Broughton, edited by His Daughter, Lady Dorchester* I, 329; Hobhouse, *Fox*, pp. 246–56, 262.

5. Lord Erskine to Grenville, May 22, 1806, in Fitzpatrick, *Manuscripts of Fortesque* VIII, 152; *Quarterly Review* 68 (June, 1841): 29; Earl of Dudley, *Letters to "Ivy" from the First Earl of Dudley*, ed. S. H. Romilly, pp. 38, 49; Charles Abbott, Lord Colchester, *The Diary and Correspondence of Charles Abbott, Lord Colchester* II, 51; Wharton, *Salons*, p. 197; Fox to John B. Church, May, 1806, David Erskine to Messrs. Le Roy Bayard and McEvers, July 1, 1806 (transcript), Jameson Papers; Willson, *Friendly Relations*, p. 54; Bindoff, Malcolm-Smith, and Webster, eds., *Diplomatic Representatives*, pp. 185–86.

6. Erskine to Fox, November 4, 1806, to Foreign Office, December 4, 6, 1806, and to Howick, February 1 (no. 3), 2, 1807, F.O. 5/52; Brant, *James Madison*, pp. 371–72, 373; Wilhelmus Bogart Bryan, *A History of the National Capital from Its Foundation through . . . the Organic Act* I, 578; Plumer, *Memorandum*, pp. 530, 533.

7. Brant, *James Madison*, pp. 374–75; Erskine to Howick, March 2, 6, 17, 28, 1807, F.O. 5/52.

8. Smelser, *Democratic Republic*, pp. 155–56. The wisdom of the treaty and hence of Jefferson's handling of it are treated according to historians' political partialities. Cf. Perkins, *Prologue to War*, pp. 120–39; Burt, *United States*, pp. 235–40, Brant, *James Madison*, pp. 376–80; Malone, *Jefferson, Second Term*, pp. 404–405, 407, 410–11, 414; Horsman, *Causes of the War*, pp. 92–95. Anthony Steel, "Impressment in the Monroe-Pinkney Negotiations, 1806–1807," *American Historical Review* 57 (1952): 352–59, like Adams, *History of the United States* III, 403–13, 434–35, 439–40, criticizes both the treaty and Jefferson's performance.

9. Erskine to Howick, March 6, 17, 28, June 3, 1807, F.O. 5/52; Smelser, *Democratic Republic*, p. 156; Aberdeen to Foster, January 13, 1807, in (Cavendish), *Two Duchesses*, p. 306; Brant, *James Madison*, pp. 377–79.

10. Stryker, *Thomas Erskine*, p. 248; Foster to his mother, November 1–3, 1807, Foster Papers.

11. Few, "Diary of Francis Few," p. 355; Madison to Monroe, May 25, 1807, in Horsman, *Causes of the War*, p. 67; Adams, *Memoirs of John Quincy Adams* I, 446, 480, IV, 129–30; Plumer, *Memorandum*, pp. 564, 635.

12. Foster to his mother, December 4, 1807, Foster Papers; Perkins, *Prologue to War*, pp. 13, 185–86; Adams, *History of the United States* IV, 56–60; Richard Wellesley, *The Wellesley Papers: The Life and Correspondence of Richard Colley Wellesley, Marquis Wellesley*, ed. the editor of the Wyndham Papers, I, 142, II, 207; Adams, *Memoirs of John Quincy Adams* III, 337; A. Aspinwall, "The Cabinet Council, 1783–1835," *Pro-*

ceedings of the British Academy, 1952, pp. 199–201, 206; Bradford Perkins, "George Canning, Great Britain, and the United States, 1807–1809," *American Historical Review* 63 (1957): 10–12; Algernon Cecil, *British Foreign Secretaries, 1807–1916: Studies in Personality and Policy*, pp. 61, 63, 65; Horsman, *Causes of the War*, pp. 117–20; Temperley, *Foreign Policy of Canning*, pp. 33, 263, 282, 288; Bagot, *George Canning* I, II; Douglas MacMurray Young, *The Colonial Office in the Early Nineteenth Century*, p. 1; Tilley and Gaselee, *Foreign Office*, p. 46.

13. Foster to his mother, March 31, June 1, 17, 1807, Foster Papers; Adams, *Memoirs of John Quincy Adams* III, 337; Madison to Monroe, May 25, 1807, Madison Papers.

14. "Orders in Council . . . An Examination of the New System," in Adams, *History of the United States* IV, 72–73.

15. Malone, *Jefferson, Second Term*, pp. 428–37; Brant, *James Madison*, pp. 380–87; Smelser, *Democratic Republic*, pp. 157–61; Perkins, *Prologue to War*, pp. 140–45; Foster, *Jeffersonian America*, p. 293; Berkeley to Bathurst, August 13, 1807, Earl Mulgrave to Bathurst, October, 1808, and other correspondence respecting Berkeley, all in Bickley, *Earl Bathurst*, pp. 27–28, 42, 63–65, 78, 79, 212; Gallatin to Nicholson, July 17, 1807, Gallatin Papers; Smith-Gallatin correspondence, July 19, 20, 1807, in Samuel Smith Papers, Library of Congress; Barclay to Canning, July 2, August 5, 1807, in Barclay, *Correspondence of Barclay*, pp. 264, 265; John Hamilton to Admiral John B. Warren, January 2, February 16, 21, 1808, Admirals' Dispatches, North America, 1814, vol. 505, British National Maritime Museum, Greenwich; James Stephen to Spencer Perceval, October 19, 1807, and "Coup d'Oeil on an American War," January–February, 1808, in Perceval Papers, British Museum.

16. Gallatin to his wife, July 10, 14, 1807, in Adams, *Albert Gallatin* pp. 358, 359; Erskine to Canning, July 2 (no. 18), 4, 17 (nos. 20 and 21), 31, September 1 (no. 24), October 5 (no. 25), November 5 (nos. 27 and 28), December 2, 1807, F.O. 5/52; Berkeley to Bathurst, August 17, 1807, in Bickley, *Earl Bathurst*, p. 65; Burt, *United States*, p. 247; Brant, *James Madison*, pp. 382, 383, 384–85, 387–89, 390–91; Perkins, *Prologue to War*, pp. 189–96; Malone, *Jefferson, Second Term*, pp. 437, 452–53, 464–66.

17. Canning to Erskine, August 3, October 25, 30, 1807, in Mayo, "Instructions," pp. 234–35; Brant, *James Madison*, pp. 387, 388, 390–91; Thomas to David Erskine, October 15, 1807, Monroe Papers; Perkins, *Prologue to War*, pp. 188–90; Horsman, *Causes of the War*, pp. 94, 121–22.

18. Adams, *History of the United States* IV, 63–68; Brant, *James Madison*, p. 389; Horsman, *Causes of the War*, pp. 108–12, 112–22; Smelser, *Democratic Republic*, pp. 161, 162; Burton Spivak, *Jefferson's English Crisis: Commerce, Embargo, and the Republican Revolution*, pp. 102–106.

19. Foster to his mother, December 4, 23, 1807, Foster Papers; Adams, *Memoirs of John Quincy Adams* I, 503, V, 95; Charles Alexander Harris, "George Henry Rose," *Dictionary of National Biography* XVII, 231–32; Adams, *History of the United States* IV, 182–83; Brant, *James Madison*, p. 416; Perkins, *Prologue to War*, p. 196; Henry B. Wheatley, ed., *The Historical and Posthumous Memoirs of Sir Nathaniel William Wraxall* III, 456–57; Duke of Richmond to Earl Bathurst, October 4, 1809, George H. Rose to Bathurst, August 2, December 23, 1812, in Bickley, *Earl Bathurst*, pp. 126, 191, 222–23; George Rose, *The Diaries and Correspondence of the Right Hon. George Rose . . .* , ed. L. V. Harcourt, I, 75, 82–84, 306–307, 369–70, 390, 430, 437–40, II, 179; Rose to Monroe, October 17, 1807, in Monroe Papers; George Ticknor, *Life, Letters, and Journals of George Ticknor*, ed. George S. Hilliard, I, 110.

20. Erskine to Canning, January 28, March 6, 1808, F.O. 5/57; Rose to Canning, December 29 (no. 2), 31 (Sep.), 1807, F.O. 5/56; Pickering to King, January 2, 3, 28, 1808, in King, *Life and Correspondence* V, 48, 49, 69; Erskine to his nephew, January 18,

1808, quoted in Adams, *History of the United States* IV, 184–85; Adams, *Albert Gallatin*, p. 397; Brant, *James Madison*, pp. 404–405; Taggart, "Letters of Samuel Taggart," pt. 1, p. 225, pt. 2, pp. 298, 307; Rose to Pickering (n.d.), 1808, Pickering Papers; Dr. Mitchell to his wife, January 29, 1807 [1808], in "Dr. Mitchell's Letters from Washington, 1801–1813," *Harper's New Monthly Magazine* 58 (1878–79): 751.

21. Madison notes on Rose negotiations, February 1–24, 1808, Madison to Armstrong, February 8, to Pinkney, February 19, March 8, 1808, in Madison, *Letters of James Madison* VIII, 1–11, 16, 18, 20; Brant, *James Madison*, pp. 405–18, 450; Canning to Rose, October 24, 1807, in Mayo, "Instructions," pp. 235–42; Horsman, *Causes of the War*, pp. 138–39; Barent Gardenier to King, January 26, King to Pickering, March 4, 1808, in King, *Life and Correspondence* V, 69, 84–85; Malone, *Jefferson, Second Term*, pp. 566–67; Rose to Canning, January 30, February 6 (Secret and Confidential), 17, 19, 25 (Secret and Confidential), 27, March 4, 19, 22 (no. 21), 1808, F.O. 5/56; *Documents Relating to New England Federalism, 1800–1815*, ed. Henry Adams, pp. 186, 191, 194, 198 and esp. Rose to Pickering, March 18, 22, 23, August 4, 1808, pp. 367–72; Pickering to Rose, March 13, Rose to Pickering, May 8, 1808, in Pickering Papers; Stoddert to McHenry, March 20, 1808, in Steiner, *Life of McHenry*, p. 542; *National Intelligencer*, January 16, 1809; Erskine to Canning, February 19, April 8, 1808, F.O. 5/57; George Rose, Sr., to Wellesley, December 19, 1809, in Rose, *Diaries of George Rose* II, 361, Bindoff, "Unreformed Diplomatic Service," p. 167; Webster, *Foreign Policy, 1815–1822*, p. 40; Bagot, *George Canning* II, 140, 148, 153; Rose to Malmesbury, April 23, 28, 1808, Malmesbury, *Diaries* II, 69–71.

22. Adams, *Memoirs of John Quincy Adams* I, 503; Admiral Berkeley to Bathurst, August 13, 17, 1807, in Bickley, *Earl Bathurst*, pp. 63, 65; John Howe to Sir George Prevost, November 27, 1808, in John Howe, "Reports of John Howe to Lt. Governor Sir George Prevost, 1808–1809," *American Historical Review* 17 (1912): 343.

23. Erskine to Canning, May 2, June 4, 1808, F.O. 5/57; Erskine to Canning, September 4 (no. 31), October 6 (no. 35), November 10, 26 (Sep.), December 3 (no. 46 and Sep.), 4, 1808, F.O. 5/58; Erskine to Canning, January 1 (nos. 1, 2), 26, February 9, 10, 1809, F.O. 5/62; Erskine to Canning, March 16, 18, 1809, F.O. 5/63; Adams, *Albert Gallatin*, pp. 381–82; Jefferson, "Anas," November 9, 1808, in *Thomas Jefferson* I, 424; Brant, *James Madison*, pp. 468f., 474–75, 477–78, 479–80; Irving Brant, *Madison the President, 1809–1817*, pp. 35–36, 41; Malone, *Jefferson, First Term*, p. 667; Malone, *Jefferson, Second Term*, pp. 632–33; Adams, *History of the United States* IV, 330–31; Spivak, *Jefferson's English Crisis*, pp. 171–72, 186, 198–225; Horsman, *Causes of the War*, pp. 134–35; John Howe to Prevost, August 5, November 27, 1808, in Howe, "Reports of John Howe," pp. 100, 143; Smith, *First Forty Years*, pp. 45, 55, 62; Wharton, *Salons*, pp. 131, 190, 191; Few, "Diary of Francis Few," pp. 350–51, 360–61; Bryan, *National Capital* I, 459, 578; Foster to his mother, December 5, 1807, Foster Papers; Samuel C. Busey, *Pictures of the City of Washington in the Past*, p. 235; Randolph to Joseph Nicholson, March 25, 1807, Nicholson Papers, Library of Congress; Neel, *Phineas Bond*, p. 155.

24. Canning to Erskine, January 23, February 6, 1809, in Mayo, "Instructions," pp. 261–268; Perkins, *Prologue to War*, pp. 211–12; Perkins, "George Canning," pp. 19–21; Notes on the Embargo, Whitbread Papers, Bedfordshire Record Office, Bedford, England.

25. Perkins, *Prologue to War*, p. 212; Brant, *Madison the President*, pp. 43–50, 75–76, 83–84; John S. Pancake, *Samuel Smith and the Politics of Business*, pp. 89–90.

26. Brant, *Madison the President*, pp. 48–50, 67; *National Intelligencer*, April 26, 1809; Erskine to Canning, April 20 (no. 20), May 4 (no. 22), June 8, 1809, F.O. 5/63.

27. Canning to Erskine, May 2, 22, 23, 30, in Mayo, "Instructions," pp. 270–77;

Willson, *Friendly Relations*, pp. 59–62; Lord Strangford to Charles Bagot, January 19, 1826, Bagot, *George Canning* II, 326; Adams, *History of the United States* V, 44, 46, 49–57, 87–95; Canning to Bathurst, March 24, April 15, 1809, in Bickley, *Earl Bathurst*, pp. 86–87, 89, 90; Brant, *Madison the President*, pp. 72–77; Temperley, *Foreign Policy of Canning*, pp. 287–88; Pancake, *Samuel Smith*, pp. 90–91; Horsman, *Causes of the War*, p. 146.

28. *American State Papers, Foreign Relations*, ed. Walter Lowrie and Mathew S. Clarke, III, 315; Brant, *Madison the President*, pp. 77, 82, 84, 89; Perkins, *Prologue to War*, pp. 103, 104, 210–19; Perkins, "George Canning," pp. 14–15; Taggart, "Letters of Samuel Taggart," p. 341; P. J. V. Rolo, *George Canning: Three Biographical Studies*, pp. 48, 200; Burt, *United States*, pp. 269–76.

29. Brant, *Madison the President*, pp. 75–77, 79, 82–84; Madison to Jefferson, August 3, 16, 1809, Erskine to Smith, July 31, August 14, 1809, in Madison, *Letters of James Madison* VIII, 64n., 65, 69; Gallatin to Erskine, August 13, 1809, in *National Intelligencer*, April 21, 1810; Gallatin to Jefferson, September 10, 1810, in Henry Adams, *Albert Gallatin* I, 458–61, 475–79, 487–88; Erskine to Gallatin, August 13, 1809, Gallatin Papers; Erskine to Jackson, August 1, 1809, F.O. 353/59; Erskine to Canning, August 6, 7, 10 (no. 32), 1809, F.O. 5/63.

30. Erskine to Canning, October 1 (Sep.), 2, November 24 (Sep.), 1809, F.O. 5/63; Wellesley to George III, December 17, 1809, in Wellesley, *Wellesley Papers* I, 292–93; Bathurst to Malmesbury, January 30, 1810 and reply February 2, 1810, in Malmesbury, *Diaries* II, 206–208; Stryker, *Thomas Erskine*, p. 495; Adams, *Memoirs of John Quincy Adams* III, 337, 431; Tayloe, *In Memoriam*, p. 7; Rush, *Residence at the Court* I, 104, 105–106; Bindoff, "Unreformed Diplomatic Service," p. 164; Wharton, *Salons*, pp. 196, 197–98; *Gentleman's Magazine and Historical Review* 43 (May, 1855): 522ff.; Bindoff, Malcolm-Smith, and Webster, *Diplomatic Representatives*, p. 186.

Francis Jackson

1. *Journal of a British Chaplain*, pp. xiii–xix.

2. *Journal of a British Chaplain*, pp. xv, xvi, xviii–xix, xxi; Henry Manners Chichester, "Francis Jackson," *Dictionary of National Biography* X, 527; Fitzpatrick, *Manuscripts of Fortesque* II, 161, 175, 196, 207, 220; Leveson Gower to his mother, November (n.d.), 1791, in Granville, *Correspondence* I, 36; Burges, *Selections from Letters*, p. 172; Bindoff, Malcolm-Smith, and Webster, *Diplomatic Representatives*, p. 96.

3. Burges, *Selections from Letters*, p. 173; Chichester, "Francis Jackson," p. 527; Fitzpatrick, *Manuscripts of Fortesque* II, 257, 297, 383, III, 129, 137, 239; Bindoff, Malcolm-Smith, and Webster, *Diplomatic Representatives*, pp. 11, 48, 96, 140; Paget, *Paget Papers* I, 109, 229, 233, 261, 292; Ward and Gooch, *Cambridge History* I, 222, 257, 262; Phillip Henry, Fifth Earl of Stanhope, *Life of the Rt. Hon. William Pitt* II, 402; Malmesbury, *Diaries* IV, 384; *Journal of a British Chaplain*, p. xxviii; Frank L. Humphreys, *Life and Times of David Humphreys* II, 198.

4. Colchester, *Diary of Charles Abbott* I, 211, 386, 388–89, 390–91; Jackson to Abbott, October 30, and to his mother, October 23, 1801, in Colchester, *Diary of Charles Abbott* I, 385–86, xlii–xliii; *Journal of a British Chaplain*, pp. xvii, xxi–xxii, xli, 8; Malmesbury, *Diaries* IV, 70–73; Alger, *Napoleon's Visitors*, pp. 20, 21, 55, 139, 161–62; Francis Jackson to his mother, October 22, 1801, George Jackson to his mother, February 25, 1802, in George Jackson, *The Diaries and Letters of Sir George Jackson KCH from the Peace of Amiens to the Battle of Talavera*, ed. Lady Jackson, I, 5–6, 68.

5. Fitzpatrick, *Manuscripts of Fortesque* VIII, 108; Douglas, *Diaries of Sylvester Douglas* II, 265; George Jackson to his mother, February 25, 1802; *Journal of a British*

Notes 243

Chaplain, pp. 232, xviii; Malmesbury, *Diaries* IV, 384; Bindoff, Malcolm-Smith, and Webster, *Diplomatic Representatives*, p. 99; Paget, *Paget Papers* II, 217–18.

6. Jackson family correspondence, in Jackson, *Diaries of George Jackson* II, 203–19; Adams, *History of the United States* IV, 62–67; John Dos Passos, *The Shackles of Power*, pp. 138–40; Temperley, *Foreign Policy of Canning*, pp. 74–75; Malmesbury, *Diaries* II, 35, 51, IV, 390, 392; Bickley, *Earl Bathurst*, pp. 65, 66; Douglas, *Diaries of Sylvester Douglas* I, 393; Rose, *Diaries of George Rose* II, 179; Rolo, *George Canning*, p. 200; Ward and Gooch, *Cambridge History* I, 362–63; Lord Gower to his mother, August 22, 1807, in George Granville Leveson Gower, *Stafford House Letters*, ed. Lord Ronald Gower, p. 57; George Pellew, *The Life and Correspondence of the Rt. Hon. Henry Addington, First Viscount Sidmouth* II, 483–84.

7. Jackson to (Hammond?), n.d., F.O. 353/60; Francis to George Jackson, May 13, 1809, George Jackson Diary, June 9, 1809, both in Jackson, *Diaries of George Jackson* II, 442, 446–47; Jackson to Canning, November 16, 1809, F.O. 5/64; Adams, *Albert Gallatin*, pp. 396, 411; Adams, *History of the United States* V, 95–97; Perkins, *Prologue to War*, p. 220; Perkins, "George Canning," p. 21; Horsman, *Causes of the War*, p. 154; Pinkney to Robert Smith, June 23, 1809, in Madison, *Letters of James Madison* VIII, 70–75; John Trumbull to Rufus King, June 12, 1809, in King, *Life and Correspondence* V, 159; Thomas Digges to Jefferson, September 11, 1809, Jefferson Papers, Library of Congress; Caesar Rodney to Madison, September 6, 1809, Madison Papers, Library of Congress; Madison to Gallatin, July 7, 1809, in Albert Gallatin, *The Writings of Albert Gallatin*, ed. Henry Adams, I, 458; Madison to Gallatin, July 30, and to Jefferson, September 11, 1809, both in Madison, *Letters of James Madison* VIII, 70–71, 76.

8. Brant, *Madison the President*, p. 81; Adams, *History of the United States* V, 115, 117, 118, 119; Willson, *Friendly Relations*, p. 66; Bond to Jackson, September 19, October 3, 1809, F.O. 353/59; Jackson to Canning, September 12, 14 (Pvt.), 1809, F.O. 5/64, 353/60; Francis to George Jackson, September 16, 1809, and to his mother, September 16, October 7, 1809, in Jackson, *Bath Archives* I, 8–10, 17–22.

9. Adams, *History of the United States* V, 118–20; Mrs. Jackson to George Jackson, June 10, 1810, Francis Jackson to his mother, October 7, 1809, to George Jackson, October 24, 1809, May 14, 1810, all in Jackson, *Bath Archives* I, 17–20, 25–27, 118–19, 138; Jackson to Canning, September 14, 1809, F.O. 353/60; Jackson to Canning, September 12, 1809, F.O. 5/64; Wharton, *Salons*, p. 197; Erskine to Canning, October 1 (Pvt.), 1809, F.O. 5/63; Francis to George Jackson, May 13, 1809, in Jackson, *Diaries of George Jackson* II, 44–46; Erskine letter, August 1, 1809 (copy), F.O. 353/59.

10. Josephine Fisher, "Francis James Jackson and Newspaper Propaganda in the United States, 1809–1810," *Maryland Historical Magazine* 30, no. 2 (June, 1935): 93–96; Jackson Papers, F.O. 353/59–61; George Jackson Diary, March(?) 7, 1810, in Jackson, *Bath Archives* I, 112–13; Jackson to Canning, September 12, 1809, F.O. 5/64.

11. Jackson to Canning, September 12, 13 (nos. 2, 3, 4), October 17 (no. 5), 1809, F.O. 5/64; Jackson to Canning, September 14 (Pvt.), 1809, F.O. 353/60; Adams, *History of the United States* IV, 129–30; Robert Knox to Jackson, September 16, 1809, F.O. 353/59.

12. Canning to Jackson, July 1, 8, 1809, in Mayo, "Instructions," pp. 277–91, 294; Jackson to Canning, September 14 (Pvt.), 1809, F.O. 353/60.

13. Madison to Smith, September 15, 1809, in Madison, *Letters of James Madison* VIII, 73–75; Jackson to Canning, October 17 (nos. 6, 7, 8), 1809, F.O. 5/64; Brant, *Madison the President*, pp. 88–89, 90–91.

14. Jackson to Canning, October 18 (nos. 9, 10), 1809, F.O. 5/64; Adams, *History of the United States* V, 123–26; Jackson to Canning, October 18 (Sep. and Secret), 1809,

F.O. 5/64; Jackson to Craig, October 21, 1809, F.O. 353/60; Francis to George Jackson, October 20–24, 1809, in Jackson, *Bath Archives* I, 22–25.

15. Brant, *Madison the President*, p. 89; Elizabeth to George Jackson, November 21, 1809, Francis Jackson to his mother, October 7, Francis Jackson to George Jackson, October 24, 1809, all in Jackson, *Bath Archives* I, 19–20, 25–27, 57–58; Jackson to Canning, October 18 (no. 9), 1809, F.O. 5/64.

16. Adams, *History of the United States* V, 127–29; Brant, *Madison the President*, pp. 94–98; Francis to George Jackson, October 26, 28, 1809, in Jackson, *Bath Archives* I, 27–29; Jackson to Canning, October 24, November 14, 1809, F.O. 5/64; Jackson to Canning, October 24 (Pvt.), 1809, F.O. 353/60.

17. Brant, *Madison the President*, pp. 98, 100–101; Adams, *History of the United States* V, 129–32; Francis to George Jackson, October 26, 1809, in Jackson, *Bath Archives* I, 27–28; Jackson to Canning, October 24, 1809, F.O. 353/60; Jackson to Canning, November 16, 1809, F.O. 5/64.

18. Brant, *Madison the President*, pp. 102–103; Oakeley to the secretary of state, November 11, 1807, in *American State Papers* III, 319; Pinkney to Wellesley, January 2, 1810, *American State Papers*, p. 354; Jackson draft, n.d., F.O. 353/60; Jackson to the secretary of state, November 13, 1809 (copy), F.O. 353/60.

19. Francis to George Jackson, November 14, 15, 20, 1809, in Jackson, *Bath Archives* I, 44–48; Jackson to Canning, November 15, 16, 1809, F.O. 5/64; Jackson to Canning (draft), November 18, 1809, F.O. 353/60; Barclay to Jackson, November 16, 1809, in Barclay, *Correspondence of Barclay*, p. 291; Jackson circular, November 13, 1809, in *American State Papers* III, 323; Jackson to Beverley, November 30, 1809, to J. H. Craig, December 14, 1809, January 2, 1810, and to Admiral John B. Warren, December 31, 1809, all in F.O. 353/60; Fisher, "Francis James Jackson," pp. 109–11.

20. Fisher, "Francis James Jackson," pp. 98–113; Jackson correspondence to and from Laird, Söderström, Luther Martin, Robertson et al., November, 1809 to January, 1810, F.O. 353/59, 353/61; Jackson to Canning and to Bathurst, November 29, December 6, 7, 13, 27 (Sep.), 28 (no. 30), 29 (no. 29), 30, 1809, F.O. 5/64.

21. Madison to Jefferson, November 6, to Congress, November 29, 1809, to George Joy, January 17, 1810, in Madison, *Letters of James Madison* VIII, 78–79, 80, 86–87; *National Intelligencer*, November 13, 15, 17, 22, 24, 1809; Brant, *Madison the President*, pp. 106–10, 120–40; McMaster, *History of the People* III, 357; Miscellaneous correspondence to and from Jackson, December 2, 1809 to May 1, 1810, F.O. 353/60 and 353/61; Stoddert to Pickering, December 6, 1809, Jackson to John Teackle, January 10, to Söderström, February 27, 1810, all in Pickering Papers; James Bayard to Andrew Bayard, February 7, 1810, in James A. Bayard, "Papers of James A. Bayard, 1796–1815," ed. Elizabeth Donnan, p. 178; Morier notes and memorandum, 1810, Additional Manuscripts, 37392, fol. 208, British Museum, London; John Lowell, *Interesting Political Discussion: The Diplomatick Policy of Mr. Madison Unveiled*; Benjamin Vaughan, *Ten Hints Addressed to Wise Men—Concerning the Dispute which Ended on November 8, 1809*; Samuel Dana, *Speech of Samuel W. Dana . . . On a Resolution Concerning Francis J. Jackson*; Pickering to King, December 8, 1809, February 5, 1810, Robert Troup to Nathaniel Pendleton, January 23, 1810, King to Gore, February 19, 1810, all in King, *Life and Correspondence* V, 187, 194–95, 210; George Jackson Diary, March 14, 1810, in Jackson, *Bath Archives* I, 98; Jackson to Foreign Office, December 7, 13, 28, 30, 1809, F.O. 5/64; Jackson to Bathurst, January 12, 22 (no. 2), 25 (nos. 6, 7), February 16, May 8, 1810, F.O. 5/69.

22. Perkins, *Prologue to War*, pp. 235–37; Brant, *Madison the President*, pp. 132–

33, 144–45; Pinkney to Wellesley, January 2, 1810, Wellesley to Pinkney, March 14, 1810, all in *American State Papers* III, 351–52, 353–56; Madison to Pinkney, January 21, 1810, in Madison, *Letters of James Madison* VIII, 92–93; Pinkney to Madison, March 23, 1810, in Henry Wheaton, *Some Account of the Life, Writings, and Speeches of William Pinkney*, pp. 440–41; Wellesley to Jackson, April 14, 1810, in Mayo, "Instructions," p. 302; Cabinet memorandum on proposed Jackson note (n.d.), Additional Manuscripts, 37291, fol. 282, British Museum; George Jackson to his mother, January 3, 1810, George Jackson Diary, December 28, 1809, January 6, 15, February 8, 11, March 14, April 11, 1810, all in Jackson, *Bath Archives* I, 29–31, 51, 60–61, 63, 71–72, 87, 89, 98, 104–105.

23. Kelsey, "Letters of Travel in the United States" Manuscript, Library of Congress; Bernard Mayo, *Henry Clay, Spokesman of the New West*, p. 325; Francis to George Jackson, October 28, 1809, January 10, 1810, in Jackson, *Bath Archives* I, 29, 78–79; Jackson to Craig, January 2, February 12, 1810, F.O. 353/59, 353/60; Jackson to Bathurst, drafts, January 20, 25, February 16, May 7, 1810, anonymous to Jackson, January 4, 27, 1810, all in F.O. 353/60; Jackson to Wellesley, January 22 (no. 2), 25 (nos. 6, 7), February 15 (no. 11), March 21, 1810, F.O. 5/69.

24. Mrs. Francis Jackson to George Jackson, November 21, 1809, and Francis to George Jackson, January 10, April 7, May 13, 1810, both in Jackson, *Bath Archives* I, 57, 78–79, 114, 117–18.

25. Adams, *History of the United States* V, 216–17; Samuel E. Morison, *Life and Letters of Harrison Gray Otis, 1765–1848* II, 20–22; Samuel E. Morison, *Harrison Gray Otis: Urbane Federalist*, pp. 311–13; Francis to George Jackson, June 22, 1810, in Jackson, *Bath Archives* I, 150–51; Jackson to Wellesley, June 19 (no. 33), 1810, F.O. 5/69.

26. Francis to George Jackson, May 1, 16, June 22, 1810, in Jackson, *Bath Archives* I, 108–11, 120, 150; Jackson to Soderström, February 27, to Pickering, March 5, 14, 16, 1810, Pickering Papers; Timothy Williams to Pickering, March 18, James McHenry to Pickering, March 15, James Laird to Pickering, March 8, Pickering to Cabot, March 19, 1810, all in Pickering Papers; King to Pickering, March 5, 1810, in King, *Life and Correspondence* V, 213; Jackson to Malmesbury, April 5, 1810, F.O. 353/60; Adams, *History of the United States* V, 218.

27. Wellesley to Jackson, April 14, 1810, in Mayo, "Instructions," pp. 302–303; Jackson to Wellesley, June 19 (no. 33), June 20 (Pvt.), August 15, 1810, F.O. 5/69; Jackson to his mother, July 11, 1810, in Jackson, *Bath Archives* I, 152–53.

28. Jackson, *Bath Archives* I, 60–62, 104–105, 128, 138, 175; George Jackson Diary; Wellesley to Jackson, June 26, July 3, 1810, in Mayo, "Instructions," pp. 303–305; Jackson to Wellesley, September 15 (no. 44), 1810, F.O. 5/69.

29. Francis to George Jackson, February 19, September 15, 1811, May 23, 1812, Francis Jackson to his mother, March 5, 1811, May 8, 1812, George Jackson to his mother, March 16, 1812, George Jackson Diary, February 28, March 19, 1811, all in Jackson, *Bath Archives* I, 212–14, 286–88, 387, II, 221, 223–24, 227, 343, 371; Jackson to Wellesley, October 17, 27, 1810, drafts, F.O. 5/69; Adams, *History of the United States* VI, 13, 19; Douglas, *Diaries of Sylvester Douglas* II, 129; Jackson to Pickering, April 24, 1811, Pickering Papers; Pickering to Jackson, April 8, 1812, Phineas Bond to Jackson, May 7, 1811, Jackson to Liverpool, August 2, 1812, all in F.O. 353/60; Hanson to Jackson, March 7, Robertson to Jackson, March 15, November 5, Hogan to Jackson, March 30, 1812, all in F.O. 353/61.

30. George Jackson to his mother, September 23, 1813, April 22, June 17, August 2, 1814, Mrs. Jackson to George Jackson, June 24, 1814, Francis to George Jackson, November 22, December 26, 1812, September 24, 28, October 13, November 13, 1813, all

in Jackson, *Bath Archives* I, 43, 448, II, 282, 363–4, 437, 439, 441, 445; Jackson to Castlereagh, July 23, 1814, (transcript), Jameson Papers; *Gentleman's Magazine and Historical Chronicle* 84, pt. 2 (1798): 198; Chichester, "Francis Jackson," p. 527.

Augustus Foster

1. Stuart, *Dearest Bess*, pp. 5–6, 76, 90, 91; Carolina Grosvenor and Lord Stuart Wortley, *The First Lady Wharncliffe and Her Family*, p. 9; Henry Morse Stephens, "Augustus Foster," *Dictionary of National Biography* VII, 492; *The Greville Memoirs*, ed. Lytton Strachey and Roger Fulford, V, 308; Douglas, *Diaries of Sylvester Douglas* I, 216, II, 82; Ethel C. Mayne, *A Regency Chapter: Lady Bessborough and Her Friends*, p. 197.

2. Stuart, *Dearest Bess*, pp. 76, 90, 91, 110, 114, 135; Augustus to George Foster, November 3, 1805, to his mother, December 30, 1804, September 23, November 9, December 20, 27, 1805, March 10, April 6, 1806, in (Cavendish) *Two Duchesses*, pp. 135, 150, 197, 240, 257–58, 274–76.

3. Foster to his mother, July 20, October 28, 1806, October 5, 1807, George Canning to Lady Elizabeth Foster, October 18, 1807, all in Foster Papers; Stoddert to McHenry, March 20, 1808, in Steiner, *Life of McHenry*, p. 542; Erskine to the Foreign Office, March 22, 1807, F.O. 5/57; Bagot, *George Canning* I, 281, 302, 303, 304–305; Elizabeth to Augustus Foster, December 5, 1809, in (Cavendish) *Two Duchesses*, pp. 328, 332, 343, 346–48; Lady Bessborough to Granville Leveson Gower, February n.d., 1811, in Granville, *Correspondence* II, 381; Bindoff, Malcolm-Smith, and Webster, *Diplomatic Representatives*, p. 151; Adams, *History of the United States* VI, 21–22; Mayne, *Regency Chapter*, p. 199; Stuart, *Dearest Bess*, pp. 147, 154, 161, 184; Hugh Stokes, *The Devonshire House Circle*, pp. 315–16.

4. Brant, *Madison the President*, p. 503; Smelser, *Democratic Republic*, pp. 196, 197; Mayo, "Instructions," p. 302; Francis to George Jackson, October 19, 1810, February 21, 1811, in Jackson, *Bath Archives* I, 105, 135, 138.

5. Brant, *Madison the President*, pp. 194–200, 207–10, 211, 229; Perkins, *Prologue to War*, pp. 244–60; Adams, *History of the United States* V, 278–80, 286, 302, VI, 4, 8; Roger H. Brown, *The Republic in Peril*, p. 245; Harry Ammon, *James Monroe: The Quest for National Identity*, p. 293; Madison to Pinkney, May 23, October 30, 1810, in Madison, *Letters of James Madison* VIII, 97, 117; Pinkney to Monroe, August 13, to Madison, December 17, 1810, in Wheaton, *William Pinkney*, pp. 444–46, 448–50, 453.

6. Brant, *Madison the President*, pp. 200–201, 229–30; Morier to the secretary of state, December 15, 1810, in *American State Papers* III, 399, 400; Morier to Wellesley, October 26 (no. 15), December 28, 1810, January 24 (no. 8), February 14 (no. 14), 1811, F.O. 5/70, 5/74; Morier to Jackson, January 24, 1811, (pt. 2) F.O. 353/11.

7. Brant, *Madison the President*, pp. 229, 262–63, 285–87; Adams, *History of the United States* VI, 12–16; Smelser, *Democratic Republic*, p. 198; Smith to Morier, December 28, 1810, in *American State Papers* III, 400; Morier to Wellesley, March 3 (no. 19), 1811, F.O. 5/74.

8. Stuart, *Dearest Bess*, p. 190; Stokes, *Devonshire House*, pp. 315–16; Adams, *History of the United States* VI, 21–22; Elizabeth to Augustus Foster, February 15, 1811, in (Cavendish) *Two Duchesses*, pp. 348–49.

9. Jackson to Pickering, April 24, 1811, in Adams, *History of the United States* VI, 22; Brant, *Madison the President*, p. 310; John Trumbull to Rufus King, February 18, April 15, June 14, 1811, in King, *Life and Correspondence* V, 240, 245, 247; Samuel Taggart to Rev. John Taylor, April 23, 1811, in Taggart, "Letters of Samuel Taggart," II, 360–61; Morier to Wellesley, May 9, 1811 (w/encl.), F.O. 5/74; John Melish, *Travels in*

the United States of America in the Years 1809, 1810, and 1811 II, 13; National Intelligencer, May 9, 1811.

10. Adams, History of the United States V, 284–85, VI, 22–24; George Dangerfield, The Era of Good Feelings, p. 89; Horsman, Causes of the War, pp. 196–98; Notes on the State of Europe, May 5, 1811, in Wellesley, Wellesley Papers II, 55; Smelser, Democratic Republic, p. 144; Perkins, Prologue to War, p. 278; Burt, United States, pp. 292–93; Francis to George Jackson, March 5, 1811, in Jackson, Bath Archives I, 226; Wellesley to Foster, April 10, 1811, in Mayo, "Instructions," pp. 310–22.

11. Foster to Wellesley, June 29, July 2, 1811, F.O. 5/76; Foster Journal; Morier-Monroe correspondence, June 26, 28, 1811, in American State Papers III, 461; George Jackson Diary, February 28, 1811, in Jackson, Bath Archives I, 221; Morier to Francis Jackson, January 24, 1811 (pt. 2) F.O. 353/11; Morier Notes, American Miscellaneous Papers, 37292, Item 208, British Museum.

12. Foster to Wellesley, July 2, 1811, F.O. 5/76; Foster Journal; Brant, Madison the President, pp. 340–41; Ammon, James Monroe, pp. 287, 292–93; Perkins, Prologue to War, pp. 279–80; Temple to Rufus King, July 4, 1811, in King, Life and Correspondence V, 248.

13. Foster to Wellesley, July 2, 5, 1811, F.O. 5/76; Adams, History of the United States VI, 37–38.

14. Foster to Wellesley, July 7 (no. 5), 18 (no. 8), 1811, F.O. 5/76; Madison to Monroe, July, August 2, 1811, in Perkins, Prologue to War, pp. 281, 282, 315–17; Adams, History of the United States VI, 39, 44; Brown, Republic in Peril, pp. 25–26, 27; Thomas Mullett to Samuel Whitbread, November 26, 1811, January 30, 1812, Whitbread Papers, Bedfordshire Record Office, Bedford, England.

15. Foster to Wellesley, July 12, August 5 (no. 10), 1811, F.O. 5/76; Paullin, "Early British Diplomats," p. 248.

16. "Solitude" stood on the site of the present Philadelphia zoo; Foster, Jeffersonian America, p. 247; Foster Journal; Foster to Wellesley, August 5 (no. 11), September 17 (no. 16), 18, 1811, F.O. 5/76.

17. Foster to Wellesley, September 17 (no. 15), November 5 (no. 20), 1811, F.O. 5/76 and 5/77; Madison to Barlow, November 17, 1811, in Madison, Letters of James Madison VIII, 170; Brant, Madison the President, pp. 364–65; Perkins, Prologue to War, pp. 354–55; Ammon, James Monroe, p. 300.

18. Brant, Madison the President, pp. 356–69, 366–72, 374.

19. Foster to Wellesley, November 9, 12 (nos. 23 and 24), 23, 26, 27 (Sep.), December 11 (no. 30), 18, 21 (no. 35), 1811, F.O. 5/77; Earl of Aberdeen to Foster, February 5, 1812, in (Cavendish), Two Duchesses, pp. 356–57; Foster-Monroe correspondence, December, 1811–January, 1812, in Manning, Diplomatic Correspondence I, 182, 608–609.

20. Brown, Republic in Peril, pp. 98–105; Brant, Madison the President, pp. 376–81, 390–404; Foster to Wellesley, February 26, 1812, F.O. 5/84; Smelser, Democratic Republic, pp. 208–209, 211–12; J. W. Griscom to William Allen, April 13, 1812, Allen & Hanbury, Ltd., Bethnal Green, London.

21. Foster to Wellesley, February 1, 2, March 9 (no. 12), 22, May 5 (Pvt. and no. 34), 15, 22, 1812, F.O. 5/84, 5/85, 5/86; Brant, Madison the President, p. 405; Perkins, Prologue to War, pp. 389–91.

22. Perkins, Prologue to War, pp. 313–15, 317–19, 324–26, 328–29; Foster Journal, esp. March 11, 18, 19, 1812; Foster to Monroe, March 11, 1812, in Manning, Diplomatic Correspondence I, 611; Brant, Madison the President, pp. 412–20; Foster to Wellesley, March 9 (Sep. and Secret), 12, 22, 24, April 1 (no. 20), 1812, F.O. 5/84, 5/85.

23. Foster, *Jeffersonian America*, p. xii; James Bayard to Andrew Bayard, January 25, 1812, in Bayard, "Papers of Bayard," 189–91; Foster Journal; Samuel Taggart to John Taylor, December 30, 1811, in Taggart, "Letters of Samuel Taggart," pp. 372–76; Abijah Bigelow to his wife, January 16, 1812, in "Letters of Abijah Bigelow, Member of Congress, to His Wife, 1810–1815," *Proceedings of the American Antiquarian Society* N.S. 40 (October, 1930): 325; Perkins, *Prologue to War*, pp. 274–75; Bond to Jackson, April 22, 1811, F.O. 353/61; Foster to Wellesley, March 12, April 24 (no. 30), 1812, F.O. 5/84, 5/85.

24. Brant, *Madison the President*, pp. 421–22, 426–30; Wellesley to Foster, January 28, 1812, in Mayo, "Instructions," 340–46; Foster to Wellesley, March 22, April 1 (no. 18), 2 (no. 22), 1812, F.O. 5/85.

25. Foster to Wellesley, February 26, April 2 (no. 22), 3, 21, 23 (nos. 27, 28), 1812, F.O. 5/85; Brant, *Madison the President*, pp. 431–32, 449–50; Foster to Charles Stuart, April (n.d.), 1812 (transcript), Jameson Papers.

26. Foster to his mother, February 3, March 13, April 18, 1812, Foster Papers; Brant, *Madison the President*, pp. 442–47, 455, 458–59 and Adams, *History of the United States* VI, 204–16; Foster Journal, April–June, 1812.

27. Perkins, *Prologue to War*, pp. 316–19, 324–28; Castlereagh to Foster, April 10, 1812, in Mayo, "Instructions," pp. 353–72; Foster to Castlereagh, May 23, 26, 28, June 6 (no. 41 and Pvt.), 8, 1812, F.O. 5/86; Horsman, *Causes of the War*, pp. 245–54, 256–58, 260; Brant, *Madison the President*, pp. 462–63, 464, 466–69.

28. Brant, *Madison the President*, pp. 470–74, 477; Horsman, *Causes of the War*, pp. 260–62.

29. Manning, *Diplomatic Correspondence* III, 201–205, 612–15; Foster Journal, June 15, 17, 18, 20, 1812; Foster to Castlereagh, June 20, July 22, August 25, 1812 and Minute of June 23, 1812, all in F.O. 5/86; Irving Brant, *James Madison, Commander-in-Chief, 1812–1836*, pp. 33–34; Foster to Barclay, June 20, 1812, in Barclay, *Correspondence of Barclay*, pp. 310–11; Madison to Jefferson, August 17, 1812, in Madison, *Letters of James Madison* VIII, 212–13; Ralph Ketcham, *James Madison, A Biography*, p. 535; Burt, *United States*, p. 313; Perkins, *Prologue to War*, pp. 415–16.

30. Monroe to Joseph Nicholson, June 23, 1812, Nicholson Papers; Library of Congress; Foster Journal, June 23–July 12, 1812; "The Abbé Correa in America, 1812–1820," *Transactions of the American Philosophical Society*, ed. Richard Beale Davis, 45, 90, 95; Foster to Castlereagh, August 25, 1812, F.O. 5/86; Foster, *Jeffersonian America*, p. 342; Henry Brougham to William Roscoe, (n.d.), 1812, Roscoe Papers, Liverpool Public Library.

31. Jameson Notes, Jameson Papers; Foster, *Jeffersonian America*, pp. 343–44; William Cobbett, ed., *The Parliamentary Debates from the Year 1803 to the Present Time* XXIV, 623–28; Granville Leveson Gower to Lady Bessborough, December 7, 1813, in Granville, *Correspondence* II, 494; Foster Notes, Foster Papers.

32. Foster to his mother, April 18, 1812, December 13, 1813, May 3, 5, August 10, (n.d.), 1814, Lady Elizabeth Foster to Foster, May 4, 1812, Mrs. George Lamb to Foster, August 31, 1812, all in (Cavendish), *Two Duchesses*, pp. 360–62, 373–74, 378, 381, 385, 394; Foster family correspondence, 1815–1819, in (Cavendish), *Two Duchesses*, pp. 399, 411, 427, 428; Webster, *Foreign Policy, 1812–1815*, pp. 307–308, 542; Foster to Bathurst, July 14, 1814, in Bickley, *Earl Bathurst*, pp. 280–81; *Greville Memoirs* I, 389, IV, 418; Ticknor, *Life of George Ticknor* II, 40, 41; Foster Notes, Foster Papers; Foster to Bayard, January 27, 1815, in Bayard, "Papers of Bayard," 376; Foster to Charles Bagot, May 28, 1816, Bagot Papers; *Gentleman's Magazine* 30 (September, 1848): 317.

Interlude

1. Horsman, *Causes of the War*, pp. 268–69; Bradford Perkins, *Castlereagh and Adams: England and the United States, 1812–1823*, pp. 154, 176–77, 183–84; Brant, *Madison, Commander-in-Chief*, pp. 375–80; Smelser, *Democratic Republic*, pp. 323–24; Woodward, *Age of Reform*, pp. 7, 8, 50; Harold Nicolson, *The Congress of Vienna*, chapters 15, 16; Adam Seybert, ed., *Statistical Annals of the United States Founded on Official Documents*, p. 287; Goldwin Smith, *A History of England*, pp. 546–51; Frank A. Updyke, *The Diplomacy of the War of 1812*, pp. 369, 373–74; Henry Goulburn to Earl Bathurst, September 2, 1814, in Dangerfield, *Era of Good Feelings*, pp. 4, 74–91; Adams, *Memoirs of John Quincy Adams* IV, 310.

Charles Bagot

1. Dangerfield, *Era of Good Feelings*, p. 77; Bagot, *George Canning* I, 234–35; T. B. Browning, "Charles Bagot," *Dictionary of National Biography*, Supp. I, 98; Granville, *Correspondence* I, 37; John Charles Dent, *The Last Forty Years: Canada Since the Union of 1841* I, 180.

2. Douglas, *Diaries of Sylvester Douglas* I, 217, 349–51; Bagot, *George Canning* I, 234–35, 238; Granville, *Correspondence* II, 14, 206; Browning, "Charles Bagot," p. 98.

3. Wellesley-Pole to Bagot, August 8, 1807, Canning to Bagot, August 8, 1807, Bagot to Canning, August 10, 1807, in Bagot, *George Canning* I, 238–44; Bindoff, "Unreformed Diplomatic Service," p. 156.

4. Countess Granville to the Duke of Devonshire, November 3, 1811, in Granville, *Correspondence* I, 29.

5. C. Jackson to Bagot, September 4, 1809, in Bagot, *George Canning* I, 320; Webster, *Foreign Policy, 1812–1815*, p. 45; Bagot to Wellington, April 30, May 22, 1814, Wellington to Bagot, May 9, 1814, Bagot Papers.

6. Bagot, *George Canning* I, 236, II, 2; Canning to Bagot, July 14, Charles Ellis to Bagot, July 22, 1815, in Bagot, *George Canning* II, 4–6, 7; Samuel F. Bemis, *John Quincy Adams and the Foundations of American Foreign Policy*, pp. 223–24; Fitzroy Somerset to Bagot, June 10, 1815, Bagot to Wellington, June 6, 1815, Bagot to Castlereagh, May 3, 1815, all in Bagot Papers.

7. Bathurst to Bagot, August 9, 10, 11, 20 (nos. 1–3), 1815, F.O. 5/108; Bagot to Castlereagh, August 14, 1815, F.O. 5/108; Adams, *Memoirs of John Quincy Adams* III, 234, 255; Morier to Baker, July 4 (Pvt.), 1815, Bathurst to Baker, September 6 (Pvt.), 1815, F.O. 5/105; Bagot to Adams, August 18, 1815, Bagot Papers; Adams to Monroe, September 19, 1815, in Manning, *Diplomatic Correspondence* III, 731–36; Wellesley-Pole to Bagot, September 25, 1815, Bagot to Binning, October 27, 1815, in Bagot, *George Canning* II, 9, 11; Perkins, *Castlereagh and Adams*, pp. 138, 149–50, 161, 197–99, 199–202, 203–204, 219; James Bayard to Richard Bayard, December 29, 1814, in Bayard, "Papers of Bayard," p. 365; Brant, *Madison, Commander-in-Chief*, pp. 375–76; Frederick Merk, *The Oregon Question: Essays in Anglo-American Diplomacy and Politics*, p. 20; Webster, *Foreign Policy, 1812–1815*, p. 44; Webster, *Foreign Policy, 1815–1822*, pp. 438–39; Dangerfield, *Era of Good Feelings*, p. 57; *Greville Memoirs* I, 127; Richard Rush, *Memoranda of a Residence at the Court of London*, pp. 335, 339; Castlereagh to Stratford Canning, August 7 (no. 2), 1820, F.O. 5/150.

8. Mary Bagot to Charles Sneyd, January 5, 1816, Sneyd Papers, University College of North Staffordshire Library (Keele); Privy Council Minutes (extract), December 4, 1815, Bagot Papers; Bagot to John Sneyd, June 12, 1816, in Bagot, *George Canning* II, 20; Morier to Baker, October 13, 1815, F.O. 5/105; Adams, *Memoirs of John Quincy*

Adams III, 3, 5, 125, 132; Paullin, "Early British Diplomats," p. 249; Samuel E. Morison, *Life in Washington a Century and a Half Ago*, p. 21; Bagot to Castlereagh, April 2 (nos. 1 and 2), 1816, F.O. 5/114; *Niles Weekly Register* 10 (March 21, 1816): 64; Baker to the Foreign Office, January 13 (no. 53), March 19 (no. 54), 1813, F.O. 5/88; Barclay to Admiral Warren, April 13, 1813, in Barclay, *Correspondence of Barclay*, p. 327; Brant, *Madison the President*, pp. 171, 367, 387, 388; Perkins, *Castlereagh and Adams*, pp. 246, 250; Morier to Baker, October 13 (Pvt.), 1815; Instructions of November 24 (no. 14), 1815, F.O. 5/105; Baker to Castlereagh, February 19 (no. 1), 25 (no. 2), 1818, F.O. 5/105; Latrobe to Jefferson (n.d.), in William Dunlap, *A History of the Rise and Progress of the Arts of Design in the United States* II, 399–401; Green, *Washington* I, 61–63, 64–68; Wharton, *Social Life*, pp. 100–102, 109–11, 178; Busey, *Pictures*, p. 46; Bryan, *National Capital* I, 626–28, 631, 636, II, 3, 32, 34, 35, 45, 66; W. H. Dobbs to William Eustis, April 10, 1815, Eustis Papers, Library of Congress; Francis Gilmer to his brother, November (n.d.), 1814, in "Abbé Correa," p. 101; Morris Birkbeck, *Notes on a Journey in America from the Coast of Virginia to the Territory of Illinois*, p. 22; John M. Duncan, *Travels through Part of the United States and Canada in 1818 and 1819* I, 257, 260; Memorial to the Prince Regent by Vice Admiral Sir Alexander Cochrane and Major General Ross (n.d.), in Codrington Papers, National Maritime Museum, Greenwich, England; Smith, *First Forty Years*, p. 109; Francis Hall, *Travels in Canada and the United States in 1816 and 1817*, pp. 327, 328; Henry Bradshaw Fearon, *Sketches of America: A Narrative of a Journey of 5000 Miles* . . . p. 289; Brant, *Madison, Commander-in-Chief*, p. 397.

    9. Bagot to Castlereagh, April 2 (nos. 1 and 2), 6, 1816; Bagot to Binning, May 6, 1816, in Bagot, *George Canning* II, 16.

    10. Ketcham, *Madison Biography*, pp. 477–78; D. B. Warden, *A Chronological and Statistical Description of the District of Columbia*, pp. 192ff.; Henry U. Addington, "Residence in the United States of America 1822, 23, 24, 25," in Sidmouth Papers, (published in part in Bradford Perkins, ed., *Youthful America: Selections from Henry Unwin Addington's Residence in the United States 1822, 23, 24, 25* . . . , University of California Publications in History, vol. 65); Hall, *Fragments of Voyages*, pp. 329–30, 331; Wharton, *Salons*, pp. 199, 203–204, 206–207; Wharton, *Social Life*, pp. 136, 163, 179, 180; Busey, *Pictures*, pp. 342, 370; Fearon, *Sketches of America*, pp. 288–89, 290, 294; Bryan, *National Capital* I, 381, 574, 627, 630, II, 1, 4, 27, 29, 70, 136, 181–82, 194, 196, 288–89; Thomas Cooper to William Roscoe, March 22, 1818, Roscoe Papers.

    11. Mary Boardman Crowninshield, *Letters of Mary Boardman Crowninshield, 1815–1816*, ed. Francis Boardman Crowninshield, pp. 16, 42, 44–45, 61, 62–63, 66–67; Anne Royall, *Sketches of History, Life, and Manners in the United States*, pp. 155–57; Duncan, *Travels through Part*, p. 253; Peel Papers, Additional Manuscripts, 40192; British Museum; Rush, *Residence at the Court* I, 296–97.

    12. Bagot to John Sneyd, June 12, 1816, to Lord Binning, May 6, 1816, in Bagot, *George Canning* II, 16, 20–21.

    13. Adams to Monroe, September 5, 1815, in Manning, *Diplomatic Correspondence* III, 729–30; Bagot to Sneyd, June 12, to Binning, May 6, 1816, in Bagot, *George Canning* II, 16, 20; Bagot to Binning, October 24, 1816, Bagot Papers; Perkins, *Castlereagh and Adams*, pp. 156–60; Webster, *Foreign Policy, 1815–1822*, p. 438; Monroe to Madison, October 18, 1817, in Monroe, *Writings* VI, 30.

    14. Dangerfield, *Era of Good Feelings*, p. 90; Bagot to Binning, May 6, June 1, 1816, in Bagot, *George Canning* II, 16, 19; Bagot to Sneyd, June 12, 1816, Bagot Papers; Stapleton to Bagot, April 11, 1816, Bagot Papers; Mary Bagot to Ralph Sneyd, August 11,

1816, Sneyd Papers; Ticknor, *Life of George Ticknor* I, 295–96; Bagot to Sneyd, June 15, 26, to Binning, October 24, 1816, in Bagot, *George Canning* II, 21, 22, 24, 34–35.

15. Bagot to Binning, October 24, 1816, Bagot Papers; Foster to Bagot, May 28, 1816, Bagot Papers.

16. Bagot to Castlereagh, May 3 (no. 12), November 9 (no. 35), 1816, F.O. 5/114, 5/115; Bryan, *National Capital* II, 168–69; Cf. Fearon, *Sketches of America*, pp. 321–22.

17. Perkins, *Castlereagh and Adams*, pp. 240–44; William A. Dunning, *The British Empire and the United States*, pp. 15–16; Madison to John Graham, June 1, 1816 (transcript), in Jameson Papers; James Morton Callahan, "The Neutrality of the American Lakes and Anglo–American Relations," in *Johns Hopkins University Studies in History and Political Science*, ser. 16, nos. 1–4, (1898), pp. 9–59; Bagot to Castlereagh, May 3 (no. 8), August 12 (no. 24, w/encl.), November 9 (no. 39), 1816, F.O. 5/114, 5/115; Bagot to Castlereagh, May 5 (no. 32), 1817, F.O. 5/122; Castlereagh to Bagot, April 23 (no. 7), September 30 (no. 16), 1816, January 31 (no. 1), 1817, F.O. 5/120; Burt, *United States*, pp. 388–89, 390–95; Manning, *Diplomatic Correspondence* III, 234–35, 254–62, 783–86, 788–92, 794–95, 802–803, 804.

18. Bagot to Castlereagh, June 4 (nos. 14, 15), July 24 (21), August 12 (nos. 23, 27), August 16 (no. 26), September 1 (nos. 30, 32), October 3 (nos. 9, 10), November 19 (no. 36), December 3 (no. 46), 1816, January 17 (no. 5), February 5 (no. 9), April 25 (no. 30), 1817, F.O. 5/114, 5/115, 5/121, 5/122; Bagot to Hamilton, March 17, 1817, F.O. 5/121; Bagot to Canning, November 1, 1817, in George Canning Papers, Archives Department, Public Library, Leeds.

19. Bushrod Washington to Bagot, June 27, 1816, Mrs. Bagot's Journal, July 28, 1816, Wellesley-Pole to Bagot, July 5, 30, 1816, Canning to Bagot, December 23, 1816, W. H. Lyttleton to Bagot, December 31, 1816, all in Bagot, *George Canning* II, 25, 26, 31, 34, 39, 40; Foster to Bagot, May 28, 1816, Baker to Bagot, June 27, 1816, Bagot to Binning, September 15, October 24, 1816, Wellesley-Pole to Bagot, September 30, 1816, Bagot to Willinck, October 4, 1816, Bagot to Sneyd, November 10, 1816, Wellesley-Pole to Bagot, October 30, 1817, all in Bagot Papers; Smith, *First Forty Years*, pp. 134–35; Bagot to William Hamilton, November 10 (Pvt.), 1816, F.O. 5/115; Hyde de Neuville, *Mémoires et Souvenirs du Baron Hyde de Neuville* II, 198; Bemis, *John Quincy Adams*, pp. 267–68.

20. Bagot to John Sneyd, March 24, 1817, in Bagot, *George Canning* II, 40; Bryan, *National Capital* II, 33–34; Wharton, *Social Life*, pp. 183, 184; Bagot to Castlereagh, March 11 (no. 11), 1817, F.O. 5/121; Ammon, *James Monroe*, pp. 367–68.

21. Bryan, *National Capital* II, 44–45; *National Intelligencer*, June 3, September 18, 1817; Bagot to Castlereagh, April 7 (no. 23), May 5 (no. 31), August 8 (no. 50), December 2 (no. 73), 1817, F.O. 5/121, 5/122, 5/123; Ammon, *James Monroe*, pp. 368, 371–79; Bagot to Sneyd, March 24, 1817, in Bagot, *George Canning* II, 40–41; Bagot to Canning, November 1, 1817, in George Canning Papers.

22. Bagot to John Sneyd, March 24, 1817, in Bagot, *George Canning* II, 40–41; Bagot to Canning, November 1, 1817, in George Canning Papers; Fearon, *Sketches of America*, p. 294; Robertson–Hyde de Neuville–Bagot–Castlereagh correspondence, Additional Manuscripts, 20119, 20120, 20200, 20201, British Museum, and Bagot Papers; Bagot to Sneyd, July 4, 1816, in Bagot, *George Canning* II, 24; Bagot to Planta, July 29, August 3, 1818 (Pvt.), F.O. 5/132; Bagot to Castlereagh, October 6 (no. 61), September 1 (Sep. and Secret), December 2 (no. 75), 1817, F.O. 5/123; Sneyd to Bagot, May 23, 1817, in Bagot, *George Canning* II, 49; Wellesley-Pole to Bagot, March 27, May 4, 13, 1817, Charles Ellis to Bagot, July 4, 1817, all in Bagot Papers; Wellington to

Mary Bagot, April 9, December 14, 1817, in Bagot, *George Canning* II, 42, 43, 63.

23. Adams, *Memoirs of John Quincy Adams* IV, 7, 138, 140, 338, V, 246; Lyttleton to Bagot, January 22, 1827, in Bagot, *George Canning* II, 362. An excellent brief sketch of John Q. Adams appears in Dangerfield, *Era of Good Feelings*, pp. 97–99; Monroe to Madison, October 18, 1817, in Monroe, *Writings* VI, 30.

24. Bemis, *John Quincy Adams*, pp. 281–86; Bagot to Castlereagh, November 7 (no. 65), 24 (Sep.), December 2 (no. 74), 1817, F.O. 5/123; Adams, *Memoirs of John Quincy Adams* IV, 11, 24–26, 93–94; Merk, *Oregon Question*, pp. 17–21; Burt, *United States*, p. 414; Rush, *Memoranda of a Residence*, pp. 94–96.

25. Bagot to Canning, November 1, 1817, December 3, 1818, in George Canning Papers; Bagot to Planta, September 2 (Pvt.), 1818, F.O. 5/133; Bagot to Castlereagh, June 2 (no. 48), 1818, F.O. 5/132; Castlereagh to Bagot, March 22 (Pvt.), 1817, F.O. 5/120; Perkins, *Castlereagh and Adams*, pp. 259–72; Bemis, *John Quincy Adams*, pp. 290–98.

26. Bagot to Canning, November 1, December 2, 1817, in George Canning Papers; Bagot to Binning, February 26, 1818, Bagot Papers; Fearon, *Sketches of America*, p. 294; Bryan, *National Capital* II, 50, 53; Paullin, "Early British Diplomats," pp. 249, 250; Adams, *Memoirs of John Quincy Adams* IV, 25, 29, 33, 304; Louisa Adams Diary, February 26, March 1, 1819, Adams Papers, Library of Congress; Hubbard, "Political and Social Life," pp. 65–66; Ammon, *James Monroe*, pp. 396–405; Bemis, *John Quincy Adams*, pp. 273–74; Morison, *Life in Washington*, pp. 23–24, 25–26; Gales and Seaton to Bagot, December 29, 1817, Bagot Papers.

27. Adams, *Memoirs of John Quincy Adams* IV, 78, 121–22; Bagot to Binning, February 26, 1818, Bagot Papers; Bagot to Castlereagh, October 6 (no. 61), December 2 (no. 75), 21 (Sep.), 1817, F.O. 5/123, January 6 (no. 7), March 3 (no. 23), April 6 (no. 28), April 7 (nos. 27, 32), 18 (no. 35), 1818, F.O. 5/130, F.O. 5/131.

28. Bagot to Castlereagh, February 5 (no. 9), April 25 (no. 30), 1817, F.O. 5/121, F.O. 5/122, January 6 (no. 7), February 8 (no. 14), April 6 (no. 28), 1818, F.O. 5/130, F.O. 5/131; Adams, *Memoirs of John Quincy Adams* IV, 48–50, 52, 62; Perkins, *Castlereagh and Adams*, pp. 283–88; Dangerfield, *Era of Good Feelings*, pp. 126–29, 134; Rush, *Memoranda of a Residence*, p. 194; Bickley, *Earl Bathurst*, p. 441; Webster, *Foreign Policy, 1815–1822*, pp. 448–49; Bemis, *John Quincy Adams*, p. 312.

29. Dangerfield, *Era of Good Feelings*, pp. 126–28, 130–36; Perkins, *Castlereagh and Adams*, pp. 288–95; Bagot to Castlereagh, April 6 (no. 28), May 6 (no. 38), June 2 (no. 47), 29 (no. 52), July 24 (nos. 56, 57), August 3 (no. 60), September 7 (no. 73), December 3 (no. 87), 1818, F.O. 5/131, F.O. 5/132, F.O. 5/133; Adams, *Memoirs of John Quincy Adams* IV, 101–102, 103, 114, 125, 126, 179–80, 184, 186–87, 337; Baker to Bagot, July 8, 1818, Bagot Papers; Webster, *Foreign Policy, 1815–1822*, pp. 449–51; Rush, *Memoranda of a Residence*, pp. 332–34, 436–39, 449–52; Bagot to Planta, July 29 (Pvt.), November 4 (Pvt.), 1818, F.O. 5/132, F.O. 5/133; Bemis, *John Quincy Adams*, pp. 313–29; Planta to Bagot, January 13, 1819, Bagot Papers; Wellesley-Pole to Bagot, January 12, 1819, Bagot, *George Canning* II, 88.

30. Bagot to Planta, February 8, May 25, 1818; Wellesley-Pole to Bagot, March 6, 1818, Planta to Bagot, March 6, May 21, 1818, Baker to Bagot, July 8, 1818, all in Bagot Papers; Bagot to Planta, July 29 (Pvt.), November 4 (Pvt.), 1818, F.O. 5/132, F.O. 5/133; Bagot to Canning, December 3, 1818, in George Canning Papers; Bagot to Binning, October 23, 1818, in Bagot, *George Canning* II, 86.

31. Bagot to Binning, September 26, 1818, Bagot to Sir Benjamin Bloomfield, September 19, 1818, both in Bagot Papers; Bagot to Canning, December 3, 1818, in George

Canning Papers, Leeds; Louisa Adams Diary, February 15, 1819, Adams Papers; Adams, *Memoirs of John Quincy Adams* IV, 177–78, 180–81, 181–82, 260.

32. Bagot to Canning, December 3, 1818, George Canning Papers; Planta to Bagot, January 13, 1819, William Hamilton to Bagot, November 14, 1818, Lord Melville to Wellesley-Pole, November 19, 1818, Joseph Delaplaine to Bagot, October 31, 1818, all in Bagot Papers; Earl Talbot to Bagot, January 17, 1819, in Bagot, *George Canning* II, 89; Rush, *Memoranda of a Residence*, pp. 453–54; Adams to Rush, May 2, 1819, in Adams, *Writings of John Quincy Adams* VI, 545–48; Adams, *Memoirs of John Quincy Adams* IV, 236–37, 238.

33. Adams, *Memoirs of John Quincy Adams* IV, 357; Bagot to Planta, March 5 (Pvt.), 1819, F.O. 5/132.

34. Perkins, *Castlereagh and Adams*, pp. 205–206; Bagot to Sir John Louis, February 3, 1819, Bagot Papers; Bagot to Castlereagh, April 14 (no. 26), 1819, F.O. 5/142; Antrobus to Bagot, April 16, 22, 1819, Bagot Papers; Antrobus to Castlereagh, May 6 (no. 3), 1819, F.O. 5/143; Christopher Hughes to Bagot, December 2, 1825, in Bagot, *George Canning* II, 298; Adams, *Memoirs of John Quincy Adams* IV, 333, 339.

35. Bloomfield to Bagot, November 25, 1819, Planta to Bagot, September 28, 1821, Bagot Papers; Temperley, *Foreign Policy of Canning*, pp. 90, 233, 287, 292, 294–95, 295–96, 332, 444; Sophia Louisa Bagot, *Links with the Past*, pp. 95, 205, 206; William Dyott, *William Dyott's Diary*, ed. Reginald W. Jeffrey, pp. 328–29; Rush, *Residence at the Court* I, 257, 258, 268, 296–97; Bagot to Binning, May 24, 1818, in Bagot, *George Canning* II, 77–78; Bagot, *George Canning* II, 94, 159, 184, 201, 223–27, 233, 234, 267–68, 270, 363–69, 372, 405, 415; Bindoff, Malcolm-Smith, and Webster, *Diplomatic Representatives*, pp. 113, 181; Browning, "Charles Bagot," pp. 98–99; *Greville Memoirs* V, 46; Harriet Martineau, *History of Thirty Years' Peace* IV, 375; John Charles Dent, *The Canadian Portrait Gallery* III, 78; Dent, *Last Forty Years* I, 181–93, 252–62.

Stratford Canning

1. E. F. Malcolm-Smith, *The Life of Stratford Canning*, pp. 35–43. The term "religious and political methodist" particularly galled Canning, who like many of his circle used the term "methodist" to denote intrusive claims to piety and morality in areas outside religion.

2. C. J. Bartlett, *Castlereagh*, p. 112; Webster, *Foreign Policy, 1812–1815*, pp. 48, 393–94; Sir Charles Petrie, *George Canning*, pp. 84–85, 103–104; Stanley Lane-Poole, *The Life of the Right Honourable Stratford Canning, Viscount de Redcliffe* I, 183–213, 278; Leo Gerald Byrne, *The Great Ambassador*, pp. 64–66; Malcolm-Smith, *Stratford Canning*, pp. 47–51.

3. Webster, *Foreign Policy, 1812–1815*, pp. 393–94; Planta to Bagot, July 12, 1816, in Bagot, *George Canning* II, 28; Lane-Poole, *Life of Stratford Canning* I, 222–80, 282–84, 287; Stratford Canning to George Canning, August 27, 1817, in Lane-Poole, *Life of Stratford Canning* I, 280–82; Byrne, *Great Ambassador*, pp. 65–73; Malcolm-Smith, *Stratford Canning*, pp. 51–63.

4. Lane-Poole, *Life of Stratford Canning* I, 285–87; S. Canning to Gally Knight, January 24, 1820, in Lane-Poole, *Life of Stratford Canning* I, 288–89; Malcolm-Smith, *Stratford Canning*, pp. 62–63.

5. Lane-Poole, *Life of Stratford Canning* I, 290–97, 298–99; Stratford Canning to Bagot, December 24, 1819, in Bagot, *George Canning* II, 95–96; Stratford Canning to Bagot, October 19, 1820, Bagot Papers; Malcolm-Smith, *Stratford Canning*, pp. 64–65; Perkins, *Castlereagh and Adams*, p. 206; Rush, *Residence at the Court* I, 191–93, 195,

257, 258, 268, 309, 322, 326, 327, 331; Bagot notes to Vaughan with comments by Stratford Canning, MS., All Souls College, Oxford, England; Adams, *Memoirs of John Quincy Adams* V, 181.

    6. Lane-Poole, *Life of Stratford Canning* I, 298–99, 319; Bagot memorandum, All Souls College; Stratford Canning to George Canning, June 25, 1823, F.O. 5/176; Castlereagh to S. Canning, Instructions No. 2 (Confidential), F.O. 5/150; Stratford Canning to Castlereagh, September 30, 1820, F.O. 5/150; Antrobus to Castlereagh, October 1, 1820, F.O. 5/149; Antrobus to Bagot, November 30, 1819, October 9, 1820, Bagot Papers.

    7. Adams, *Memoirs of John Quincy Adams* V, 181; Canning to Castlereagh, November 20, 1820, F.O. 5/150; Lane-Poole, *Life of Stratford Canning* I, 300; John Palmer, *Journal of Travels in the United States of North America and Lower Canada*, pp. 30–31; *Baron Klinkowström's America, 1813–1820*, trans. and ed. Franklin D. Scott, pp. 30–31; K. E. Greenwood, "Washington in 1820," typed MS., Washington Collection, Library of Congress; Bryan, *National Capital* II, 14, 15, 16; James F. Cooper, *Notions of the Americans Picked up by a Travelling Bachelor* I, 12, 21, 26.

    8. Stratford Canning to Bagot, October 19, 1820, Antrobus to Bagot, October 9, 1820, A. St. John Baker to Bagot, April 3, 1820, all in Bagot Papers; Stratford Canning to Castlereagh, October 9, 1820, Stratford Canning Papers; Stratford Canning to Castlereagh, October 16, 1820, F.O. 5/150; Adams, *Memoirs of John Quincy Adams* V, 187.

    9. Hugh G. Soulsby, "The Right of Search and the Slave Trade in Anglo-American Relations, 1814–1862," *Johns Hopkins University Studies in Historical and Political Science*, ser. 51, no. 2 (1933): 13–14, 16, 20, 21–22; Webster, *Foreign Policy, 1815–1822*, pp. 454–65; Frank J. Klingberg, "The Anti-Slavery Movement in England," *Yale Historical Publications* 17 (1926): 130, 131–70; Castlereagh to Canning, August 7 (no. 3), 1820, F.O. 5/150; Adams, *Memoirs of John Quincy Adams* IV, 335–37, V, 181–84.

    10. Adams, *Memoirs of John Quincy Adams* V, 189–91, 191–93, 193–95; Canning to Castlereagh, October 3 (no. 2), 28 (no. 7), 30 (Sep.), 1820, F.O. 5/150; Bemis, *John Quincy Adams*, p. 270; Byrne, *Great Ambassador*, p. 78.

    11. Thomas Cooper to William Roscoe, May 18, 1819, Roscoe Papers; Canning to Castlereagh, November 20 (no. 13), 1820, F.O. 5/150; Canning to Fazakerley, November 14, 1820, in Lane-Poole, *Life of Stratford Canning* I, 316–17; Baker to Bagot, November 1, 1818, Bagot Papers; Adams, *Memoirs of John Quincy Adams* V, 214, 215, 216–19, 222–23, 225–26; Canning to Castlereagh, October 30 (no. 8), 31, December 6, 18, 30 (no. 20), 1820, F.O. 5/150; Castlereagh to Canning, August 9 (no. 4), 1820, F.O. 5/150.

    12. Adams, *Memoirs of John Quincy Adams* V, 218, 225–26, 232–34; Canning to Castlereagh, January 2 (no. 1), 21 (no. 2), 1821, F.O. 5/157; Bemis, *John Quincy Adams*, pp. 417–24; Soulsby, "Right of Search," pp. 21–24; Webster, *Foreign Policy, 1815–1822*, p. 465.

    13. Adams, *Memoirs of John Quincy Adams* V, 237, 243–60, 320, 412, 447–50, 466, 472, VI, 39, 41, 90–91, 120–21, 140, 154; Canning to Castlereagh, January 28, 30 (Sep.), 1821, F.O. 5/157; Perkins, *Castlereagh and Adams*, pp. 278–81; Bemis, *John Quincy Adams*, pp. 488–93; Canning to Planta (Pvt.), February 6, 1821, F.O. 5/157, June 15, 1821, in Canning Papers, Library of Congress.

    14. Adams, *Memoirs of John Quincy Adams* V, 62; Singleton, *White House* I, 149–50; *Klinkowström's America*, pp. 28–29; Morison, *Life in Washington*, p. 24; Ingersoll Diary, February, 1823, Library of Congress; Lane-Poole, *Life of Stratford Canning* I, 314–15; Canning to his sister, April 24, 1821, in Lane-Poole, *Life of Stratford Canning* I, 321; Diary of R. G. Gladstone, MS. 84, Aetheneum Library, Liverpool; Canning to Castlereagh, February 19, March 7 (no. 13), 8 (nos. 14, 15, 16 and Pvt.), April 27, June 4

(no. 32), 1821, F.O. 5/157, 5/158; Ammon, *James Monroe*, pp. 444-45; Addington, "Residence," p. 30.

15. Baker to Bagot, April 18, 1821, in Bagot Papers; Canning to Planta, March 8, July 30, 1821, to Richard Wellesley, September 1, 1823, in Lane-Poole, *Life of Stratford Canning* I, 318, 319, 320-21; Canning to his sister, April 24, July 2, 1821, in Lane-Poole, *Life of Stratford Canning*, pp. 320, 322; Stratford to William Canning, April 29, 1821, in Lane-Poole, *Life of Stratford Canning*, p. 322; Canning to his mother, April 23, 1821, April 25, 1822, in Lane-Poole, *Life of Stratford Canning*, pp. 322, 324; Stratford to George Canning, April 2, 1821, in George Canning Papers, Leeds; Canning to Bagot, October 9, 1821, Bagot Papers; Canning to Castlereagh, July 30 (Sep.), 1821, F.O. 5/158.

16. Baker to Bagot, April 18, 1821, Planta to Bagot, January 20, 1821, Canning to Bagot, July 28, 1821, all in Bagot Papers; Canning to his mother, July 2, October 5, 1821, in Lane-Poole, *Life of Stratford Canning* I, 326-28; Canning to Planta, April 2, 1821, in Lane-Poole, *Life of Stratford Canning* I, 324; Stratford Canning, "Notes on a Tour of Harper's Ferry," Stratford Canning Papers.

17. Adams, *Memoirs of John Quincy Adams* V, 320; Bemis, *John Quincy Adams*, pp. 356-58; Canning to Londonderry, April 27, June 5, July 30 (Sep.), 1821, F.O. 5/158; Castlereagh to Canning, March 25, April 10, 1821, F.O. 5/156; Canning to Planta (Pvt.), June 15, 1821, Stratford Canning Papers; Canning to Planta, April 3, 1821, in Lane-Poole, *Life of Stratford Canning* I, 309-10; Canning to Bagot, July 28, 1821, Bagot Papers. Like Bagot, Canning, when writing to England privately, used sarcasm heavily, especially in describing those he disliked. Curiously, neither Dangerfield nor Bemis recognizes the scathing irony in the minister's description of the Adams July 4 speech. Bemis, *John Quincy Adams*, p. 358, and Dangerfield, *Era of Good Feelings*, p. 269. Canning's private letters make it clear that he was furious and was using his favorite weapon.

18. Stratford to George Canning, September 29, 1821, in Lane-Poole, *Life of Stratford Canning* I, 304-306, 317-18; Canning to Bagot, October 9, 1821, Baker to Bagot, August 6, 1821, both in Bagot Papers; Canning to Planta, June 15, 1821 (photostat), Stratford Canning Papers, Library of Congress; Canning to Lord Ellenborough, October 10, 1821, Stratford Canning Papers; Canning to Robertson, September 21, 1821, in George Canning Papers, Leeds; Canning to Londonderry, September 4 (Confidential), 1821, F.O. 5/159 and George Canning Papers, Leeds; Canning to Londonderry, August 31 (Sep.), September 4 (no. 47), October 1 (Sep.), December 4 (no. 63), 1821, F.O. 5/159.

19. Ammon, *James Monroe*, pp. 493-94, 497-500, 501; Canning to Lord Ellenborough, October 10, 1821, Canning to Robert Wilmot, November 7, 1822, both in Stratford Canning Papers; Stratford to George Canning, July 28, 1821, Bagot Papers; Canning to Londonderry, February 8 (no. 10), May 8 (no. 34), 1822, F.O. 5/166, 5/168.

20. Stratford to George Canning, April 2, 1821, January 3, 1822, in George Canning Papers, Leeds; Canning to Planta, June 15, 1821, April 28, 1822 (photostats), Library of Congress; Canning to Bagot, July 28, 1821, January 3, 1822, Bagot Papers; Adams, *Memoirs of John Quincy Adams* V, 458, 459-60; Rufus King to Charles King, December 23, to Christopher Gore, December 25, to J. A. King, December 28, 1821, in King, *Life and Correspondence* VI, 431-32, 433; Canning to Londonderry, December 31 (Sep. and Confidential w/encl.), 1821, F.O. 5/159; Lane-Poole, *Life of Stratford Canning* I, 313.

21. Canning to Londonderry, February 7 (no. 5), 8 (no. 6), April 2 (no. 25), May 8 (no. 30), June 29, July 16, 1822; Canning to Bathurst, October 28 (no. 5), December 4 (nos. 12, 13), 1822, F.O. 5/166, 5/168, 5/169; Canning to Bagot, May 8, 1822, in Bagot, *George Canning* II, 26; Adams, *Memoirs of John Quincy Adams* VI, 13-14; Dangerfield, *Era of Good Feelings*, pp. 259-63; Perkins, *Castlereagh and Adams*, pp. 232-37; Bemis, *John Quincy Adams*, p. 425; Lane-Poole, *Life of Stratford Canning* I, 309-10;

Canning to Undersecretary Wilmot, November 7, 1822, F.O. 352/8; Louisa Adams Diary, December 22, 24, 1822; Canning to Bathurst, December 28 (Confidential), 1822, F.O. 5/169.

22. Byrne, *Great Ambassador*, pp. 81, 83; Lane-Poole, *Life of Stratford Canning* I, 33; Canning to the Columbian Harmonic Society, February 11, 1822, F.O. 353/8; Joseph Delaplane to Canning, February 22, 1822, F.O. 353/8; Canning to Daniel Webster, Webster Papers (microfilm), University of Tennessee, Knoxville; Canning to Barclay, January 25, 1822, in Canning Papers (photostat), Library of Congress; William Lee to Mary Lee, June 9, 28, 1822, in Lee, *Yankee Jeffersonian*, pp. 193, 200; Louisa Adams Diary, December 9, 1822.

23. Adams, *Memoirs of John Quincy Adams* VI, 35–39, 41–42, 81–84; Lane-Poole, *Life of Stratford Canning* I, 328–34; Canning to Bathurst, October 7, 28 (no. 5), December 4 (no. 12), 1822, F.O. 5/169; Canning to Planta, October 1, 1822, in Lane-Poole, *Life of Stratford Canning* I, 333–34.

24. Ammon, *James Monroe*, pp. 509–10, 512–13; Byrne, *Great Ambassador*, p. 27; Stratford to George Canning, January 4, 1823, in Canning Papers, Leeds; Stratford to George Canning, January 8 (Sep.), 1823, F.O. 5/175; Stratford to George Canning, January 10, 1823, in Canning Papers, Library of Congress; Stratford to George Canning, March 12, 1823, in George Canning Papers, Leeds; Canning to Bagot, March 30, 1823, in Bagot, *George Canning* II, 160–66; Louisa Adams Diary, January 20, 1823; Ingersoll Diary, February, 1823.

25. Stratford to George Canning, February 10, March 12, June 6, 1823, in George Canning Papers, Leeds; George to Stratford Canning, October 11 (nos. 5, 6, 8), 1822, F.O. 5/165; Stratford to George Canning, January 1 (nos. 3, 4), 11 (no. 10 Secret), February 7 (no. 18), 8 (no. 20), March 10 (no. 28), 19, 31, April 22 (nos. 40, 41), June 6 (nos. 54, 56), July 7 (no. 69), 1823, F.O. 5/175, 5/176; Bemis, *John Quincy Adams*, pp. 427–31.

26. Stratford to George Canning, March 12, April 9, in Stratford Canning Papers, F.O. 353/8; Stratford Canning to Bagot, March 20, 1823, Bagot Papers; Adams, *Memoirs of John Quincy Adams* VII, 216; Dangerfield, *Era of Good Feelings*, pp. 259–63, 281, 284; Perkins, *Castlereagh and Adams*, pp. 234–38; Stratford to George Canning, February 8 (no. 21), 10 (no. 24), March 12 (no. 30), April 1 (no. 37), 22 (no. 42), May 24, June 6 (nos. 54, 56), F.O. 5/175, 5/176; George Canning to Bagot, March 30, 1823, Bagot Papers; H. W. V. Temperley, "The Later American Policy of George Canning," *American Historical Review* 12 (July, 1906): 789, 790; George to Stratford Canning, November 11 (no. 9), 1822, July 11 (no. 14), 1823, F.O. 5/165.

27. Dangerfield, *Era of Good Feelings*, pp. 266–67, 277–81; Stratford to George Canning, May 3 (no. 47), 24, June 6 (nos. 54, 56), 1823, F.O. 5/176; Adams, *Memoirs of John Quincy Adams* VI, 151–54, esp. 153; Stratford to George Canning, May 6, 27, June 6, 1823, in George Canning Papers, Leeds; Bemis, *John Quincy Adams*, p. 375.

28. Adams, *Memoirs* VI, 147, 156, 157; George to Stratford Canning, May 10, 1823, in George Canning Papers, Leeds; *Niles Weekly Register*, July 5, 1823.

29. Stratford to George Canning, June 25, July 7 (no. 69 and Sep.), August 4, 1823, F.O. 5/176; Addington to Canning, August 12, 1823, F.O. 5/177; Stratford to George Canning, July 7, August 8, September 9, 1823, Stratford Canning to Planta, July 30, 31, 1823, all in George Canning Papers, Leeds; Dangerfield, *Era of Good Feelings*, pp. 284–90; George Dangerfield, *The Awakening of American Nationalism, 1815–1828*, pp. 257–62; Canning to Planta, February 6 (Pvt.), 1824, F.O. 5/157; Adams, *Memoirs of John Quincy Adams* VII, 328; Canning to Bagot, September 19, 1823, in Bagot, *George Canning* II, 200; Bemis, *John Quincy Adams*, p. 379; George Canning to Bagot, August 27, 1823, January 9, 1824, in Bagot, *George Canning* II, 199–200, 207–209.

30. Stratford to George Canning, March 23, 1824, in George Canning Papers, Leeds; Stratford Canning to Bagot, January 23, July 25, 1824, in Bagot, *George Canning* II, 220–21, 271; Stratford to George Canning, June 3, 1824, in George Canning Papers, Leeds; Lane-Poole, *Life of Stratford Canning* I, 336; Bemis, *John Quincy Adams*, pp. 432–34, 443; Malcolm-Smith, *Stratford Canning*, pp. 83ff.; Byrne, *Great Ambassador*; Lane-Poole, *Life of Stratford Canning* I, 339ff., II; Bindoff, Malcolm-Smith, and Webster, *Diplomatic Representatives*, pp. 61, 62, 105, 113, 127, 139, 145, 161, 168, 169, 170; Strangford to Bagot, August 30, 1825, in Bagot, *George Canning* II, 292; Ward and Gooch, *Cambridge History* II, 365; Charles C. F. Greville, *The Greville Memoirs: A Journal of the Reigns of King George IV and King William IV*, ed. Henry Reeve, II, 146–47, 203; Sir Ernest Satow, *A Guide to Diplomatic Practice*, pp. 204–205, 206, 207; Bindoff, "Unreformed Diplomatic Service," p. 168; Temperley, *Foreign Policy of Canning*, pp. 332, 342–43; Addington, "Residence," pp. 86–90; Stanley Lane-Poole, "Stratford Canning," *Dictionary of National Biography* VIII, 437–44.

Bibliography

PRIMARY MATERIAL

Manuscript Collections

GREAT BRITAIN
Bedford. Bedfordshire Record Office. Samuel Whitbread Papers.
Edinburgh. University of Edinburgh. Liston Papers.
Exeter. Devon Record Office. Sidmouth Papers.
Greenwich. Greenwich Naval Museum. Admirals' Dispatches, North America, vol. 505, 1814. Personal Papers, Codrington Papers.
———. National Maritime Museum. Personal Papers, Admiral Sir John Borlase Warren correspondence with Lord Melville.
Keele. University College of North Staffordshire Library. Sneyd Manuscripts.
Kendal. Levens Hall. Bagot Papers.
Leeds. Public Library, Archives Department. George Canning Papers.
Liverpool. Aetheneum Library. Diary of R. G. Gladstone.
———. Public Library. Roscoe Papers.
London. British Museum. Aberdeen Papers. Perceval Papers.
———. Morier notes and memorandum, 1810, Additional Manuscripts 37291 and 37392, folders 209 and 28.
———. London School of Economics. Letters of Eminent Statesmen Collection. Hammond MS. No. 581.
———. Public Record Office. F.O. 353/59, 353/60, 353/61, Jackson Papers. F.O. 5 Series, Dispatches of and Instructions to the British Ministers to the United States. Lord Lascelles MSS., George Canning Correspondence (transcripts). Margaret Hammond Collection (transcripts). Stratford Canning Papers.
North Riding. York County Records Office, Northallerton. Beresford-Pierce MSS.
Oxford. All Souls College. Bagot Notes to Vaughan.

UNITED STATES
Boston. Massachusetts Historical Society. Pickering Papers.
Knoxville. University of Tennessee. Daniel Webster Papers (microfilm).

Washington, D.C. Library of Congress. Adams Papers. Henry Adams, Transcripts of the Dispatches of the British Ministers to the United States. Baldwin Papers. Stratford Canning Papers, Miscellaneous Personal Papers. Andrew Ellicott Papers. Eustis Papers. Augustus Foster, "Notes and Recollections Respecting the States in the Years 1805–06–07 and 1811–1812." Augustus Foster, "Part of a Journal in the United States of America, 1811–1812, Containing Allusions to the Declaration of War." Gallatin Papers. K. E. Greenwood, "Washington in 1820," Washington Collection. Ingersoll Diary. John Franklin Jameson Papers. Jefferson Papers. William Jones Papers. Kelsey Papers, "Letter of Travel in the United States." Liston Papers. McHenry Papers. Madison Papers. Nicholson Papers. Samuel Smith Papers. Edward Thornton, Correspondence with Bland Burges, Thornton Papers. Edward Thornton Memoir. Mrs. William Thornton Diary.

Books

Adams, Abigail. *Letters of Mrs. Adams, the Wife of John Adams, with an Introductory Memoir by Her Grandson, Charles Francis Adams.* Boston, Wilkins Carter and Co., 1848.

———. *New Letters of Abigail Adams, 1788–1801, with an Introduction by Stewart Mitchell.* Cambridge, Mass.: Houghton Mifflin, 1947.

Adams, John. *Diary and Autobiography of John Adams.* Edited by Lyman H. Butterfield. Cambridge, Mass.: Belknap Press, 1961.

Adams, John Quincy. *Memoirs of John Quincy Adams, Comprising Portions of His Diary from 1795 to 1848.* Edited by Charles Francis Adams. 12 vols. Philadelphia: J. B. Lippincott, 1874–77.

———. *The Writings of John Quincy Adams.* Edited by Worthington Chauncey Ford. 7 vols. New York: Macmillan, 1913–1917.

Ames, Fisher. *The Works of Fisher Ames, with a Selection from His Speeches and Correspondence.* Edited by Seth Ames. 2 vols. Boston: Little, Brown, 1854.

Auckland, Lord William. *The Journals and Correspondence of William, Lord Auckland.* Edited by the Right Hon. and Right Reverend Bishop of Bath and Wells. 4 vols. London: R. Bentley, 1861–62.

Bagot, Captain Joscelin. *George Canning and His Friends.* 2 vols. London: J. Murray, 1909.

Baker, William Spohn. *Washington after the Revolution, 1784–99.* 2 vols. Philadelphia: J. B. Lippincott, 1898.

Barclay, Thomas. *Selections from the Correspondence of Thomas Barclay.* Edited by George Lockhart Rives. New York: Harper and Brothers, 1894.

Bickley, Francis, comp. *Reports on the Manuscripts of Earl Bathurst Preserved at Cirencester.* Historical Manuscripts Commission, vol. LXVI. London, 1923.

Birbeck, Morris. *Notes on a Journey in America from the Coast of Virginia to the Territory of Illinois.* 4th ed. London: James Ridgeway, 1818.

Blane, William Newnham. *An Excursion through the United States and Canada, 1822–23*. London: printed for Baldwin, Craddock, and Joy, 1824.

Brown, Everett Somerville. *The Missouri Compromise and Presidential Politics, 1820–1825, Letters from William Plumer, Jr.*, St. Louis: Missouri Historical Society, 1926.

Burges, Sir James Bland. *Selections from the Letters and Correspondence of Sir James Bland Burges, Bart. . . .* Edited by James Hutton. London: J. Murray, 1885.

Castlereagh, Robert, Viscount. *Memoirs and Correspondence of Castlereagh*. 16 vols. London: H. Calburn, 1850–53.

[Cavendish, Georgiana]. *Extracts from the Correspondence of Georgiana, Duchess of Devonshire*. Edited by the earl of Bessborough. London: J. Murray, 1865.

Cobbett, William. *Letters from William Cobbett to Edward Thornton, 1797 to 1800*. Edited by G. D. H. Cole. Oxford: Oxford University Press, 1937.

Colchester, Charles Abbott, Lord. *The Diary and Correspondence of Charles Abbott, Lord Colchester*. Edited by Charles Abbott, Lord Colchester. 3 vols. London: J. Murray, 1861.

Cooper, James Fenimore. *Notions of the Americans Picked up by a Travelling Bachelor*. 2 vols. Philadelphia: Carey, Lee, and Carey, 1828.

Cornwallis, Charles, First Marquis. *Correspondence of Charles, First Marquis of Cornwallis*. Edited by Charles Ross. London: J. Murray, 1859.

Creevey, Thomas. *The Creevey Papers: A Selection from the Correspondence and Diaries of the Late Thomas Creevey, M.P.* Edited by Sir Herbert Maxwell. 2 vols. London, J. Murray, 1903.

Crowninshield, Mary Boardman. *Letters of Mary Boardman Crowninshield, 1813–1816, Edited by Francis Boardman Crowninshield*. Cambridge, Mass.: printed at the Riverside Press, 1905.

Cutler, Manasseh. *Life, Journals, and Correspondence of Reverend Manasseh Cutler*. Edited by William P. and Julia P. Cutler. 2 vols. Cincinnatti: R. Clarke and Co., 1888.

Davis, John. *Travels of Four Years and a Half in the United States of America during 1798, 1799, 1800, 1801, and 1802*. Edited by A. J. Morrison. New York: Henry Holt and Co., 1909.

Documents Relating to New England Federalism, 1800–1813. Edited by Henry Adams. Boston: Little, Brown, 1877.

Douglas, Sylvester. *The Diaries of Sylvester Douglas, Lord Glenbervie*. Edited by Francis Bickley. 2 vols. London: Constable and Co., 1928.

Dudley, John William Ward, First Earl of Dudley. *Letters to "Ivy" from the First Earl of Dudley*. Edited by Samuel Henry Romilly. London: Longmans, Green, and Co., 1905.

Duncan, John Morison. *Travels through Part of the United States and Canada in 1818 and 1819*. 2 vols. New York: W. B. Gilley, 1823.

Dyott, William. *Dyott's Diary*. Edited by Reginald W. Jeffery. 2 vols. London: Constable and Co., 1907.

Fearon, Henry Bradshaw. *Sketches of America: A Narrative of a Journey of 5000 Miles.* . . . London: printed for Longman, Hurst, Rees, Orme, and Brown, 1818.
Fitzpatrick, Walter, ed. *Report on the Manuscripts of J. B. Fortesque, Esq. Preserved at Dropmore.* 13th Report of the Historical Manuscripts Commission. 10 vols. London, 1892–1927.
Foster, Augustus. *Jeffersonian America: Notes on the United States of America Collected in the Years 1805–1806–1807 and 1811–1812.* Edited by Richard Beale Davis. San Marino, Calif.: Huntington Library, 1954.
Gallatin, Albert. *The Writings of Albert Gallatin.* Edited by Henry Adams. 3 vols. Philadelphia: J. B. Lippincott, 1879.
The Glenbervie Journals. Edited by Walter Sichel. London: Constable and Co., 1910.
Gower, Lord Ronald. *Stafford House Papers.* London: Kegan, Paul, and Co., 1891.
Granville, Lord Leveson Gower (First Earl of Granville) *Private Correspondence 1781 to 1821.* Edited by Castalia, Countess Granville. London: J. Murray, 1916.
The Greville Memoirs. Edited by Lytton Strachey and Roger Fulford. 8 vols. London: Macmillan, 1938.
The Greville Memoirs: A Journal of the Reigns of King George IV and King William IV. Edited by Henry Reeve. 2 vols. New York: D. Appleton, 1887.
Hall, Captain Basil. *Fragments of Voyages and Travels.* London: E. Moxon, 1852.
Hall, Frances. *Travels in Canada and the United States in 1816 and 1817.* London: printed for Longman, Hurst, Rees, Orme, and Brown, 1818.
Hamilton, Alexander. *The Papers of Alexander Hamilton.* Edited by Harold C. Syrett et al. 26 vols. New York: Columbia University Press, 1961–1979.
Hyde de Neuville, Jean Guillaume, Baron. *Mémoirs et souvenirs du Baron Hyde de Neuville.* 3 vols. Paris: E. Plon, Nourrit, 1892.
Irving, Washington. *Washington Irving's Diary: Spain, 1828–29.* Edited by Clara Louise Penny. New York: Hispanic Society of America, 1926.
Jackson, George. *The Diaries and Letters of Sir George Jackson, KCH from the Peace of Amiens to the Battle of Talavera.* Edited by Lady Jackson. 2 vols. London: Richard Bentley and Son, 1873.
———. *The Bath Archives: A Further Selection of the Diaries and Letters of Sir George Jackson . . . from 1809 to 1816.* Edited by Lady Jackson. London: R. Bentley and Son, 1873.
Janson, Charles William. *The Stranger in America.* London: printed for J. Cundee, 1807.
Jay, John. *The Correspondence and Public Papers of John Jay.* Edited by Henry P. Johnson. 4 vols. New York: G. P. Putnam's Sons, 1890–93.
Jefferson, Thomas. *The Writings of Thomas Jefferson.* Collected and edited by Paul L. Ford. 10 vols. New York: G. P. Putnam's Sons, 1892–99.
The Journal of a British Chaplain in Paris during the Peace Negotiations of

Bibliography 263

1801–1802. Edited by Alexander Meyrick Broadley. London: Chapman and Hall, 1913.
Keith, Sir Robert Murray. *Memoirs and Correspondence of Sir Robert Murray Keith.* . . . Edited by Mrs. Gillespie Smythe. 2 vols. London: H. Colburn, 1894.
King, Rufus. *The Life and Correspondence of Rufus King.* Edited by Charles R. King. 6 vols. New York: G. P. Putnam's Sons, 1894–1900.
Klinkowström, Alex Leonard. *Baron Klinkowström's America, 1818–1820.* Translated and edited by Franklin D. Scott. Evanston, Ill.: Northwestern University Press, 1952.
Knight, Henry Cogswell [Arthur Singleton]. *Letters from the South and West.* Boston: Richardson and Lord, 1824.
Lambert, John. *Travels through Canada and the United States in 1806, 1807, and 1808.* 3 vols. Printed for C. Craddock and W. Joy, 1810.
Lee, William. *A Yankee Jeffersonian: Selections from the Diary and Letters of William Lee of Massachusetts.* Edited by Mary Lee Mann. Cambridge, Mass.: Belknap Press of Harvard University Press, 1958.
Madison, Dolley. *Memoirs and Letters of Dolley Madison, Edited by Her Grand-Niece.* Boston: Houghton Mifflin, 1887.
Madison, James. *The Writings of James Madison.* Edited by Gaillard Hunt. 9 vols. New York: G. P. Putnam's Sons, 1900–1910.
Malmesbury, James Harris, First Earl of. *Diaries and Correspondence of James Harris, First Earl of Malmesbury, Edited by His Grandson, the Third Earl.* 4 vols. London: R. Bentley, 1844.
Mayo, Bernard. *Henry Clay, Spokesman of the New West.* Boston: Houghton, Mifflin and Co., 1837.
Melish, John. *Travels in the United States of America in the Years 1809, 1810 and 1811.* 2 vols. Philadelphia: Thomas and George Palmer, 1812.
Miles, William Augustus. *The Correspondence of W. A. Miles on the French Revolution, 1789–1817.* Edited by Reverend Charles Popham Miles. 2 vols. London: Longmans Green and Co., 1890.
Monroe, James. *The Writings of James Monroe.* Edited by Stanislaus Murray. 7 vols. New York: G. P. Putnam's Sons, 1898–1903.
Moore, Thomas. *The Letters of Thomas Moore.* Edited by Wilfred S. Dowden. 2 vols. Oxford: Clarendon Press, 1964.
———. *Memoirs, Journals, and Correspondence of Thomas Moore.* Edited by Right Hon. Lord John Russell, M.P. 8 vols. London: Longmans, Brown, Green, and Longmans, 1853–56.
Moreau de St. Mery's American Journey, 1793–98. Translated and edited by Kenneth Roberts and Anna M. Roberts, New York, Garden City: Doubleday, 1947.
Morison, Samuel E. *Life in Washington a Century and a Half Ago.* Washington, D.C.: The Cosmos Club, 1968.
Morris, Gouverneur. *Life of Gouverneur Morris, with Selections from His Correspondence.* Edited by Jared Sparks. 3 vols. Boston: Gray and Bowen, 1832.

———. *The Diary and Letters of Gouverneur Morris.* Edited by Anne C. Morris. 2 vols. London: K. Paul French, 1889.
Paget, Arthur. *The Paget Papers: Diplomatic and Other Correspondence of the Right Hon. Sir Arthur Paget, GCB, 1794–1807.* Arranged and edited by Augustus B. Paget, GCB. 2 vols. London: W. Heinemann, 1896.
Palmer, John. *Journal of Travels in the United States of North America and Lower Canada.* London: Sherwood, Neely, and Jones, 1818.
Plumer, William. *Memorandum of Proceedings in the United States Senate, 1803–1807.* Edited by Everett Somerville Brown. New York: Macmillan, 1923.
Rose, George. *The Diaries and Correspondence of the Right Hon. George Rose.* Edited by L. Vernon Harcourt. 2 vols. N.p.: R. Bentley, 1860.
[Royall, Anne]. *Sketches of History, Life, and Manners in the United States.* New Haven: Printed for the author, 1826.
Rush, Benjamin. *Letters of Benjamin Rush.* Edited by Lyman H. Butterfield. 2 vols. Princeton, N.J.: Princeton University Press, 1951.
Rush, Richard. *Memoranda of a Residence at the Court of London, from 1819 to 1825.* Philadelphia: Carey, Lee and Blanchard, 1833.
———. *A Residence at the Court of London.* 2 vols. London: 2nd ser., R. Bentley, 1845.
Scott, Captain James. *Recollections of a Naval Life.* 3 vols. London: L. Bentley, 1834.
Scott, Walter. *The Journal of Sir Walter Scott.* Edited by W. E. K. Anderson. Oxford: Clarendon Press, 1972.
Smith, John Cotton. *The Correspondence and Miscellanies of John Cotton Smith.* Edited by William W. Andrews. New York: Harper and Brothers, 1847.
Smith, Mrs. Samuel Harrison. *The First Forty Years of Washington Society Portrayed by the Family Letters of Mrs. Samuel Harrison Smith.* Edited by Gaillard Hunt. New York: Charles Scribner's Sons, 1906.
Statistical Annals of the United States Founded on Official Documents. Edited by Adam Seybert. New York: B. Franklin, 1818, reprinted 1969.
Stuart, James. *Three Years in North America.* 2 vols. Edinburgh: printed for R. Caddell, 1833.
Sutcliff, Robert. *Travels in Some Parts of North America in the Years 1804, 1805, and 1806.* York, England: printed by C. Peacock, 1811.
Temple, William Johnstone. *Diaries of William Johnstone Temple, 1780–1796.* Edited by Lewis Bettany. Oxford: Clarendon Press, 1929.
Ticknor, George. *Life, Letters, and Journals of George Ticknor.* Edited by George S. Hilliard. 2 vols. Boston: J. Osgood and Co., 1878.
Tudor, Henry. *Narrative of a Tour in North America . . . in a Series of Letters . . . 1831–32.* London: J. Duncan, 1834.
Twining, Thomas. *Travels in America 100 Years Ago.* New York: Harper, 1893.
Tyler, Lyon G. *Letters and Times of the Tylers.* 3 vols. Richmond, Va.: Whittel and Shepperson, 1884–96.

Bibliography

Washington, George. *Diaries of George Washington.* Edited by John C. Fitzpatrick. 4 vols. Boston: Houghton Mifflin, 1925.
Weld, Isaac. *Travels through the States of North America and the Provinces of Upper and Lower Canada during the Years 1795, 1796, and 1797.* 2 vols. London: printed for J. Stockdale, 1799.
Wellesley, Richard. *The Wellesley Papers: The Life and Correspondence of Richard Colley Wellesley, Marquis Wellesley.* Edited by the editor of the Wyndham Papers. 2 vols. Herbert Jenkins, 1914.
Wilson, Sir Robert Thomas. *General Wilson's Journal, 1812–1814.* Edited by Anthony Brett James. London: Kember, 1964.

Official Documents, Tables, and Pamphlets

American State Papers: Documents Legislative and Executive of the Congress of the United States, Class III (Foreign Relations). Edited by Walter Lowrie and Matthew S. Clarke. 6 vols. Washington, D.C., 1832.
Cobbett, William. *Cobbett's Political Register.* October 12, 1805, April 10, 1830.
———. *Porcupine's Works.* 12 vols. London, 1801.
"Correspondence of the French Ministers to the United States, 1791–1797." Edited by Frederick Jackson Turner. *American Historical Association Annual Report,* 1903, vol. II.
Dana, Samuel. *Speech of Samuel W. Dana . . . on a Resolution Concerning Francis J. Jackson.* Washington, D.C., 1810.
"Documents on the Blount Conspiracy, 1795–1797." Edited by Frederick Jackson Turner. *American Historical Review* 10: 574–606.
Lowell, John. *Interesting Political Discussion: The Diplomatick Policy of Mr. Madison Unveiled.* N.p., 1810.
Manning, William R., ed. *The Diplomatic Correspondence of the United States: Canadian Relations, 1784–1860.* 4 vols. Washington, D.C., 1940–45.
Mayo, Bernard, ed. "Instructions to the British Ministers to the United States, 1791–1812." *American Historical Association Annual Report,* 1936, vol. III. Washington, D.C., 1941.
Niles Weekly Register. March 21, 1816, July 25, 1823.
The Parliamentary Debates from the Year 1803 to the Present Time. Edited by William Cobbett. London, 1813.
The Quarterly Review 68 (June, 1841): 20–57.
Statistical Tables Exhibiting the Commerce of the United States with European Countries from 1790 to 1860. Washington, D.C., 1893.
Vaughan, Benjamin. *Ten Hints Addressed to the Wise Men—Concerning the Dispute Which Ended on November 8, 1809.* Boston, 1810.

Principal Periodicals

Gentleman's Magazine (variously titled)
Georgetown *Museum*

New York *Argus*
Philadelphia *Aurora*
Washington *National Intelligencer*

Articles

Aspinwall, A. "The Cabinet Council, 1783–1835." *Proceedings of the British Academy* 38 (1952): 45–252.

Bindoff, S. T. "The Unreformed Diplomatic Service, 1812–1860." *Transactions of the Royal Historical Society*, 4th series, 18 (1935): 143–72.

Bristed, John. "The Resources of the United States of America." Review in *Quarterly Review* 61: 1–24.

Browning, T. B. "Charles Bagot." *Dictionary of National Biography*, Supp. I: 98–99.

Bulwer, P. L. "The Diplomatic Service." *New Monthly Magazine and Literary Journal* 1 (1833): 418–29.

Callahan, James Morton. "The Neutrality of the American Lakes and Anglo-American Relations." *Johns Hopkins University Studies in History and Political Science*, series 16, nos. 1–4.

Cecil, Algernon. "The Foreign Office." In *The Cambridge History of British Foreign Policy*. Edited by A. W. Ward and G. P. Gooch. Vol. III. London, 1922–23.

Chichester, Henry Manners. "Francis Jackson." *Dictionary of National Biography* X, 527.

Clarfield, Gerard. "Postscript to the Jay Treaty: Timothy Pickering and Anglo-American Relations, 1795–1797." *William and Mary Quarterly*, 3rd series, 23: 106–20.

Coemmerer, H. Paul. "The Sesquicentennial of the Laying of the Cornerstone of the United States Capitol by George Washington." *Records of the Columbia Historical Society* 44–45: 161–89.

Cowan, Helen J. "Selkirk's Work in Canada." *Canadian Historical Review* 9: 299–308.

Fisher, Josephine. "Francis James Jackson and Newspaper Propaganda in the United States, 1809–1810." *Maryland Historical Magazine* 30, no. 2 (June, 1935): 93–113.

Harris, Charles Alexander. "George Henry Rose." *Dictionary of National Biography* XVII, 231–32.

Hay, Thomas Robson. "Charles Williamson and the Burr Conspiracy." *Journal of Southern History* 2 (1935): 175–210.

Hill, Edwin C. "Historical Sketch of Washington, D.C." (typescript) Washington: Library of Congress (n.d.).

Hubbard, Robert J. "Political and Social Life in Washington during the Administration of President Monroe." *Transactions of the Oneida Historical Society* 11: 56–73.

Jones-Parry, E. "Undersecretaries of State for Foreign Affairs, 1782–1855." *English Historical Review* 49: 308–20.

Bibliography

Kyte, George W. M. "Robert Liston and Anglo-American Cooperation 1796–1800." *Proceedings of the American Philosophical Society* 93, no. 3: 259–66.
Lane-Poole, Stanley. "Stratford Canning." *Dictionary of National Biography* VIII, 431–44.
Lee, Sidney. "George Hammond." *Dictionary of National Biography* VIII, 1125–26.
Lyon, E. Wilson. "The Directory and the United States." *American Historical Review* 43: 514–32.
Manning, William Ray. "The Nootka Sound Controversy." *American Historical Association Annual Report* (1904): 279–478.
Mugridge, Donald H. "Augustus Foster and His Book." *Records of the Columbia Historical Society* 53–56: 327–52.
Osborne, John Ball. "The Removal of the Government of Washington." *Records of the Columbia Historical Society* 3: 136–60.
Paullin, Charles O. "Early British Diplomats in Washington." *Records of the Columbia Historical Society* 44–45: 241–62.
Perkins, Bradford. "George Canning, Great Britain, and the United States, 1807–1809." *American Historical Review* 63: 1–22.
Power, D'Arcy. "Robert Liston." *Dictionary of National Biography* XI, 1236–37.
Reade, Leslie. "George III to the United States Sendeth Greetings." *History Today* 3, no. 11: 770–80.
Smelser, Marshall. "The Federalist Period as an Age of Passion." *American Quarterly* 10: 391–419.
———. "The Jacobin Phrenzy: The Menace of Monarch, Plutocracy, and Anglophilia, 1789–1798." *Review of Politics* 21 (1933): 239–58.
Soulsby, Hugh G. "The Right of Search and the Slave Trade in Anglo-American Relations, 1814–1862." *Johns Hopkins University Studies in Historical and Political Science*, series 51, no. 2 (1933).
Steel, Anthony. "Impressment in the Monroe-Pinkney Negotiations, 1806–1807." *American Historical Review* 57 (1952): 352–59.
Stephens, Henry Morse. "David Erskine." *Dictionary of National Biography* VI, 819–20.
———. "Augustus Foster." *Dictionary of National Biography* VII, 492.
Temperley, H. W. V. "The Later American Policy of George Canning." *American Historical Review* 12 (1906): 779–97.
Turner, Frederick Jackson. "English Policy toward America in 1790–1791." *American Historical Review* 7 (July, 1902): 706–35, 8 (October, 1902): 78–86.
Veitch, G. S. "William Huskisson and the Controverted Elections at Liskead in 1802 and 1804." *Transactions of the Royal Historical Society*, 4th series, 13: 206–11.
Wright, Esmond. "Robert Liston, Second British Minister to the United States." *History Today* 11: no. 2.

BIBLIOGRAPHY

SECONDARY MATERIAL

Books

Abernethy, Thomas. *The Burr Conspiracy.* New York: Oxford University Press, 1954.

Adams, Henry. *The Education of Henry Adams.* New York: Charles Scribner's Sons, 1928.

———. *History of the United States of America in the Administrations of Jefferson and Madison.* 9 vols. New York: Charles Scribner's Sons, 1889–91.

———. *The Life of Albert Gallatin.* New York: P. Smith, 1943 [reprint of 1879 edition].

Albion, Robert G. and Jennie Barnes. *Sea Lanes in Wartime, the American Experience, 1775–1942.* New York: W. W. Norton, 1942.

Alger, John Goldworth. *Napoleon's British Visitors and Captives, 1801–1815.* New York: James Potts and Co., 1904.

Ammon, Harry. *James Monroe: The Quest for National Identity.* New York: McGraw-Hill, 1971.

Ashton-Gwatkin, Frank. *The British Foreign Service.* Syracuse, N.Y.: Syracuse University Press, 1951.

Bagot, Sophia Louisa. *Links with the Past.* London: E. Arnold, 1902.

Bartlett, C. J. *Castlereagh.* London: Macmillan, 1966.

Bemis, Samuel Flagg. *Jay's Treaty: A Study in Commerce and Diplomacy.* New York: Macmillan, 1923.

———. *John Quincy Adams and the Foundations of American Foreign Policy.* New York: Alfred A. Knopf, 1949.

Benjamin, Lewis Saul. *The Life and Letters of William Cobbett in England and America.* 2 vols. London: J. Lane, 1913.

Berkeley, Edmund, and Dorothy Smith. *John Beckley, Zealous Partisan in a Nation Divided.* Philadelphia: American Philosophical Society, Memoirs of the American Philosophical Society, 1973.

Beveridge, Albert. *The Life of John Marshall.* 4 vols. Boston: Houghton-Mifflin, 1916–1919.

Bigham, Clive. *The Prime Ministers of Britain.* London: J. Murray, 1924.

Bindoff, S. T., E. F. Malcolm-Smith, C. K. Webster, eds. *British Diplomatic Representatives, 1789–1852.* Camden Society Publications, 3rd series, vol. 50.

Bowman, Albert H. *The Struggle for Neutrality: Franco-American Diplomacy during the Federalist Era.* Knoxville, Tenn: University of Tennessee Press, 1974.

Boyd, Julian P. *Number 7: Alexander Hamilton's Secret Attempt to Control American Foreign Policy.* Princeton, N.J.: Princeton University Press, 1964.

Brant, Irving. *James Madison, Secretary of State, 1800–1809.* New York: Bobbs Merrill Co., 1952.

———. *James Madison the President, 1809–1817.* New York: Bobbs Merrill Co., 1956.

Bibliography

———. *James Madison, Commander-in-Chief, 1812–1836.* New York: Bobbs Merrill Co., 1961.
Brown, Roger H. *The Republic in Peril: 1812.* New York: Columbia University Press, 1964.
Brown, Stuart Gerry. *The First Republicans.* Syracuse, N.Y.: Syracuse University Press, 1954.
Bryan, Wilhelmus Bogart. *A History of the National Capital from Its Foundation through the Period of the Adoption of the Organic Act.* 2 vols. New York: Macmillan, 1914–1916.
Burt, A. L. *The United States, Great Britain and British North America from the Revolution to the Establishment of Peace after the War of 1812.* New Haven: Yale University Press, 1940.
Busey, Samuel C. *Pictures of the City of Washington in the Past.* W. Ballantyne and Sons: Washington, 1898.
Byrne, Leo Gerald. *The Great Ambassador.* Columbus, Ohio: Ohio State University Press, 1964.
Cecil, Algernon. *British Foreign Secretaries, 1807–1916: Studies in Personality and Policy.* Port Washington, N.Y.: Kennekat Press, 1971.
Childe-Pemberton, William S. *The Earl Bishop.* London: Hurst and Blackett, Ltd., 1925.
Coleridge, Ernest Hartley. *The Life of Thomas Coutts, Banker.* 2 vols. London: John Lane, 1920.
Conway, Moncure D. *Omitted Chapters of History Disclosed in the Life and Papers of Edmund Randolph.* New York: G. P. Putnam's Sons, 1888.
Costigan, Giovanni. *Sir Robert Wilson: A Soldier of Fortune in the Napoleonic Wars.* Madison, Wis.: University of Wisconsin Studies in the Social Sciences and History, no. 6., 1932.
Cross, Jack L. *London Mission: The First Critical Years.* East Lansing, Mich.: Michigan State University Press, 1932.
Cunningham, Noble E., Jr., *The Jeffersonian Republicans: The Formation of Party Organization, 1789–1801.* Chapel Hill, N.C.: University of North Carolina Press, 1957.
Dangerfield, George. *The Awakening of American Nationalism, 1815–1828.* New York: Harper and Row, 1965.
———. *The Era of Good Feelings.* New York: Harcourt Brace, 1952.
Darling, Arthur Burr. *Our Rising Empire, 1763–1803.* New Haven, Conn.: Yale University Press, 1940.
Dauer, Manning J. *The Adams Federalists.* Baltimore: Johns Hopkins University Press, 1953.
De Conde, Alexander. *Entangling Alliance: Politics and Diplomacy under George Washington.* Durham, N.C.: Duke University Press, 1958.
———. *The Quasi-War: The Politics and Diplomacy of the Undeclared War with France, 1797–1801.* New York: Scribner's, 1966.
Dent, John Charles. *The Canadian Portrait Gallery.* 4 vols. London and Toronto: J. B. Magurn, 1880–81.
Dos Passos, John. *The Shackles of Power.* New York: Doubleday, 1966.

Dunlap, William A. *A History of the Rise and Progress of the Arts of Design in the United States.* 3 vols. New York: R. Blom, 1965.

Dunning, William A. *The British Empire and the United States.* New York: Charles Scribner's Sons, 1914.

Eaton, Clement. *Henry Clay and the Art of American Politics.* Boston: Little, Brown, 1957.

Escott, Thomas. *The Story of British Diplomacy—Its Makers and Movements.* London: T. F. Unwin, 1908.

Festing, Gabrielle. *John Hookham Frere and His Friends.* London: J. Nisbet and Co., Ltd., 1899.

Freeman, Douglas Southall. *George Washington: A Biography.* 7 vols. New York: Scribner, 1948.

Gibbs, George. *Memoirs of the Administrations of Washington and Adams.* 2 vols. New York: W. Van Norten, printer, 1846.

Green, Constance McLaughlin. *Washington, Village and Capital, 1800–1878.* Princeton, N.J.: Princeton University Press, 1962.

Grosvenor, Caroline, and Lord Stuart Wortley. *The First Lady Wharncliffe and Her Family.* 2 vols. London: W. Heinemann, 1927.

Hertslet, Sir Edward. *Recollections of the Old Foreign Office.* London: J. Murray, 1901.

Hobhouse, Christopher. *Fox.* London: Constable and Co., 1947.

Hobhouse, John Cam [Baron Broughton]. *Recollections of a Long Life by Lord Broughton, Edited by His Daughter, Lady Dorchester.* 6 vols. London: J. Murray, 1909–1911.

Horsman, Reginald. *The Causes of the War of 1812.* New York: A. S. Barnes, 1962.

———. *The War of 1812.* New York: Alfred A. Knopf, 1969.

Humphreys, Frank L. *Life and Times of David Humphreys.* 2 vols. New York: G. P. Putnam's Sons, 1917.

Jones, Reverend C. A. *History of Dedham.* Colchester: Wiles and Son, 1907.

Jones, Ray. *The Nineteenth Century Foreign Office: An Administrative History.* London: London School of Economics and Political Science, 1971.

Ketcham, Ralph. *James Madison: A Biography.* New York: Macmillan, 1971.

Klingberg, Frank J. *The Anti-Slavery Movement in England.* New Haven: Yale University Press, 1926.

Lane-Poole, Stanley. *Life of the Right Hon. Stratford Canning, Viscount de Redcliffe.* 2 vols. London: Longmans, Green, and Co., 1888.

Lester, Malcolm. *Anthony Merry Redivivus: A Reappraisal of the British Minister to the United States, 1803–1806.* Charlottesville, Va.: University Press of Virginia, 1978.

MacDonald, Forrest. *The Presidency of George Washington.* Lawrence, Kans.: University of Kansas Press, 1974.

Malcolm-Smith, E. F. *The Life of Stratford Canning.* London: Ernest Benn, 1933.

Malmesbury, James Howard Harris, Third Earl of Malmesbury. *Memoirs of an Ex-Minister—An Autobiography.* London: Longmans, Green, and Co., 1885.

Malone, Dumas. *Jefferson and the Rights of Man*. Boston: Little, Brown, 1957.
———. *Jefferson the President, First Term, 1801–1805*. Boston: Little, Brown, 1970.
———. *Jefferson, the President, Second Term, 1805–1809*. Boston: Little, Brown, 1974.
Martineau, Harriet. *History of the Thirty Years' Peace*. 4 vols. London: Saunders and Otley, 1874.
———. *Society in America*. New York: Saunders and Otley, 1837.
Masterson, William H. *William Blount*. Baton Rouge: Louisiana State University Press, 1954.
Masterson, William H., ed. *The John Gray Blount Papers*, III. Raleigh, N.C.: State Department of Archives and History, 1965.
McMaster, John Bach. *A History of the People of the United States from the Revolution to the Civil War*. 8 vols. New York: D. Appleton Co., 1883–1913.
Mayne, Ethel C. *A Regency Chapter: Lady Bessborough and Her Friends*. London: Macmillan, 1939.
Merk, Frederick. *The Oregon Question: Essays in Anglo-American Diplomacy and Politics*. Cambridge, Mass.: Belknap Press of Harvard University Press, 1967.
Miller, John C. *Crisis in Freedom: The Alien and Sedition Acts*. Boston: Little, Brown and Co., 1951.
Moore, Virginia. *The Madisons: A Biography*. New York: McGraw-Hill, 1979.
Morison, Samuel E. *Harrison Gray Otis: Urbane Federalist*. Boston: Houghton Mifflin, 1969.
———. *Life and Letters of Harrison Gray Otis, 1765–1848*. 2 vols. Boston: Houghton Mifflin, 1913.
Mowat, R. B. *The Diplomatic Relations of Great Britain and the United States*. London: E. Arnold and Co., 1925.
Neel, Joanne Lowe. *Phineas Bond: A Study in Anglo-American Relations, 1786–1812*. Philadelphia: University of Pennsylvania Press, 1968.
Nicolson, Harold. *The Congress of Vienna*. New York: Viking Press, 1965.
Pancake, John S. *Samuel Smith and the Politics of Business*. Tuscaloosa: University of Alabama Press, 1972.
Pellew, George. *The Life and Correspondence of the Right Hon. Henry Addington, First Viscount Sidmouth*. 3 vols. London: J. Murray, 1847.
Perkins, Bradford. *Castlereagh and Adams, England and the United States, 1812–1823*. Berkeley: University of California Press, 1964.
———. *The First Rapprochement: England and the United States, 1795–1805*. Philadelphia: University of Pennsylvania Press, 1955.
———. *Prologue to War: England and the United States, 1805–1812*. Berkeley: University of California Press, 1974.
Peterson, Merrill D. *Thomas Jefferson and the New Nation: A Biography*. New York: Oxford University Press, 1970.
Petrie, Sir Charles. *George Canning*. London: Eyre and Spottiswood, 1932.

Philbrick, Francis S. *The Rise of the West, 1754–1830.* New York: Harper and Row, 1965.
Platt, Desmond C. M. *Finance, Trade, and Politics in British Foreign Policy, 1815–1914.* Oxford: Clarendon Press, 1968.
Plumer, William, Jr. *Life of William Plumer.* Edited by A. P. Peabody. Boston: Phillips, Sampson and Co., 1857.
Poore, Ben Perley. *Perley's Reminiscences of Sixty Years in the National Metropolis.* 2 vols. Philadelphia: Hubbard Brothers, 1886.
Ritcheson, Charles R. *Aftermath of Revolution: British Policy toward the United States, 1783–1795.* Dallas: Southern Methodist University Press, 1969.
Rolo, P. J. V. *George Canning: Three Biographical Studies.* London: Macmillan, 1965.
Satow, Sir Ernest. *A Guide to Diplomatic Practice.* 2 vols. London: Longmans, Green, and Co., 1922.
Schachner, Nathan. *Aaron Burr.* New York: Frederick A. Stokes Co., 1937.
———. *The Founding Fathers.* New York: Putnam, 1954.
Singleton, Esther. *The Story of the White House.* 2 vols. New York: McClure and Co., 1907.
Small, John. *Castles and Mansions of the Lothians.* 2 vols. Edinburgh: William Paterson, 1883.
Smelser, Marshall. *The Democratic Republic, 1801–1815.* New York: Harper and Row, 1968.
Smith, Goldwin. *A History of England.* New York: Scribner, 1966.
Smith, James Morton. *Freedom's Fetters: The Alien and Sedition Laws and American Civil Liberties.* Ithaca, N.Y.: Cornell University Press, 1956.
Smith, Page. *John Adams.* 2 vols. New York: Doubleday, 1962.
Spivak, Burton. *Jefferson's English Crisis: Commerce, Embargo, and the Republican Revolution.* Charlottesville: University Press of Virginia, 1979.
Stanhope, Phillip Henry. Fifth Earl of. *Life of the Right Hon. William Pitt.* 4 vols. London: J. Murray, 1861–62.
Stapleton, Augustus G. *The Political Life of George Canning.* 3 vols. London: Longmans, Rees, Orme, Brown, and Green, 1831.
Steiner, Bernard C. *The Life and Correspondence of James McHenry.* Cleveland, Ohio: Burrows Brothers Co., 1907.
Stokes, Hugh. *The Devonshire House Circle.* London: H. Jenkins, Ltd., 1917.
Stryker, Lloyd Paul. *For the Defense: Thomas Erskine, the Most Enlightened Liberal of His Times.* New York: Doubleday, 1947.
Stuart, Dorothy Margaret. *Dearest Bess: The Life and Times of Lady Elizabeth Foster.* London: Methuen, 1955.
Tayloe, Benjamin Ogle. *In Memoriam: Benjamin Tayloe.* New York: Sherman and Co., printers, 1872.
Temperley, Harold W. V. *The Foreign Policy of George Canning, 1822–1827.* London: G. Bell and Sons, 1925.
Tickell, John. *The History of the Town and County of Kingston-upon-Hull.* Kingston: T. Lee and Co., 1798.

Bibliography 273

Tilley, Sir John, and Stephen Gaselee. *The Foreign Office.* New York: G. P. Putnam's Sons, 1933.

Updyke, Frank A. *The Diplomacy of the War of 1812.* Baltimore, Md.: Johns Hopkins University Press, 1915.

Walters, Raymond, Jr. *Albert Gallatin, Jeffersonian Financier and Diplomat.* New York: Macmillan, 1957.

Ward, Sir Adolphus W., and G. P. Gooch, eds. *The Cambridge History of British Foreign Policy.* 3 vols. Cambridge: Cambridge University Press, 1922–23.

Warden, David B. *A Chronological and Statistical Description of the District of Columbia.* Paris: printed by Smith, 1816.

Webster, Charles Kingsley. *The Art and Practice of Diplomacy.* London: London School of Economics and Political Science, 1961.

———. *The Foreign Policy of Castlereagh, 1812–1815.* London: G. Bell and Sons, Ltd., 1931.

———. *The Foreign Policy of Castlereagh, 1815–1822.* London: G. Bell and Sons, Ltd., 1925.

Wharton, Anne Hollingsworth. *Salons, Colonial and Revolutionary.* Philadelphia: J. B. Lippincott Co., 1900.

———. *Social Life in the Early Republic.* Philadelphia: J. B. Lippincott Co., 1903.

Wheatley, Henry B., ed. *The Historical and Posthumous Memoirs of Sir Nathaniel Wilson Wraxall.* 5 vols. London: Bickers and son, 1884.

Wheaton, Henry. *Some Accounts of the Life, Writings, and Speeches of William Pinkney.* New York: E. Bliss and E. White, 1826.

Willson, Beckles. *Friendly Relations: A Narrative of Britain's Ministers and Ambassadors to America, 1791–1930.* Boston: Little, Brown and Co., 1934.

Wilmot, Catherine. *An Irish Peer on the Continent, 1801–1803.* Edited by Thomas U. Sadleir. London: Williams and Norgate, 1920.

Wilson, Bird. *Memoir of the Life of the Right Reverend William White, D.D., Bishop of the Protestant Episcopal Church in the State of Pennsylvania.* Philadelphia: J. Kay, Jr. and brother, 1839.

Woodward, Ernest Llewellyn. *The Age of Reform, 1815–1870.* Oxford: Clarendon Press, 1938.

Wright, J. Leitch, Jr. *Britain and the American Frontier, 1783–1815.* Athens: University of Georgia Press, 1975.

Yonge, Charles Duke. *The Life and Administration of Robert Banks, Second Earl of Liverpool.* 3 vols. London: Macmillan Co., 1868.

Young, Douglas MacMurray. *The Colonial Office in the Early Nineteenth Century.* London: published for the Royal Commonwealth Society by Longmans, 1961.

Young, James Sterling. *The Washington Community, 1800–1828.* New York: Columbia University Press, 1966.

Articles

Addington, Henry U. "Youthful America: Selections from Henry Unwin Addington's *Residence in the United States of America, 1822, 23, 24, 25.*" Edited by Bradford Perkins, *University of California Publications in History*, 65, 1960.

Bayard, James A. "Papers of James A. Bayard, 1796–1815." Edited by Elizabeth Donnan. *American Historical Association Annual Report* 2, 1913.

Bigelow, Abijah. "Letters of Abijah Bigelow, Member of Congress, to his Wife, 1810–1815." *Proceedings of the American Antiquarian Society*, n.s. 40: 305–406.

Bond, Phineas. "Letters of Phineas Bond." Edited by John Franklin Jameson. *American Historical Association Annual Report*, 1896, 513–659; 1897, 454–568.

"The Abbé Correa in America, 1812–1820." Edited by Richard Beale Davis. *Transactions of the American Philosophical Society*, n.s. 45, 87–197.

Erskine, D. M. "D. M. Erskine: Letters from America, 1798–1799." Edited by Patricia Holbert Menk. *William and Mary Quarterly*, 3rd series, 6 (1949): 251–84.

Few, Francis. "The Diary of Francis Few, 1808–1809." Edited by Noble Cunningham, Jr. *Journal of Southern History* 29 (1963): 345–61.

Gordon, William. "Letters of William Gordon." Edited by Worthington Chauncey Ford. *Proceedings of the Massachusetts Historical Society* 63: 563–66.

Hawkins, Benjamin. "Letters of Benjamin Hawkins." *North Carolina Historical Review* 12: 259.

Howe, John. "Reports of John Howe to Lt. Governor Sir George Prevost, 1808–1809." *American Historical Review* 17 (1912): 70–102, 332–64.

[Jefferson correspondence.] *American Historical Review* 33 (1928): 834.

[Liston correspondence.] *Massachusetts Historical Society Collections*, series 8: 6.

Macon, Nathaniel, John Steele, and William Barry Grove. "Letters of Nathaniel Macon, John Steele, and William Barry Grove." Edited by Kemp P. Battle. *James Sprunt Historical Monographs*, 3 (1902): 49–52.

Mason, Jonathan. "Diary of the Hon. Jonathan Mason." *Proceedings of the Massachusetts Historical Society*, 2nd series, 2: 5–34.

Mitchell, Samuel Latham. "Doctor Mitchell's Letters from Washington, 1801–1813." *Harper's New Monthly Magazine* 58 (1878–79): 740–55.

Taggart, Samuel. "Letters of Samuel Taggart." Edited by George Henry Haynes. *Proceedings of the American Antiquarian Society*, n.s. 33: 113–226, 297–438.

"Unpublished Letters from North Carolinians to Jefferson." Edited by Elizabeth Gregory McPherson. *North Carolina Historical Review* 12: 252–83.

Index

Adair, Robert, 198, 200
Adams, Abigail, 45, 59–60
Adams, Henry, 7, 150
Adams, John, 9, 11, 48; Blount-Chisholm affair and, 40, 41; Liston on, 44–45; Thornton on, 56, 61, 62; Erskine on, 99
Adams, John Quincy: on British ministers, 7; and Hammond, 22, 28; and Erskine, 120; as American minister to Britain, 174, 185; as secretary of state, 187–220; and Bagot, 187, 192–95; and S. Canning, 204, 220
Addington, Henry U., 200, 217, 220, 224
Addington ministry, 57, 64, 67, 83, 123
Adet, Pierre, 35, 37
Alexander, Elizabeth. *See* Canning, Elizabeth
Allen, Margaret. *See* Hammond, Margaret
Ambrister, Robert, 190–91, 193
Americans: Hammond on, 12, 28, 63; H. Liston on, 35–36; Thornton on, 56, 63; E. Merry on, 91; Erskine on, 99; F. Jackson on, 127, 139; Foster on, 91; G. Canning on, 174; Bagot on, 180, 189, 203; S. Canning on, 210–12
American Trade Act, 214, 218
Amiens, Peace of, 63, 64, 67, 73, 100
Anglo-American relations, 4–5, 7; under Hammond, 11, 14–17, 23, 27–28; under Liston, 44, 46, 48, 52; under Thornton, 57, 64–68, 70; under Merry, 70, 87–98; under Erskine, 98–99, 104–109, 115; under F. Jackson, 121–42; under Foster, 148–65; in war years, 164, 165, 168–70; under Bagot, 175–95; under S. Canning, 202–24
Anglo-French relations, 17–22, 87, 101, 102
Anglo-Spanish relations, 31, 72
Anti-Jacobin Review, 28, 48
Antrobus, Crawfurd, 183, 194, 202–203, 208, 209
Arbuthnot, Alexander, 190–91, 193
Auckland, Baron. *See* Eden, William
Aurora, 47, 70

Bache, Benjamin F., 46, 47
Bagot, Charles, 171–95; early life, 171; marriage, 172; appointed minister, 172–75; arrival in America, 176; popularity, 178–79, 183, 184, 189, 193–95; professional relationships, 187–200; role in Great Lakes negotiations, 182–88; role in A. Jackson affair, 191–93; illness of, 193; departure from America, 193–95; later career, 195; death, 195; effect on successors, 203, 206
Bagot, Mary Charlotte Anne (née Wellesley-Pole), 172–75, 178, 183, 193
Baker, Anthony St. John: and Foster, 150, 159, 162, 165; and Bagot, 176, 203
Barclay, Thomas, 60, 112, 115
Bentinck, William, duke of Portland, 71, 104, 172
Berkeley, George Cranfield, 106–108, 112, 116, 172
Berlin Decree. *See* Bonaparte, Napoleon
Blount, William, 37–40
Bonaparte, Napoleon, 57–58, 64, 87,

106, 123, 146; Bayonne Decree, 112; Berlin Decree, 101–103, 147; Milan Decree, 109, 147; Russian campaign, 158, 165, 172, 173, 199
Bond, Phineas: and Hammond, 8, 10–12, 17, 19, 25–27; and Thornton, 12, 54–55, 60; and Erskine, 98, 115; and Pickering, 142
Bowles, William Augustus, 14, 46, 48
Brent, Senator, 159, 164
British ministers. See ministers to America, British. See also names of individual ministers
Burges, James Bland, 11, 27, 54
Burr, Aaron: and Thornton, 60, 61, 63, 66, 68; and Merry, 76, 82, 88–89, 93

cabinet: American, 15, 23, 27, 107, 177, 184–85, 205; British, 3–4, 8, 20, 141, 151, 163, 175
Cadore, duke of (French minister), 147, 148, 150, 151
Cadwalader, Frances. See Erskine, Frances
Calhoun, John C., 185, 212
Canada, 9, 51; boundary disputes, 63, 183, 188; Indians in, 14, 20, 21
Canning, Elizabeth (née Alexander), 221
Canning, George, 84–85; as foreign secretary, 4, 104, 115; and Hammond, 27–28; and Erskine, 104–20, 125; and Bagot, 172–74; and S. Canning, 105, 197
Canning, Harriet (née Raikes), 201
Canning, Stratford, 196–222; early life, 196–200; arrival in America, 201; personality, 203, 206–208, 213; professional duties, 203–15, 224; professional relationships, 105, 197–98, 202–207; eagerness to leave post, 217; departure from America, 220; later career, 221–22; marriage, 221; death, 222
Carmarthen, marquis of. See Osborne, Francis
Castlereagh, Viscount. See Stewart, Robert
Central America, 182–83, 186, 190, 208, 214
Chesapeake affair. See ships, *Chesapeake*
Chisholm, John, 37–40, 88

Clay, Henry, 156–59, 184, 185, 202, 212
Clinton, De Witt, 84, 161
Cobbett, William, 5; and Hammond, 27–35; and Liston, 43, 48; and Thornton, 55; and Merry, 74
Cockburn, George, 75–76
Columbia River Basin, 206, 208, 211
commerce. See trade
Congress, 9, 20, 25, 40, 81, 218; Eleventh, 146; Twelfth, 156, 164; Fourteenth, 177; Fifteenth, 188–90; Sixteenth, 204–205; Eighteenth, 212
Constantinople, 30–31, 36, 51, 122. See also Ottoman Empire
Convention of 1800, 45
Convention of 1818, 188
"Copenhagen Jackson." See Jackson, Francis
correspondence, personal: Hammond, 12, 18; Liston, 44; Erskine, 97, 99; F. Jackson, 124, 125, 132, 135, 140–41; Foster, 113, 162; Bagot, 174, 179–80, 182, 186; professional: Bond to Hammond, 8; Hammond to Grenville, 12, 13, 16, 20, 23; Hammond and Jefferson, 14, 20, 54; Grenville to Hammond, 16–19, 23–25; Liston to Hammond, 39, 41; Liston to Grenville, 39, 40, 44, 50; Grenville to Liston, 50; Jenkinson to Thornton, 57; Thornton to Jenkinson, 66, 67; Merry and Fox, 94; Erskine to Howick, 102; Erskine to Canning, 106; F. Jackson and Madison, 130–36; F. Jackson to Canning, 135; F. Jackson and Wellesley, 141; Foster to Wellesley, 152, 156, 157; Wellesley to Foster, 149, 156, 160; Castlereagh to Foster, 163; Foster to Castlereagh, 161–64; Bagot to Castlereagh, 181, 183, 185; Castlereagh to Bagot, 186, 188; Bagot and Planta, 192–93; Bagot and Monroe, 182; S. Canning to G. Canning, 219; S. Canning to Castlereagh, 210; Castlereagh to S. Canning, 201. See also individual letters cited on pages 226–55
Crawford, William H., 175, 181, 185
Cutler, Manasseh, 91

Decatur, Stephen, 177, 180
de Garambouville, Louis-Marie Turreau.

Index

See Turreau de Garambouville, Louis-Marie
de Neuville, Guillaume-Jean Hyde. *See* Hyde de Neuville, Guillaume-Jean
Denmark, 95, 109, 124, 125, 166, 197–98
de Ternant, Jean. *See* Ternant, Jean de
Diplomatic Service, British, 4–6. *See also* Foreign Office *and names of individual diplomats*
disunion theory, 62, 63, 82
Dorchester, Lord, 10, 20–23
Douglas, Thomas, earl of Selkirk, 10, 94
Downing Street. *See* Foreign Office *and names of individual diplomats*
Duane, William, 44, 47

East Florida. *See* Florida
Eden, William, Baron Auckland, 6, 101
Embargo Act, 110, 114
Erskine, David, 95, 97–120; early life, 98–99; marriage, 100; arrival in America, 101; popularity, 103, 104, 112, 113; professional relationships, 103, 105–106, 110, 112–20, 127, 128, 135; disobedience to Canning's instructions, 115–19; departure from America, 119–20; later career, 120; death, 120
Erskine, Frances (née Cadwalader), 100, 101
Erskine, Thomas, 98–100
etiquette. *See* protocol

Federalists, 6; and Hammond, 15–16, 22; and Liston, 41, 48; and Thornton, 60; and Jackson, 129, 136–38, 140; and Foster, 149, 153, 158
Florida, 9, 38, 65, 150, 152, 185, 190; East Florida, 82, 87, 155; West Florida, 147–48
Foreign Office, 3–8. *See also names of individual diplomats*
forts, 11, 21, 34, 187–88
Foster, Albinia Jane (née Hobart), 166
Foster, Augustus John, 144–67; early life, 144–45; as secretary of legation, 86, 91, 92, 116; personality, 144, 148–49, 160, 166; popularity, 153, 159–61, 165; professional relationships, 103, 105, 145, 149, 150; departure from America, 165; later career, 165–67; marriage, 166; death, 167
Foster, Elizabeth (née Hervey), 86, 95, 144–46, 154, 166
Fox, Charles James, 3, 28, 93–94, 100–101
Franco-American relations, 8; under Hammond, 16–20, 23; under Liston, 36–37, 42–45, 57–58; under Thornton, 57, 58, 61, 66; under Merry, 87; under Erskine, 101–102, 112, 114; under Foster, 152, 155, 160, 163; under Canning, 213

Gallatin, Albert, 58, 62, 157, 169; and Erskine, 99, 107, 119; and Jackson, 126; and Bagot, 188
George III, 4, 8, 116, 210; and Jackson, 124, 134, 135, 142
George IV, 4, 142, 148–50
Georgetown, 36, 58, 60, 127, 202
Gerry, Elbridge, 42, 140, 162
Ghent, Treaty of, 174, 186, 187, 214, 224
Gore, Christopher, 19, 139–40
Great Lakes, 9, 11, 182, 188
Grenville, William Wyndham, Lord, 9, 16–19, 23, 24, 50. *See also* Ministry of All the Talents

Hamilton, Alexander, 14, 15, 32, 82
Hammond, George, 5, 8–29; early life, 10–11; arrival in America, 11, 13–14, 27, 54; personality, 12, 13, 20–22; professional relationships, 13–16, 20, 21, 24, 54, 96; recall, 25; travels, 16, 19; marriage, 18; unpopularity, 20–22, 26–28, 32; departure from America, 27; later career, 27–28; death, 28; effect on successors, 11, 28, 29
Hammond, Margaret (née Allen), 18, 22, 27
Harris, James, earl of Malmesbury, 6, 67, 122
Harrowby, Lord. *See* Ryder, Dudley
Hawkesbury, Lord. *See* Jenkinson, Robert Banks
Hervey, Elizabeth. *See* Foster, Elizabeth
Hobart, Albinia Jane. *See* Foster, Albinia Jane
Hyde de Neuville, Guillaume-Jean, 184, 187, 191, 213

impressment: and Hammond, 18, 19, 22; and Liston, 33–34, 41; and Thornton, 64, 68, 69; and Merry, 81, 87; and Erskine, 108, 109; and Foster, 154; and S. Canning, 204

Indians, American, 9, 32, 90, 92; British involvements with, 13, 14, 18, 20, 37–38, 183

Instructions. *See* correspondence, professional

Jackson, Andrew, 191–93, 212
Jackson, Elizabeth, 123, 127, 132, 139, 142
Jackson, Francis James, 73, 109, 119, 121–43; early life, 121–23; marriage, 123; professional relationships, 122, 149; nicknamed "Copenhagen Jackson," 124–25; unpopularity, 123, 138, 142; departure from America, 137–42; death, 143
Jay's Treaty, 23, 24–26; American reaction to, 31–33; French reaction to, 37, 223
Jefferson, Thomas: Britons' perceptions of, 14–16, 63, 179; Hammond and, 13–15, 20; Thornton and, 54, 56–57, 60–63; Merry and, 76–77, 80, 86; Erskine and, 99, 199; Bagot and, 188; Canning and, 210
Jenkinson, Robert Banks, Baron Hawkesbury, 5, 57, 173; and Thornton, 62, 64, 65; and Merry, 122

Keith, Sir Robert Murray, 6, 10–11
King, Rufus, 57; and Hammond, 19, 21; and Liston, 34, 40, 47; as minister to Britain, 67, 68; and Merry, 73–74, 122; and S. Canning, 208

Latin America, 182–83, 186, 190, 208
Leathes, Elizabeth. *See* Merry, Elizabeth
Liston, Henrietta (née Marchant), 31–33, 40–43, 48, 49, 51, 55
Liston, Robert, 30–52; early life, 30–31; marriage, 31; arrival in America, 32, 33; popularity, 32–34, 37; travels, 36, 41, 48–49; personal problems, 41, 49–50; professional problems, 37–41, 44, 45, 47–50; successes, 45–46; recall, 50; departure from America, 51; later career, 51, 52; death, 52; influence on successors, 55–56, 74–75
Londonderry, marquis of. *See* Stewart, Robert, Viscount Castlereagh
Louisiana, 38, 63–66, 68, 81, 190
Loyalist debt issue: and Hammond, 9, 10, 13, 19; and Liston, 46, 49; and Thornton, 64; and Merry, 73

McHenry, James, 37, 48
Macon's Bill, 146, 147, 151
Madison, Dolley (née Payne), 77, 79, 132, 151, 178
Madison, James, 20, 125, 147–48; and Thornton, 62, 63, 68, 69; and Merry, 81–83, 90; and Erskine, 104, 112, 114–19; and F. Jackson, 126, 130–36; and Foster, 151–65
Malmesbury, James, earl of. *See* Harris, James
Marchant, Henrietta. *See* Liston, Henrietta
Marshall, John, 42, 48
Merry, Anthony, 72–95; early life, 72–73; nicknamed "Toujours Gai," 73; marriage, 74; personality, 73, 75, 90; arrival in America, 76; personal problems, 82–83, 90; professional relationships, 73–83, 85–88, 90; recall, 93; departure from America, 93–95; later career, 95–96; death, 96; effect on successors, 98, 103
Merry, Elizabeth (née Leathes), 74, 76, 78, 90, 91, 95
Milbanke, Anne Isabella, 149, 160, 162, 166, 199
ministers to America: British, 7, 9–10, 98; French, 11, 18, 35, 38, 44, 104, 147; Portuguese, 35, 46; Spanish, 35, 104; Tunisian, 80, 92
Ministry of All the Talents, 93, 100, 104
Missouri, 205
Mobile Act, 81
Monroe, James: and Hammond, 24; and Thornton, 66; and Foster, 148–51, 160, 165; and Bagot, 184–94; and S. Canning, 209, 221
Moodie, Benjamin, 60, 190

Moore, Tom, 75–76
Morier, John Philip, 138, 141, 142, 146–48, 150
Morris, Gouverneur, 31, 58–59
Mulgrave, Lord. *See* Phipps, Henry

Napoleon I. *See* Bonaparte, Napoleon
National Intelligencer, 79, 88; and Erskine, 109; and Jackson, 134, 136, 140, 149; and Bagot, 177, 195. *See also* newspapers
navy, British, 81, 143. *See also* ships, British
neutrality, 17, 110, 163
New England, 62, 158, 159
New Orleans. *See* Louisiana
newspapers, American: and Hammond, 21; and Liston, 41, 46; and F. Jackson, 128–29, 135–36; and Foster, 149, 153; and Bagot, 192; and S. Canning, 202, 211, 212
Niagara Falls, 49, 141
Nicholls, Edward, 190, 192
Nonintercourse Act of 1809, 114, 116, 117, 136
Nootka Sound, 9, 72

Oakeley, Charles, 116, 131, 134, 135, 141
Onís, Chevalier Luis, 133, 154, 178, 187, 190
Orders in Council: of 1793, 17, 19; of 1795, 25–26; of 1806, 86–87; of 1807, 103, 109, 115–20; of 1811, 150–52, 155
Oregon, 187–88
Osborne, Francis, marquis of Carmarthen, 9, 10, 121
Ottoman Empire: Liston in, 30–31, 41; S. Canning in, 198, 215, 221–22

Pahlen, Count (Russian minister), 153, 154
"Palace," the, 58, 59, 64, 79, 103, 166–67, 177. *See also* White House
Paris, Treaty of, 9, 10, 36
Perceval, Spencer, 5, 104, 148–50, 161, 163, 173
Philadelphia: as capital, 12, 16, 18, 34, 46, 53; as "dirty nest of philosophy," 140
Phipps, Henry, Lord Mulgrave, 5, 87

Pichon, Louis André, 64, 65, 77, 80
Pickering, Timothy: Hammond and, 24, 26, 27; Liston and, 33–34, 40, 48, 51; professional relations of, with Britons, 90, 104, 111, 112, with French, 37, 43
Pinckney, Charles Cotesworth, 37, 41, 42, 154
Pinkney, William, 115, 117, 125, 136, 137, 150
Pitt, William, 8–10, 83–84, 87, 89, 122
Planta, Joseph, 4, 5, 192–93, 199, 207
Plumer, William, 90, 104
Poletica (Russian minister), 210, 213, 217
Porter, Peter, 155, 157
Portland, duke of. *See* Bentinck, William
Portugal, 146, 156, 160–61, 203–204
prize courts, 19, 46, 64. *See also* impressment; ships
protocol: Washingtonian, 34, 35; Jeffersonian, 61–62, 77–83; Madisonian, 127, 130, 132, 176; Monroeite, 188–89, 207. *See also* social life

Quarterly Review, 5, 28, 199

Randolph, Edmund, 20–23, 157, 159
Randolph, John, 89–90, 113, 208
Reign of Terror, 16, 20, 54
Republicans, 15, 43, 60; and Thornton, 62, 63; and F. Jackson, 138–39; and Foster, 149, 151, 156, 159, 162, 166
Rose, George, 84, 110–12, 145
Rule of 1756, 87, 115, 116
Rush, Benjamin, 48, 120
Rush, Richard, 34, 182, 185, 188, 194, 215, 220–21
Russell, Jonathan, 152, 158
Russia, 158, 165, 172, 173, 199, 221
Ryder, Dudley, Lord Harrowby, 5, 84, 87

Santo Domingo, 45, 63, 64
Selkirk, Lord. *See* Douglas, Thomas
Serrurier, Louis, 155, 159, 178
ships: British, 17, 19; French, 17, 212; American, 19, 110, 182; *Tankersley*, 25; *Jean Bart*, 26; *Thistle*, 27; *Assistance*, 32; *Andromache*, 51; *Phaeton*, 75–76; *Cambrian*, 84; *Leander*, 89; *Chesapeake*, 106–108, 114–16, 125, 147,

150–52, 154, 172; *Leopard*, 107; Danish, 109; *L'Africaine*, 120, 126; *Venus*, 141, 142; *Minerva*, 149; *President*, 150; *Hornet*, 155, 163; *Ontario*, 187, 206; *Spartan*, 201; *Francis Freeling*, 223

Simcoe, John Graves, 10, 14, 21, 23

slave trade, 203, 205, 208, 214, 218, 221. *See also* impressment

Smith, Robert, 113, 116, 119, 130–36, 148, 157

social life: in Philadelphia, 12, 16, 34–35, 48; in Washington, 69–70, 77, 79, 83, 91–92, 139, 207–209; of Hammond, 12, 16, 18; of Listons, 32, 34, 35, 48; of Thornton, 69–70; of Merrys, 77, 79, 83, 91–92; of Jacksons, 139; of Foster, 153, 159–61; of Bagot, 183, 184; of S. Canning, 207–209, 217. *See also* protocol

Soderström, Richard, 80, 128, 135, 154

South America, 182–83, 186, 190, 208, 214

South Carolina, 42

Spain, 65, 72, 122, 148, 182, 214–15, 219. *See also* Florida

Stanhope, Lady Hester, 198–99, 213

Stephen, James, 86, 105, 149, 175

Stewart, Robert, Viscount Castlereagh, 4, 161, 175, 199, 200, 217

Stuart, Gilbert, 48, 55, 145

Switzerland, 199, 200, 215

Temple, Sir John, 10, 32

Ternant, Jean de, 11, 18

Thornton, Edward, 53–71; early life, 53–54; personality, 55, 57, 64; as secretary of legation, under Hammond, 11, 16, 54, 55; under Liston, 31, 32, 41, 42; as vice consul, 19, 54, 55; professional relationships, 11, 16, 54–57, 64, 117; departure from America, 68, 70, 82; later career, 71; death, 71; effect on successors, 63

Thornton, William, 65, 70, 177

Tories, 5, 12, 20–22, 27, 83–84, 120. *See also names of individual diplomats*

"Toujours Gai." *See* Merry, Anthony

trade: Anglo-American, 9, 17, 25–26, 84, 87, 109, 148, 149, 152, 170, 189; Franco-American, 115, 116, 152

travel: Hammond's, 16, 19; Listons', 36, 41–42, 48–49; Erskine's, 99; Jackson's, 141; Bagots', 183; S. Canning's, 210, 216

Tunisian diplomats, 80, 92

Turkey. *See* Ottoman Empire

Turreau de Garambouville, Louis-Marie, 85, 92, 113

War in Disguise. *See* Stephen, James

War of 1812, 157, 164–67

Washington, George: Hammond on, 13, 16; Liston on, 34, 44, 49; Thornton on, 56, 62

Washington, Martha (Custis, née Dandridge), 34, 49

Washington (city): descriptions, 58, 59, 69, 70, 78–79, 112–13, 176–77, 224; Hammond on, 19; Liston on, 36, 42, 51; Erskine on, 98, 99; Foster on, 92, 145; F. Jackson on, 126–27; S. Canning on, 201, 202, 211

Wellesley, Arthur, 172–75

Wellesley, Richard Colley, 5, 137–42, 148, 161, 172

Wellesley-Pole, Mary Charlotte Anne. *See* Bagot, Mary Charlotte Anne

West Florida. *See* Florida

West Indies, 9, 46, 64; American trade involving, 17, 25–26, 84, 87, 109, 163, 186, 214, 219

Whigs, 98, 117, 118, 120, 135

White House, the, 177, 207. *See also* Palace, the

Williamson, Charles, 76, 82, 85

Wolcott, Oliver, 22, 26, 58, 59

Wood, Gabriel, 126–28, 165

Woodbine, George, 190, 192

XYZ affair, 42–43, 56

yellow fever, 19, 46, 217

d'Yrujo, Carlos Martinez, 35, 39, 40, 65, 77, 78, 134

www.ingramcontent.com/pod-product-compliance
Lightning Source LLC
Chambersburg PA
CBHW030306080526
44584CB00012B/456